THE CLAY SANSKRIT LIBRARY
FOUNDED BY JOHN & JENNIFER CLAY

GENERAL EDITOR

SHELDON POLLOCK

EDITED BY

ISABELLE ONIANS

WWW.CLAYSANSKRITLIBRARY.ORG
WWW.NYUPRESS.ORG

Artwork by Robert Beer.
Typeset in Adobe Garamond Pro at 10.25 : 12.3 +*pt.*
Editorial input from Dániel Balogh, Ridi Faruque,
Chris Gibbons, Tomoyuki Kono & Eszter Somogyi.
Printed and Bound in Great Britain by
TJ Books Ltd, Cornwall on acid free paper

MAHĀBHĀRATA

BOOK SEVEN

DROṆA

VOLUME TWO

EDITED AND TRANSLATED BY

Vaughan Pilikian

NEW YORK UNIVERSITY PRESS

JJC FOUNDATION

2009

First Edition 2009

The Clay Sanskrit Library is co-published by
New York University Press
and the JJC Foundation.

Further information about this volume
and the rest of the Clay Sanskrit Library
is available at the end of this book
and on the following websites:
www.claysanskritlibrary.org
www.nyupress.org

ISBN 978-0-8147-6776-4

Library of Congress Cataloging-in-Publication Data
Mahābhārata. Droṇaparvan. English & Sanskrit.
Mahābhārata. Book seven, Droṇa /
translated by Vaughan Pilikian. -- 1st ed.
p. cm.-- (The Clay Sanskrit Library)
Includes bibliographical references and index.
Epic Poetry.
In English and Sanskrit (romanized) on facing pages;
includes translation from Sanskrit.
ISBN 978-0-8147-6776-4
I. Title. II. Title: Drona.
BL1138.242.D76E5 2006
294.5'92304521--dc22
2006022412

CONTENTS

CSL CONVENTIONS

Sanskrit Alphabetical Order

Vowels:	*a ā i ī u ū ṛ ṝ ḷ ḹ e ai o au ṃ ḥ*
Gutturals:	*k kh g gh ṅ*
Palatals:	*c ch j jh ñ*
Retroflex:	*ṭ ṭh ḍ ḍh ṇ*
Dentals:	*t th d dh n*
Labials:	*p ph b bh m*
Semivowels:	*y r l v*
Spirants:	*ś ṣ s h*

Guide to Sanskrit Pronunciation

a	b*u*t
ā, â	f*a*ther
i	s*i*t
ī, î	f*ee*
u	p*u*t
ū, û	b*oo*
ṛ	vocalic *r*, American p*ur*dy or English p*re*tty
ṝ	lengthened *ṛ*
ḷ	vocalic *l*, ab*le*
e, ê, ē	m*a*de, esp. in Welsh pronunciation
ai	b*i*te
o, ô, ō	r*o*pe, esp. Welsh pronunciation; Italian s*o*lo
au	s*ou*nd
ṃ	*anusvāra* nasalizes the preceding vowel
ḥ	*visarga*, a voiceless aspiration (resembling the English *h*), or like Scottish lo*ch*, or an aspiration with a faint echoing of the last element of the preceding vowel so that *taiḥ* is pronounced *taih*^{i}
k	lu*ck*
kh	blo*ckh*ead
g	*g*o
gh	bi*gh*ead
ṅ	a*n*ger
c	*ch*ill
ch	mat*chh*ead
j	*j*og
jh	aspirated *j*, he*dgeh*og
ñ	ca*ny*on
ṭ	retroflex *t*, *t*ry (with the tip of tongue turned up to touch the hard palate)
ṭh	same as the preceding but aspirated
ḍ	retroflex *d* (with the tip

	of tongue turned up to touch the hard palate)
ḍh	same as the preceding but aspirated
ṇ	retroflex *n* (with the tip of tongue turned up to touch the hard palate)
t	French *t*out
th	ten*t h*ook
d	*d*inner
dh	guil*dh*all
n	*n*ow
p	*p*ill
ph	u*ph*eaval
b	*b*efore
bh	a*bh*orrent
m	*m*ind
y	*y*es
r	trilled, resembling the Italian pronunciation of *r*
l	*l*inger
v	*w*ord
ś	*sh*ore
ṣ	retroflex *sh* (with the tip of the tongue turned up to touch the hard palate)
s	hi*ss*
h	*h*ood

CSL Punctuation of English

The acute accent on Sanskrit words when they occur outside of the Sanskrit text itself, marks stress, e.g., Ramáyana. It is not part of traditional Sanskrit orthography, transliteration, or transcription, but we supply it here to guide readers in the pronunciation of these unfamiliar words. Since no Sanskrit word is accented on the last syllable it is not necessary to accent disyllables, e.g., Rama.

The second CSL innovation designed to assist the reader in the pronunciation of lengthy unfamiliar words is to insert an unobtrusive middle dot between semantic word breaks in compound names (provided the word break does not fall on a vowel resulting from the fusion of two vowels), e.g., Maha·bhárata, but Ramáyana (not Rama·áyana). Our dot echoes the punctuating middle dot (·) found in the oldest surviving samples of written Indic, the Ashokan inscriptions of the third century BCE.

The deep layering of Sanskrit narrative has also dictated that we use quotation marks only to announce the beginning and end of every direct speech, and not at the beginning of every paragraph.

CSL Punctuation of Sanskrit

The Sanskrit text is also punctuated, in accordance with the punctuation of the English translation. In mid-verse, the punctuation will not alter the sandhi or the scansion. Proper names are capitalized. Most Sanskrit meters have four "feet" (*pāda*); where possible we print the common *śloka* meter on two lines. In the Sanskrit text, we use French *Guillemets* (e.g., *«kva saṃcicīrṣuḥ?»*) instead of English quotation marks (e.g., "Where are you off to?") to avoid confusion with the apostrophes used for vowel elision in sandhi.

SANDHI

Sanskrit presents the learner with a challenge: *sandhi* (euphonic combination). Sandhi means that when two words are joined in connected speech or writing (which in Sanskrit reflects speech), the last letter (or even letters) of the first word often changes; compare the way we pronounce "the" in "the beginning" and "the end."

In Sanskrit the first letter of the second word may also change; and if both the last letter of the first word and the first letter of the second are vowels, they may fuse. This has a parallel in English: a nasal consonant is inserted between two vowels that would otherwise coalesce: "a pear" and "an apple." Sanskrit vowel fusion may produce ambiguity.

The charts on the following pages give the full sandhi system.

Fortunately it is not necessary to know these changes in order to start reading Sanskrit. All that is important to know is the form of the second word without sandhi (pre-sandhi), so that it can be recognized or looked up in a dictionary. Therefore we are printing Sanskrit with a system of punctuation that will indicate, unambiguously, the original form of the second word, i.e., the form without sandhi. Such sandhi mostly concerns the fusion of two vowels.

In Sanskrit, vowels may be short or long and are written differently accordingly. We follow the general convention that a vowel with no mark above it is short. Other books mark a long vowel either with a bar called a macron (*ā*) or with a circumflex (*â*). Our system uses the

VOWEL SANDHI

Final vowels: →	a	ā	i	ī	u	ū	ṛ	e	ai	o	au	Initial vowels:
	' â	" â	y a	y a	v a	v a	r a	e '	ā a	o '	āv a	a
	' ā	" ā	y ā	y ā	v ā	v ā	r ā	a ā	ā ā	a ā	āv ā	ā
	' ê	" ê	' î	" î	v i	v i	r i	a i	ā i	a i	āv i	i
	' ē	" ē	' ī	" ī	v ī	v ī	r ī	a ī	ā ī	a ī	āv ī	ī
	' ô	" ô	y u	y u	' û	" û	r u	a u	ā u	a u	āv u	u
	' ō	" ō	y ū	y ū	' ū	" ū	r ū	a ū	ā ū	a ū	āv ū	ū
	a' r	a" r	y ṛ	y ṛ	v ṛ	v ṛ	' ṝ̂	a ṛ	ā ṛ	a ṛ	āv ṛ	ṛ
	' âi	" âi	y e	y e	v e	v e	r e	a e	ā e	a e	āv e	e
	' āi	" āi	y ai	y ai	v ai	v ai	r ai	a ai	ā ai	a ai	āv ai	ai
	' âu	" âu	y o	y o	v o	v o	r o	a o	ā o	a o	āv o	o
	' āu	" āu	y au	y au	v au	v au	r au	a au	ā au	a au	āv au	au

CONSONANT SANDHI

Permitted finals: k	ṭ	t	p	ṅ	n	m	*(Except āḥ/aḥ)* ḥ/r	āḥ	aḥ	*Initial letters:*
k	ṭ	t	p	ṅ	n	ṃ	ḥ	āḥ	aḥ	k/kh
g	ḍ	d	b	ṅ	n	ṃ	r	ā	o	g/gh
k	ṭ	c	p	ṅ	ṃś	ṃ	ś	āś	aś	c/ch
g	ḍ	j	b	ṅ	ñ	ṃ	r	ā	o	j/jh
k	ṭ	ṭ	p	ṅ	ṃṣ	ṃ	ṣ	āṣ	aṣ	ṭ/ṭh
g	ḍ	ḍ	b	ṅ	ṇ	ṃ	r	ā	o	ḍ/ḍh
k	ṭ	t	p	ṅ	ṃs	ṃ	s	ās	as	t/th
g	ḍ	d	b	ṅ	n	ṃ	r	ā	o	d/dh
k	ṭ	t	p	ṅ	n	ṃ	ḥ	āḥ	aḥ	p/ph
g	ḍ	d	b	ṅ	n	ṃ	r	ā	o	b/bh
ṅ	ṇ	n	m	ṅ	n	ṃ	r	ā	o	*nasals* (n/m)
g	ḍ	d	b	ṅ	n	ṃ	r	ā	o	y/v
g	ḍ	d	b	ṅ	n	ṃ	*zero*[1]	ā	o	r
g	ḍ	l	b	ṅ	l̃[2]	ṃ	r	ā	o	l
k	ṭ	c ch	p	ṅ	ñ ś/ch	ṃ	ḥ	āḥ	aḥ	ś
k	ṭ	t	p	ṅ	n	ṃ	ḥ	āḥ	aḥ	ṣ/s
gg h	ḍḍ h	dd h	bb h	ṅ	n	ṃ	r	ā	o	h
g	ḍ	d	b	ṅ/ṅṅ[3]	n/nn[3]	m	r	ā	a[4]	*vowels*
k	ṭ	t	p	ṅ	n	m	ḥ	āḥ	aḥ	*zero*

[1]ḥ or r disappears, and if a/i/u precedes, this lengthens to ā/ī/ū. [2]e.g. tān+lokān=tāl̃ lokān.
[3]The doubling occurs if the preceding vowel is short. [4]Except: aḥ+a=o '.

macron, except that for initial vowels in sandhi we use a circumflex to indicate that originally the vowel was short, or the shorter of two possibilities (*e* rather than *ai*, *o* rather than *au*).

When we print initial *â*, before sandhi that vowel was	*a*
î or *ê*,	*i*
û or *ô*,	*u*
âi,	*e*
âu,	*o*
ā,	*ā*
ī,	*ī*
ū,	*ū*
ē,	*ī*
ō,	*ū*
ai,	*ai*
āu,	*au*
’, before sandhi there was a vowel *a*	

When a final short vowel (*a*, *i*, or *u*) has merged into a following vowel, we print ’ at the end of the word, and when a final long vowel (*ā*, *ī*, or *ū*) has merged into a following vowel we print ” at the end of the word. The vast majority of these cases will concern a final *a* or *ā*. See, for instance, the following examples:

What before sandhi was *atra asti* is represented as	*atr’ âsti*
atra āste	*atr’ āste*
kanyā asti	*kany” âsti*
kanyā āste	*kany” āste*
atra iti	*atr’ êti*
kanyā iti	*kany” êti*
kanyā īpsitā	*kany” ēpsitā*

Finally, three other points concerning the initial letter of the second word:

(1) A word that before sandhi begins with *ṛ* (vowel), after sandhi begins with *r* followed by a consonant: *yatha” rtu* represents pre-sandhi *yathā ṛtu*.

(2) When before sandhi the previous word ends in *t* and the following word begins with *ś*, after sandhi the last letter of the previous word is *c*

and the following word begins with *ch*: *syāc chāstravit* represents pre-sandhi *syāt śāstravit*.

(3) Where a word begins with *h* and the previous word ends with a double consonant, this is our simplified spelling to show the pre-sandhi form: *tad hasati* is commonly written as *tad dhasati*, but we write *tadd hasati* so that the original initial letter is obvious.

COMPOUNDS

We also punctuate the division of compounds (*samāsa*), simply by inserting a thin vertical line between words. There are words where the decision whether to regard them as compounds is arbitrary. Our principle has been to try to guide readers to the correct dictionary entries.

Exemplar of CSL Style

Where the Devanagari script reads:

कुम्भस्थली रक्षतु वो विकीर्णसिन्धूररेणुर्द्विरदाननस्य ।
प्रशान्तये विघ्नतमश्छटानां निष्ठ्यूतबालातपपल्लवेव ॥

Others would print:

kumbhasthalī rakṣatu vo vikīrṇasindūrareṇur dviradānanasya /
praśāntaye vighnatamaśchaṭānāṃ niṣṭhyūtabālātapapallaveva //

We print:

kumbha|sthalī rakṣatu vo vikīrṇa|sindūra|reṇur dvirad'|ānanasya
praśāntaye vighna|tamaś|chaṭānāṃ niṣṭhyūta|bāl'|ātapa|pallav" êva.

And in English:

May Ganésha's domed forehead protect you! Streaked with vermilion dust, it seems to be emitting the spreading rays of the rising sun to pacify the teeming darkness of obstructions.

("Nava·sáhasanka and the Serpent Princess" I.3)

INTRODUCTION

It is understood that being alive always means the death of someone else.
—Antonin Artaud[1]

WE ARE AT A pause in the action of the epic. Evening and the death of Árjuna's son have slowed for a brief time the ferocious pace of the war. Back in the Pándava camp, the seer and bard Vyasa has just finished telling King Yudhi·shthira the story of the birth of Death, hoping to ease the king's suffering with philosophy. Now he presents him with an example from the past. Vyasa tells Yudhi·shthira about a king called Srínjaya, whose son is abducted and hideously murdered by a demented band of robbers. Vyasa recounts how when Srínjaya went to see the sage Nárada to seek solace in his despair, Nárada quite heartlessly berated him for indulging his anguish and ridiculed his dead son's achievements as against those of Srínjaya's own forefathers. Over the course of the next seventeen cantos, Vyasa repeats the compendium of grand sacrifices held by the kings of old that Nárada recounted to illustrate his point to Srínjaya. We are left reeling by the excesses of this seemingly bizarre and distracting interlude. We might reasonably question its insertion at this juncture in the wider story.[2]

Vyasa's discourse moves far out of the action of the epic and into the world in which the epic evolved. His ornate description of the grandeur and extravagance of the rites of the ancient kings invokes the Vedas, those four great dark monoliths that loom at the origin of ancient Indian thought and culture, and the sacrifice, the very essence of Vedic cosmology.[3] It is difficult to overstate the importance of the sacrifice in Vedic India. Its basic form is in principle simple enough: the destruction and dispersion of property in an act of ritual largesse. But its meaning is so fundamental to the Vedic worldview that it is very hard to grasp.[4] Contrary to what we might assume, sacrifice is everywhere. All that is participates within it. Sacrifice permeates the world obscurely and mysteriously, branching through its abysses invisibly like capillaries through the human body, and bearing in its corpuscles a latent energy that can only be tapped with diligence and caution: the practice of sacrifice is an esoteric and meticulous science that succeeds only through the skill and erudition of its practitioners. We might say that sacrifice is the instrument panel wired up to the mechanism of the cosmos. Understanding how to read and manipulate it can yield vast but hazardous power.

Central to the theory of sacrifice in the Veda is the flight beyond death. All creatures are born mortal: even the gods were destined to die, and it was only through their mastery of sacrifice that they achieved immortality. Indeed it is their success that the mortal sacrificer aims to mimic, and for this he needs priests, and the craft of the priests: ritual. Through stylizing a series of otherwise everyday acts, ritual transforms these acts into a heightened gestural language marked off from the domain of diurnal existence. The ritual is worked in a third space between the temporal space of the world and the eternal space of heaven. Through the correct deployment of ritual action, the Vedic priest can enable the sacrificer to make a return journey to heaven while still alive in preparation for what will happen when he dies.

In no sense is this an abstract notion. The cosmology that the journey traverses is material and real. Its dividing line is the solar axis: all that is beneath the sun dies and all that is above it lives, and lives forever.[5]

Our evidence for this theory comes from the only texts we have that predate the epics—the four Vedas and their commentaries. This corpus contains the liturgy, its explanation and the instructions for its ritual enactment, but nothing more. For a huge span of preliterate time it was around the rite that the collective memory had crystallized: it was through ritual alone that the culture remembered and recorded itself. Even when written down Vedic mythology was preserved by the tradition only to the extent that it explained why a ritual took the form that it did. This does not mean, as has often been said, that the Veda has no history in it. In the Veda, ritual is the armature on which history is sculpted. But a necessary paradox is entailed, as ritual is founded on the abolition of profane time. If history seems to disappear, that is because it must: the Veda records a history devoted in its ideal to arresting the very passage of sublunary existence.

In this sense Vyasa's litany of rites sound exactly how we would expect a Vedic priest's royal chronicle to sound. What matters in Vyasa's account is not the loss of life, but rather its plenitude. The fact that he gives his peroration at this point in the narrative draws a symmetry between the dead warrior and the munificent king. In the end, Nárada resurrects Sríñjaya's son because he has died without fulfilling his earthly life. In contrast, Abhimányu remains dead because he has seen life through to its ultimate abundance, its violent and explosive conclusion. He has already reached heaven. His acts are done, and they have been sanctified. He has achieved what only the solemn rites or the mortification of the flesh achieve: escape from the arc of time.[6] Abhimányu has cut across the winding trails of ancient ritual with the unique velocity of the warrior, and according to Vyasa it is absurd for those he has left behind to mourn him.

If at first this seems obtuse, on closer inspection it need not. Though the action of the battle appears profane, war is connected to sacrifice as ritual, a correspondence the epic's bards well understood. Warriors blaze like pyres or suns and in so doing bring to mind the burning heat generated in the austerities of holy men or the ritual fires of the sacrifice. In the Veda, the sacrifice is sometimes described as a chariot or a boat that carries the sacrificer to heaven, and in the epic fighters become rafts on the sea of battle, or are called *raṇa/dīkṣitān*, "initiates of war," anointed for the fighting as a king might be anointed for his coronation. The very plain on which the two sides contend is described in the Veda as the altar of the gods. Though the poets of the epic would inevitably draw on the Veda as a store of metaphor, their choices are more than merely felicitous, because in the language of ritual, correspondences are a technical apparatus that yoke disparate things and charge their equivalence with transcendent meaning. A warrior is *tyakta/jīvita/yodhin*: he abandons life. In so doing, he moves like the sacrificer through a violent and hazardous expenditure of energy into a special order of being severed from the profane. In both sacrifice and war, life and death are brought into extreme and volatile proximity in the risky and difficult attempt to clarify their true significance.

The many connections between the conceptual framework of the Veda and the structuring principles of the epic also go some way to explain this volume's second enigma. In light of the fact that Dauhshásani strikes the blow that kills Abhimányu, it seems bizarre that Árjuna should decide Jayad·ratha is the real culprit in the crime of his son's death. But there is a precedent for the forces at work here. In the Veda, life is a kind of theft from death. To be alive implies a debt that can only be paid through sacrifice, when something else that lives is destroyed in the sacrificer's place.[7] This is never an easy compromise. The Bráhmanas tell us that man himself is the only true sacrifice, and that all other victims are substitutes for him.[8] The art of sacrifice thus becomes a deflection of the violence that somehow emanates from being alive onto another's head: it is death evaded. In some sense, then, Jayad·ratha is Árjuna's fatal opposite, both providentially, as they are each rivals for Rudra's favour and Dráupadi's hand,[9] and pragmatically, since Árjuna sets his own life against Jayad·ratha's.[10] There is something of the pure or primordial sacrifice to what Árjuna proposes—yet there is also something disturbed, even delirious about it.[11] While Vyasa's discourse tries to fix the relationship between war and sacrifice, Árjuna's oath, a sort of cracked parody of the seer's words, violently disrupts it. It can be read as a kind of negative prayer: in a lengthy formulation running exactly counter to the description of Abhimányu's ascent to heaven, Árjuna describes the descent he will make into hell should he fail to avenge his son's death.

It is a promise that quakes with a wild and feverish anger that overwhelms Vyasa's cool speculations.

With Árjuna's oath the Vedic correspondences in the epic begin to give out. In the Veda, ritualisation is about control. Though war in the epic can be ritualised with some success, it cannot be controlled, since it is driven most fundamentally by the limitless irrationality of human behaviour, of which Árjuna's vendetta is a prime example.[12] It is precisely that which is inexplicable in Árjuna's decision to identify Jayad·ratha as the focus of his rage that defines the fatal strategy of the epic hero, and throws him out of balance with the Vedic cosmos. That fatal strategy is revenge.

Vyasa's Vedic interpretation of events can help us to understand the universe of the "Maha·bhárata" but it can never explain it. Nor, indeed, can the epic's rising deities. Scholars have often seen Krishna as some sort of key to the epic's deeper "meaning," perhaps because of his self-disclosure as omnipotent being in the "Gita."[13] This regularly misguided predilection first takes root in the very text of the epic itself. Those around Krishna often turn to him in search of answers or help, and receive little useful advice in response. When he encounters Duryódhana clad in his magic armour, it is Árjuna and not Krishna who understands why his arrows cannot pierce through it.[14] Krishna has to contend with exactly the same mysteries that perplex the rest of the epic's cast, mysteries expressed in the prismatic seams of the Sanskrit language, where the meaning of things glitters with a restless, alien light. Krishna describes Árjuna's encounter with Duryódhana as a *dyūta*, a "dice game," reminding us of the gamble that brought this entire conflict into being, but he also says repeatedly that it is *diṣṭi* that has brought Árjuna and Duryódhana together at this particular moment in time. Translating *diṣṭi* as "fate" happily captures in English similar ambiguities to those present in the Sanskrit, but in etymology the two terms are quite separate. Fate is spoken: it is oracular. Against this, *diṣṭi* comes from the verb √*diś*, to "indicate" or "point out." Both *diṣṭi* and *dyūta*, the two terms to which Krishna resorts in order to frame the action unfolding before him are vast, diaphanous words evoking the day (*dyu*),[15] and the sky (*diś/dyu*), the source of the day's light. They are everywhere and nowhere, too transparent and too luminous to be themselves visible. Whatever power directs the action from above the sun is too bright and amorphous to be seen or shaped into language below.

So Krishna gets it wrong. Far from being Árjuna's grand opportunity to "tear out the root" of his sufferings, his encounter with Duryódhana descends into bathos as Árjuna's arrows clatter uselessly off Duryódhana's armour, while Duryódhana taunts him back and prances about to little effect. We might say that Krishna tries to "ritualise" the encounter, but the moment he wants to freeze slips away, lost forever in the stream of time. This is typical of the plight in which the epic's actors find themselves. In the world of the epic, time can no longer be transfigured as it once could. For time hides its secrets even from the gods. Though it has a logic, the epic's characters are not to know that logic: instead it binds them *pare vidhau*, in a dictate they can never understand. Again, this conundrum has a metaphysical significance. The very cosmology of the epic is so obscure it swallows up any human attempt to give life or the afterlife a meaning. Even the celestial *svarga* of the Veda has become in the epic a confusing, labyrinthine place, a House of Yama divided into hells and heavens of different orders to which all dead heroes are bound, regardless of what they have done.[16]

What we are left with is the radical separation of that which once seemed so close. The structure of agonistic Vedic sacrifice is still present in the epic, but its foundations in word and rite are little more than ghostly remains. Before the epic, literature was *śruti*, a holy throb of language heard only by those inspired enough to listen. By the time of the "Maha·bhárata" it is *smṛti*, the memorial work of man.[17] A faultline separates the epic from its past. Again and again its action bursts out of control and resort is made to the old language that matched human life against the cosmos in some hope of reasserting order within it. But all such efforts are doomed to failure. The fracture in creation itself that Vedic sacrifice tried to bridge has grown into a chasm. Perhaps inevitably, man loses his footing. He is thrown back upon himself and can find nothing to comfort him but the old stories of the priests.

What remains in the end is private tragedy: life this side of the sun's path. It is Subhádra's devastating lament that silences all the rhetoric before it. With its extraordinary intensity of feeling, her speech gives the lie to the common opinion that the characters in the "Maha·bhárata" are little more than epic formulae, archetypes lacking personality or nuance. Subhádra knows full well to where Abhimányu is bound but she is a bereaved mother and it means nothing to her:

> *Though you are gone I can see you yet like some splendour in a dream. O this brief life of ours is as fleeting as a bubble in water. Your young wife's mate has been torn from her and she drowns in sorrow. How will I bear her up? O my son you have left too early. You have abandoned me in the summer of our lives and I am still so hungry to have you.* (78.17–19)

From where Subhádra stands the exuberances of the battlefield with its rising and falling suns seem like so much star-death, a trail of ash, the mere testament of a violence that glows dimly under the morbid sign of glory. Here as elsewhere the "Maha·bhárata" presents us with its skewed vision of life, a double perspective that renders inexplicable the real significance of the conflict between the Pándavas and Káuravas. In the epic, the greatest mystery is not, as it was in the Veda, the technology of the sacrifice, but the secret machinery of the human heart. As Sánjaya puts it, we cannot know if these men are fighting because they are "so devoted to the warrior's calling" or simply "so besotted with death." It is instructive to recall that beside all the Vedic analogies in the epic, the battle is also described in profane terms: as a *raṅga*, a crimson playhouse, a painted stage where the actors remain masked to one another and even to themselves. Here they must play out their destinies whether or not their gestures and words are their own, left to puzzle over success and failure with neither divine guidance nor supernatural explanation to help them understand. Not unlike ourselves.

Argument

The book begins in the aftermath of Abhimányu's death. It is evening. Vyasa has just finished describing to Yudhi·shthira the origins of Death and now he goes on to narrate histories of the philosopher kings as they once were told to King Sríñjaya after losing his own son. Yudhi·shthira listens to the sage and his burden lifts a little.

Árjuna and Krishna make their way back to the Pándava camp surrounded by dreadful portents. As soon as he sees the silent faces of his brothers, Árjuna realises Abhimányu is dead. He flies into a wild rage, and accuses his brothers of cowardice and betrayal. Yudhi·shthira tells Árjuna that he and the other Pándavas were kept from their nephew's side by Jayad·ratha's counterattack. Árjuna collapses in anguish and his brothers revive him. When he regains consciousness, Árjuna says he holds Jayad·ratha responsible for Abhimányu's death and vows that he will either kill Jayad·ratha the following day or build a pyre and throw himself into its flames.

Jayad·ratha learns from his spies of Árjuna's oath and he is terrified of what the coming day holds for him. He considers abandoning the war entirely and returning home. Jayad·ratha demands that Duryódhana afford him special protection on the battlefield. Duryódhana is keen to see Árjuna's plans frustrated and he immediately guarantees Jayad·ratha his best men. Drona too reassures Jayad·ratha that he will not allow him to be harmed.

Back among the tents of the Pándavas, Krishna castigates Árjuna for his rash public pronouncement, but Árjuna rebuffs his friend and sends him away to comfort Subhádra.

Krishna can do little: his sister is inconsolable. He returns to the Pándava camp and performs his nocturnal observances with Árjuna. They retire to their beds and Krishna resolves to do all that he can to ensure Árjuna's success in the coming battle. Later that night Árjuna dreams that he and Krishna journey to Rudra's mountain retreat where the deity teaches him how to mount the apocalyptic Pashu·pata attack.

The next morning Drona lays out his troops in the shape of an arum flower and stations Jayad·ratha in its hidden centre to ensure that Árjuna is kept away from him until sundown. The battle begins once again. Árjuna makes straight for Drona and demands that he surrender Jayad·ratha to him. Drona refuses and drives his former pupil back. Árjuna breaks away into the array and heads in search of his quarry regardless. Uttamáujas and Yudha·manyu follow on behind to guard his wheels, but Krita·varman blocks them, and Árjuna and Krishna press on alone.

Rampaging through the Káurava formation, Árjuna seems unstoppable. Duryódhana goes to find Drona at the vanguard and accuses him once again of secretly assisting the Pándava cause. Drona counters that his task is to capture the Pándava king and that Duryódhana should distract Árjuna so that he can do so. Drona gives Duryódhana a suit of enchanted armour to protect him from Pandu's son. The battle continues on two fronts: though the Pándavas at the frontline manage to split apart Drona's formation, Duryódhana holds back Árjuna with the help of the other Káurava champions. The sun drops lower in the sky, and still Árjuna cannot get any nearer to Jayad·ratha. The battle rages on.

Dramatis Personæ

Árjuna: the middle Pándava, son of Indra and Kunti also known as Bibhátsu, the Despiser / Dhanan·jaya, the Victor / Guda·kesha, Pigtails / Jishnu, the Conquering Sun / Kirítin, the Crowned Warrior / Kauntéya, son of Kunti / Savya·sachin, the Lefthanded Archer / Paka·shásani, the Guardian's Son / Pándava, son of Pandu / Partha, son of Pritha / Phálguna, the Red Star Fighter / Víjaya, the Champion.

Bhima·sena: the second Pándava, son of Vayu and Kunti also known as Bhima / Kauntéya, son of Kunti / Pándava, son of Pandu / Partha, son of Pritha / Vrikódara, Dogbelly.

Drona: teacher of the Pándavas and Káuravas and commander of the Káurava armies also known as Achárya, the Teacher / Bharadvája, son of Bharad·vaja / Shonáshva, warrior of the red horses.

Duryódhana: Dhrita·rashtra's eldest son and Yudhi·shthira's rival also known as Dhartaráshtra son of Dhrita·rashtra / Suyódhana.

Indra: warrior god of the Vedas also known as Mahéndra, Great Indra / Puran·dara, Scourge of Men / Shakra, The Mighty / Shata·kratu, God of a Hundred Hecatombs / Vásava, Lord of the Vasus.

Krishna: the Vrishni chieftain, Árjuna's driver, and incarnation of Vishnu also known as Áchyuta, the Unfallen / Go·vinda, the Herdsman / Hrishi·kesha, Bristles / Janárdana, Stirrer of Hearts / Késhava, Longhair / Madhu·súdana, slayer of Madhu / Pundaríkáksha, Lotuseye / Shauri, grandson of Shura / Varshnéya, scion of Vrishni / Vasudéva, son of Vasu·deva / Vishvak·sena, the Almighty.

Rudra: fierce deity of the Vedas also known as Bhava, the Origin / Hara, the Destroyer / Mahéshvara, the Great Lord / Shánkara, the Blessed God / Sharva, the God Who Kills With Arrows / Try·ámbaka, the Three Eyed God / Várada, the Giver / Vrisha·dhvaja or Vrishánka, the god that bears the mark of the bull / (see canto 80 for more of Rudra's names).

YUDHI·SHTHIRA: ELDEST OF THE PÁNDAVAS, SON OF DHARMA AND KUNTI also known as Ajáta·shatru, the matchless king / Dharma·raja, the righteous king / Kauntéya, son of Kunti / Partha, son of Pritha / Pándava, son of Pandu.

Concordance of Canto Numbers with the Critical Edition

CSL	CE
55.1	—
72.1	50.1
75.1	53.1
76.1	53.31
77.1	54.1
80.1	57.1
81.1	57.60
82.1	58.1
88.1	64.1
89.1	64.29
90.1	65.1

Notes

1 From a letter Artaud sent to Jean Paulhan in 1932.

2 In fact, the Critical Edition excises entirely cantos 55–71, identifying them as a corrupted recursion of material that appears in Book Twelve of the epic.

3 The Veda considered as a whole is the vast corpus of texts in Vedic, the most ancient form of the Sanskrit language, precursor of the Classical Sanskrit in which the "Maha·bhárata" is written. Contained in the corpus are the Vedas themselves, which are collections of the liturgical poetry that lie at the centre of the system, and the prose books of Bráhmanas, Arányakas and Sutras, which comment or speculate upon these collections. All

of this literature was originally oral, transmitted down the centuries by distinct theological schools. The texts were committed to manuscript some time between 1500 BCE and 500 BCE, although even these very general dates are controversial.

4 Though there is no space to go in depth into the matter here, it should be mentioned that the Vedic corpus is divided into different schools, each with rival ideas and beliefs. The tradition's inner contradictions often render strict generalisations about Vedic cosmology untenable.

5 For a brilliant and unsurpassed survey of the Vedic conception of sacrifice, see LÉVI's study *Le Doctrine du Sacrifice dans les Brāhmaṇas* (1898). One of the leading contemporary scholars on the Veda is STEPHANIE JAMISON: her insightful and learned books perform the rare feat of being immensely informative and entirely accessible to the non-specialist.

6 Vyasa is not the only character in the epic to observe the significance of this achievement. Drona and Krishna both reiterate his conclusions. See cantos 74 and 77.

7 Even from the earliest period of the written Veda, sacrificial offerings were being "downgraded" from what the rituals once demanded, and through later periods the value perceived to inhere in an offering continues to decline, while its ritual significance is intensified. Some commentators have seen this tendency as a process by which the violence of sacrifice is "cooled" through ritual. See for example HEESTERMAN (1993). Though interesting in themselves, many of HEESTERMAN's conclusions are conjectural.

8 It is Praja·pati, the primordial Creator, who forms the world out of himself by incarnating the sacrifice. See the chapter on Praja·pati in LÉVI (1898).

9 In Book Three of the epic Jayad·ratha happens across Dráupadi in the Pándavas' forest retreat, and while the Pándavas are out hunting he makes off with her. Bhima later captures Jayad·ratha

and ritually humiliates him in front of Dráupadi. It is this experience that drives Jayad·ratha to seek Rudra's favour in order to withstand the Pándavas in battle, which in turn leads indirectly to Abhimányu's death. But there is a further parallel between Jayad·ratha and Árjuna: Abhimányu's mother Subhádra is "abducted" by Árjuna in much the same way as Jayad·ratha abducts Dráupadi, although here it happens at the instigation of Subhádra's brother Krishna. One wonders if the union between Árjuna and Subhádra remains in some way transgressive. After all, when Abhimányu dies Árjuna despatches Krishna to comfort Subhádra rather than going to see her himself. For more on these abducted brides, see Jamison (1996: 226–35).

10 Though everyone takes Árjuna's vow very seriously, Krishna's response to it implies that he does not believe Árjuna can keep his word. He castigates him for what he considers a poorly-judged piece of bravado.

11 That Árjuna will set himself alight if he fails to make good his oath has explicitly Vedic connotations, fire being the primary medium through which a Vedic sacrifice is committed.

12 Yudhi·shthira has an important influence on Árjuna's response to Abhimányu's death. He is careful about where to place the emphasis in his account of the events that led up to it: he glosses over Dauhshásani's role and pointedly mentions that Jayad·ratha has received from Rudra the magical ability to restrain the Pándavas. What Yudhi·shthira has to explain is why the Pándavas failed to protect Abhimányu, not who it was that actually killed him. Thus it is partly because his brother feels the need to excuse his own shortcomings that Árjuna in the end trains his anger almost entirely on Jayad·ratha.

13 Such commentators could learn a great deal from the second-century gnostic exegetes of the Old Testament who read with mordant irony Yahweh's statement "I am the Lord, and there is none else, there is no God beside me" (Isaiah 45:5).

14 Árjuna is so foxed by Krishna's seeming ignorance on this point that he accuses him of dissembling. See 103.14.

15 This association is not purely phonological. There seems to be an etymological connection between √*div*, meaning most commonly "to play, gamble" and the notion of "shining," perhaps by way of the sense of "spreading" or "increasing" or being drunk or mad: lit with some kind of inner fervour.

16 The eschatology of the dead warrior does not follow a system in the "Maha·bhárata." Vyasa states that Abhimányu is *punar/bhāva/gata*, "returned to being," a compound with an ominous resemblance to the *punar/mṛtyu* "repeated death" opposed in the Veda to eternal life in heaven.

17 The Vedic Sutras are also considered *smṛti*: but these are the youngest parts of the Vedic corpus, and it is likely that their authors were working in the same time period as the epic's first scribes.

Bibliography

THE "MAHA·BHÁRATA" IN SANSKRIT

The Mahābhārata. Edited by N. SIROMANI and N. GOPALA. Calcutta: Baptist Mission Press, 1834–9.

The Mahābhāratam. Edited by R KINJAWADEKAR. Poona: Chitraśāla Prakāśana, 1929–37.

The Mahābhārata. Critically edited by V.K. SUKTHANKAR, S.K. BELVALKAR, P.L. VAIDYA et al. Poona: Bhandarkar Oriental Research Institute, 1933–66.

THE "MAHA·BHÁRATA" IN TRANSLATION

The Mahabharata of Krishna-Dwaipayana Vyasa. K.M. GANGULI (trans) [early editions ascribed to the publisher, P.C. ROY]. Calcutta: Bharata Press, 1884–99.

FURTHER READING AND REFERENCES

ARTAUD, A. 1993. *The Theatre and its Double.* London: Calder.

HEESTERMAN, J. 1993. *The Broken World of Sacrifice.* Chicago: University of Chicago Press.

JAMISON, S. 1991. *The Ravenous Hyenas and the Wounded Sun.* Ithaca: Cornell University Press.

———. 1996. *Sacrificed Wife, Sacrificer's Wife.* Oxford: Oxford University Press.

LÉVI, S. 1898. *La Doctrine du Sacrifice dans les Brāhmaṇas.* Paris: E. Leroux.

OBERLIES, T. 2003. *A Grammar of Epic Sanskrit.* Berlin: Walter de Gruyter.

PILIKIAN, V. 2006. *Maha·Bhárata, Drona, Volume One.* Clay Sanskrit Library. New York: New York University Press & JJC Foundation.

SØRENSEN, S. 1904–25. *An Index to the Names in the Mahābhārata.* London: Williams and Norgate.

MAHA·BHÁRATA

BOOK SEVEN

DRONA

VOLUME TWO

55–73

THE DEATH OF ABHIMÁNYU (CONTINUED)

SAMJAYA uvāca:

55.1 ŚRUTVĀ MṚTYU|samutpattiṃ
karmāṇy an|upamāni ca
dharma|rājaḥ punar vākyaṃ
prasādy' âinam ath' âbravīt.

YUDHIṢṬHIRA uvāca:

gurabaḥ puṇya|karmāṇaḥ Śakra|pratima|vikramāḥ
sthāne rāja'|rṣayo, brahmann, kiyanto mṛtyunā hatāḥ?
bhūya eva tu māṃ tathyair vacobhir abhibṛṃhaya.
rāja'|rṣīṇāṃ purāṇānāṃ samāśvāsaya karmabhiḥ.
kiyatyo dakṣiṇā dattāḥ? kaiś ca dattā mah"|ātmabhiḥ
rāja'|rṣibhiḥ puṇya|kṛdbhis? tad bhavān prabravītu me.

VYĀSA uvāca:

55.5 Śaibyasya nṛ|pateḥ putraḥ Sṛñjayo nāma nāmataḥ
sakhāyau tasya c' âiv' ôbhau' ṛṣī Parvata|Nāradau.
tau kadā cid gṛhaṃ tasya praviṣṭau tad|didṛkṣayā.
vidhivac c' ârcitau tena prītau tatr' ōṣatuḥ sukham.
taṃ kadā cit sukh'|āsīnaṃ tābhyāṃ saha śuci|smitā
duhit" âbhyāgamat kanyā Sṛñjayaṃ vara|varṇinī.
tay" âbhivāditaḥ kanyām abhyanandad yathā|vidhi
tat|sa|liṅgābhir āśīrbhir iṣṭābhir abhitaḥ sthitām.
tāṃ nirīkṣy' âbravīd vākyaṃ Parvataḥ prahasann iva.
«kasy' êyaṃ capal'|âpāṅgī sarva|lakṣaṇa|saṃmatā?
55.10 ut' āho bhāḥ svid arkasya? jvalanasya śikhā tv iyam?
śrīr hrīḥ kīrtir dhṛtiḥ puṣṭiḥ siddhiś candramasaḥ prabhā.»

SÁNJAYA spoke:

THE GOOD KING listened to the sage tell of the origins 55.1
of Death and of her strange deeds. He bowed to him and said these words.

YUDHI·SHTHIRA spoke:

O holy one. What kind of men were they who were called the philosopher kings? Death has long since overcome them. I know that they were wise and noble in deed and that they were brave as Indra. Tell me more of their history for in doing so you succour my spirit. Ease my heart with tales of these royal seers of old. What were their offerings? Who were the great wise kings so pious and extravagant? O mighty one, tell me more.

VYASA spoke:

The king of Shibi had a son by the name of Srínjaya who 55.5
was a friend to the saints Párvata and Nárada. They both came to his home to visit him. He welcomed them with propriety and they stayed with him as his guests. One day during their sojourn they were sitting with Srínjaya when his beautiful daughter approached them, a sweet smile on her lips. She stopped before them and greeted them cordially and politely and with all fitting grace. Párvata's eyes widened. He spoke to her playfully.

"To whom does this perfect creature belong? Love flutters about her eyes. I feel the light of the sun on my face. 55.10
Or is it the dancing light of a flame? No. The moon I see before me, all lustred in a radiant blush, its curve so perfectly smooth."

evaṃ bruvāṇaṃ deva'|rṣiṃ nṛpatiḥ Sṛñjayo 'bravīt.
«mam' êyaṃ bhagavan kanyā. matto varam abhīpsati.»
Nāradas tv abravīd enaṃ
«dehi mahyam imāṃ nṛ|pa,
bhāry'|ârthaṃ su|mahac chreyaḥ
prāptuṃ ced icchase nṛ|paḥ.»
«dadān'» îty eva saṃhṛṣṭaḥ Sṛñjayaḥ prāha Nāradam.
Parvatas tu su|saṃkruddho Nāradaṃ vākyam abravīt.
«hṛdayena mayā pūrvaṃ vṛtāṃ vai vṛtavān asi.
yasmād vṛtā tvayā vipra mā gāḥ svargaṃ yath"|ēpsayā.»
55.15 evam ukto Nāradas taṃ pratyuvāc' ôttaraṃ vacaḥ.
«mano|vāg|buddhi|sambhāṣā dattā codaka|pūrvakam.
pāṇigrahaṇa|mantrāś ca prathitaṃ vara|lakṣaṇam
na tv eṣā niścitā niṣṭhā, niṣṭhā sapta|padī smṛtā.
an|utpanne ca kāry'|ârthe māṃ tvaṃ vyāhṛtavān asi.
tasmāt tvam api na svargaṃ gamiṣyasi mayā vinā.»
anyo|'nyam evaṃ śaptvā vai tasthatus tatra tau tadā.
atha so 'pi nṛ|po viprān pān'|ācchādana|bhojanaiḥ
putra|kāmaḥ paraṃ śaktyā yatnen' ôpācarac chuciḥ.
55.20 tasya prasannā vipr'|êndrāḥ kadā cit putram īpsavaḥ
tapaḥ|sv'|âdhyāya|niratā veda|ved'|âṅga|pāra|gāḥ
sahitā Nāradaṃ prāhur «dehy asmai putram īpsitam.»
tath" êty uktvā dvijair uktaḥ Sṛñjayaṃ Nārado 'bravīt.

As the heavenly seer flattered her so King Srínjaya explained.

"O holy one this is my daughter. She wants me to find her a husband."

Nárada interjected. "Let her be my bride o majesty, if you are keen that she enjoy the kind of union a king's daughter deserves."

Srínjaya was well pleased and he gave his daughter to the seer. But Párvata was furious and hurled these words at Nárada.

"You have stolen one whom my heart possessed. For that o bard I will bar your path to heaven."

Nárada replied to Párvata's threat with words finely composed. 55.15

"When I asked him, the girl's father promised her to me in mind, word and soul. The offer of her hand makes it clear that I am to be her husband, but nothing is certain and our covenant will only be ratified with seven steps around the fire. You rail against an oath unsealed. And for that, you will not reach heaven without my blessing."

An awkward silence followed these insults and the pure-hearted king tried hard to placate the two wise men. He brought them food, gifts and fine garments, for he wanted above all to be granted a son. Indeed there were many great seers immersed in the mysteries of the Veda and devoted to their scholarship and meditation who had been touched by Srínjaya's kindness. They knew that he yearned for an heir and one day these holy men went together to Nárada and told him to give the king the son they felt he deserved. 55.20

«tubhyaṃ prasannā rāja'|rṣe putram īpsanti brāhmaṇāḥ.
varaṃ vṛṇīṣva bhadraṃ te yādṛśaṃ putram īpsitam.»
tath" ôktaḥ prāñjalī rājā putraṃ vavre guṇ'|ânvitam
yaśasvinaṃ kīrtimantaṃ tejasvinam ariṃ|damam,
yasya mūtraṃ purīṣaṃ ca kledaḥ svedaś ca kāñcanam.
Suvarṇaṣṭhīvir ity evaṃ tasya nām' âbhavat kṛtam.
tasmin vara|pradānena vardhaty a|mitaṃ dhanam.
kārayām āsa nṛ|patiḥ sauvarṇaṃ sarvam īpsitam:
55.25 gṛha|prākāra|durgāṇi brāhmaṇ'|âvasathāny api
śayy"|āsanāni yānāni sthālī|piṭhara|bhājanam.
tasya rājño 'pi yad veśma bāhyāś c' ôpaskarāś ca ye,
sarvaṃ tat kāñcana|mayaṃ kālena parivardhitam.
atha dasyu|gaṇāḥ śrutvā dṛṣṭvā c' âinaṃ tathā|vidham
sambhūya tasya nṛ|pateḥ samārabdhāś cikīrṣitum.
ke cit tatr' âbruvan: «rājñaḥ putraṃ gṛhṇīma vai svayam.
so 'sy' ākaraḥ kāñcanasya. tasya yatnaṃ carāmahe.»
tatas te dasyavo lubdhāḥ praviśya nṛpater gṛham
rāja|putraṃ tato jahruḥ Suvarṇaṣṭhīvinaṃ balāt.
55.30 gṛhy' âinam an|upāya|jñā nītv" âraṇyam a|cetasaḥ
hatvā viśasya c' âpaśyan lubdhā vasu na kiṃ cana.
tasya prāṇair vimuktasya naṣṭaṃ tad vara|daṃ vasu.
dasyavaś ca tad" ânyo|'nyaṃ jaghnur mūrkhā vi|cetasaḥ.
hatvā paras|paraṃ naṣṭāḥ kumāraṃ c' âdbhutaṃ bhuvi

Nárada assented to the twiceborn and went to speak with Srínjaya.

"Philosopher and king the brahmins tell me you are in their favour and they want you to have a son. I will grant your wish. Tell me yourself what kind of a boy you would like him to be."

At the seer's words the king raised his hands in gratitude and described a son of the finest stock, a boy whom in glory, splendour and strength his rivals would not match. He asked that his son would flow from every orifice with gold. And so it was that the boy was born as He Who Spits Gold. His gifts made him a mine of untold wealth. Whatever the king wished might take on the glitter of gold he
could now transform: houses, walls and citadels, the homes 55.25
of the brahmins, seats and thrones and chariots, cauldrons and pots and plates, all of the king's palaces and all of his jewels in time turned to gold. But a band of thieves heard about the king and saw in what luxury he lived. They began to plot together against him, and muttered to one another: "We should take the king's son for ourselves. Let us steal him away. It is from this boy that the king gets his gold."

Greed drove them on and they broke into the royal chambers and seized the prince named He Who Spits Gold.
They had no plan but they ran to a wood with their booty 55.30
and madly dashed out the boy's brains and cut his body into pieces. No treasure appeared to their foolish eyes. For when the child ceased to breathe the miracle of his trove was no more. The simpletons who had killed him lost their minds and murdered one another for it was their lot to destroy themselves once they had squandered that young wonder

a|sambhāvyaṃ gatā ghoraṃ narakaṃ duṣṭa|kāriṇaḥ.
taṃ dṛṣṭvā nihataṃ putraṃ vara|dattaṃ mahā|tapāḥ
vilalāpa su|duḥkh'|ārto bahudhā karuṇaṃ nṛpaḥ.
vilapantaṃ niśamy' âtha putra|śoka|hataṃ nṛpam
pratyadṛśyata deva'|rṣir Nāradas tasya saṃnidhau.
55.35 uvāca c' âinaṃ duḥkh'|ārtaṃ vilapantam a|cetasam
Sṛñjayaṃ Nārado 'bhyetya. tan nibodha Yudhiṣṭhira.
«kāmānām a|vitṛptas tvaṃ, Sṛñjay', êha mariṣyasi
yasya c' âite vayaṃ gehe uṣitā brahma|vādinaḥ.
Āvikṣitaṃ Maruttaṃ ca mṛtaṃ Sṛñjaya śuśruma.
Saṃvarto yājayām āsa spardhayā vai Bṛhaspateḥ,
yasmai rāja'|rṣaye prādād dhanaṃ sa bhagavān prabhuḥ.
haimaṃ Himavataḥ pādaṃ yiyakṣor vividhaiḥ savaiḥ
yasya s'|Êndr'|âmara|gaṇā Bṛhaspati|puro|gamāḥ
devā viśva|sṛjaḥ sarve yajan'|ânte samāsate.
55.40 yajña|vāṭasya sauvarṇāḥ sarve c' āsan paricchadāḥ
yasya sarvaṃ tadā hy annaṃ mano|'bhiprāya|gaṃ śuci
kāmato bubhujur viprāḥ
sarve c' ânn'|ârthino dvi|jāḥ:
payo dadhi ghṛtaṃ kṣaudraṃ
bhakṣyaṃ bhojyaṃ ca śobhanam.
yasya yajñeṣu sarveṣu vāsāṃsy ābharaṇāni ca
īpsitāny upatiṣṭhante prahṛṣṭān veda|pāra|gān.
marutaḥ pariveṣṭāro Maruttasy' âbhavan gṛhe.

of all the world. Now they dwell deep in a hated and dismal hell with others as cruel of deed.

When the king laid his eyes on his son's corpse he was struck with terrible sorrow and he wept in pain for the loss of what the gods had given him. He was shattered by the death of his son and the divine seer came to his side to comfort him. The king was mad with anguish and crushed by 55.35
despair. Coming very close the seer looked at him intently. Think o Yudhi·shthira upon these words that Nárada spoke to him then.

"Srínjaya. Though we speakers of secrets dwell with you here, you too will die and leave this world and it will not have been enough for you. O Srínjaya, we hear of a man named Marútta son of Avíkshita. He lived long ago. Brihas·pati's rival Samvárta was his priest, and the great and illustrious king was good to the mighty seer.* Many were the rites during which he made his eager offerings to the golden slopes of snowy Himálaya, and Indra and the gods who created the world and crowds of other immortals with Brihas·pati among them all thronged his halls.* Upon the 55.40
sacrificial ground the tools and bowls had been fashioned in gold and all the twiceborn priests who were hungry ate their fill there, in a pure and agreeable feast of milk and curds and ghee, of honey sweets and other fine morsels. At all Marútta's ceremonies cloaks and jewels were piled high and his magi took away with them whatever they pleased. None but the very divinities of the wind were servants in his home.

Āvikṣitasya rāja'|rṣer viśve devāḥ sabhā|sadaḥ
yasya vīryavato rājñaḥ su|vṛṣṭyā sasya|sampadaḥ.
55.45 havirbhis tarpitā yena samyak|kḷptair div'|âukasaḥ
ṛṣīṇāṃ ca pitṝṇāṃ ca devānāṃ sukha|jīvinām,
brahma|carya|śruti|mukhaiḥ sarvair dānaiś ca sarvadā,
śayan'|āsana|pānāni svarṇa|rāśīś ca dus|tyajāḥ
tat sarvam a|mitaṃ vittaṃ dattaṃ viprebhya icchayā.
so 'nudhyātas tu Śakreṇa prajāḥ kṛtvā nir|āmayāḥ
śraddadhāno jitāl̐ lokān gataḥ puṇya|duho 'kṣayān
sa|prajaḥ sa|nṛ|p'|âmātyaḥ sa|dār'|âpatya|bāndhavaḥ.
yauvanena sahasr'|âbdaṃ Marutto rājyam anvaśāt.
sa cen mamāra, Sṛñjaya, catur|bhadrataras tvayā,
putrāt puṇyataras tubhyaṃ, mā putram anutapyathāḥ
a|yajvānam a|dākṣiṇyam abhi, Śvaity', êti vyāharan.»

NĀRADA uvāca:

56.1 SUHOTRAṂ NĀMA rājānaṃ mṛtaṃ, Sṛñjaya, śuśruma
eka|vīram a|dhṛṣyantam amarair abhivīkṣitum,
yaḥ prāpya rājyaṃ dharmeṇa ṛtvig|brahma|purohitān
apṛcchad ātmanaḥ śreyaḥ pṛṣṭvā teṣāṃ mate sthitaḥ.
prajānāṃ pālanaṃ dharmo dānam ijyā dviṣaj|jayaḥ
etat Suhotro vijñāya dharmeṇ' âicchad dhan'|āgamam.
dharmeṇ' ārādhayad devān bāṇaiḥ śatrūñ jayaṃs tathā
sarvāṇy api ca bhūtāni sva|guṇair apy arañjayat,
56.5 yo 'bhuktv" êmāṃ vasumatīṃ mlecch'|āṭavika|varjitām,

In the halls of the great and wise king the gods themselves tarried. His crops flourished in warm rain. The sky's 55.45
denizens were in thrall to what he gave through the fire to the departed seers and fathers and beings that dwell in bliss, and to the great sacrifices he made as a perfect and taintless servant of the Veda. For of his own free will he opened his kitchens, his rooms, his wells, his priceless treasuries and all of his measureless wealth to the brahmins. He had Indra's favour. Only when his subjects were free from every evil did he pass to the undying worlds that flow with bliss which his rites had opened to him, and with him went his wives and children and kin, his ministers and all his empery.

Marútta's vigour kept him king for a thousand years. O Srínjaya, if even he had to die and he four times more blessed than you and more pious than your son then I say to you do not suffer for your child. Cry not the name of one whose life was so miserly and so profane."

NÁRADA spoke:

O SRÍNJAYA. WE know of a king now gone called Suhótra 56.1
so unique that even the gods did not dare raise their eyes to him. He built his kingdom on justice. But that was not enough for him and in search of longevity he decided to seek the help of priests and seers.

Suhótra knew to protect his kingdom and he knew what was right. He understood that he should as much give and sacrifice as throw down his adversaries and he sought to shore up his wealth without neglecting what was incumbent on him. So he paid the gods in obeisance and his enemies in arrows and every creature in his power flourished and

yasmai vavarṣa parjanyo hiraṇyaṃ parivatsarān.
hairaṇyās tatra vāhinyaḥ svairinyo vyavahan purā
grāhān karkaṭakāṃś c' âiva matsyāṃś ca vividhān bahūn.
kāmān varṣati parjanyo rūpāṇi vividhāni ca
sauvarṇāny a|prameyāni vāpyaś ca krośa|saṃmitāḥ.
sahasraṃ vāmanān kubjān nakrān makara|kacchapān
sauvarṇān vihitān dṛṣṭvā tato 'smayata vai tadā.
tat suvarṇam a|paryantaṃ rāja'|rṣiḥ Kurujāṅgale
ījāno vitate yajñe brāhmaṇebhyo hy amanyata.
56.10 so 'śva|medha|sahasreṇa rāja|sūya|śatena ca
puṇyaiḥ kṣatriya|yajñaiś ca prabhūta|vara|dakṣiṇaiḥ
kāmya|naimittik'|âjasrair iṣṭāṃ gatim avāptavān.
sa cen mamāra, Sṛñjaya, catur|bhadrataras tvayā,
putrāt puṇyataras tubhyaṃ, mā putram anutapyathāḥ
ayajvānam adākṣiṇyam abhi Śvaity' êti vyāharan.

NĀRADA uvāca:

57.1 RĀJĀNAṂ PAURAVAṂ vīraṃ mṛtaṃ, Sṛñjaya, śuśruma
sahasraṃ yaḥ sahasrāṇāṃ śvetān aśvān avāsṛjat.
tasy' âśva|medhe rāja'|rṣer deśād deśāt sameyuṣām
śikṣ"|âkṣara|vidhi|jñānāṃ n' āsīt saṃkhyā vipaścitām.
veda|vidyā|vrata|snātā vadānyāḥ priya|darśanāḥ
su|bhikṣ"|ācchādana|gṛhāḥ su|śayy'|āsana|vāhanāḥ
naṭa|nartaka|gandharvaiḥ pūrṇakair vardhamānakaiḥ

grew as it would. In his realm of plenty went no rogue or 56.5
vagabond and the clouds above it rained gold for years and years. Down streams ever gold fared sharks and crabs and shoals of fish. Dreams and colours rained down and filled lakes of gold so vast their breadth could not be reckoned and when Suhótra looked upon the minnows, crocodiles, sharks, dolphins and turtles glittering beyond number in their waters he was truly pleased.

It is said that during an immense sacrifice at Kuru·jángala the wise king gave to the brahmins his bright and bursting
kingdom. He performed horse sacrifices and royal conse- 56.10
crations and ceremonies of war one after the other and each time rewarded his priests with all that they could want. The rituals appointed by day or by want and the rites that are everlasting he made his assiduous work and through them he set foot upon the gloried path to heaven.

O Srínjaya, if even Suhótra had to die and he four times more blessed than you and more pious than your son then I say to you do not suffer for your child. Cry not the name of one whose life was so miserly and so profane.

NÁRADA spoke:

O SRÍNJAYA. WE know of a mighty king and seer now 57.1
gone whose name was Páurava and who let loose thousands upon thousands of white horses. While the rites were being worked there was no accounting of the wise men and keepers of the rules and rhymes of ritual who had gathered to see them through. These reverend and learned men who lived by oath and lore Páurava furnished with chambers and with clothes and with provisions, with fine beds and couches and

nity'|ôdyogaiś ca krīḍadbhis tatra sma pariharṣitāḥ.
57.5 yajñe yajñe yathā|kālaṃ dakṣiṇāḥ so 'tyakālayat
dvipā daśa|sahasr'|ākhyāḥ pramadāḥ kāñcana|prabhāḥ
sa|dhvajāḥ sa|patākāś ca rathā hema|mayās tathā.
yaḥ sahasraṃ sahasrāṇāṃ kanyā hema|vibhūṣitāḥ
dhūrya|jñ'|âśva|gaṇ'|ārūḍhāḥ sa|gṛha|kṣetra|go|śatāḥ,
śataṃ śata|sahasrāṇi svarṇa|mālī mah"|ātmanām
gavā sahasr'|ânucarān dakṣiṇām atyakālayat
hema|śṛṅgyo raupya|khurāḥ sa|vatsāḥ kāṃsya|dohanāḥ.
dāsī|dāsa|khar'|ôṣṭrāṃś ca prādād ājāvikaṃ bahu.
ratnānāṃ vividhānāṃ ca vividhāṃś c' ânna|parvatān
tasmin saṃvitate yajñe dakṣiṇām atyakālayat.
57.10 tatr' âsya gāthā gāyanti ye purāṇa|vido janāḥ.
aṅgasya yajamānasya sva|dharm'|âdhigatāḥ śubhāḥ
guṇ'|ôttarās tu kratavas tasy' āsan sārvakāmikāḥ.
sa cen mamāra, Sṛñjaya, catur|bhadrataras tvayā,
putrāt puṇyataras tubhyaṃ, mā putram anutapyathāḥ
a|yajvānam a|dākṣiṇyam abhi Śvaity' êti vyāharan.

NĀRADA uvāca:

58.1 ŚIBIM AUŚĪNARAṂ c' âpi mṛtaṃ, Sṛñjaya, śuśruma
ya imāṃ pṛthivīṃ sarvāṃ carmavat paryaveṣṭayat
s'|âdri|dvīp'|ârṇava|vanāṃ ratha|ghoṣeṇa nādayan
sa Śibir vai ripūn nityaṃ mukhyān nighnan sapatna|jit,

carriages, with dancers and actors and musicians to play for them without cease while urns and platters were laid before them. And the brahmins were well pleased.

At every occasion Páurava payed his priests as he ought. 57.5
He gave them wild elephants too numerous to name and glittering with gold and he gave them chariots fashioned of gold trailing pennants and flags. He gave them thousands upon thousands of girls, each clad in gold and riding behind a team of mildtempered horses, each bringing with her a palace and an estate and a hundredhead of oxen. He gave them cows in vast numbers garlanded in gold, with horns of gold and silver hooves and milk pails made of copper and farmhands to care for them. He gave them slaves and concubines and donkeys and camels and flocks of sheep and goats. And he raised up mountains of meat and fowl and jewels of every hue and these were his payments to his priests for their office. Those who know the myths of old 57.10
sing songs in his name. Páurava's were works of purity and perfection and the most wondrous virtue and they brought about all that he had meant to come to pass.

O Srínjaya, if even Páurava had to die and he four times more blessed than you and more pious than your son then I say to you do not suffer for your child. Cry not the name of one whose life was so miserly and so profane.

NÁRADA spoke:

O SRÍNJAYA. WE hear of a king now gone who once 58.1
clasped the whole of this wide earth in his embrace. The grind of his chariot's wheels echoed across the mountains and lakes and resounded over jungle and archipelago. King

tena yajñair bahu|vidhair iṣṭaṃ paryāpta|dakṣiṇaiḥ
sa rājā vīryavān dhīmān avāpya vasu puṣkalam
sarva|mūrdh'|âbhiṣiktānāṃ sammataḥ so 'bhavad yudhi,
ayajac c' âśva|medhair yo vijitya pṛthivīm imām.
58.5 nir|argalair bahu|phalair niṣka|koṭi|sahasra|daḥ
hasty|aśva|paśubhir dhānyair mṛgair go|j'|âvibhis tathā
vividhāṃ pṛthivīṃ pūṇyaṃ Śibir brāhmaṇasāt karot.
yāvatyo varṣato dhārā, yāvatyo divi tārakāḥ,
yāvatyāh sikatā Gāṅgyo, yāvan Meror mah"|ôpalāḥ,
udanvati ca yāvanti ratnāni prāṇino 'pi ca
tāvatīr adadad gā vai Śibir Auśīnaro 'dhvare.
no yantāraṃ dhuras tasya
kaṃ cid anyaṃ Prajāpatiḥ
bhūtaṃ bhavyaṃ bhavantaṃ vā
n' âdhyagacchan nar'|ôttamam.
tasy' āsan vividhā yajñāḥ sarva|kāryaiḥ samanvitāḥ
hema|yūp'|āsana|gṛhā hema|prākāra|toraṇāḥ
58.10 śuci svādv anna|pānaṃ ca brāhmaṇāḥ prayut'|âyutāḥ
nānā|bhakṣyaiḥ priya|kathāḥ payo|dadhi|mahā|hradāḥ.
tasy' āsan yajña|vāṭeṣu nadyaḥ śubhr'|ânna|parvatāḥ
pibata snāta khādadhvam iti yad rocate janāḥ.

Shibi of the Ushi·naras was a formidable warrior who cast down the very greatest of his rivals , and so after many rites full of gifts he built the prosperous kingdom he had set out to found. When he was revered among those crowned like he, with the world at his feet he began to stage his grander ceremonies.

His rites were immense and he spared nothing. He 58.5
poured forth coins and trinkets of gold, elephants and horses, kine and corn, deer and cows and calves and goats. Thus he gave his broad and happy land to the twiceborn. Count the raindrops in the rain, the stars in the sky, the grains of sand in the Ganges or stones on Meru. Count all the glittering stones and creatures that teem in the oceans and still you will not have the number of cattle that Shibi of the Ushi·naras let go in those rites. Praja·pati never gave us another like to him. Time could not touch this great one: not past nor future nor the days in which he lived. His sacrifices were ornate and replete. They were conducted in temples of gold where the thrones and pillars were fashioned of gold, with gold the archways and gold the vessels his priests
held in their hands. The food and drink of those feasts were 58.10
sweet and pure and the brahmins came to attend in multitudes. In his hallowed grounds voices sang in the air and there were victuals and lakes of milk and curd and fresh water and mountains of the finest fruits. All who were there were told to bathe and drink and eat, to feast upon whatever they found.

yasmai prādād varaṃ Rudras tuṣṭaḥ puṇyena karmaṇā
a|kṣayaṃ dadato vittaṃ śraddhā kīrtis tathā kriyāḥ
yath" ôktam eva bhūtānāṃ priyatvaṃ svargam uttamam.
etāl̄ labdhvā varān iṣṭāñ Śibiḥ kāle divaṃ gataḥ.
sa cen mamāra, Sṛñjaya, catur|bhadrataras tvayā,
putrāt puṇyataras tubhyaṃ, mā putram anutapyathāḥ
a|yajvānam a|dākṣiṇyam abhi Śvaity' êti vyāharan.

NĀRADA uvāca:

59.1 RĀMAṂ DĀŚARATHIṂ c' âiva mṛtaṃ, Sṛñjaya, śuśruma
yaṃ prajā anvamodanta pitā putrān iv' āurasān
a|saṃkhyeyā guṇā yasmin n' āsann amita|tejasi.
yaś catur|daśa varṣāṇi nideśāt pitur a|cyutaḥ
vane vanitayā sārdham avasal̄ Lakṣmaṇ'|âgra|jaḥ,
jaghāna ca Janasthāne rākṣasān manu|ja'|rṣabhaḥ
tapasvināṃ rakṣaṇ'|ârthaṃ sahasrāṇi catur|daśa.
tatr' âiva vasatas tasya Rāvaṇo nāma rākṣasaḥ
jahāra bhāryāṃ Vaidehīṃ sammohy' âinaṃ sah'|ânujam.
59.5 tam āgas|kāriṇaṃ Rāmaḥ Paulastyam a|jitaṃ paraiḥ
jaghāna samare kruddhaḥ pur" êva Tryambako 'ndhakam
sur'|âsurair avadhyaṃ taṃ deva|brāhmaṇa|kaṇṭakam.
jaghāna sa mahā|bāhuḥ Paulastyaṃ sa|gaṇaṃ raṇe.

Rudra was so moved by Shibi's piety that the god granted the king fame, faith, wealth and power without end. And he gave him the highest heaven which is the love of all men. So it was that when the time came for Shibi to leave this earth he had all the gifts that any man could desire.

O Srínjaya, if even Shibi had to die and he four times more blessed than you and more pious than your son then I say to you do not suffer for your child. Cry not the name of one whose life was so miserly and so profane.

NÁRADA spoke:

O SRÍNJAYA. WE hear of a king now gone whose subjects 59.1
loved him as fathers love their children. He was Rama son of Dasha·ratha. His virtues cannot be summed. They blaze yet in his memory.

Rama lived with his bride in the wilderness for fourteen years and he passed his time there without complaint because his father had decreed it. It was the taurine Rama brother of Lákshmana who slew fourteen thousand demons in Jana·sthana to protect the holy men who dwelt there. But one day during Rama's stay in the forest the demon Rávana tricked him and his brother and snatched away Vaidéhi his
wife. Rama was the only man able to stop Pulástya's savage 59.5
child and in fury he struck him down in battle as once the Three Eyed God had struck down Ándhaka, thorn to deity and brahmin whom neither god nor demon could hitherto defeat. With his two strong arms Rama crushed Paulástya and all those who followed him.

sa praj"|ânugraham kṛtvā tri|daśair abhipūjitaḥ
vyāpya kṛtsnaṃ jagat kīrtyā sura'|ṛṣi|gaṇa|sevitaḥ
sa prāpya vividhaṃ rājyaṃ sarva|bhūt'|ânukampakaḥ
ājahāra mahā|yajñaṃ prajā dharmeṇa pālayan
nir|argalaṃ sa|jārūthyam aśva|medha|śataṃ vibhuḥ.
ājahāra sur'|ēśasya haviṣā mudam āvahat
anyaiś ca vividhair yajñair īje bahu|guṇair nṛ|paḥ.
59.10 kṣut|pipāse 'jayad Rāmaḥ sarva|rogāṃś ca dehinām
satataṃ guṇa|sampanno dīpyamānaḥ sva|tejasā.
ati sarvāṇi bhūtāni Rāmo Dāśarathir babhau.
ṛṣīṇāṃ devatānāṃ ca mānuṣāṇāṃ ca sarvaśaḥ
pṛthivyāṃ saha|vāso 'bhūd Rāme rājyaṃ praśāsati.
n' âhīyata tadā prāṇaḥ prāṇināṃ na tad anyathā
prāṇ'|âpāna|samānāś ca Rāme rājyaṃ praśāsati.
paryadīpyanta tejāṃsi tad|anarthāś ca n' âbhavan
dīrgh'|āyuṣaḥ prajāḥ sarvā yuvā na mriyate tadā.
59.15 vedaiś caturbhiḥ samprītāḥ prāpnuvanti div'|âukasaḥ
havyaṃ kavyaṃ ca vividhaṃ niṣpūrtaṃ hutam eva ca.
a|daṃśa|maśakā deśā naṣṭa|vyāla|sarīsṛpāḥ
n' âpsu prāṇa|bhṛtāṃ mṛtyur n' â|kāle jvalano 'dahat.
a|dharma|rucayo lubdhā mūrkhā vā n' âbhavaṃs tadā
prajāḥ śiṣṭ'|êṣṭa|karmāṇaḥ sarve varṇās tad" âbhavan.
sva|dhā pūjāṃ ca rakṣobhir Janasthāne praṇāśite
prādān nihatya rakṣāṃsi pitṛ|devebhya īśvaraḥ.

Rama was kind to his subjects and favoured by the gods
and his borderless fame drew the heavenly seers into his
sanctuary. The warrior king cared for all the creatures that
lived in his broad kingdom and staged grand rites to keep
his people safe. His horse sacrifices spared nothing but were
numerous and replete with all the ordinances of ritual. His
fire offerings kept the lord of the gods at peace and his many
other ceremonies were of an extravagance that befits a king.
Rama drove out hunger, thirst and disease from his king- 59.10
dom, such a man was he. His brilliance radiated about him.

None could be said to have shone like Rama son of
Dasha·ratha. While he ruled the earth it was a home shared
by men, seers and gods. The breath of the living never ex-
pired nor could it have been otherwise so long as he was
king. Lights burned bright and there was no calamity and
life was without flaw. People lived long and no one died
young. The gods in heaven were placated with the four 59.15
Vedas and were sent oblations and offerings and gifts. The
air of Rama's land was empty of flies and gnats and its soil
free from all creeping evil. Nothing drowned in water or
was consumed in fire. There were none who were crooked
or selfish or foolish but every man no matter what his station did what was ordained for him. For when the king
had driven out the demons who had ravaged Jana·sthana he
held rituals of blessing for the gods and for those who were
no more.

sahasra|putrāḥ puruṣā daśa|varṣa|śat'|āyuṣaḥ
na ca jyeṣṭhāḥ kaniṣṭhebhyas tadā śrāddhāny akārayan.
59.20 śyāmo yuvā lohit'|âkṣo matta|mātaṅga|vikramaḥ
ājānu|bāhuḥ su|bhujaḥ siṃha|skandho mahā|balaḥ
daśa varṣa|sahasrāṇi daśa varṣa|śatāni ca
sarva|bhūta|manaḥ|kānto Rāmo rājyam akārayat.
«Rāmo Rāmo Rāma» iti prajānām abhavat kathā.
rāmād rāmaṃ jagad abhūd Rāme rājyaṃ praśāsati.
catur|vidhāḥ prajā Rāmaḥ svargaṃ nītvā divaṃ gataḥ
ātmānaṃ sampratiṣṭhāpya rāja|vaṃśam ih' âṣṭadhā.
sa cen mamāra, Sṛñjaya, catur|bhadrataras tvayā,
putrāt puṇyataras tubhyaṃ, mā putram anutapyathāḥ
a|yajvānam a|dākṣiṇyam abhi Śvaity' êti vyāharan.

NĀRADA uvāca:

60.1 BHAGĪRATHAṂ CA rājānaṃ mṛtaṃ, Sṛñjaya, śuśruma
yena Bhāgīrathī Gaṅgā cayanaiḥ kāñcanaiś citā,
yaḥ sahasraṃ sahasrāṇāṃ kanyā hema|vibhūṣitāḥ
rājñaś ca rāja|putrāṃś ca brāhmaṇebhyo hy amanyata.
sarvā ratha|gatāḥ kanyā rathāḥ sarve catur|yujaḥ
rathe rathe śataṃ nāgāḥ sarve vai hema|mālinaḥ,
sahasram aśvāś c' âik'|âikaṃ gajānāṃ pṛṣṭhato 'nvayuḥ
aśve aśve śataṃ gāvo gavāṃ paścād ajāvikam.
60.5 ten' ākrāntā jan'|âughena dakṣiṇā bhūyasīr dadat
upahvare 'tivyathitā tasy' âṅke niṣasāda ha.
tathā Bhāgīrathī Gaṅgā urvaśī c' âbhavat purā

Men were gifted with a thousand sons and each lived
for a thousand years, yet even the very old never had to
lay the young to rest. Dark Rama built his kingdom as 59.20
the centuries rolled past and he was beloved of every being
within it. From wonder to wonder the world turned beneath his lustrous rule and all his subjects sang the name
of the redeyed and muscled youth with a lion's shoulders
and the might of an elephant in musth. When he had led
every one of his subjects to heaven he departed for the skies
himself. Behind him he left eight full bloodlines of future
kings.

O Srínjaya, if even Rama had to die and he four times more blessed than you and more pious than your son then I say to you do not suffer for your child. Cry not the name of one whose life was so miserly and so profane.

NÁRADA spoke:

O SRÍNJAYA. THERE was a king now gone whose name 60.1
was Bhagi·ratha. He was the father of Ganges for he filled
her to her banks with a glittering hoard. King Bhagi·ratha
gave to his brahmins thousands upon thousands of his sons
and princes and daughters and all of them were tricked out
in gold. Every one of the girls came riding on a chariot
and each chariot was drawn by a team of four and behind
each chariot came a hundred elephants bound in gold. And
behind the elephants came a thousand horses and behind
each horse came a hundred cows, and behind the cows came
sheep and goats. The throng pressed against the river, and 60.5
so that she might yield a gift yet greater she roiled in her
courses and settled into the curve they made. And so it was

duhitṛtvaṃ gatā rājñaḥ putratvam agamat tadā.
tāṃ tu gāthāṃ jaguḥ prītā gandharvāḥ sūrya|varcasaḥ
pitṛ|deva|manuṣyāṇāṃ śṛṇvatāṃ valgu|vādinaḥ.

Bhagīrathaṃ yajamānam Aikṣvākuṃ bhūri|dakṣiṇam
Gaṅgā samudra|gā devī vavre pitaram īśvaram.
tasya s'|Êndraiḥ sura|gaṇair devair yajñaḥ sv|alaṃ|kṛtaḥ
samyak parigṛhītaś ca śānta|vighno nir|āmayaḥ.
60.10 yo ya iccheta vipro vai yatra yatr' ātmanaḥ priyam
Bhagīrathas tathā prītas tatra tatr' ânayad vaśī.
n' â|deyaṃ brāhmaṇeṣv āsīd yasya yat syāt priyaṃ dhanam
so 'pi vipra|prasādena brahma|lokaṃ gato nṛ|paḥ.
yena yātā makha|mukhe diś"|āśāv iha pāda|pāḥ
ten' âvasthātum icchanti taṃ gatvā rājam īśvaram.

sa cen mamāra, Sṛñjaya, catur|bhadrataras tvayā,
putrāt puṇyataras tubhyaṃ, mā putram anutapyathāḥ
a|yajvānam a|dākṣiṇyam abhi Śvaity' êti vyāharan.

NĀRADA UVĀCA:

61.1 DILĪPAṂ VAI c' Âilavilaṃ mṛtaṃ, Sṛñjaya, śuśruma
yasya yajña|śateṣv āsan prayut'|âyutaśo dvijāḥ
tantra|jñān'|ârtha|sampannā yajvānaḥ putra|pautriṇaḥ.
ya imāṃ vasu|sampūrṇāṃ vasudhāṃ vasudh'|âdhipaḥ
ījāno vitate yajñe brāhmaṇebhyo hy amanyata.

that Ganges Bhagi·rathi grew broad as the dawn. After being like the king's daughter she became a kind of son.* So sing the sunbright spirits in harmonies divine to fill the ears of ancestors and gods and men.

As the generous heir of Ikshváku worked his rites and as the goddess wound down to the sea she swallowed up the king her father. The gods and immortals and Indra himself ringed his perfect ceremony and its violence was cooled and its pollution washed away.

If there was something Bhagi·ratha owned no matter 60.10
how dear and one of his brahmins desired it, the good king would give it away without heed. His greatest gift to the brahmins was the river herself and when he had given her away the king went with the blessing of the priests up to the holy realm. For as the things that grow in the earth take root in a happy place where they can hope to see the sky so it is that whoever goes to the shining king of heaven goes there to abide with him*and to endure.

O Srínjaya, if even Bhagi·ratha had to die and he four times more blessed than you and more pious than your son then I say to you do not suffer for your child. Cry not the name of one whose life was so miserly and so profane.

NÁRADA spoke:

O SRÍNJAYA. WE hear of a king now gone named Dilípa 61.1
son of Ílavila. He held rite after rite and he had a battery of the twiceborn to perform them, venerable priests and patriarchs who knew the arts and secrets of magic. As the rites were arraigned this regent of the earth would give his rich and fertile realm away to the twiceborn. At Dilípa's

Dilīpasya ca yajñeṣu kṛtaḥ panthā hiraṇmayaḥ.
taṃ Dharmam iva kurvāṇāḥ s'|Êndrā devāḥ samāgaman.
caṣālaṃ pracaṣālaṃ ca yasya yūpe hiraṇmaye
nṛtyante 'psarasas tasya ṣaṭ|sahasrāṇi saptadhā,
yatra vīnāṃ vādayati prītyā Viśvāvasuḥ svayam.
61.5 sarva|bhūtāny amanyanta rājānaṃ satya|śīlinam
rāga|khaṇḍava|bhojyaiś ca mattāḥ pathiṣu śerate.
tad etad adbhutaṃ manye anyair na sadṛśaṃ nṛ|paiḥ
yad apsu yudhyamānasya cakre na paripetatuḥ.
rājānaṃ dṛḍha|dhanvānaṃ Dilīpaṃ satya|vādinam
ye 'paśyan bhūri|dākṣiṇyaṃ te 'pi svarga|jito narāḥ
pañca śabdā na jīryante Khaṭṭāṅgasya niveśane
svādhyāya|ghoṣo jyā|ghoṣaḥ pibat' âśnīta khādata.
sa cen mamāra, Sṛñjaya, catur|bhadrataras tvayā,
putrāt puṇyataras tubhyaṃ, mā putram anutapyathāḥ
a|yajvānam a|dākṣiṇyam abhi Śvaity' êti vyāharan.

NĀRADA uvāca:

62.1 MĀNDHĀTĀ CED Yauvanāśvo mṛtaḥ, Sṛñjaya, śuśruma
dev'|âsura|manuṣyāṇāṃ trailokya|vijayī nṛ|paḥ,
yaṃ devāv aśvinau garbhāt pituḥ pūrvaṃ cakarṣatuḥ.
mṛgayāṃ vicaran rājā tṛṣitaḥ klānta|vāhanaḥ
dhūmaṃ dṛṣṭv" āgamat sattraṃ pṛṣad|ājyam avāpa saḥ.
taṃ dṛṣṭvā Yuvanāśvasya jaṭhare sūnutāṃ gatam

rituals there was always a path paved in gold, and Indra would bring the gods there as if to Dharma himself, while around the sacrificial stake with its golden ring and clasp* vast crowds of *ápsaras*es* would dance. There would be six times seven thousand of them, and Vishva·vasu himself would play for them upon the strings of his ringing lute.
Later they would all lay down upon the ground, drunk on 61.5
the feasting, and all of them proclaim the king a man of peerless virtue.

Dilípa's chariot was a miracle like no other for its wheels as they passed through water left no mark. He was a man of extravagant gifts, his bow was strong and his words were true and to bask in his presence was to push wide heaven's gates. For there were five sounds that echoed forever in the palace of Khattánga: these were the voice of incantation, the sigh of the bow, and the calls to drink, to eat and to feast.

O Srínjaya, if even Dilípa had to die and he four times more blessed than you and more pious than your son then I say to you do not suffer for your child. Cry not the name of one whose life was so miserly and so profane.

NÁRADA spoke:

O SRÍNJAYA. WE hear of another king now gone named 62.1
Mandhátri son of Yuvanáshva, a man whose triumphs crossed the triple world of gods, demons and men. He was born when the twin Horse Gods drew him from his father's belly. One day Yuvanáshva was wandering thirsty from the hunt with his strength spent when he saw the smoke rising

garbhādd hi jahratur devāv aśvinau bhiṣajāṃ varau.
tam dṛṣṭvā pitur utsaṅge śayānaṃ deva|varcasam
anyo|'nyam abruvan devāḥ «kam ayaṃ dhāsyat'?» îti vai.
62.5 «mām ev' âyaṃ dhayatv agre» iti ha sm' āha Vāsavaḥ.
tato 'ṅgulibhyo h' Îndrasya prādur āsīt payo 'mṛtam.
«māṃ dhāsyat'» îti kāruṇyād yad Indro hy anvakampayat
tasmāt tu Māndhāt" êty evaṃ nāma tasya tu taiḥ kṛtam.
tatas tu dhārāḥ payaso ghṛtasya ca mah"|ātmanaḥ
tasy' āsye Yauvanāśvasya pāṇir Indrasya c' âsravat.
apibat pāṇim Indrasya sa c' âpy ahn" âbhyavardhata.
so 'bhavad dvā|daśa|samo dvā|daś'|âhena vīryavān.
imāṃ ca pṛthivīṃ kṛtsnām ek'|âhnā sa vyajījayat
dharm'|ātmā dhṛtimān vīraḥ satya|saṃdho jit'|êndriyaḥ.
62.10 Janamejayaṃ Sudhanvānaṃ Gayaṃ Pūruṃ Bṛhadratham
Asitaṃ ca Nṛgaṃ c' âiva Māndhātā dhanuṣo 'jayat.
udeti ca yataḥ sūryo yatra ca pratitiṣṭhati
tat sarvaṃ Yauvanāśvasya Māndhātuḥ kṣetram ucyate.
so 'śva|medha|śatair iṣṭvā rāja|sūya|śatena ca
adadad rohitān matsyān brāhmaṇebhyo viśāṃ pate.
hairaṇyān yojan'|ôtsedhān āyatān daśa|yojanam
bahu|prakārān su|svādūn bhakṣya|bhojy'|ânna|parvatān
atiriktaṃ brāhmaṇebhyo bhuñjāno hīyate janaḥ.
bhakṣy'|ânna|pāna|nicayāḥ śuśubhus tv anna|parvatāḥ

from a *soma* sacrifice. Coming nearer, he found an oblation and drank it. When the Horse Gods saw the draught become a child within Yuvanáshva's stomach they reached right inside him and using their healing magic they drew the baby forth into the world.

The immortals looked upon the boy as he lay in his father's lap splendid as a god and they wondered how to keep him alive.

"He must drink from my fingertips," said Vásava. 62.5

Divine milk flowed from Indra's fingers. Because he had
taken pity on the child with the words "Drink from my
hands," the gods decided to call the boy Mandhátri.* Jets
of milk and ghee streamed from the kind god's fingers and
into Mandhátri's mouth and he drank and grew quite suddenly in size. In twelve days he had become strong as twelve
men and in the day that followed he conquered the whole
of the earth. He became a master of himself, a pillar of
truth, a hardy warrior in whom order reigned. Bow in hand 62.10
Mandhátri laid low Janam·éjaya, Sudhánvan, Gaya, Puru
and Brihad·ratha. Even Ásita and Nriga fell before him. The
whole of the land from where the sun rose to where it set
he called his kingdom.

O lord of this realm. Mandhátri slew hundreds of horses in sacrifice and held a hundred times the rituals of a king. To his priests he gave *ruhi* fish, and raised up mountains of food a mile high and ten miles wide, scattered with gold and full of all kinds of victuals and morsels. All of it was sweet and delicious. The needs of his people were always second to the needs of the brahmins. Flowing down those mountains between heaps of food and drink wondrous to

ghṛta|hradāḥ sūpa|paṅkā dadhi|phenā guḍ'|ôdakāḥ.
rurudhuḥ parvatān nadyo madhu|kṣīra|vahāḥ śubhāḥ.
62.15 dev'|âsurā narā yakṣā gandharv'|ôraga|pakṣiṇaḥ
viprās tatr' āgatāś c' āsan veda|ved'|âṅga|pāra|gāḥ.
brāhmaṇā ṛṣayaś c' âpi n' āsaṃs tatr' â|vipaścitaḥ.
samudr'|ântāṃ vasumatīṃ vasu|pūrṇāṃ ca sarvataḥ
sa tāṃ brāhmaṇasāt kṛtvā jagām' âstaṃ tadā nṛ|paḥ
gataḥ puṇya|kṛtāṃ lokān vyāpya sva|yaśasā diśaḥ.
sa cen mamāra, Sṛñjaya, catur|bhadrataras tvayā,
putrāt puṇyataras tubhyaṃ, mā putram anutapyathāḥ
a|yajvānam a|dākṣiṇyam abhi Śvaity' êti vyāharan.

NĀRADA UVĀCA:

63.1 YAYĀTIṂ NĀHUṢAṂ c' âiva mṛtaṃ, Sṛñjaya, śuśruma.
rāja|sūya|śatair iṣṭvā so 'śva|medha|śatena ca
puṇḍarīka|sahasreṇa vāja|peya|śatais tathā
atirātra|sahasreṇa cāturmāsyaiś ca kāmataḥ
agni|ṣṭomaiś ca vividhaiḥ sattraiś ca prājya|dakṣiṇaiḥ,
a|brāhmaṇānāṃ yad vittaṃ pṛthivyām asti kiṃ cana
tat sarvaṃ parisaṃkhyāya tato brāhmaṇasāt karot.
Sarasvatī puṇyatamā nadīnāṃ
tathā samudrāḥ saritaḥ s'|âdrayaś ca
ījānāya puṇyatamāya rājñe
ghṛtaṃ payo duduhur Nāhuṣāya.
63.5 vyūḍhe dev'|âsure yuddhe kṛtvā deva|sahāyatām

behold came rivers of milk and honey, rushing over beds of broth and bubbling with curd and swirling with molasses into pools of ghee. Gods, men and demons, spirits, *gan-* 62.15
dhárvas,* snakes and birds and anchorites deepversed in the Veda body and limb all flocked to his rites. All his priests were seers steeped in learning. Only when he had brought his vast and flourishing kingdom down to the sea's edge and given it to the twiceborn and spread his fame far and wide did that lord of men finally set like the sun and depart for paradise.

O Srínjaya, if even Mandhátri had to die and he four times more blessed than you and more pious than your son then I say to you do not suffer for your child. Cry not the name of one whose life was so miserly and so profane.

NÁRADA spoke:

O SRÍNJAYA. WE hear of another monarch now gone 63.1
named Yayáti son of Náhusha. He slew hundreds of horses in sacrifice and held a hundred times the rituals that befit a king. A thousand times he staged the Rite of the Lotus and the Drink of Battle, the Night Passage and the Four Month Cycle. Whenever he was in need he sacrificed. His fire offerings were many and his *soma* rituals rich with gifts. Whatever there was on earth that did not belong to the holy he reckoned up and rendered to them. He was so devout that Sarásvati the holiest of rivers who already poured her rocky waters into his kingdom flowed for Yayáti with milk and ghee. When the gods and demons donned their armour to 63.5

caturdhā vyabhajat sarvāṃ caturbhyaḥ pṛthivīm imām.
yajñair nānā|vidhair iṣṭvā prajām utpādya c' ôttamām
Devayānyāṃ c' Āuśanasyāṃ Śarmiṣṭhāyāṃ ca dharmataḥ,
dev'|âraṇyeṣu sarveṣu vijahār' âmar'|ôpamaḥ
ātmanaḥ kāma|cāreṇa dvitīya iva Vāsavaḥ.
yadā n' âdhyagamac chāntiṃ kāmānāṃ sarva|vedavit
tato gāthām imāṃ gītvā sa|dāraḥ prāviśad vanam.
yat pṛthivyāṃ vrīhi|yavaṃ hiraṇyaṃ paśavaḥ striyaḥ,
n' âlam ekasya tat sarvam iti matvā śamaṃ vrajet.
63.10 evaṃ kāmān parityajya Yayātir dhṛtim etya ca
Pūruṃ rājye pratiṣṭhāpya prayāto vanam īśvaraḥ.
sa cen mamāra, Sṛñjaya, catur|bhadrataras tvayā,
putrāt puṇyataras tubhyaṃ, mā putram anutapyathāḥ
a|yajvānam a|dākṣiṇyam abhi Śvaity' êti vyāharan.

NĀRADA uvāca:

64.1 NĀBHĀGAM AMBARĪṢAṂ ca mṛtaṃ, Sṛñjaya, śuśruma
yaḥ sahasraṃ sahasrāṇāṃ rājñāṃ c' âikas tv ayodhayat.
jigīṣamāṇāḥ saṃgrāme samantād vairiṇo 'bhyayuḥ
astra|yuddha|vido ghorāḥ sṛjantaś c' â|śivā giraḥ.
bala|lābhād vaśī|kṛtya teṣāṃ śastra|balena ca
chattr'|āyudha|dhvaja|rathāṃś chittvā prāsān gata|vyathaḥ,
ta enaṃ mukta|saṃnāhāḥ prārthayan jīvit'|âiṣiṇaḥ
śaraṇyam īyuḥ śaraṇaṃ tava sma iti vādinaḥ.

do battle, he proclaimed allegiance to the former and divided the whole of his fourfold kingdom into its parts for them.

After his many rites and after Sharmíshtha and Deva·yani daughter of Úshanas had both borne him perfect children, Yayáti went wandering at whim through the holy groves like a second Vásava. He was a wise and learned man and when he found that his desires would never be at peace he took his wife and departed for the forest with this very hymn in his heart: As the whole of this earth with all the rice barley gold goats and girls it contains will never be enough for a man, so must one seek to know this and to know peace.
And so indeed the great man cast off his desires and found 63.10
a deeper beatitude, and leaving his son to rule in his place headed even deeper into the jungle.

O Srínjaya, if even Yayáti had to die and he four times more blessed than you and more pious than your son then I say to you do not suffer for your child. Cry not the name of one whose life was so miserly and so profane.

NÁRADA spoke:

WE HEAR OF ANOTHER king now gone named Ambarísha 64.1
son of Nabhága who though but a single man warred with a million kings. His enemies were formidable chieftains versed in war and bowcraft and they came at him in battle wild and baying for blood. He was not afraid. With the force of his arm and blade he cut down their cars and totems, their parasols and swords and spears and he laid them low. Stripped of their armour and fearing for their lives they begged for mercy. And o king he showed them

64.5 sa tu tān vaśa|gān kṛtvā jitvā c' êmāṃ vasuṃ|dharām
īje yajña|śatair iṣṭair yathā|śāstraṃ tath" ân|agha.
bubhujuḥ sarva|sampannam annam anye janāḥ sadā
tasmin yajñe tu vipr'|êndrāḥ su|tṛptāḥ param'|ârcitāḥ.
modakān pūrik"|âpūpān svādu|pūrṇāś ca śaṣkulīḥ
karambhān pṛthu|mṛdvīkā annāni su|kṛtāni ca
sūpān maireyak'|âpūpān rāga|khāṇḍava|pānakān
mṛṣṭ'|ânnāni su|yuktāni mṛdūni surabhīṇi ca
ghṛtaṃ madhu payas toyaṃ dadhīni rasavanti ca
phalaṃ mūlaṃ ca su|svādu dvijās tatr' ôpabhuñjate.
64.10 madanīyāni pānāni viditvā c' ātmanaḥ sukham
apibanta yathā|kāmaṃ pāna|pā gīta|vāditaiḥ.
tatra sma gāthā gāyanti kṣībā hṛṣṭāḥ paṭhanti ca
Nābhāga|stuti|saṃyuktā nanṛtuś ca sahasraśaḥ.
teṣu yajñeṣv Ambarīṣo dakṣiṇām atyakālayat
rājñāṃ śata|sahasrāṇi daśa prayuta|yājinām.
hiraṇya|kavacān sarvāñ śveta|cchattra|prakīrṇakān
hiraṇya|syandan'|ārūḍhān s'|ânuyātra|paricchadān
ījāno vitate yajñe dakṣiṇām atyakālayat.
mūrdh'|âbhiṣiktāṃś ca nṛ|pān rāja|putra|śatāni ca
sa|daṇḍa|kośa|nicayān brāhmaṇebhyo hy amanyata.
64.15 «n' âivaṃ pūrve janāś cakrur na kariṣyanti c' âpare
yad Ambarīṣo nṛ|patiḥ karoty a|mita|dakṣiṇaḥ»
ity evam anumodante prītā yasya maha"|rṣayaḥ.

clemency. His foes subdued, he brought the whole of the 64.5
wide earth beneath his dominion and then o sinless one following what the holy books dictate he began the work of
sacrifice. Ceremonies he held beyond number.

Men came to his rites and enjoyed extravagant feasts,
and among them the brahmins were held in the highest
esteem. There were sweetmeats, lemon loaves, fine pastries
made of molasses and oats and raisins. There were sauces
and cakes made with liquor, honeyballs rolled in sugar and
sweet drinks and all of it was soft to the bite and fragrant
and daintily arranged. There was the most delicious ghee
and there was honey, milk, fresh water, curds, vegetables
and ripe fruit. The brahmins ate their fill. They drank spirits 64.10
until they could drink no more and sang to the strains of
lutes and at last took to the roads in their thousands, drunk
and happy and dancing and chanting their praise to Nabhága's son.

At his rites Ambarísha gave the brahmins hundreds of
thousands of his own vassals, men who themselves had
staged many of their own rites, who wore golden armour
and carried white parasols and rode on golden chariots and
brought retainers and servants along with them. All these
anointed rulers of men were sent by Ambarísha with their
treasuries and sceptres and hundreds of princes across to the
brahmins as the rites went on. No man of old had shown 64.15
such generosity and none to come will ever show the same.
For all the gifts without end that King Ambarísha gave them
the great sages of his time loved him well.

sa cen mamāra, Sṛñjaya, catur|bhadrataras tvayā,
putrāt puṇyataras tubhyaṃ, mā putram anutapyathāḥ
a|yajvānam a|dākṣiṇyam abhi Śvaity' êti vyāharan.

NĀRADA uvāca:

65.1 ŚAŚABINDUṂ CA rājānaṃ mṛtaṃ, Sṛñjaya, śuśruma
īje sa vividhair yajñaiḥ śrīmān satya|parākramaḥ.
tasya bhāryā|sahasrāṇāṃ śatam āsīn mah"|ātmanaḥ
ek'|âikasyāṃ ca bhāryāyāṃ sahasraṃ tanay" âbhavan.
te kumārāḥ parākrāntāḥ sarve niyuta|yājinaḥ
rājānaḥ kratubhir mukhyair ījānā veda|pāra|gāḥ.
hiraṇya|kavacāḥ sarve sarve c' ôttama|dhanvinaḥ
sarve 'śva|medhair ījānāḥ kumārāḥ Śāśabindavāḥ.
65.5 tān aśva|medhe rāj'|êndro brāhmaṇebhyo 'dadat pitā.
śataṃ śataṃ ratha|gajā ek'|âikaṃ pṛṣṭhato 'nvayuḥ
rāja|putraṃ, tadā kanyās tapanīya|svalaṃkṛtāḥ,
kanyāṃ kanyāṃ śataṃ nāgā, nāge nāge śataṃ rathāḥ,
rathe rathe śataṃ c' âśvā vājino hema|mālinaḥ,
aśve aśve sahasraṃ gā, gavāṃ paścā śat'|āvikāḥ.

etad dhanam a|paryantam aśva|medhe mahā|makhe
Śaśabindur mahā|bhāgo brāhmaṇebhyo hy amanyata.
vārkṣāś ca yūpā yāvanta aśva|medhe mahā|makhe
te tath" âiva punaś c' ânye tāvantaḥ kāñcan" âbhavan.
65.10 bhakṣy'|ânna|pāna|nicayāḥ parvatāḥ krośam ucchritāḥ
tasy' âśva|medhe nirvṛtte rājñaḥ śiṣṭās trayo|daśa.

O Srínjaya, if even Ambarísha had to die and he four times more blessed than you and more pious than your son then I say to you do not suffer for your child. Cry not the name of one whose life was so miserly and so profane.

NÁRADA spoke:

O SRÍNJAYA. WE hear of a king now gone named Shasha· 65.1
bindu. He was blessed and brave and his offerings were
prodigious. The great man had many thousands of wives
and to each of them were born a thousand sons, and all
of them were bold and devout young men who as kings
worked the solemn rites and steeped themselves in the Veda's
lore. All wore golden armour and bore the finest bows and
all of them slew horses at the ceremonies they gave. And 65.5
the great king their father gave them to his brahmins at just
such a rite. The king's sons were brought forth and behind
each of them went elephants and chariots in vast numbers,
and then came his daughters clad in firebeaten gold, and
behind each of his daughters went a hundred elephants,
and behind each elephant a hundred cars, and behind each
car a hundred swift horses decorated with gold, and behind
each horse a thousand oxen, and behind each ox a hundred
goats.

Great was the rite and great the feast at which Shasha·
bindu gave from his enormous wealth gifts that cannot be
surpassed. Great was the rite and great the feast where he
hewed twice as many stakes as the ceremony demanded,
and every one of them plated in gold, where he raised into 65.10
the sky mountains of food and drink a league high, of which
by the rite's end a range thirteen wide stood yet untouched.

tuṣṭa|puṣṭa|jan'|ākīrṇāṃ śānta|vighnām an|āmayām
Śaśabindur imāṃ bhūmiṃ ciraṃ bhuktvā divaṃ gataḥ.
sa cen mamāra, Sṛñjaya, catur|bhadrataras tvayā,
putrāt puṇyataras tubhyaṃ, mā putram anutapyathāḥ
a|yajvānam a|dākṣiṇyam abhi Śvaity' êti vyāharan.

NĀRADA uvāca:

66.1 GAYAṂ c' Āmūrtarayasaṃ mṛtaṃ, Sṛñjaya, śuśruma
yo vai varṣa|śataṃ rājā huta|śiṣṭ'|āśano 'bhavat.
tasmai hy Agnir varaṃ prādāt tato vavre varaṃ Gayaḥ
tapasā brahma|caryeṇa vratena niyamena ca.
«gurūṇāṃ ca prasādena vedān icchāmi veditum.
sva|dharmeṇ' â|vihiṃsy' ânyān dhanam icchāmi c' âkṣayam.
vipreṣu dadataś c' âiva śraddhā bhavati nityaśaḥ
an|anyāsu sa|varṇāsu putra|janma ca me bhavet.
66.5 annaṃ me dadataḥ śraddhā dharme me ramatāṃ manaḥ
a|vighnaṃ c' âstu me nityaṃ dharma|kāryeṣu, pāvaka.»
«tathā bhaviṣyat'» îty uktvā tatr' âiv' ântar|adhīyata
Gayo hy avāpya tat sarvaṃ dharmeṇ' ârīn ajījayat.
sa darśa|paurṇamāsābhyāṃ kāleṣv āgrayaṇena ca
cāturmāsyaiś ca vividhair yajñaiś c' âvāpta|dakṣiṇaiḥ
ayajac chraddhayā rājā parisaṃvatsarān śatam.
gavāṃ śata|sahasrāṇi śatam aśva|śatāni ca
śataṃ niṣka|sahasrāṇi gavāṃ c' âpy ayutāni ṣaṭ
utthāy' ôtthāya samprādāt parisaṃvatsarān śatam.

Only when the earth was free from any plague or violence and full of flourishing and happy souls and Shasha·bindu had drunk deep of life did he at last depart for heaven.

O Srínjaya, if even Shasha·bindu had to die and he four times more blessed than you and more pious than your son then I say to you do not suffer for your child. Cry not the name of one whose life was so miserly and so profane.

NÁRADA spoke:

O SRÍNJAYA. WE hear of a king now gone named Gaya 66.1
son of Amúrta·rayas who lived for a hundred years on what food remained after the sacrifices were over. For his power and piety and for his vows and his discipline, Agni offered him a reward. Gaya chose what it would be.

"O Burning One. I want to learn the Veda at the feet of masters. I seek the undying wealth of one who finds it within his being not to harm another. I will forever honour the twiceborn with gifts and may I have children with
women of my station who will be true to me. May I hold 66.5
ceremonies and feasts and treat those who enjoy them, as is right. May all my rites be undisturbed."

"So will it be," said Agni and disappeared, and so it was that Gaya received all that he asked for and one by one his enemies fell at his feet. For a hundred years more the king offered sacrifices every morning and on the days of the full and new moons. He faithfully followed the Four Month Cycle and his rituals were numerous and extravagant. Again and again he offered up huge herds of oxen and horses and heaps of gold coins and so many cows they could not be reckoned. Thus the century passed. Like Soma and Ángiras

nakṣatreṣu ca sarveṣu dadan nakṣatra|dakṣiṇāḥ
īje ca vividhair yajñair yathā Somo ’ṅgirā yathā.
66.10 sauvarṇāṃ pṛthivīṃ kṛtvā ya imāṃ maṇi|śarkarām
viprebhyaḥ prādadad rājā so ’śva|medhe mahā|makhe.
jāmbūnada|mayā yūpāḥ sarve ratna|paricchadāḥ
Gayasy’ āsan samṛddhās tu sarva|bhūta|mano|harāḥ.
sarva|kāma|samṛddhāṃś ca prādāt tāṃś ca Gayas tadā
brāhmaṇebhyaḥ prahṛṣṭebhyaḥ sarva|bhūtebhya eva ca.
sa|samudra|vana|dvīpa|nadī|nada|vaneṣu ca
nagareṣu ca rāṣṭreṣu divi vyomni ca ye ’vasan
bhūta|grāmāś ca vividhāḥ saṃtṛptā yajña|sampadā.
Gayasya sadṛśo yajño n’ âsty anya iti te ’bruvan.
66.15 ṣaṭ|triṃśad|yojan’|āyāmā triṃśad yojanam āyatā
paścāt puraś caturviṃśad vedī hy āsīdd hiraṇmayī
Gayasya yajamānasya muktā|vajra|maṇi|stṛtā.
prādāt sa brāhmaṇebhyo ’tha vāsāṃsy ābharaṇāni ca
yath”|ôktā dakṣiṇāś c’ ânyā viprebhyo bhūri|dakṣiṇaḥ.
yatra bhojana|śiṣṭasya parvatāḥ pañca|viṃśatiḥ,
kulyāḥ kuśala|vāhinyo rasānām abhavaṃs tadā,
vastr’|ābharaṇa|gandhānāṃ rāśayaś ca pṛthag|vidhāḥ,
yasya prabhāvāc ca Gayas triṣu lokeṣu viśrutaḥ
vaṭaś c’ âkṣayya|karaṇaḥ puṇyaṃ brahma|saraś ca tat.
sa cen mamāra, Sṛñjaya, catur|bhadrataras tvayā,
putrāt puṇyataras tubhyaṃ, mā putram anutapyathāḥ
a|yajvānam a|dākṣiṇyam abhi Śvaity’ êti vyāharan.

before him he spread his rites upon the earth to match the stars above and gave as the almanacs dictated.

Great were the feasts whereat this king for whom the 66.10
dust of the land glittered with jewels gave gifts to the brahmins who came to him. All the broad posts driven into Gaya's hallowed ground were covered in rivergold and studded with jewels beautiful to behold. Gaya gave them to the brahmins and to other men besides and they were delighted for these stakes were charms that would grant their every desire. On the coast and in the jungles, by the lakes and in the rivers and marshes and forests, in the cities and in the kingdoms of the air and the sky every kind of thing that lived was replenished by his worship.

It was said that there was no rite on earth that could compare to one of the grandest ceremonies that Gaya performed. His altar then was three hundred miles wide, three 66.15
hundred and sixty miles high and two hundred and forty miles deep and all of it was covered in gold and sprent with pearls and diamonds and gemstones. True to his words he gave his priests garments and treasure and jewellery and piles of other gifts. The ceremony spread Gaya's renown across the triple world. Where once there were mountains of food and rivers flowing rich with nectar and bright piles of cloaks and bangles and perfume, there now grows a banyan tree beside a pool of hallowed water. Its branches never wither.

O Sríñjaya, if even Gaya had to die and he four times more blessed than you and more pious than your son then I say to you do not suffer for your child. Cry not the name of one whose life was so miserly and so profane.

NĀRADA uvāca:

67.1 SĀṂKṚTIṂ RANTIDEVAṂ ca mṛtaṃ, Sṛñjaya, śuśruma
yasya dvi|śata|sāhasrā āsan sūdā mah"|ātmanaḥ.
gṛhān abhyāgatān viprān atithīn pariveṣakāḥ
pakv'|â|pakvaṃ divā|rātraṃ var'|ânnam amṛt'|ôpamam.
nyāyen' âdhigataṃ vittaṃ brāhmaṇebhyo hy amanyata
vedān adhītya dharmeṇa yaś cakre dviṣato vaśe.
upasthitāś ca paśavaḥ svayaṃ yaṃ saṃśita|vratam
bahavaḥ svargam icchanto vidhivat sattra|yājinam.
67.5 nadī mahānasād yasya pravṛttā carma|rāśitaḥ.
tasmāc Carmaṇvatī pūrvam agni|hotre 'bhavat purā.
brāhmaṇebhyo 'dadan niṣkān sauvarṇān sa prabhāvataḥ,
tubhyaṃ niṣkaṃ, tubhyaṃ niṣkam iti ha sma prabhāṣate.
tubhyaṃ, tubhyam iti prādān niṣkān niṣkān sahasraśaḥ
tataḥ punaḥ samāśvāsya niṣkān eva prayacchati.
«alpaṃ dattaṃ may" âdy'» êti niṣka|koṭiṃ pradāya saḥ
ek' âhnā dāsyati punaḥ ko 'nyas tat sampradāsyati.
dvija|pāṇi|viyogena duḥkham me śāśvataṃ mahat
bhaviṣyati na saṃdeha evaṃ rāj" âdadad vasu.
67.10 sahasraśaś ca sauvarṇān vṛṣabhān go|śat'|ânugān
s'|âṣṭaṃ śataṃ suvarṇānāṃ niṣkam āhur dhanaṃ tadā
adhyardha|māsam adadad brāhmaṇebhyaḥ śataṃ samāḥ.
agni|hotr'|ôpakaraṇaṃ yajñ'|ôpakaraṇaṃ ca yat
ṛṣibhyaḥ karakān kumbhān sthālīḥ piṭharam eva ca

NÁRADA spoke:

O SRÍNJAYA. WE hear of a king now gone named Ranti·deva son of Sánkriti whose palace held two hundred thousand cooks. The twiceborn stayed as guests with the king's family in his home and were attended by his servants, and day and night he set before the twiceborn the finest food steaming and fresh and fine as ambrosia. To the brahmins he gave many things, all of which he had come by justly. He was a man who had studied the Veda and thus had with the honour brought his enemies low. One after another the animals stepped up to the blade* and offered themselves to heaven for Ranti·deva's vows were severe and his ceremonies were faithful to scripture. Once during a fire ritual he held a river of juice formed from the great heap of animal skins laid up in his scullery, and so it was that the Charmánvati got its name.* 67.1 67.5

A coin for you, a coin for you, he would say as he gave away all the gold he had to the brahmins. Coin after coin followed his refrain: thousands of them left his fingers then. Take this little gift from me, he would say, holding out a chest full of gold. In a single day he would give away all that another king owned. He knew that if he were to lose the help of the brahmins it would be a catastrophe for him and so the king resolved to give away all he had.

They say that the coins he gave away were worth a thousand golden bulls, each with a hundred cows and eight hundred ingots of gold. Every fortnight for a hundred years to his priests he gave tools for the fire sacrifice and tools for other rites and urns and pots and pans and cauldrons, sedans, couches and cars, palaces, houses and the timber of 67.10

śayan'|âsana|yānāni prāsādāṃś ca gṛhāṇi ca
vṛkṣāṃś ca vividhān dadyād annāni ca dhanāni ca.
sarvaṃ sauvarṇam ev' āsīd Rantidevasya dhīmataḥ.
tatr' âsya gāthā gāyanti ye purāṇa|vido janāḥ.
Rantidevasya tāṃ dṛṣṭvā samṛddhim atimānuṣīm,
«n' âitādṛśaṃ dṛṣṭa|pūrvaṃ Kubera|sadaneṣv api
67.15 dhanaṃ ca pūryamāṇaṃ naḥ kiṃ punar manujeṣv api:
vyaktaṃ Vasvokasār" êyam» ity ūcus tatra vismitāḥ.
Sāṃkṛte Rantidevasya yāṃ rātrim atithir vaset
ālabhyanta tadā gāvaḥ sahasrāṇy eka|viṃśatiḥ.
tatra sma sūdāḥ krośanti su|mṛṣṭa|maṇi|kuṇḍalāḥ
sūpaṃ bhūyiṣṭham aśnīdhvaṃ n' âdya māṃsaṃ yathā purā.
Rantidevasya yat kiṃ cit sauvarṇam abhavat tadā
tat sarvaṃ vitate yajñe brāhmaṇebhyo hy amanyata.
pratyakṣaṃ tasya havyāni pratigṛhṇanti devatāḥ
kavyāni pitaraḥ kāle sarva|kāmān dvij'|ôttamāḥ.
67.20 sa cen mamāra, Sṛñjaya, catur|bhadrataras tvayā,
putrāt puṇyataras tubhyaṃ, mā putram anutapyathāḥ
a|yajvānam a|dākṣiṇyam abhi Śvaity' êti vyāharan.

NĀRADA uvāca:

68.1 DAUṢYANTIṂ Bharataṃ c' âpi mṛtaṃ, Sṛñjaya, śuśruma
karmāṇy a|su|karāṇy anyaiḥ kṛtavān yaḥ śiśur vane.
him'|âvadātān yaḥ siṃhān nakha|daṃṣṭr'|āyudhān balī
nir|vīryāṃs tarasā kṛtvā vicakarṣa babandha ca.
krūrāṃś c' ôgratarān vyāghrān damitvā c' âkarod vaśe
manaḥ|śilā iva śilāḥ saṃyuktā jatu|rāśibhiḥ
vyāl'|âdīṃś c' âtibalavān su|pratīkān gajān api
daṃṣṭrāsu gṛhya vimukhān śuṣk'|āsyān akarod vaśe.

every tree, and yet other gifts and provisions besides. Those who know the myths of old sing that all that wise Ranti·deva owned was gold. Men said that Ranti·deva's treasuries dwarfed even Kubéra's. Could such enormous and awesome 67.15
wealth be found in the vaults of Vasv·okasára? Any guest who stayed with Ranti·deva at the palace of Sánkriti left with herds of cattle, one for every night he had been there. With polished jewels glinting in their ears the cooks would bring a guest rich broths to drink rather than the dry meat that he had known elsewhere.

Whatever things of worth that Ranti·deva possessed he gave to the brahmins in sacrifice. The gods came and received their share, the departed fathers took theirs and in the fullness of time the best of the twiceborn had all that they desired from him.

O Srínjaya, if even Ranti·deva had to die and he four 67.20
times more blessed than you and more pious than your son then I say to you do not suffer for your child. Cry not the name of one whose life was so miserly and so profane.

NÁRADA spoke:

O SRÍNJAYA. We hear of a king now gone called Bharata 68.1
son of Dushyánta whose deeds as a child in the wilderness were like to none. Snowwhite leopards snapped and swiped but were no match for his might and without even a struggle he laid them low and bound them. Crueler and more savage still were the striped tigers red as orpiment under bands of lac. He turned them into pets. He found other beasts of prey, elephants with great curling trunks, and with wild force took them in his jaws until they gasped and lay

68.5 mahiṣān apy atibalo balino vicakarṣa ha
siṃhānāṃ ca su|dṛptānāṃ śatāny ādamayad balāt.
balinaḥ sṛmarān khaḍgān nānā|sattvāni c' âpy uta
kṛcchra|prāṇaṃ vane baddhvā damayitv' âpy avāsṛjat.
taṃ sarva|daman' êty āhur dvijās ten' âsya karmaṇā.
taṃ pratyaṣedhaj jananī «mā sattvāni vijījahi.»
so 'śva|medha|śaten' êṣṭvā Yamunām anu vīryavān
tri|śat'|âśvān Sarasvatyāṃ Gaṅgām anu catuḥ|śatān,
so 'śva|medha|sahasreṇa rāja|sūya|śatena ca
punar īje mahā|yajñaiḥ samāpta|vara|dakṣiṇaiḥ.
68.10 agni|ṣṭom'|âtirātrābhyām ukthyā viśva|jitā api
vāja|peya|sahasrāṇāṃ sahasraiś ca su|saṃvṛtaiḥ
iṣṭvā Śākuntalo rājā tarpayitvā dvijān dhanaiḥ
sahasraṃ yatra padmānāṃ Kaṇvāya Bharato dadau
Jāmbūnadasya śuddhasya kanakasya mahā|yaśāḥ.
yasya yūpaḥ śata|vyāmaḥ
pariṇāhena kāñcanaḥ
samāgamya dvijaiḥ sārdhaṃ
s'|Êndrair devaiḥ samucchritaḥ.
sv|alaṃ|kṛtān rājamānān sarva|ratnair mano|haraiḥ
hairaṇyān aśvān dvi|radān rathān uṣṭrān aj'|âvikaṃ
dāsī|dāsaṃ dhanaṃ dhānyaṃ gāḥ sa|vatsāḥ payasvinīḥ
grāmān gṛhāṇi kṣetrāṇi vividhāṃś ca paricchadān
68.15 koṭī|śat'|âyutāṃś c' âiva brāhmaṇebhyo hy amanyata
cakravartī hy a|dīn'|ātmā jitārir hy ajitaḥ paraiḥ.

still at his feet. He came across strong buffalo but he was 68.5
stronger and he tamed the majestic lion in its pride. In the woods for sport he held down and bound bucking stags and rhinoceros and other creatures besides and then let them all loose again. And so the twiceborn call him the Great Tamer. Only when his mother told him to stop his campaign against the creatures did Bharata turn to his solemn tasks.

He sacrificed a hundred horses on the banks of the Yámuna and then three hundred by the Sarásvati and four hundred more by the Ganges. Then he began again, and slew a thousand more horses in sacrifice and held a hundred
times the rituals of a king. In ceremonies of fire and cer- 68.10
emonies by night Shakúntala's son poured out his potent libations to the chant of the hymns. A hundred times he held the Drink of Battle. All the while Bharata showered his priests in coins: to Kanva alone he gave a billion medallions of the purest Jambu gold. Indra and the gods joined the brahmins there and they set up a stake where the animals would be slain and it was a hundredfathom high and plated in gold. Horses arrayed in silver and crusted in jewels to dazzle the eye Bharata gave to the brahmins, then elephants and chariots and buffalo and sheep, slaves and concubines and other spoils, and corn and milkgiving cows and their calves, and estates and dwellings and land and garments of every hue and all of these things in numbers too huge to
reckon. He was a true emperor, a conqueror, a nemesis: a 68.15
soul undimmed.

sa cen mamāra, Sṛñjaya, catur|bhadrataras tvayā,
putrāt puṇyataras tubhyaṃ, mā putram anutapyathāḥ
a|yajvānam a|dākṣiṇyam abhi Śvaity' êti vyāharan.

NĀRADA uvāca:

69.1 PṚTHUṂ VAINYAṂ ca rājānaṃ mṛtaṃ, Sṛñjaya, śuśruma
yam abhyaṣiñcan sāmrājye rāja|sūye maha"|rṣayaḥ.
yatnataḥ prathit" êty ūcuḥ sarvān abhibhavan Pṛthuḥ
kṣatān nas trāsyate sarvān ity evaṃ kṣatriyo 'bhavat.
Pṛthuṃ Vainyaṃ prajā dṛṣṭvā «raktāḥ sm'» êti yad abruvan
tato rāj' êti nām' âsya anurāgād ajāyata.
a|kṛṣṭa|pacyā pṛthivī āsīd Vainyasya kāma|dhuk
sarvāḥ kumbha|dugho gāvaḥ puṭake puṭake madhu.
69.5 āsan hiraṇ|mayā darbhāḥ sukha|sparśāḥ sukh'|āvahāḥ
teṣāṃ cīrāṇi saṃvītāḥ prajās teṣv eva śerate.
phalāny amṛta|kalpāni mūlāni ca madhūni ca
teṣām āsīt tad" āhāro, nir|āhārāś ca n' âbhavan.
a|rogāḥ sarva|siddh'|ârthā manuṣyā hy a|kuto|bhayāḥ
nyavasanta yathā|kāmaṃ vṛkṣeṣu ca guhāsu ca.
pravibhāgo na rāṣṭrāṇāṃ purāṇāṃ c' âbhavat tadā
yathā|sukhaṃ yathā|kāmaṃ tath" âitā muditāḥ prajāḥ.
tasya saṃstambhitā hy āpaḥ samudrān abhiyāsyataḥ
parvatāś ca dadur mārgaṃ dhvaja|bhaṅgaś ca n' âbhavat.
69.10 taṃ vanas|patayaḥ śailā dev'|âsura|nar'|ôragāḥ
sapta'|rṣayaḥ puṇya|janā gandharv'|âpsaraso 'pi ca
pitaraś ca sukh'|âsīnam abhigamy' êdam abruvan.

O Srínjaya, if even Bharata had to die and he four times more blessed than you and more pious than your son then I say to you do not suffer for your child. Cry not the name of one whose life was so miserly and so profane.

NÁRADA spoke:

O SRÍNJAYA. WE know of a king now gone called Prithu 69.1
son of Vena whom great seers anointed at his imperial coronation. Men celebrated the broad dominion that earned
him his name. He kept safe their lands and so they called
him regent. They whom Prithu son of Venu ruled adored
him and because they adored him they named him lord.
Under Prithu the whole of the earth yielded its bounty
unfurrowed by the plough, and all its cows yielded pail after
pail of sweet milk at the merest touch of the farmer's hand.
The grass in the meadows was gold and soft beneath hand 69.5
and foot and the people wove it into quilts for their beds.
Honey and fruits and roots tasted of ambrosia and all were
in abundance nor was there ever any want. Man lived in
cave or wood or wherever he pleased and there was no fear,
disease or lack. There were no walls around kingdoms or
cities and all the king's subjects were contented and fulfilled
and lived together in harmony. The seas petrified to support his tread, the mountains laid themselves open when he
passed and his flag was never cast into the dust. One day as 69.10
he sat in peace all the trees, rocks and snakes, men, demons
and gods, the Seven Seers and the Holy Ones, *gandhárvas*
and *ápsarases* and ancestors all stood before him, and they
spoke to him.

«samrāḍ asi kṣatriyo 'si rājā goptā pit" âsi naḥ.
dehy asmabhyaṃ mahā|rāja prabhuḥ sann īpsitān varān
yair vayaṃ śāśvatīs tṛptīr vartayiṣyāmahe sukham.»
tath" êty uktvā Pṛthur Vainyo gṛhītv" Âjagavaṃ dhanuḥ
śarāṃś c' â|pratimān ghorāṃś, cintayitv" âbravīn mahīm.
«ehy ehi vasudhe kṣipraṃ kṣar' âibhyaḥ kāṅkṣitaṃ payaḥ.
tato dāsyāmi bhadraṃ te annaṃ yasya yath"|ēpsitam.»

VASUDH" ôvāca:

69.15 duhitṛtvena māṃ vīra saṃkalpayitum arhasi.

tath" êty uktvā Pṛthuḥ sarvaṃ vidhānam akarod vaśī.
tato bhūta|nikāyās tāṃ vasudhāṃ duduhus tadā.
tāṃ vanas|patayaḥ pūrvaṃ samuttasthur dudhukṣavaḥ.
s" âtiṣṭhad vatsalā vatsaṃ dogdhṛ|pātrāṇi c' êcchatī.
vatso 'bhūt puṣpitaḥ śālaḥ,
plakṣo dogdh" âbhavat tadā,
chinna|prarohaṇaṃ dugdhaṃ
pātram audumbaraṃ śubham.
udayaḥ parvato vatso Merur dogdhā mahā|giriḥ,
ratnāny oṣadhayo dugdhaṃ pātram aśmamayaṃ tathā.
dogdhā c' āsīt tadā devo dugdham ūrjas|karaṃ priyam.
69.20 asurā duduhur madyam āma|pātre tu te tadā,
dogdhā Dvimūrdhā tatr' āsīd vatsaś c' āsīd Virocanaḥ.
kṛṣiṃ ca sasyaṃ ca narā duduhuḥ pṛthivī|tale,
Svāyambhuvo Manur vatsas teṣāṃ dogdh" âbhavat Pṛthuḥ.
alābu|pātre ca tadā viṣaṃ dugdhā vasuṃ|dharā,

"You are our emperor. You are our ruler, our master, protector, father. O great king use your omnipotence to grant us the most coveted gifts of all: that we might dwell in peace so deep that it will never leave us."

Prithu son of Vena nodded and thought for a moment and he lifted up his bow Ájagava and its arrows so terrible and sublime and spoke then to the earth.

"Come come o Earth and flow now with the milk these creatures desire. With your blessing I will give them the cornucopia they crave."

THE EARTH spoke:

You must be gentle with me o king. Do not forget that I 69.15
am your daughter.

Prithu heard her and with care made good his promise. The earth was like a cow pining for her calf and waiting for the milker and his pails, and all that lived began to draw milk from her. First the great trees of the forests rose up eager to drink. The blossoming *sal* tree became the calf, the *bo* tree became the milker. The buds bursting open became the milk and the fine wood of the fig tree's trunk the pail.

Then the mountain in the east became the calf and the great peak Meru the milker, minerals and plants the milk and the pail was made of rock. With a god to milk the
earth the milk was sweet and rich. Then the demons Dvi· 69.20
murdhan and Viróchana became milker and calf and the milk they brought forth was moonshine in a rough clay pot. Manu son of Svayámbhu became the calf and Prithu their milker and men drew corn and grain from the soil. Then Dhrita·rashtra became the milker and Tákshaka the cow

Dhṛtarāṣṭro 'bhavad dogdhā teṣāṃ vatsas tu Takṣakaḥ.
sapta'|ṛṣibhir brahma dugdhā tathā c' â|kliṣṭa|karmabhiḥ,
dogdhā Bṛhaspatiḥ pātraṃ chando vatsaś ca soma|rāṭ.
antar|dhānaṃ c' āma|pātre dugdhā puṇya|janair Virāṭ,
dogdhā Vaiśravaṇas teṣāṃ vatsaś c' āsīd Vṛṣadhvajaḥ.
69.25 puṇya|gandhān padma|pātre gandharv'|âpsaraso 'duhan,
vatsaś Citrarathas teṣāṃ dogdhā Viśvaruciḥ prabhuḥ.
sva|dhāṃ rajata|pātreṣu duduhuḥ pitaraś ca tām,
vatso Vaivasvatas teṣāṃ Yamo dogdh" ântakas tadā.
evaṃ nikāyais tair dugdhā payo 'bhīṣṭaṃ hi sā virāṭ,
yair vartayanti te hy adya pātrair vatsaiś ca nityaśaḥ.
yajñaiś ca vividhair iṣṭvā Pṛthur Vainyaḥ pratāpavān
saṃtarpayitvā bhūtāni sarvaiḥ kāmair manaḥ|priyaiḥ
hairaṇyān akarod rājā ye ke cit pārthivā bhuvi.
tān brāhmaṇebhyaḥ prāyacchad aśva|medhe mahā|makhe.
69.30 ṣaṣṭi nāga|sahasrāṇi ṣaṣṭi nāga|śatāni ca
sauvarṇān akarod rājā brāhmaṇebhyaś ca tān dadau.
imāṃ ca pṛthivīṃ sarvāṃ maṇi|ratna|vibhūṣitām
sauvarṇām akarod rājā brāhmaṇebhyaś ca tān dadau.
sa cen mamāra, Sṛñjaya, catur|bhadrataras tvayā,
putrāt puṇyataras tubhyaṃ, mā putram anutapyathāḥ
a|yajvānam a|dākṣiṇyam abhi Śvaity' êti vyāharan.

and the earth brought forth poison into a calabash. Then Brihas·pati became milker, the meter the pail, the moon the calf and the abyss was milked by the Seven Seers in rites played out unending. Then Kubéra became the milker and Vrisha·dhvaja the calf and the Holy Ones drew from the
earth the milk that made them invisible. Then Chitra·ratha 69.25
became the calf and great Vishva·ruchi the milker and the *gandhárvas* and *ápsarases* drew delicate fragrances into the lotus their pail. Then Vaivásvata became the calf and Yama who brings the end the milker and so the ancestors poured out benediction into pails of silver. Thus one by one did all of creation draw the precious milk from the earth, each with his own calf and pail.

With rites beyond number the blazing Prithu son of Vena furnished his people with all that pleased their hearts, and at a great feast during a great sacrifice of horses the king took all that his vassals had and chased those things in gold and
gave them to the twiceborn. To the brahmins went scores 69.30
and then hundreds and then thousands of elephants and each of them was decorated with gold. The king covered the whole earth in gemstones and jewels and gave the whole gleaming sphere to his priests.

O Srínjaya, if even Prithu had to die and he four times more blessed than you and more pious than your son then I say to you do not suffer for your child. Cry not the name of one whose life was so miserly and so profane.

NĀRADA uvāca:

70.1 RĀMO MAHĀ|TAPĀḤ śūro vīra|loka|namas|kṛtaḥ
Jāmadagnyo 'py atiyaśā a|vitṛpto mariṣyati.
yasmād yaman upary eti bhūmiṃ kurvann imāṃ sukhām
na c' āsīd vikriyā yasya prāpya śriyam an|uttamām,
yaḥ kṣatriyaiḥ parāmṛṣṭe vatse pitari c' â|bruvan
tato 'vadhīt Kārtavīryam a|jitaṃ samare paraiḥ.
kṣatriyāṇāṃ catuḥ|ṣaṣṭim ayutāni sahasraśaḥ
tadā mṛtyoḥ sametāni ekena dhanuṣ" âjayat.
70.5 brahma|dviṣāṃ c' âtha tasmin sahasrāṇi catur|daśa
punar anyān nijagrāha Dantakrūraṃ jaghāna ha.
sahasraṃ muśalen' āghnan sahasram asin' âvadhīt
udbandhanāt sahasraṃ tu Haihayāḥ samare hatāḥ.
sa|rath'|âśva|gajā vīrā nihatās tatra śerate
pitur vadh'|â|marṣitena Jāmadagnyena dhīmatā.
nijaghne daśa|sāhasrān Rāmaḥ paraśunā tadā.
na hy amṛśyata tā vāco yās tair bhṛśam udīritāḥ.
«Bhṛgau Rām' âbhidhāv'» êti yad" ākrandan dvij'|ôttamāḥ
tataḥ Kāśmīra|Daradān Kunti|Kṣudraka|Mālavān
70.10 Aṅga|Vaṅga|Kaliṅgāṃś ca Videhāṃs Tāmraliptakān
Rakṣovāhān Vītihotrāṃs Trigartān Mārttikāvatān
Śibīn anyāṃś ca rājanyān deśād deśāt sahasraśaḥ
nijaghāna śitair bāṇair Jāmadagnyaḥ pratāpavān.

NÁRADA spoke:

MIGHTY RAMA son of Jamad·agni is a fiery hero of wild 70.1
renown admired by great men. Yet he too will die unappeased.

Because he crosses the earth to bear it up and bring peace he has earned his glory and none will measure or demean it. When warlords killed his father and son, without saying a word he sought out Karta·virya whom none had been able to beat before and he slew him. Then by the hundreds and thousands the warlords were rounded up to die and fell
before his bow. He killed fourteen thousand more for their 70.5
vile impiety and spite: it was Rama who slew Danta·krura.

The son of Jamad·agni was resolved. He would not brook his father's murder. A thousand of the Háihayas fell beneath his club, a thousand beneath his sword and a thousand more before his bow and they all laid down dead among their elephants, horses and cars. Nor would Rama brook the taunts he heard and ten thousand more fell beneath the head of his axe. The hierophants cried out for Bhrigu's blood and then with his sharp shafts the blazing son of Jamad·agni brought them down: Kashmíras, Dáradas, Kuntis, Kshúdrakas and Málavas, Angas, Vangas and Kalíngas, Vidéhas, Tamra·líptakas, Raksho·vahas and
Viti·hotras and Tri·gartas and Marttikávatas, Shibis and a 70.10
thousand other peoples that came from every place on the earth.

koṭī|śata|sahasrāṇi kṣatriyāṇāṃ sahasraśaḥ
indra|gopaka|varṇasya bandhujīva|nibhasya ca
rudhirasya parīvāhān pūrayitvā sarāṃsi ca
sarvān aṣṭā|daśa|dvīpān vaśam ānīya Bhārgavaḥ
īje kratu|śataiḥ puṇyaiḥ samāpta|vara|dakṣiṇaiḥ
vedīm aṣṭa|nav'|ôtsedhāṃ sauvarṇāṃ vidhi|nirmitām
sarva|ratna|śataiḥ pūrṇāṃ patākā|śata|mālinīm.
70.15 grāmy'|âraṇyaiḥ paśu|gaṇaiḥ sampūrṇāṃ ca mahīm imām
Rāmasya Jāmadagnyasya pratijagrāha Kaśyapaḥ.
tataḥ śata|sahasrāṇi dvip'|êndrān hema|bhūṣaṇān
nir|dasyuṃ pṛthivīṃ kṛtvā śiṣṭ'|êṣṭa|jana|saṃkulām
Kaśyapāya dadau Rāmo haya|medhe mahā|makhe.
tri|sapta|kṛtvaḥ pṛthivīṃ kṛtvā niḥ|kṣatriyāṃ prabhuḥ
iṣṭvā kratu|śatair vīro brāhmaṇebhyo hy amanyata.
sapta|dvīpāṃ vasumatīṃ Mārīco 'gṛhṇata dvijaḥ.
Rāmaṃ provāca «nirgaccha vasudhāto mam' ājñayā.»
sa Kaśyapasya vacanāt protsārya saritāṃ patim
iṣupātair yudhāṃ śreṣṭhaḥ kurvan brāhmaṇa|śāsanam
adhyāvasad giri|śreṣṭhaṃ Mahendraṃ parvat'|ôttamam.
70.20 evaṃ guṇa|śatair juṣṭo Bhṛgūṇāṃ kīrti|vardhanaḥ
Jāmadagnyo 'py atiyaśā mariṣyati mahā|dyutiḥ.
tvayā catur|bhadra|taraḥ putrāt puṇyataras tava.
a|yajvānam a|dākṣiṇyaṃ mā putram anutapyathāḥ.

Rama filled the rivers and lakes of the world with the
blood of the teeming dead and their waters turned scarlet
as noonflower and cochineal. When all the eighteen islands
of the world were his, Bhárgava fashioned an altar by the 70.15
ancient precepts and built it high and golden and studded
with a rainbow of gems and he bound it with a hundred
prayer rags. He consecrated it with a chain of holy rites
rich in offerings. This broad land flocked with animals from
field and from forest was the gift of Jamad·agni's son to
Káshyapa. Now that the world was purged of evil and full
only of the happy and the good Rama held a great sacrifice
of horses, and during the feast gave to his archpriest a hundred thousand elephants all bedecked in gold.

So it was that the bold and mighty king emptied the
land of warriors twentyone times over and then gave it to
the brahmins in a hundred rites. To Marícha's son alone he
gave dominion over all the seven continents. And one day
Káshyapa told Rama that the time had come for him to go
forth from the world. Rama obeyed and the great warrior
parted the ocean's waters with a wall of his arrows and went
to dwell on Mahéndra's towering peak.

Jamad·agni's son is a man of the rarest virtue whose deeds 70.20
are celebrated beyond bounds and have cast the fame of the
Bhrigus far and wide. Despite his glories Rama too will die,
but he is four times more blessed than you and more pious
than your son. I say to you: do not suffer for a boy so miserly
and so profane.

ete catur|bhadratarās tvayā bhadra|śat'|âdhikāḥ
mṛtā nara|vara|śreṣṭhā mariṣyanti ca, Sṛñjaya.

VYĀSA uvāca:

71.1 PUṆYAM ĀKHYĀNAM āyuṣyaṃ śrutvā ṣo|ḍaśa|rājikam
a|vyāharan nara|patis tūṣṇīm āsīt sa Sṛñjayaḥ.
tam abravīt tath" āsīnaṃ Nārado bhagavān ṛṣiḥ.
«śrutaṃ kīrtayato mahyaṃ gṛhītaṃ te, mahā|dyute,
āho svid antato naṣṭaṃ śrāddhaṃ śūdrī|patāv iva?»
sa evam uktaḥ pratyāha prāñjaliḥ Sṛñjayas tadā.
«etac chrutvā, mahā|bāho, dhanyam ākhyānan uttamam
rāja'|rṣīṇāṃ purāṇānāṃ yajvanāṃ dakṣiṇāvatām
71.5 vismayena hate śoke tamas' îv' ârka|tejasā
vipāpm" âsmy a|vyath'|ôpeto. brūhi kiṃ karavāṇy aham.»

NĀRADA uvāca:

diṣṭy" âpahṛta|śokas tvaṃ. vṛṇīṣv' êha yad icchasi.
tat tat prapatsyase sarvaṃ: na mṛṣā|vādino vayam.

SṚÑJAYA uvāca:

eten' âiva pratīto 'haṃ, prasanno yad bhavān mama.
prasanno yasya bhagavān na tasy' âst' îha dur|labham.

O Srínjaya. These kings with their hundred gifts were all four times more blessed than you yet death took them all as it will ever take even the very greatest who live.

VYASA spoke:

King Srínjaya sat listening to the holy lives of the six- 71.1
teen kings and he did not say a word. He sat very still. The reverend seer Nárada then spoke to the king.

"O illustrious king. You have heard these noble histories. Have you understood them? Or have they been lost to you, as a man's duties to his forefathers are lost when he marries below his station?"

At Nárada's question Srínjaya raised his hands in reverence and replied.

"O great one. You have described to me the rites and offerings and the immaculate lives of the ancient philosopher
kings. As the sun's rays banish darkness my anguish and de- 71.5
spair have left me, and wonder has banished my grief. Tell me what I can do in return."

NÁRADA spoke:

It is right that your grief has left you. But tell me what you desire yourself. I say that as sure as I stand before you it will be yours.

SRÍNJAYA spoke:

I have heard all I need, and you have given me your grace. O master the things of this world are easy for any whom your holiness illuminates.

NĀRADA uvāca:

mṛtaṃ dadāmi te putraṃ dasyubhir nihataṃ vṛthā
uddhṛtya narakāt kaṣṭāt paśuvat prokṣitaṃ yathā.

VYĀSA uvāca:

prādur āsīt tataḥ putraḥ Sṛñjayasy' âdbhuta|prabhaḥ
prasannena' ṛṣiṇā dattaḥ Kubera|tanay'|ôpamaḥ.
71.10 tataḥ saṃgamya putreṇa prītimān abhavan nṛ|paḥ
īje ca kratubhiḥ puṇyaiḥ samāpta|vara|dakṣiṇaiḥ.
a|kṛt'|ârthaś ca bhītaś ca na ca sāṃnāhiko hataḥ
a|yajvā hy an|apatyaś ca tato 'sau jīvitaḥ punaḥ.
śūro vīraḥ kṛt'|ârthaś ca pratāpy' ârīn sahasraśaḥ
Abhimanyur gato vīraḥ pṛtan"|âbhimukho hataḥ.
brahma|caryeṇa yān kāṃś cit prajñayā ca śrutena ca
iṣṭaiś ca kratubhir yānti tāṃs te putro 'kṣayān gataḥ.
vidvāṃsaḥ karmabhiḥ puṇyaiḥ svargam īhanti nityaśaḥ
na tu svargād ayaṃ lokaḥ kāmyate svarga|vāsibhiḥ.
71.15 tasmāt svarga|gataṃ putram Arjunasya hataṃ raṇe
na c' ēh' ānayituṃ śakyaṃ. kiṃ cid a|prāpyam īhitam.

yāṃ yogino dhyāna|vivikta|darśanāḥ
prayānti yāṃ c' ôttama|yajvino janāḥ
tapobhir iddhair anuyānti yāṃ tathā
tām akṣayāṃ te tanayo gato gatim.
antāt punar|bhāva|gato virājate
rāj" êva vīro hy amṛt'|ātma|raśmibhiḥ
tām aindavīm ātma|tanuṃ dvij'|ôcitāṃ
gato 'bhimanyur na sa śokam arhati.

NÁRADA spoke:

Then I give you back the son who died in vain at the hands of thieves. I raise him from the dark of hell, anointed like a lamb to the altar.

VYASA spoke:

And so it was that like a vision or like a shade Sríñjaya's
son appeared before them at the kind sage's bidding. The 71.10
king embraced his son and wild with delight he held great
and holy rites full of the very finest of gifts.

Sríñjaya's son did not die in his armour. He died afraid
and undone and before he could have children or sacrifice
and so he was brought back to life. But Abhimányu was a
hero mighty and resolute and only when he had burnt a
hole in his enemy a thousand men wide was he struck down
in the thick of battle. Your nephew has joined the undying
ones who pass on through piety and learning, lore and sacrifice. Wise men strive without end to live right and reach
heaven and none who dwell there covet anything in this
world. Árjuna's son died in battle and now he is in heaven. 71.15
If a thing cannot be then it is foolish to yearn for it.

Eremites deep in meditation
And men who work the solemn rites
Walk to eternity through the fires they kindle:
Your boy now treads their path.
Death has brought him back to life
Radiant with what it cannot touch.
Abhimányu we know lives the moon's life now:
There is no call to pity him.

evaṃ jñātvā sthiro bhūtvā jahy arīn dhairyam āpnuhi
jīvanta eva naḥ śocyā na tu svarga|gato 'n|agha.
śocato hi, mahā|rāja, agham ev' âbhivardhate.
tasmāc chokaṃ parityajya śreyase prayated budhaḥ.
71.20 praharṣam abhimānaṃ ca sukha|prāptiṃ ca cintayan
etad buddhvā budhāḥ śokaṃ na śokaḥ śoka ucyate.
evaṃ viddhi samuttiṣṭha prayato bhava mā śucaḥ.
śrutas te sambhavo mṛtyos tapāṃsy an|upamāni ca
sarva|bhūta|samatvaṃ ca cañcalāś ca vibhūtayaḥ.
Sṛñjayasya tu taṃ putraṃ mṛtaṃ saṃjīvitaṃ punaḥ
evaṃ vidvan, mahā|rāja, mā śucaḥ, sādhayāmy aham.

etāvad uktvā bhagavāṃs tatr' âiv' ântar|adhīyata.
vāg|īśāne bhagavati Vyāse vy|abhra|nabhaḥ|prabhe
gate matimatāṃ śreṣṭhe samāśvāsya Yudhiṣṭhiram,
71.25 pūrveṣāṃ pārthiv'|êndrāṇāṃ mah"|Êndra|pratim'|âujasām
nyāy'|âdhigata|vittānāṃ tāṃ śrutvā yajña|sampadam
sampūjya manasā vidvān vi|śoko 'bhūd Yudhiṣṭhiraḥ.
punaś c' âcintayad dīnaḥ «kiṃ svid vakṣye Dhanaṃjayam?»

SAṂJAYA uvāca:

72.1 TASMINN AHANI nirvṛtte ghore prāṇa|bhṛtāṃ kṣaye
āditye 'staṃ gate śrīmān saṃdhyā|kāla upasthite
vyapayāteṣu vāsāya sainyeṣu, Bharata'|rṣabha,
hatvā Saṃśaptaka|vrātān divyair astraiḥ kapi|dhvajaḥ
prāyāt sva|śibiraṃ Jiṣṇur jaitram āsthāya taṃ ratham.
gacchann eva ca Govindaṃ s'|âśru|kaṇṭho 'bhyabhāṣata.

Hear me and find your strength and find the courage to face your foes. O pure one it is the living who deserve your tears and not the dead in heaven. O great king the pain of mourning can only become worse. Be wise and throw off
your grief. Concentrate on better things. Wise men who 71.20
have pondered the nature of joy pride and greed understand the pain that is sorrow and they no longer call it such. Be like them and raise yourself up. Rouse yourself and cease to mourn. I have told you of the origin of death, of her fierce penance and her even treatment of the living. I have shown you how all that is must fade. Understand the meaning of Shvaitya's resurrection, my king. Be at peace.

Vyasa was like a cloudless sky and he spoke so well that the illustrious king heard the seer and took his words to heart. Then the brilliant sage bid farewell and disappeared and left Yudhi·shthira consoled by his tale of the godlike
majesty and power of those kings of old, of their great rites 71.25
and their hallowed treasuries. His mind now full of their stories the wise king felt for a moment freed from his grief. But then his spirits sunk as he fell to thinking what he would tell Dhanan·jaya.

SÁNJAYA spoke:

O ILLUSTRIOUS KING. That terrible day that had been 72.1
the last for so many was now itself at an end. The sun had gone down and the twilight was deepening fast. All the soldiers had returned to camp except for Jishnu. O bull of the Bharatas a chariot that carried the sign of the monkey rolled back through the dusk alone. Behind it slain lay the Beholden, dead by Árjuna's celestial shafts. As Árjuna made

«kiṃ nu me hṛdayaṃ trastaṃ vākyaṃ sajjati Keśava,
syandanti c' âpy an|iṣṭāni gātraṃ sīdati c' âpy uta.
72.5 an|iṣṭaṃ c' âiva me śliṣṭaṃ hṛdayān n' âpasarpati,
bhuvi ye dikṣu c' âtyugrā utpātās trāsayanti mām.
bahu|prakārā dṛśyante sarva ev' âgha|śaṃsinaḥ
api svasti bhaved rājñaḥ s'|âmātyasya guror mama.»

VĀSUDEVA uvāca:

vyaktaṃ śivaṃ tava bhrātuḥ s'|âmātyasya bhaviṣyati.
mā śucaḥ. kiṃ cid ev' ânyat stok'|ân|iṣṭaṃ bhaviṣyati.

SAṂJAYA uvāca:

tataḥ saṃdhyām upāsy' âiva vīrau vīr'|âvasādane
kathayantau raṇe vṛttaṃ prayātau ratham āsthitau.
tataḥ sva|śibiraṃ prāptau hat'|ānandaṃ hata|tviṣam
Vāsudevo 'rjunaś c' âiva kṛtvā karma su|duṣkaram.
72.10 dhvast'|ākāraṃ samālakṣya śibiraṃ para|vīra|hā
Bībhatsur abravīt Kṛṣṇam a|sva|stha|hṛdayas tataḥ.
«nadanti n' âdya tūryāṇi maṅgalyāni, Janārdana,
miśrā dundubhi|nirghoṣaiḥ śaṅkhāś c' āḍambaraiḥ saha.
vīṇā n' âiv' âdya vādyante śamyā|tāla|svanaiḥ saha
maṅgalyāni ca gītāni na gāyanti paṭhanti ca
stuti|yuktāni ramyāṇi mam' ānīkeṣu bandinaḥ.
yodhāś c' âpi hi māṃ dṛṣṭvā nivartante hy adho|mukhāḥ.
karmāṇi ca yathā|pūrvaṃ kṛtvā n' âbhivadanti mām.
api svasti bhaved adya bhrātṛbhyo mama Mādhava.
na hi śudhyati me bhāvo dṛṣṭvā sva|janam ākulam.

his way back suddenly he felt sorrow choke him. He turned to the Herdsman and spoke.

"O Késhava my heart trembles. These words catch in my throat. Strange things dance before my eyes and my blood runs cold. A shadow has passed across me and it will not 72.5
lift. I see things in heaven and earth that trouble me and make me afraid. They are omens in different shapes but all of them presage evil. I hope my brother the king and those with him have not come to harm."

VASUDÉVA spoke:

Be assured that it goes well with your brother and the rest of them. Fear not. These omens are trifling things.

SÁNJAYA spoke:

The two heroes bowed to the dusk and though troubled they fell to talking about the battle just passed and continued on their way. Vasudéva and Árjuna had achieved mighty things that day. But soon they came near a camp de-
void of light or celebration. Árjuna felt an abyss open in his 72.10
heart. The nemesis of the Kurus looked across the doomsome scene and turned to Krishna and spoke.

"The drums are silent, Janárdana. I do not hear the horns or kettles or timpani that should fanfare our return. The lutes are silent, silent the cymbals and gongs. No voice welcomes us with song nor do the heralds cry out my return. Look there. My men see me but they lower their eyes and withdraw. Each one does the same. They do not call over to me. O Mádhava I hope all is well with my brothers. This strange behaviour does little to ease my mood.

72.15 api Pāñcāla|rājasya Virāṭasya ca, māna|da,
sarveṣāṃ c' âiva yodhānāṃ sāmagryaṃ syān mam' Âcyuta?
na ca mām adya Saubhadraḥ prahṛṣṭo bhrātṛbhiḥ saha
raṇād āyāntam ucitaṃ pratyudyāti hasann iva.»

SAMJAYA uvāca:

evaṃ saṃkathayantau tau praviṣṭau śibiraṃ svakam
dadṛśāte bhṛś'|â|sva|sthān Pāṇḍavān naṣṭa|cetasaḥ.
dṛṣṭvā bhrātṝṃś ca putrāṃś ca vi|manā vānara|dhvajaḥ
a|paśyaṃś c' âiva Saubhadram idaṃ vacanam abravīt.
«mukha|varṇo '|prasanno vaḥ sarveṣām eva lakṣyate.
na c' Âbhimanyuṃ paśyāmi. na ca māṃ pratinandatha.
72.20 mayā śrutaś ca Droṇena cakra|vyūho vinirmitaḥ,
na ca vas tasya bhett" âsti vinā Saubhadram arbhakam.*
na c' ôpadiṣṭas tasy' āsīn may" ânīkād vinirgamaḥ.
kaccin na bālo yuṣmābhiḥ par'|ânīkaṃ praveśitaḥ.
bhittv" ânīkaṃ mah"|êṣv|āsaḥ pareṣāṃ bahuśo yudhi
kaccin na nihataḥ śete Saubhadraḥ para|vīra|hā?
lohit'|âkṣaṃ mahā|bāhuṃ jātaṃ siṃham iv' âdriṣu
Upendra|sadṛśaṃ, brūta, katham āyodhane hataḥ?
su|kumāraṃ mah"|êṣv|āsaṃ Vāsavasy' ātmaj'|ātmajam
sadā mama priyaṃ, brūta, katham āyodhane hataḥ?
72.25 Subhadrāyāḥ priyaṃ putraṃ Draupadyāḥ Keśavasya ca
Ambāyāś ca priyaṃ nityaṃ ko 'vadhīt kāla|mohitaḥ?

O my friend. Has the same fate that afflicts King Viráta 72.15
come to blight me and my own? Saubhádra has not come out to see me. He knows I am on my way back. By now he should have run out here with a smile on his face and my brothers at his heels."

SÁNJAYA spoke:

Muttering to each other Árjuna and Krishna entered the camp. The Pándavas were there and their faces wore expressions of despair and devastation. Árjuna's flags fluttered in the wind. He glanced about for Saubhádra. He looked at his brothers and his nephews and terror clutched at him and he spoke.

"You are all so pale and sad. Where is Abhimányu? Are
you not pleased to see me back? I know that today Drona 72.20
had the Kurus in the array of the wheel and I know that there was only one among you who could break it. My little Saubhádra.

But I never taught him how to return from a breach. I pray that you did not send my boy into the enemy line. I pray that my son Saubhádra did not go forth to slay your enemies and break the Kuru line with his bow. Only to be struck down dead.

Tell me of my boy. My boy with the red eyes and broad shoulders of a mountain lion. He could not die in battle. He is like Indra's brother. He is the son of Indra's son. Tell me of my dear child who though only a boy bears a bow
like a man. How could he be killed in battle? Who in these 72.25
dark days would be mad enough to strike down Subhádra's beloved, beloved too forever of Dráupadi Késhava and

sadṛśo Vṛṣṇi|vīrasya Keśavasya mah"|ātmanaḥ
vikrama|śruta|māhātmyaiḥ katham āyodhane hataḥ?
Vārṣṇeyī|dayitaṃ śūraṃ mayā satata|lālitam
yadi putraṃ na paśyāmi yāsyāmi Yama|sādanam.
mṛdu|kuñcita|keś'|ântaṃ bālaṃ bāla|mṛg'|êkṣaṇam
matta|dvi|rada|vikrāntaṃ śāla|potam iv' ôdgatam
smit'|âbhibhāṣiṇaṃ śāntaṃ guru|vākya|karaṃ sadā
bālye 'py a|bāla|karmāṇaṃ priya|vākyam a|matsaram
72.30 mah'|ôtsāhaṃ mahā|vīryaṃ dīrgha|rājīva|locanam
bhakt'|ânukampinaṃ dāntaṃ na ca nīc'|ânusāriṇam
kṛta|jñaṃ jñāna|sampannaṃ kṛt'|âstram a|nivartinam
yuddh'|âbhinandinaṃ nityaṃ dviṣatām bhaya|vardhanam
sveṣāṃ priya|hite yuktaṃ pitṝṇāṃ jaya|gṛddhinam,
na ca pūrva|prahartāraṃ saṃgrāme naṣṭa|sambhramam,
yadi putraṃ na paśyāmi yāsyāmi Yama|sādanam.
ratheṣu gaṇyamāneṣu gaṇitaṃ taṃ mahā|ratham
may" âdhyardha|guṇaṃ saṃkhye taruṇaṃ bāhu|śālinam
Pradyumnasya priyaṃ nityaṃ Keśavasya mam' âiva ca,
yadi putraṃ na paśyāmi yasyāmi Yama|sādanam.
72.35 su|nasaṃ su|lalāṭ'|ântaṃ sv|akṣi|bhrū|daśana|cchadam
a|paśyatas tad|vadanaṃ kā śāntir hṛdayasya me?
tantrī|svana|sukhaṃ ramyaṃ puṃs|kokila|sama|dhvanim
a|śṛṇvataḥ svanaṃ tasya kā śāntir hṛdayasya me?
rūpaṃ c' â|pratimaṃ tasya tridaśeṣv atidurlabham
a|paśyato hi vīrasya kā śāntir hṛdayasya me?

Amba? How could a boy who in courage and cunning and
strength is a match for the mighty Vrishni lord be slain?

If I cannot see my son again then I will leave this life.
Day after day his mother and I have held him in our arms.
My boy with his deer's eyes and long soft curls, tall as a
sapling, strong as an elephant but always mild of tongue
and gentle and respectful of his elders. My boy who though
a child has left childish things behind him. My wellspo-
ken and unselfish and vigorous and lively boy with his deep 72.30
blue lotus gaze. My boy with his measured mind and his
contempt for the petty in soul and his love for the great of
heart. My brave and clever boy whose wit is as sharp as his
sword, who brings joy to his fellows and terror to his foes
and who dreams of nothing but his uncles' victory and the
preservation of his kin. My son who has never struck a man
before being struck himself. My boy who never feared the
fight. If I cannot see my son again then I will leave this life.

If I cannot see my boy whose skill has made him a warrior
among warriors and who in battle is half again as good as I.
Beloved child of mine and beloved ever to Késhava and to
Pradyúmna. If I cannot see you again then I will leave this
life.

What peace can there ever be in my heart if I cannot see 72.35
my boy's noble face, his perfect eyes and brow and smile?
What peace can there ever be in my heart if I cannot hear
his voice, gentle and sweet as a chord on a lute, sonorous as
the cuckoo's call? What peace can there ever be in my heart
if I cannot any more look upon his form more handsome
even than the figure of a god? My boy who was always so
polite and so courteous, and who hung on his elders' every

abhivādana|dakṣaṃ taṃ pitṝṇāṃ vacane ratam
n' âdy' âhaṃ yadi paśyāmi kā śāntir hṛdayasya me?
su|kumāraḥ sadā vīro mah'|ârha|śayan'|ôcitaḥ
bhūmāv a|nāthavac chete nūnaṃ nāthavatāṃ varaḥ?
72.40 śayānaṃ samupāsanti yaṃ purā parama|striyaḥ
bhramantyo vipraviddh'|âṅgam upāsanty a|śivāḥ śivāḥ?
yaḥ purā bodhyate suptaḥ sūta|māgadha|bandibhiḥ
bodhayanty adya taṃ nūnaṃ śvāpadā vikṛtaiḥ svaraiḥ?
chatra|cchāyā|samucitaṃ tasya tad vadanaṃ śubham
nūnam adya rajo|dhvastaṃ raṇa|reṇuḥ kariṣyati?
hā putrak' â|vitṛptasya satataṃ putra|darśane
bhāgya|hīnasya kālena yathā me nīyase balāt.
sā ca Saṃyamanī nūnaṃ sadā su|kṛtināṃ gatiḥ
sva|bhābhir mohitā ramyā tvay" âtyarthaṃ virājate.
72.45 nūnaṃ Vaivasvataś ca tvāṃ Varuṇaś ca priy'|âtithim
Śatakratur Dhaneśaś ca prāptam arcanty a|bhīrukam.»
evaṃ vilapya bahudhā bhinna|poto vaṇig yathā
duḥkhena mahat" āviṣṭo Yudhiṣṭhiram apṛcchata.
«kaccit sa kadanaṃ kṛtvā pareṣāṃ, Kuru|nandana,
svar gato 'bhimukhaḥ saṃkhye yudhyamāno nara'|rṣabhaiḥ?
sa nūnaṃ bahubhir yattair yudhyamāno nara'|rṣabhaiḥ
a|sahāyaḥ sahāy'|ârthī mām anudhyātavān dhruvam.
pīḍyamānaḥ śarais tīkṣṇaiḥ Karṇa|Droṇa|Kṛp'|ādibhiḥ
nānā|liṅgaiḥ su|dhaut'|âgrair mama putro 'lpa|cetanaḥ,
72.50 iha me syāt paritrāṇaṃ pit" êti sa punaḥ punaḥ
iti vipralapan manye nṛśaṃsair bhuvi pātitaḥ.

word. If from this day I can no more look upon him then what peace can there ever be in my heart?

Does a great prince forever worthy of the finest pillows on earth and the hardiest guardians lie abandoned in the dirt? Does a boy whose bed was tended by the most deli- 72.40
cate hands in the world lie pierced with arrows, his body a bed for dogs? Do the wild cries of beasts now echo in the dead ears of one who once was woken from slumber by the chords of harp and song? Does the dust of the earth taint a radiant countenance worthy only of a parasol's shade? O never did I have enough of looking at you and now because these evil days cannot hold hope you are being torn from my arms.

The path to Yama's home lies open to life's paragons and
it blazes with wild light for you. Vaivásvata and Váruna and 72.45
Shata·kratu and Kubéra will welcome you there. O my fearless child. They will sing your praises when you come before them."

Árjuna wailed out like a poor man whose mean things had been sucked into the sea.* In a flood of grief he turned to Yudhi·shthira.

"Speak o joy of the Kurus. Is my son in heaven? When their bulls charged did he stand his ground and blast them and fall? When their bulls charged and bore down upon him friendless and needing a friend I know he would have been thinking of me. As the arrows loosed by Karna and Drona and Kripa rained down and stabbed with their polished points again and again the thought would have come 72.50
into his child's mind, even as those devils knocked him to the earth: My father will look after me.

atha vā mat|prasūtaḥ sa svasrīyo Mādhavasya ca
Subhadrāyāṃ ca sambhūto, na c' âivaṃ vaktum arhati.
vajra|sāra|mayaṃ nūnaṃ hṛdayaṃ su|dṛḍhaṃ mama
a|paśyato dīrgha|bāhuṃ rakt'|âkṣaṃ yan na dīryate.
kathaṃ bāle mah"|êṣv|āsā nṛśaṃsā marma|bhedinaḥ
svasrīye Vāsudevasya mama putre 'kṣipañ śarān?
yo māṃ nityam a|dīn'|ātmā pratyudgamy' âbhinandati
upāyāntaṃ ripūn hatvā, so 'dya māṃ kiṃ na paśyati?
72.55 nūnaṃ sa patitaḥ śete dharaṇyāṃ rudhir'|ôkṣitaḥ,
śobhayan medinīṃ gātrair āditya iva pātitaḥ.
Subhadrām anuśocāmi yā putram a|palāyinam
raṇe vinihataṃ śrutvā śok'|ārtā vai vinaṃkṣyati.
Subhadrā vakṣyate kiṃ mām Abhimanyum a|paśyatī
Draupadī c' âiva duḥkh'|ārte te pi vakṣyāmi kiṃ v aham?
vajra|sāra|mayaṃ nūnaṃ hṛdayaṃ yan na yāsyati
sahasradhā vadhūṃ dṛṣṭvā rudatīṃ śoka|karśitām.
dṛptānāṃ Dhārtarāṣṭrāṇāṃ siṃha|nādo mayā śrutaḥ,
Yuyutsuś c' âpi Kṛṣṇena śruto vīrān upālabhan.
72.60 ‹a|śaknuvanto Bībhatsuṃ
bālaṃ hatvā mahā|rathāḥ
kiṃ modadhvam a|dharma|jñāḥ
Pāṇḍavaṃ dṛśyatāṃ balam?
kiṃ tayor vi|priyaṃ kṛtvā Keśav'|Ârjunayor mṛdhe
siṃhavan nadatha prītāḥ śoka|kāla upasthite?
āgamiṣyati vaḥ kṣipraṃ phalaṃ pāpasya karmaṇaḥ.
a|dharmo hi kṛtas tīvraḥ kathaṃ syād a|phalaś ciram?›

No. These words do not fit my son, Mádhava's nephew,
Subhádra's very soul. Will I never again see his bright eyes,
his strong arms? My heart must be made of diamond that
it does not break apart. How could those monsters raise
their bows and drive their arrows into the body of a child?
My child, Vasudéva's nephew. My boy who would come out
and whose smiles and high spirits would lift my own when
I returned from waging death on my foes. What? He will
not, this time? He lies fallen in a pool of blood on the earth. 72.55
Brightening the dust with his lifestuff like a toppled sun.

O Subhádra I pity you. His mother will perish in sorrow when she hears that her son has died a lonely death. When Abhimányu does not come to her she will ask me why. And Dráupadi, what will I say to you when sorrow swallows you up? My heart must be made of diamond if it will not break into a thousand pieces when I see her sodden and buckled with grief.

I heard the proud sons of Dhrita·rashtra cheer. But it was
Krishna who heard Yuyútsu upbraid his kin. "You cannot
overcome Bibhátsu but now you have struck his son you
rejoice? O heroes let the Pándavas look upon your crimes.
Well then. Look with your twisted gaze upon the Pándava 72.60
army and rejoice in the evil done to Késhava and Árjuna
this day. Roar with delight for the time of your sorrow is at
hand. Soon you will reap the harvest of this poison crop for
no crime this foul can escape respite for long."

iti tān paribhāṣan vai vaiśyā|putro mahā|matiḥ
apāyāc chastram utsṛjya kopa|duḥkha|samanvitaḥ.
kim|artham etan n' ākhyātaṃ tvayā Kṛṣṇa raṇe mama?
adhakṣaṃ tān ahaṃ krūrāṃs tadā sarvān mahā|rathān.»

SAMJAYA uvāca:

72.65 putra|śok'|ārditaṃ Pārthaṃ dhyāyantaṃ s'|âsru|locanam
nigṛhya Vāsudevas taṃ putr'|ādhibhir abhiplutam
«m" âivam» ity abravīt Kṛṣṇas tīvra|śoka|samanvitam.
«sarveṣām eṣa vai panthāḥ śūrāṇām a|nivartinām
kṣatriyāṇāṃ viśeṣeṇa yeṣāṃ yuddhena jīvikā.
eṣā vai yudhyamānānāṃ śūrāṇām a|nivartinām
vihitā sarva|śāstra|jñair gatir matimatāṃ vara.
dhruvaṃ hi yuddhe maraṇaṃ śūrāṇām a|nivartinām.
gataḥ puṇya|kṛtāṃ lokān Abhimanyur na saṃśayaḥ.
etac ca sarva|vīrāṇāṃ kāṅkṣitaṃ Bharata'|rṣabha
saṃgrāme 'bhimukho mṛtyuṃ prāpnuyād iti māna|da.
72.70 sa ca vīrān raṇe hatvā rāja|putrān mahā|balān
vīrair ākāṅkṣitaṃ mṛtyuṃ saṃprāpto 'bhimukhaṃ raṇe.
mā śucaḥ, puruṣa|vyāghra. pūrvair eṣa sanātanaḥ
dharma|kṛdbhiḥ kṛto dharmaḥ kṣatriyāṇāṃ raṇe kṣayaḥ.
ime te bhrātaraḥ sarve dīnā Bharata|sattama
tvayi śoka|samāviṣṭe nṛ|pāś ca su|hṛdas tava.
etāṃs ca vacasā sāmnā samāśvāsaya, māna|da.
viditaṃ veditavyaṃ te. na śokaṃ kartum arhasi.»

He may be a commoner's son but Yuyútsu is no fool. With more angry words he cast down his sword and walked away in shame and grief. O Krishna why did you not tell me that this had happened before, while we were still fighting? I would have burnt all their lawless kind from the earth."

SÁNJAYA spoke:

Another wave of despair crashed against Partha and tears 72.65
filled his eyes as he thought of his son. He convulsed with grief. Krishna son of Vasu·deva put his hands on him and spoke.

"Do not do this. All warriors who are brave and strong walk the same path and those who live by war never stray from it. The brave and the strong take this path because it is ordained for them by men wise enough to know the dictates of this world and you are the best of their number. The brave and the strong can be certain to die in battle. But o bull of the Bharatas have no doubt: Abhimányu dwells now in the land of the pure of heart, the place where every hero yearns to go and the reason why a warrior seeks to meet
death on the field. O friend. Abhimányu slew the bold and 72.70
mighty sons of kings and came face to face with death as a hero should: in the dance of war.* O tiger in the forest of men do not mourn. This has been the way since days of old. Those who know the order of things do what is given them and warriors are given the mayhem of war. O best of all the Bharatas all of your brothers and kings and friends are with you in the pit of your grief. Brave friend you must hearten us all with some words of hope. You must understand that you should let your sorrow go."

evam āśvāsitaḥ Pārthaḥ Kṛṣṇen' âdbhuta|karmaṇā
tato 'bravīt tadā bhrātṝn sarvān Pārthaḥ sa|gadgadān.
72.75 «sa dīrgha|bāhuḥ pṛthv|aṃso dīrgha|rājīva|locanaḥ
Abhimanyur yathā vṛttaḥ śrotum icchāmy ahaṃ tathā.
sa|nāga|syandana|hayān drakṣyadhvaṃ nihatān mayā
saṃgrāme s'|ânubandhāṃs tān mama putrasya vairiṇaḥ.
katham ca vaḥ kṛt'|âstrāṇāṃ sarveṣāṃ śastra|pāṇinām
Saubhadro nidhanaṃ gacched Vajriṇ' âpi samāgataḥ?
yady evam aham ajñāsyam a|śaktān rakṣaṇe mama
putrasya Pāṇḍu|Pāñcālān mayā gupto bhavet tataḥ.
kathaṃ ca vai ratha|sthānāṃ śara|varṣāṇi muñcatām
nīto 'bhimanyur nidhanaṃ kad|arthī|kṛtya vaḥ paraiḥ?
72.80 aho vaḥ pauruṣaṃ n' âsti na ca vo 'sti parākramaḥ,
yatr' Âbhimanyuḥ samare paśyatāṃ vo nipātitaḥ.
ātmānam eva garheyaṃ yad ahaṃ vai su|durbalān
yuṣmān ājñāya niryāto bhīrūn a|kṛta|niścayān.
āho svid bhūṣaṇ'|ârthāya varma śastr'|āyudhāni vaḥ,
vācaś ca vaktuṃ saṃsatsu, mama putram a|rakṣatām?»
evam uktvā tato vākyaṃ tiṣṭhaṃś cāpa|var'|âsimān
na sm' âśakyata Bībhatsuḥ kena cit prasamīkṣitum.
tam antakam iva kruddhaṃ niḥśvasantaṃ muhur muhuḥ
putra|śok'|âbhisaṃtaptam aśru|pūrṇa|mukhaṃ tadā,
72.85 na bhāṣituṃ śaknuvanti draṣṭuṃ vā suhṛdo 'rjunam,
anyatra Vāsudevād vā jyeṣṭhād vā Pāṇḍu|nandanāt.
sarvāsv avasthāsu hi tāv Arjunasya mano|'nugau
bahu|mānāt priyatvāc ca tāv enaṃ vaktum arhataḥ.
tatas taṃ putra|śokena bhṛśaṃ pīḍita|mānasam
rājīva|locanaṃ kruddhaṃ rājā vacanam abravīt.

Somehow Krishna had managed to console Partha a little. His brothers stammered but fell silent. Then Partha spoke.

"I want now to hear of my son. My boy with his broad 72.75
shoulders and strong arms and deep blue eyes. I want to hear what happened to him. Then watch as I pluck my son's killers and all their friends from elephant, car and horse and destroy them.

All of you with swords and bows drawn and yet still my boy was laid low. Was he battling Indra? If I had known that the Pandus and Panchálas could not look after my son then I would have made sure to myself. Did you stand in your chariots clouding the sky with arrows while they dragged
him down and rolled him in the earth? There is not a man 72.80
among you. Are you such cowards? Did you stand and gawp when they knocked my son down? Then I should blame myself for leaving him in the hands of such pitiful and timid weaklings. Do you carry these swords and bows and wear this armour to look pretty? Do you save your speeches for feasts? Betrayers of my son. Speak to me."

Árjuna broke off and brandished his bow and bright sword. His face was full of tears. He stood there gasping,
angry as death and burning in pain for his son. None of his 72.85
companions could look him in the eye. Only Vasudéva and Pandu's heir could meet his gaze. In this terrible moment they alone could comfort Árjuna and could find words to express their sympathy and love and reach through his rage and shattering despair. Yudhi·shthira turned to his bluelotuseyed brother and spoke.

YUDHIṢṬHIRA uvāca:

73.1 TVAYI YĀTE, mahā|bāho, Saṃśaptaka|balaṃ prati
prayatnam akarot tīvram Ācāryo grahaṇe mama.
vyūḍh'|ânīkā vayaṃ Droṇaṃ vārayāmaḥ sma sarvaśaḥ
prativyūhya rath'|ânīkaṃ yatamānaṃ tathā raṇe.
sa vāryamāṇo rathibhir mayi c' âpi su|rakṣite
asmān abhijagām' āśu pīḍayan niśitaiḥ śaraiḥ.
te pīḍyamānā Droṇena Droṇ'|ânīkaṃ na śaknumaḥ
prativīkṣitum apy ājau bhettuṃ tat kuta eva tu.
73.5 vayaṃ tv a|pratimaṃ vīrye sarve Saubhadram ātma|jam
uktavantaḥ sma taṃ «tāta bhindhy anīkam» iti prabho.
sa tathā codito 'smābhiḥ sad|aśva iva vīryavān
a|sahyam api taṃ bhāraṃ voḍhum ev' ôpacakrame.
sa tav' âstr'|ôpadeśena vīryeṇa ca samanvitaḥ
prāviśat tad balaṃ bālaḥ suparṇa iva sāgaram.
te 'nuyātā vayaṃ vīraṃ Sātvatī|putram āhave
praveṣṭu|kāmās ten' âiva yena sa prāviśac camūm.
tataḥ Saindhavako rājā kṣudras tāta Jayadrathaḥ
vara|dānena Rudrasya sarvān naḥ samavārayat.
73.10 tato Droṇaḥ Kṛpaḥ Karṇo Drauṇiḥ Kausalya eva ca
Kṛtavarmā ca Saubhadraṃ ṣaḍ rathāḥ paryavārayan.
parivārya tu taiḥ sarvair yudhi bālo mahā|rathaiḥ
yatamānaḥ paraṃ śaktyā bahubhir vi|rathī|kṛtaḥ.
tato Dauḥśāsaniḥ kṣipraṃ tathā tair vi|rathī|kṛtam
saṃśayaṃ paramaṃ prāpya diṣṭ'|ânten' âbhyayojayat.
sa tu hatvā sahasrāṇi nar'|âśva|ratha|dantinām
aṣṭau ratha|sahasrāṇi nava danti|śatāni ca
rāja|putra|śahasre dve vīrāṃś c' â|lakṣitān bahūn,
Bṛhadbalaṃ ca rājānaṃ svargeṇ' ājau prayojya ha

YUDHI·SHTHIRA spoke:

O WARRIOR. AFTER you had left to fight the Beholden, 73.1
the Teacher made a fierce effort to capture me. We ranged
our lines to meet him and managed to rebuff his attempt. I
was well protected and Drona momentarily at bay, but soon
after he rallied and struck us hard with his whetted shafts.
We strained beneath his counterattack and could barely see
his line for arrows let alone find some way to break through
it. O great one we agreed that your boy had no equal among 73.5
us and so we asked the child to open up Drona's array.

Though it was a heavy burden to harness to him Abhimányu like a young stallion was keen and rearing to draw it.
The arts you taught him and the courage he was born with
stood him in good stead and like a heron diving into the
sea he plunged into Drona's array. We were close behind
Sátvati's daring boy, hoping to rush through the gap that he
forced open. But the murderous Jayad·ratha king of Sindhu
had a pact with Rudra and so he was able to hold us back
while Drona, Kripa, Karna, Ashvattháman, Kausálya and 73.10
Krita·varman brought their six chariots in around Saubhádra. Surrounded by all six of their deadly cars the boy fought
back as best he could but soon they had him out on the
open earth. Dauhshásani saw him so and could not believe
his luck and though he struck the fatal blow Abhimányu's
fate was by then already sealed.

He tore their army apart before he fell. In their thousands horses cars and beasts fell before him. Eight thousand chariots, nine hundred elephants, two thousand sons of kings and heroes beyond number. He sent King Brihad·bala beyond this dusty earth. Only after these feats did he go to

tataḥ parama|dharm'|ātmā diṣṭ'|ântam upajagmivān.
73.15 etāvad eva nirvṛttam asmākaṃ śoka|vardhanam.
sa c' âivaṃ puruṣa|vyāghraḥ svarga|lokam avāptavān.

tato 'rjuno vacaḥ śrutvā dharma|rājena bhāṣitam
«hā putra» iti niḥśvasya vyathito nyapatad bhuvi.
viṣaṇṇa|vadanāḥ sarve parivārya Dhanaṃjayam
netrair a|nimiṣair dīnāḥ pratyavaikṣan paras|param.
pratipadya tataḥ saṃjñāṃ Vāsaviḥ krodha|mūrchitaḥ,
kampamāno jvareṇ' êva niḥśvasaṃś ca muhur muhuḥ
pāṇiṃ pāṇau viniṣpiṣya śvasamāno 'śru|netravān
unmatta iva vipreksann idaṃ vacanam abravīt.

ARJUNA uvāca:

73.20 satyaṃ vaḥ pratijānāmi śvo smi hantā Jayadratham
na ced vadha|bhayād bhīto Dhārtarāṣṭrān prahāsyati,
na c' âsmāñ śaraṇaṃ gacchet Kṛṣṇaṃ vā puruṣ'|ôttamam
bhavantaṃ vā mahā|rāja śvo 'smi hantā Jayadratham.
Dhārtarāṣṭra|priya|karaṃ mayi vismṛta|sauhṛdam
pāpaṃ bāla|vadhe hetuṃ śvo 'smi hantā Jayadratham.
rakṣamāṇāś ca taṃ saṃkhye ye māṃ yotsyanti ke cana
api Droṇaḥ Kṛpo rājan chādayiṣyāmi tāñ śaraiḥ.
yady etad evaṃ saṃgrāme na kuryāṃ puruṣa'|rṣabhāḥ
mā sma puṇya|kṛtāl̃ lokān prāpnuyāṃ śūra|saṃmatān.
73.25 ye lokā mātṛ|hantṝṇāṃ ye c' âpi pitṛ|ghātinām
guru|dāra|ratānāṃ ye piśunānāṃ ca ye sadā,
sādhūn asūyatāṃ ye ca ye c' âpi parivādinām
ye ca nikṣepa|hartṝṇāṃ ye ca viśvāsa|ghātinām,
bhukta|pūrvāṃ striyaṃ ye ca nindatām agha|śaṃsinām
brahma|ghnānāṃ ca ye lokā ye ca go|ghātinām api,

meet the destiny that drew his perfect soul. His death is a 73.15
choking misery for us. But he was a tiger. Even as we mourn
him he leaves the forest of men and sets foot in paradise.

Árjuna had been listening quietly to his brother's words but all of a sudden he cried out for his son and fell trembling to the earth. His brothers stepped in grimly around him and bleak of eye glanced at one another. Then Indra's son seemed to light on an idea and he rose up again quaking with anger. He shook as if in a fever and his breath came slowly. Tears welled in his eyes. Clenching and unclenching his hands he looked about him as if out of his mind and spoke these words between shallow gasps.

ÁRJUNA spoke:

I swear to you that tomorrow I will kill Jayad·ratha. Per- 73.20
haps he will so fear for his life that he will abandon Dhrita·
rashtra's sons and come to seek my mercy or the mercy of
great Krishna or o great king your own. But if he does not,
then tomorrow I will slay him.

I speak of one who has traded our old friendship for Duryódhana's favour. Jayad·ratha's crime is child murder and for that tomorrow I will slay him. If anyone tries to stop me whether Drona or Kripa or anyone else then o king see them vanish beneath my darts.

O mighty warriors here gathered know that if I fail in
this task I will never set foot in the realms of the blessed
to which we all aspire. Instead I will go to where men who 73.25
murder their mothers and fathers go. Where men who se-
duce their teachers' wives go, men who lie and hurl insults,

pāyasaṃ vā yav'|ânnaṃ vā śākaṃ kṛsaram eva vā
saṃyāv'|āpūpa|māṃsāni ye ca lokā vṛth" âśnatām,
tān ahnāy' âdhigaccheyaṃ na cedd hanyāṃ Jayadratham.
ved'|âdhyāyinam atyarthaṃ saṃśitaṃ vā dvij'|ôttamam
avamanyamāno yān yāti vṛddhān sādhūn gurūṃs tathā,
73.30 spṛśato brāhmaṇaṃ gāṃ ca
pāden' âgniṃ ca yā bhavet
y" âpsu śleṣma purīṣaṃ ca
mūtraṃ vā muñcatāṃ gatiḥ,
tāṃ gaccheyaṃ gatiṃ kaṣṭāṃ
na cedd hanyāṃ Jayadratham.
nagnasya snāyamānasya yā ca vandhy'|âtither gatiḥ
utkocināṃ mṛṣ"|ôktīnāṃ vañcakānāṃ ca yā gatiḥ,
sv'|ātm'|âpahāriṇāṃ yā ca yā ca mithy"|âbhiśaṃsinām
bhṛtyaiḥ saṃdiśyamānānāṃ putra|dār"|āśritais tathā,
a|saṃvibhajya kṣudrāṇāṃ
yā gatir miṣṭam aśnatām,
tāṃ gaccheyaṃ gatiṃ ghorāṃ
na cedd hanyāṃ Jayadratham.
saṃśritaṃ v" âpi yas tyaktvā sādhuṃ tad|vacane ratam
na bibharti nṛśaṃs'|ātmā nindate c' ôpakāriṇam,
73.35 arhate prātiveśyāya śrāddhaṃ yo na dadāti ca
an|arhebhyaś ca yo dadyād vṛṣalī|pataye tathā,
madya|po bhinna|maryādaḥ kṛta|ghno bhrātṛ|nindakaḥ:
teṣāṃ gatim iyāṃ kṣipraṃ na cedd hanyāṃ Jayadratham.
dharmād apetā ye c' ânye mayā n' âtr' ânukīrtitāḥ
ye c' ânukīrtitās teṣāṃ gatim kṣipram avāpnuyām
yadi vyuṣṭām imāṃ rātriṃ śvo na hanyāṃ Jayadratham.

men whose children despise them, who take bribes and betray trust, who spurn women they have defiled, who venerate evil, who kill brahmins and cows, who glut themselves at banquets pouring heaps of barleycakes and sweetmeats down their necks. If I do not kill Jayad·ratha I will go to 73.30
meet the men who mock devotion, who despise piety, who insult the old, the wise and the learned, who muddy with their tread a brahmin or a cow or the fire, who spit and piss and shit where fresh water runs. If I do not kill Jayad·ratha may I go the way of men who bathe naked, of idle guests, of the corrupt, of liars and deceivers, of suicides, of the impudent, of those who bow to their servants or cower behind their wives and children, who do not share their sweets with the poor. May I go the same way as every one of these turbid souls, if I do not kill Jayad·ratha.

There are fools who cast out holy men seeking their shelter and lose their blessing, who abuse and starve servants, who ignore the deaths of neighbours and instead give to 73.35
fools and hypocrites. May I go their way: the way of the drunk, the dissolute, the damned. May I go the way of the man who spurns his brother, if I do not kill Jayad·ratha. If this night ends and day breaks and I do not kill Jayad·ratha then I will go the same way as all of these wretches and of any others who have strayed from what is right and whose sins I have not spoken.

imāṃ c' âpy aparāṃ bhūyaḥ pratijñāṃ me nibodhata:
yady asminn a|hate pāpe sūryo 'stam upayāsyati
ih' âiva sampraveṣṭ" âhaṃ jvalitaṃ jāta|vedasam.

asura|sura|manuṣyāḥ pakṣiṇo v" ôragā vā
pitṛ|rajani|carā vā brahma|deva'|rṣayo vā
caram a|caram ap' îdaṃ yat paraṃ c' âpi tasmāt
tad api mama ripuṃ taṃ rakṣituṃ n' âiva śaktāḥ.
73.40 yadi viśati rasā|talaṃ tad|agryaṃ
viyad api deva|puraṃ diteḥ puraṃ vā
tad api śara|śatair ahaṃ prabhāte
bhṛśam Abhimanyu|ripoḥ śiro 'bhihartā.

evam uktvā vicikṣepa Gāṇḍīvaṃ savya|dakṣiṇam.
tasya śabdam atikramya dhanuḥ|śabdo 'spṛśad divam.
Arjunena pratijñāte Pāñcajanyaṃ Janārdanaḥ
pradadhmau tatra saṃkruddho Devadattaṃ ca Phālgunaḥ.

sa Pāñcajanyo 'cyuta|vaktra|vāyunā
bhṛśaṃ su|pūrṇ'|ôdara|niḥsṛta|dhvaniḥ
jagat sa|pātāla|viyad|dig|īśvaraṃ
prakampayām āsa yug'|âtyaye yathā.

tato vāditra|ghoṣāś ca prādur āsan sahasraśaḥ
siṃha|nādāś ca Pāṇḍūnāṃ pratijñāte mah"|ātmanā.

Mark me, for to make good my vow I make it stronger. If tomorrow the sun sets and this devil still lives then I will cast myself into the fire to which all things in truth belong.

No mortal or immortal, man, bird or serpent,
No ghost or nightwalker, god, seer or priest,
Nothing within or beyond the still or shifting world
Will keep my quarry from me.
Let him flee helldeep, 73.40
Let him hide on high with deity or demon:
With a hundred arrows come daybreak
I will tear off the head of Abhimányu's killer.

Árjuna rapped Gandíva against the earth to one side and then the other and the cracks echoed out and touched the sky. The Stirrer of Men sounded Pancha·janya and the Red Star Fighter raised up Deva·datta.

Pancha·janya filled with Áchyuta's gale
And from the shell's lip rose a note
That shook the world from pit to peak
As if to augur its end.

Then the thunder of a thousand drums and the roar of a thousand voices rolled out across the Pandu host. Their champion had made his vow.

74–84

THE VOW

SAMJAYA uvāca:

74.1 ŚRUTVĀ TU TAṂ mahā|śabdaṃ
Pāṇḍūnāṃ putra|gṛddhinām
cāraiḥ pravedite tatra
samutthāya Jayadrathaḥ
śoka|saṃmūḍha|hṛdayo duḥkhen' âbhipariplutaḥ
majjamāna iv' â|gādhe vipule śoka|sāgare
jagāma samitiṃ rājñāṃ Saindhavo vimṛśan bahu.
sa teṣāṃ nara|devānāṃ sakāśe parivedayan
Abhimanyoḥ pitur bhītaḥ sa|vrīḍo vākyam abravīt.
«yo 'sau Pāṇḍoḥ kila kṣetre jātaḥ Śakreṇa kāminā
sa ninīṣati dur|buddhir māṃ kil' âiṣaṃ Yama|kṣayam.
74.5 tat svasti vo 'stu yāsyāmi sva|gṛhaṃ jīvit'|ēpsayā
atha v" âstra|pratibalās trāta māṃ kṣatriya'|rṣabhāḥ.
Pārthena prārthitaṃ vīrās te saṃdatta mam' â|bhayam.
Droṇa|Duryodhana|Kṛpāḥ Karṇa|Madr'|ēśa|Bāhlikāḥ
Duḥśāsan'|ādayaḥ śaktās trātum mām antak'|ārditam.
kim aṅga punar ekena Phālgunena jighāṃsatā
na trāyeyur bhavanto māṃ samastāḥ patayaḥ kṣiteḥ.
praharṣaṃ Pāṇḍaveyānāṃ śrutvā mama mahad bhayam
sīdanti mama gātrāṇi mumūrṣor iva pārthivāḥ.
vadho nūnaṃ pratijñāto mama Gāṇḍīva|dhanvanā
tathā hi hṛṣṭāḥ krośanti śoka|kāle sma Pāṇḍavāḥ.
74.10 tan na devā na gandharvā n' âsur'|ôraga|rākṣasāḥ
utsahante 'nyathā kartuṃ. kuta eva nar'|âdhipāḥ?
tasmān mām anujānīta: bhadraṃ vo 'stu nara'|rṣabhāḥ
a|darśanaṃ gamiṣyāmi na māṃ drakṣyanti Pāṇḍavāḥ.»

SÁNJAYA spoke:

THERE WERE SPIES in the Pandu camp, and they re- 74.1
turned to Jayad·ratha and explained the reason for the
rumbles he heard. Jayad·ratha rose up flushed with panic.
His heart was in tumult. He felt as if a vast and fathomless
sea of despair was opening under his feet. Thinking desperately about what to do he brought together the other kings
and told that godlike company what he knew and confessed
his fear of Abhimányu's father. There was shame in his voice
when he spoke.

"The man born from Indra's desire and Pandu's wife is
in dark spirits: he plots to send me off to Death's kingdom.
I fear for my life. My fellow chieftains, I ask either that 74.5
with your blessing I may return home or if you think your
weapons can match his that you use your might to protect
me, and stop Partha from doing me the harm he so yearns
to inflict. If death came to take me then Drona, Duryódhana and Kripa, Karna, the King of Madra and Bahlíka
and Duhshásana and all our other champions would together be able to fend him off. So perhaps the combined
strength of you high majesties of the earth can thwart the
Red Star Fighter when he comes for my head. But o kings I
have heard the Pándavas' strange celebrations and they have
bedded in me a deep unease. My body shakes as if death
were already close. The Pándavas cry with joy in their hour
of despair, and they do so because Gandíva's master has
vowed to kill me. No god or *gandhárva*, no demon, serpent 74.10
or devil can stand against him. How then will mere kings?
I ask you o bulls in this world of men: give me your leave to

evaṃ vilapamānaṃ taṃ bhayād vyākula|cetasam
ātma|kārya|garīyastvād rājā Duryodhano 'bravīt.
«na bhetavyaṃ. nara|vyāghra, ko hi tvāṃ, puruṣa'|rṣabha,
madhye kṣatriya|vīrāṇāṃ tiṣṭhantaṃ prārthayed yudhi?
ahaṃ Vaikartanaḥ Karṇaś, Citraseno Viviṃśatiḥ,
Bhūriśravāḥ, Śalaḥ, Śalyo, Vṛṣaseno dur|āsadaḥ,
74.15 Purumitro, jayo, Bhojaḥ, Kāmbojaś ca Sudakṣiṇaḥ,
Satyavrato mahā|bāhur, Vikarṇo, Durmukhaś ca ha,
Duḥśāsanaḥ, Subāhuś ca Kāliṅgaś c' âpy udāyudhaḥ,
Vind'|Ânuvindāv Āvantyau, Droṇo Drauṇiś ca Saubalaḥ,
ete c' ânye ca bahavo nānā|janapad'|ēśvarāḥ
sa|sainyās tv" âbhiyāsyanti. vyetu te mānaso jvaraḥ.
tvaṃ c' âpi rathināṃ śreṣṭhaḥ svayaṃ śūro 'mita|dyute
sa kathaṃ Pāṇḍaveyebhyo bhayaṃ paśyasi, Saindhava?
akṣauhiṇyo daś' âikā ca
madīyās tava rakṣaṇe
yatnād yotsyanti. mā bhais tvaṃ,
Saindhava. vyetu te bhayam.»
74.20 evam āśvāsito, rājan, putreṇa tava Saindhavaḥ
Duryodhanena sahito Droṇaṃ rātrāv upāgamat.
upasaṃgrahaṇaṃ kṛtvā Droṇāya sa, viśāṃ pate,
upopaviśya praṇataḥ paryapṛcchad idaṃ tadā.
nimitte dūra|pātitve laghutve dṛḍha|vedhane
mama bravītu, bhagavān, viśeṣaṃ Phalgunasya ca.
vidyā|viśeṣam icchāmi jñātum, Ācārya, tattvataḥ
Arjunasy' ātmanaś c' âiva. yathātathyam pracakṣva me.

vanish from here and away from the hungry eyes of Pandu's children."

Jayad·ratha was witless with fear and his words lacked sense. But King Duryódhana had his own concerns, and with these in mind he replied.

"Do not be afraid. You are a tiger, a bull in this world of men. Who could lay a hand on you when flanked in battle by such fierce companions? We are all at your side: I and Karna born of the sun, Chitra·sena and Vivínshati, Bhuri·shravas, Shala and Shalya, deadly Vrisha·sena and Puru· 74.15
mitra, Jaya and Bhoja, Sudákshina lord of the Kambójas, mighty Satya·vrata, Vikárna, Dúrmukha and Duhshásana. Subáhu is here, Kalínga draws his sword. Here are Vinda and Anuvínda princes of Avánti, and Drona and Drauni, Sáubala and all the other chieftains of tribes too numerous to name. They and all their soldiery will be fighting at your side. Let this fever pass. O great one you are yourself a marvel, a man of vaunting might, a master of war. How can you be afraid of the Pándavas, Sáindhava? I will command eleven of my legions to protect you and you alone. Have no fear, Sáindhava. Let this fever pass."

O majesty, Sáindhava took heart from your son's words 74.20
and a little cheered he went in the night to see Drona. O lord of these lands, Jayad·ratha knelt before Drona and came closer and bowed once again and then asked him a question.

"O master. Tell me Phálguna's secret. How he is so quick, how his arrows fly so far and bite so deep. I want to know the very nature of Árjuna's being. Tell me the truth about him."

DROṆA uvāca:

samam ācāryakaṃ, tāta, tava c' âiv' Ârjunasya ca.
yogād duḥkh'|ôṣitatvāc ca tasmāt tvatto 'dhiko 'rjunaḥ.
74.25 na tu te yudhi saṃtrāsaḥ kāryaḥ Pārthāt kathaṃ cana.
ahaṃ hi rakṣitā, tāta, bhayāt tvāṃ n' âtra saṃśayaḥ.
na hi mad|bāhu|guptasya prabhavanty amarā api.
vyūhayiṣyāmi taṃ vyūhaṃ yaṃ Pārtho na tariṣyati.
tasmād yudhyasva. mā bhais tvaṃ. sva|dharmam anupālaya.
pitṛ|paitāmahaṃ mārgam anuyāhi mahā|ratha.
adhītya vidhivad vedān agnayaḥ su|hutās tvayā
iṣṭaṃ ca bahubhir yajñair na te mṛtyur bhayaṃ|karaḥ.
dur|labhaṃ mānuṣair mandair mahā|bhāgyam avāpya tu
bhuja|vīry'|ârjitāl̃ lokān divyān prāpsyasy an|uttamān.
74.30 Kuravaḥ Pāṇḍavāś c' âiva Vṛṣṇayo 'nye ca mānavāḥ
ahaṃ ca saha putreṇa a|dhruvā iti cintyatām.
paryāyeṇa vayaṃ sarve kālena balinā hatāḥ
para|lokaṃ gamiṣyāmaḥ svaiḥ svaiḥ karmabhir anvitāḥ.
tapas taptvā tu yāl̃ lokān prāpnuvanti tapasvinaḥ
kṣatra|dharm'|āśritā vīrāḥ kṣatriyāḥ prāpnuvanti tān.

SAṂJAYA uvāca:

evam āśvāsito rājan Bhāradvājena Saindhavaḥ
apānudad bhayaṃ Pārthād yuddhāya ca mano dadhe.
tataḥ praharṣaḥ senānāṃ tav' âpy āsīd viśām pate
vāditrāṇāṃ dhvaniś c' ôgraḥ siṃha|nāda|ravaiḥ saha.

DRONA spoke:

My son. I taught you both. Árjuna's skill has been hardened in the fire of his suffering and he can overreach you.
In tomorrow's battle no one will be able to save you from 74.25
Partha's grasp except I. Be at peace my son. Even the gods could not snatch you from the safety of my arms. I will form an array that Partha will not cross. So fight on unafraid, cleave to your calling. Follow o mighty one the path of your father and grandfather. Study the Veda and tend the fires and observe your rites and you will have nothing to fear from death. Rise to a destiny above the reach of frailer souls and you will find the perfect realms of heaven, realms only
a mighty stride can reach. Remember that no man whether 74.30
Kuru Pándava Vrishni or any other race stands a chance against me and my son.

The wheel of time turns on and in the end we all must die: but we go to the next world with what we have done in this one. Great ascetics pass through curtains of flame to reach the same demesne as warriors worth the name who follow the law of their kind.

SÁNJAYA spoke:

Sáindhava was gladdened by what Bharadvája said and o majesty he cast aside his fear of Pritha's son and made up his mind to fight. And o lord of men when the troops heard of his decision the air filled with their drums and roars and cries of delight.

SAMJAYA uvāca:

75.1 PRATIJÑĀTE TU Pārthena Sindhu|rāja|vadhe tadā
Vāsudevo mahā|bāhur Dhanamjayam abhāṣata.
«bhrātṝṇāṃ matam ājñāya tvayā vācā pratiśrutam
‹Saindhavaṃ śvo 'smi hant"› êti tat sāhasam idaṃ kṛtam.
a|saṃmantrya mayā sārdham atibhāro 'yam udyataḥ.
kathaṃ nu sarva|lokasya n' âvahāsyā bhavemahi?
Dhārtarāṣṭrasya śibire mayā praṇihitāś carāḥ.
ta ime śīghram āgamya pravṛttiṃ vedayanti naḥ.
75.5 tvayā vai sampratijñāte Sindhu|rāja|vadhe prabho
siṃha|nādaḥ sa|vāditraḥ su|mahān iha taiḥ śrutaḥ.
tena śabdena vitrastā Dhārtarāṣṭrāḥ sa|bāndhavāḥ
‹n' â|kasmāt siṃha|nādo 'yam› iti matvā vyavasthitāḥ.
su|mahāñ śabda|sampātaḥ Kauravāṇāṃ mahā|bhuja
āsīn nāg'|âśva|pattīnāṃ ratha|ghoṣaś ca bhairavaḥ.
Abhimanyor vadhaṃ śrutvā ‹dhruvam ārto Dhanaṃjayaḥ
rātrau niryāsyati krodhād› iti matvā vyavasthitāḥ.
tair yatadbhir iyaṃ satyā śrutā satyavatas tava
pratijñā Sindhu|rājasya vadhe rājīva|locana.
75.10 tato vi|manasaḥ sarve trastāḥ kṣudra|mṛgā iva
āsan Suyodhan'|âmātyāḥ sa ca rājā Jayadrathaḥ
ath' ôtthāya sah' âmātyair dīnaḥ śibiram ātmanaḥ
āyāt Sauvīra|Sindhūnām īśvaro bhṛśa|duḥkhitaḥ.
sa mantra|kāle saṃmantrya sarvā naiḥśreyasīḥ kriyāḥ
Suyodhanam idaṃ vākyam abravīd rāja|saṃsadi.

SÁNJAYA spoke:

LATER THAT NIGHT mighty Vasudéva spoke to Dhanan·jaya about his promise to slay the Sindhu king. 75.1

"Your vow to kill Sáindhava tomorrow was a rash one. You knew what your brothers wanted to hear, but the burden you have shouldered is great and you did not even ask my advice before making your decision. We will be the laughing stock of the whole world.

I have spies in Duryódhana's camp, and they have just
now returned and brought me news. The clamour of drums 75.5
and voices that met your oath crossed the field to their ears. O mighty one the report of soldiers' cries and grinding wheels travelled from here and boomed among the men horses and beasts of the Káurava camp. Duryódhana and his thugs were perplexed for at first they could not understand its cause. They knew that Dhanan·jaya would have heard his son was dead and would pass the night frozen in fury. But as they wondered to themselves what was happening, they heard the truth of what was afoot. They learned that with your blue eyes burning you had vowed to kill the
Sindhu king. Suyódhana and his brothers and King Jayad· 75.10
ratha skipped in terror like fawns. In deep distress the lord of the Sauvíras and Sindhus rose up and went with his ministers into his tent. There they deliberated on what they might do. When the time came for the evening counsel Jayad·ratha stood before the assembled kings and turned to Suyódhana and spoke.

‹mam' âsau putra|hant" êti śvo 'bhiyātā Dhanaṃjayaḥ.
pratijñāto hi senāyā madhye tena vadho mama.
tāṃ na devā na gandharvā n' âsur'|ôraga|rākṣasāḥ
utsahante 'nyathā kartuṃ pratijñāṃ Savyasācinaḥ.
75.15 te māṃ rakṣata saṃgrāme mā vo mūrdhni Dhanaṃjayaḥ
padaṃ kṛtv' âpnuyāl lakṣyaṃ tasmād atra vidhīyatām.
atha rakṣā na me saṃkhye kriyate Kuru|nandana
anujānīhi māṃ rājan gamiṣyāmi gṛhān prati.›
evam uktas tv avāk|śīrṣo vi|manāḥ sa Suyodhanaḥ
śrutvā taṃ samayaṃ tasya dhyānam ev' ânvapadyata.
tam ārtam abhisamprekṣya rājā kila sa Saindhavaḥ
mṛdu c' ātma|hitaṃ c' âiva s'|âpekṣam idam uktavān.
‹n' êha paśyāmi bhavatāṃ tathā|vīryaṃ dhanur|dharam
yo 'rjunasy' âstram astreṇa pratihanyān mah"|āhave.
75.20 Vāsudeva|sahāyasya Gāṇḍīvaṃ dhunvato dhanuḥ
ko 'rjunasy' âgratas tiṣṭhet sākṣād api Śatakratuḥ?
Maheśvaro 'pi Pārthena śrūyate yodhitaḥ purā
padātinā mahā|vīryo girau Himavati prabhuḥ.
Dānavānāṃ sahasrāṇi hiraṇya|pura|vāsinām
jaghān' âika|rathen' âiva deva|rāja|pracoditaḥ.
samāyukto hi Kaunteyo Vāsudevena dhīmatā
s'|âmarān api lokāṃs trīn hanyād iti matir mama.
so 'ham icchāmy anujñātuṃ rakṣituṃ vā mah"|ātmanā
Droṇena saha|putreṇa vīreṇa, yadi manyase.›
75.25 sa rājñā svayam Ācāryo bhṛśam atr' ârthito, 'rjuna.
saṃvidhānaṃ ca vihitaṃ rathāś ca kila sajjitāḥ.
Karṇo, Bhūriśravā, Drauṇir, Vṛṣasenaś, ca dur|jayaḥ

"Dhanan·jaya sees me as his son's killer and tomorrow he will come to find me. He has promised the Pándavas that I will die at his hand. If the Lefthanded Archer has said a thing will be, then no god or *gandhárva*, no demon, snake
or ghost can make it otherwise. Either ensure that I am safe 75.15
tomorrow lest Dhanan·jaya tread on my crown and make good his oath, or if you cannot guarantee my protection then o joy of the Kurus allow me to leave for home."

Suyódhana listened to Jayad·ratha's condition. He could understand his vassal's fear, and he hung his head in despair. Sáindhava saw how desolate the king looked and when he repeated his demand he chose his words with care.

"I have described Árjuna's rare quality. I see none among us who might match this warrior arrow for arrow in the
great battle to come. Would even Shata·kratu stand a chance 75.20
against the man that wields Gandíva and rides with Vasudéva? It is said that Pritha's mighty son once climbed snowy Himálaya to spar with Mahéshvara hand to hand. Bidden by the king of the gods he singlehandedly cast down a horde of Danu's children that dwelled in the golden city. While Vasudéva stands unrelenting at his car's reins I would say that Kunti's son could conquer the whole of the triple world, and not even the gods could hope to stop him. That is why I beg you to promise me that the great Drona and his son will do all they can to keep him from me."

Árjuna, the king did not hesitate. The plan was hatched 75.25
and the Teacher was told what he must do. Now his six best warriors have been prepared for the task: Karna, Bhuri·shravas, Drauni, hardy Vrisha·sena, Kripa and the Madra

Kṛpaś ca, Madra|rājaś ca ṣaḍ ete 'sya puro|gamāḥ.
śakaṭaḥ padmakaś c' ârdha|vyūho Droṇena nirmitaḥ,
padma|karṇika|madhya|sthaḥ sūcī|pārśve Jayadrathaḥ.
sthāsyate rakṣito vīraiḥ Sindhu|rāṭ sa su|durmadaḥ
dhanuṣy astre ca vīrye ca prāṇe c' âiva tath" âurase.
a|viṣahyatamā hy ete niścitāḥ Pārtha ṣaḍ rathāḥ.
etān a|jitvā ṣaḍ rathān n' âiva prāpyo Jayadrathaḥ.
75.30 teṣām ek'|âikaśo vīryaṃ ṣaṇṇāṃ tvam anucintaya.
sahitā hi nara|vyāghrā na śakyā jetum añjasā.
bhūyas tu mantrayiṣyāmi nītim ātma|hitāya vai
mantra|jñaiḥ sacivaiḥ sārdhaṃ suhṛdbhiḥ kārya|siddhaye.»

ARJUNA uvāca:

76.1 ṢAḌ RATHĀN Dhārtarāṣṭrasya manyase yān bal'|âdhikān
teṣāṃ vīryaṃ mam' ârdhena na tulyam iti me matiḥ.
astram astreṇa sarveṣām eteṣāṃ Madhusūdana
mayā drakṣyasi nirbhinnaṃ Jayadratha|vadh'|âiṣiṇā.
Droṇasya miṣataś c' âhaṃ sa|gaṇasya vilapyataḥ
mūrdhānaṃ Sindhu|rājasya pātayiṣyāmi bhū|tale.
yadi Sādhyāś ca Rudrāś ca Vasavaś ca sah'|Âśvinaḥ,
Marutaś ca sah' Êndreṇa viśve devāḥ sah'|ēśvarāḥ,
76.5 pitaraḥ saha|gandharvāḥ su|parṇāḥ sāgar'|ādayaḥ,
dyaur viyat pṛthivī c' êyaṃ diśaś ca sa|dig|īśvarāḥ,
grāmy'|âraṇyāni bhūtāni sthāvarāṇi carāṇi ca
trātāraḥ Sindhu|rājasya bhavanti Madhusūdana
tath" âpi bāṇair nihataṃ śvo draṣṭ" âsi raṇe mayā.
satyena ca śape Kṛṣṇa tath" âiv' āyudham ālabhe
yasya goptā mah"|êṣv|āsas tasya pāpasya durmateḥ.

chieftain. Splinter and lotus* are the arrays Drona will choose and at the tip of the needle and the very pericarp of the flower he will place Jayad·ratha. The Sindhu king is afraid. His weaponcraft and vigour and lifeblood ebb from him. But o Partha his six guardians are impossible to beat, and unbeaten they will keep you at bay.

Think on the valour of each of those six, one by one. They 75.30
are tigers in the forest of men and we will not overcome them in a fair fight. You must do what you must do. But I would rather for your own sake that you had sought counsel from those friends of yours who might have given it."

ÁRJUNA spoke:

LET ME TELL you about the six you call Duryódhana's 76.1
champions. Their might combined is not worth half of mine. Tomorrow you will see o Madhu·súdana how I match them arrow for arrow as I go to kill Jayad·ratha. While Drona and his cronies look on in anguish I will drop the Sindhu king's head in the dust. Let the Sadhyas, the Rudras and the Vasus, the Ashvins and Indra's storm gods, let all the gods and god kings and the departed dead and the *gan-* 76.5
dhárvas, let all that rule over the sky the air the earth the sea and every quarter of the world, let all the animals from farm and jungle, let all things animate and inanimate come together tomorrow to save the Sindhu king and still Madhu·súdana you will watch my arrows take his life. O Krishna I will break the fool's accursed bow in two whoever is there to protect him. Suyódhana thinks Drona holds the dice in this contest.* Well Késhava I will fight him off first. And

tam eva prathamaṃ Droṇam abhiyāsyāmi Keśava,
tasmin dyūtam idaṃ baddhaṃ manyate sa Suyodhanaḥ.
tasmāt tasy' âiva sen"|âgraṃ bhittvā yāsyāmi Saindhavam.
draṣṭ" âsi śvo mah"|êṣv|āsān nārācais tigma|tejitaiḥ
śṛṅgāṇ' îva girer vajrair dīryamāṇān mayā yudhi.
76.10 nara|nāg'|âśva|dehebhyo visraviṣyati śoṇitam
patadbhyaḥ patitebhyaś ca vibhinnebhyaḥ śitaiḥ śaraiḥ.
Gāṇḍīva|preṣitā bāṇā mano|'nila|samā jave
nṛ|nāg'|âśvān vi|deh'|âsūn kartāraś ca sahasraśaḥ.
Yamāt Kuberād Varuṇād Indrād Rudrāc ca yan mayā
upāttam astraṃ ghoraṃ tad draṣṭāro 'tra narā yudhi.
Brāhmeṇ' âstreṇa c' âstrāṇi hanyamānāni saṃyuge
mayā draṣṭ" âsi sarveṣāṃ Saindhavasy' âbhirakṣiṇām
śara|vega|samutkṛttai rājñāṃ Keśava mūrdhabhiḥ
āstīryamāṇāṃ pṛthivīṃ draṣṭ" âsi śvo mayā yudhi.
76.15 kravy'|âdāṃs tarpayiṣyāmi, drāvayiṣyāmi śātravān,
suhṛdo nandayiṣyāmi pramathiṣyāmi Saindhavam.
bahv āgas|kṛt ku|sambandhī pāpa|deśa|samudbhavaḥ
mayā Saindhavako rājā hataḥ svāñ śocayiṣyati.
sarva|kṣīr'|ânna|bhoktāraṃ pāpā|cāraṃ raṇ'|âjire
mayā sa|rājakaṃ bāṇair bhinnaṃ drakṣyasi Saindhavam.
tathā prabhāte kart" âsmi yathā Kṛṣṇa Suyodhanaḥ
n' ânyaṃ dhanur|dharaṃ loke maṃsyate mat|samaṃ yudhi.
Gāṇḍīvaṃ ca dhanur divyaṃ yoddhā c' âhaṃ, nara'|ṛṣabha,
tvaṃ ca yantā Hṛṣīkeśa kiṃ nu syād a|jitaṃ mayā?
76.20 tava prasādād bhagavan kiṃ n' âvāptaṃ raṇe mama
a|viṣahyaṃ, Hṛṣīkeśa? kiṃ jānan māṃ vigarhase?
yathā lakṣmīḥ sthirā candre samudre ca yathā jalam
evam etāṃ pratijñāṃ me satyāṃ viddhi Janārdana.

when I have smashed his army in the van I will seek out Sáindhava.

Tomorrow you will see their very mightiest ripped asunder in the fierce heat of my darts like mountains in lightning. Blood will flow from dead soldiers and dead horses 76.10
and dead elephants falling and fallen and broken by my whetted shafts. The arrows that fly from Gandíva quick as thought or wind will snatch body and soul from all the living things they strike. Yama and Kubéra, Váruna, Indra and Rudra have all schooled me in the deadliest arts: tomorrow men shall see what I have learned. Heaven's Attack will curve above the battle field and whatever Sáindhava's protectors raise against it will fail.

Tomorrow you will see the earth scattered with the heads
of kings ripped clean away by the force of my arrows. I will 76.15
rout my foes and feed the carrioneaters, and give all those dear to me reason to rejoice. I will grind Sáindhava into the dust. Tomorrow as I requite his gross evils that illbefriended hellspawn of a king will have just a little time to mourn his own. No more will Sáindhava feast on children or wade in sin. Tomorrow you will see him and his suzerain pinned to the earth by my shafts.

At dawn o Krishna I will be the warrior whom Suyódhana deems to have no peer. O bull in the herd of men, if it is I who draw the magic bow Gandíva and Hrishi·kesha
who drives my steeds then what battle will I not win? What 76.20
can I not do in the fray with your holy grace upon me, Hrishi·kesha? You know the answer and yet you reproach me? O Stirrer of Men a vow that I make is as certain as

m" âvamaṃsthā mam' âstrāṇi.
m" âvamaṃsthā dhanur dṛḍham.
m" âvamaṃsthā balaṃ bāhvor.
m" âvamaṃsthā Dhanaṃjayam.
tath" âbhiyāmi saṃgrāmaṃ na jīyeyaṃ jayāmi ca.
tena satyena saṃgrāme hataṃ viddhi Jayadratham.
dhruvaṃ vai brāhmaṇe satyaṃ, dhruvā sādhuṣu saṃnatiḥ,
śrīr dhruv" âpi ca yajñeṣu, dhruvo Nārāyaṇe jayaḥ.

SAṂJAYA uvāca:

76.25 evam uktvā Hṛṣīkeśaṃ svayam ātmānam ātmanā
saṃdideś' Ârjuno nardan Vāsaviḥ Keśavaṃ prabhum.
«yathā prabhātāṃ rajanīṃ kalpitaḥ syād ratho mama
tathā kāryaṃ tvayā, Kṛṣṇa. kāryaṃ hi mahad udyatam.»

SAṂJAYA uvāca:

77.1 TĀṂ NIŚĀṂ duḥkha|śok'|ārtau niḥśvasantāv iv' ôragau
nidrāṃ n' âiv' ôpalebhāte Vāsudeva|Dhanaṃjayau.
Nara|Nārāyaṇau kruddhau jñātvā devāḥ sa|Vāsavāḥ,
vyathitāś cintayām āsuḥ kiṃ svid etad bhaviṣyati.
vavuś ca dāruṇā vātā rūkṣā ghor'|âbhiśaṃsinaḥ
sa|kabandhas tath" āditye parighaḥ samadṛśyata.
śuṣk'|âśanyaś ca niṣpetuḥ sa|nirghātāḥ sa|vidyutaḥ
cacāla c' âpi pṛthivī sa|śaila|vana|kānanā.
77.5 cukṣubhuś ca, mahā|rāja, sāgarā makar'|ālayāḥ
pratisrotaḥ pravṛttāś ca tathā gantuṃ samudra|gāḥ.
rath'|âśva|nara|nāgānāṃ pravṛttam adhar'|ôttaram
kravy'|âdānāṃ pramod'|ârthaṃ Yama|rāṣṭra|vivṛddhaye.

the mark in the moon or the brine in the sea. Scorn not my arrows. Scorn not my stout bow nor the strength in my arms. Scorn not Dhanan·jaya. I ride victorious into battle and none will challenge me.

Mark me when I say that Jayad·ratha is good as dead. As surely as truth dwells in the holy man, humility in the wise and wealth in sacrifice so too does triumph dwell in Naráyana.

SÁNJAYA spoke:

Thus did Indra's son fairly upbraid Hrishi·kesha, though 76.25
he spoke almost as if he addressed himself. He bellowed his final words at Késhava.

"Arraign my chariot at first light. O Krishna. A great task lies before you."

SÁNJAYA spoke:

THAT NIGHT Vasudéva and Dhanan·jaya could get no 77.1
sleep. Sighing like snakes they toiled in pain and suffering. Indra and the gods saw the fury gathering in Nara and Naráyana. They were troubled to witness it and wondered what would come of it.

At dusk a band of dark cloud had settled across the descending sun and at night the winds blew dry and moaning and full of foreboding. Lightning flared in the sky and there was thunder but no rain fell. O majesty, the ground trembled beneath the trees in the groves and the copses, and
beneath the rocks on the mountains. The sea where the fish 77.5
live roiled and the rivers that wound down towards it began to flow uphill. All through the camps went the howls of beasts scenting blood on the wind. Death was opening

vāhanāni śakṛn|mūtre mumucū ruruduś ca ha
tān dṛṣṭvā dāruṇān sarvān utpātāl̐ loma|harṣaṇān.
sarve te vyathitāḥ sainyās tvadīyā Bharata'|rṣabha
śrutvā mahā|balasy' ôgrāṃ pratijñāṃ Savyasācinaḥ.
atha Kṛṣṇaṃ mahā|bāhur abravīt Pākaśāsaniḥ.
«āśvāsaya Subhadrāṃ tvaṃ bhaginīṃ snuṣayā saha.
77.10 snuṣāṃ c' âsyā vayasyāś ca viśokāḥ kuru, Mādhava.
sāmnā satyena yuktena vacas" āśvāsaya, prabho.»
tato 'rjuna|gṛhaṃ gatvā Vāsudevaḥ su|durmanāḥ
bhaginīṃ putra|śok'|ārtām āśvāsayata duḥkhitām.

VĀSUDEVA uvāca:

mā śokaṃ kuru, Vārṣṇeyi, kumāraṃ prati sa|snuṣā.
sarveṣāṃ prāṇināṃ bhīru niṣṭh" âiṣā kāla|nirmitā.
kule jātasya dhīrasya kṣatriyasya viśeṣataḥ
sadṛśaṃ maraṇaṃ hy etat tava putrasya. mā śucaḥ.
diṣṭyā mahā|ratho dhīraḥ pitus tulya|parākramaḥ
kṣātreṇa vidhinā prāpto vīr'|âbhilaṣitāṃ gatim.
77.15 jitvā su|bahuśaḥ śatrūn preṣayitvā ca mṛtyave
gataḥ puṇya|kṛtāṃ lokān sarva|kāma|duho '|kṣayān.
tapasā brahma|caryeṇa śrutena prajñay" âpi ca
santo yāṃ gatim icchanti tāṃ prāptas tava putrakaḥ.
vīra|sūr vīra|patnī tvaṃ vīra|jā vīra|bāndhavā.
mā śucas tanayaṃ, bhadre. gataḥ sa paramāṃ gatim.

the doors to his kingdom. The horses saw all these prodigies so ghastly and terrific and their bowels churned and they whinnied and o bull of the Bharatas your men all shivered to think of the darkling promise the mighty Lefthanded Archer had made. The brawny Guardian's Son spoke then to Krishna.

"O Mádhava. Go to your sister Subhádra and to Abhi- 77.10
mányu's widow and try to lift their spirits. Make their hearts a little lighter o great one. Find some words of comfort for them and for their friends."

Vasudéva went with a heavy tread back to Árjuna's palace. There he found his sister crushed by grief and racked with longing for her son. He did what he could to console her.

VASUDÉVA spoke:

O daughter of the rams.* Neither you nor his widowed wife should grieve for your son. Time shapes this same dread darkness for all things that breathe. Your son's death was a noble one and because he was noble and brave and above all a king's son he is all the less to be mourned. He was a great warrior and he was as bold as his father and since his nature compelled him to do as he did we know that he has
gone the way that all heroes long to go. He drove a thou- 77.15
sand enemies from this life. He has found the lands of the blessed where nothing fades and where all our yearnings are appeased. Inner fire, purity and learning and dedication are the means others use to reach the places where your son has gone. You are the mother of a warrior, the wife of a warrior, the daughter of a warrior, the sister of warriors. Know better than to mourn one who has risen so high.

prāpsyate c' âpy asau pāpaḥ Saindhavo bāla|ghātakaḥ
asy' âvalepasya phalaṃ sa|suhṛd|gaṇa|bāndhavaḥ.
vyuṣṭāyāṃ tu var'|ārohe rajanyāṃ pāpa|karma|kṛt
na hi mokṣyati Pārthāt sa praviṣṭo 'py Amarāvatīm.
77.20 śvaḥ śroṣyate śiras tasya Saindhavasya raṇe hṛtam
Samantapañcakād bāhyaṃ. vi|śokā bhava. mā rudaḥ.
kṣatra|dharmaṃ puras|kṛtya gataḥ śūraḥ satāṃ gatim
yāṃ gatiṃ prāpnuyām' êha ye tv anye śastra|jīvinaḥ.
vyūḍh'|ôrasko mahā|bāhur a|nivartī ratha|praṇut
gatas tava var'|ārohe putraḥ svargaṃ. jvaraṃ jahi.
anujātaś ca pitaraṃ mātṛ|pakṣaṃ ca vīryavān
sahasraśo ripūn hatvā hataḥ śūro mahā|rathaḥ.
āśvāsayan snuṣāṃ rājñi mā śucaḥ kṣatriye bhṛṣam.
śvaḥ priyaṃ su|mahac chrutvā vi|śokā bhava, nandini.
77.25 yat Pārthena pratijñātaṃ tat tathā, na tad anyathā.
cikīrṣitaṃ hi te bhartur na bhavej jātu niṣphalam.

yadi ca manu|ja|pannagāḥ piśācā
rajani|carāḥ pata|gāḥ sur'|âsurāś ca
raṇa|gatam abhiyānti Sindhu|rājaṃ
na sa bhavitā saha tair api prabhāte.

SAMJAYA UVĀCA:

78.1 ETAC CHRUTVĀ vacas tasya Keśavasya mah"|ātmanaḥ
Subhadrā putra|śok'|ārtā vilalāpa su|duḥkhitā.

Sáindhava the childmurderer and all his kin and kind will tomorrow reap reward for his savagery and hubris. O fair one at the first blush of dawn Partha's grasp will close upon him and he too will set out for the house of the gods.

Tomorrow word will come to you that Sáindhava has lost 77.20
his head in the battle at Samánta·pánchaka. So cast aside this sorrow. Do not weep. Your great son honoured his calling and walked a noble path whereon only we who spend our leaves cleaving to justice can hope to tread. Your boy found the way to heaven in his armour, riding on and on into the fray and sweeping his foes before him as he went. Let your fever lift. Your child fought hard for his mother and father and he died after his adversaries had already departed this life. Console the daughter left to you. You have royal blood o queen: warrior blood. Do not suffer so. Instead be glad, for tomorrow the revenge that fills your heart
will be exacted and your suffering will be at an end. Partha 77.25
always keeps his word. When your husband sets out to do a thing there can be no doubt: it will come to pass.

> Whether men, serpents or ghosts,
> Fiends, winged things, gods or goblins
> Fly into battle with the Sindhu king
> Soon after dawn they all will fall.

SÁNJAYA spoke:

SUBHÁDRA LISTENED to what mighty Késhava said. But 78.1
she was deep in sorrow. She wailed in lamentation for her lost son.

«hā putra mama mandāyāḥ katham ety' âsi saṃyugam
nidhanaṃ prāptavāṃs, tāta, pitus tulya|parākramaḥ?
katham indīvara|śyāmaṃ su|daṃṣṭraṃ cāru|locanam
mukhaṃ te dṛśyate, vatsa, guṇṭhitaṃ raṇa|reṇunā?
nūnaṃ śūraṃ nipatitaṃ tvāṃ paśyanty a|nivartinam
su|śiro|grīva|bāhv|aṃsaṃ vyūḍh'|ôraskaṃ nat'|ôdaram
78.5 cār'|ûpacita|sarv'|âṅgaṃ sv|akṣaṃ śastra|kṣat'|ôkṣitam
bhūtāni tvāṃ nirīkṣante nūnaṃ candram iv' ôditam.

śayanīyaṃ purā yasya spardhy'|āstaraṇa|saṃvṛtam
bhūmāv adya kathaṃ śeṣe vipraviddhaḥ sukh'|ôcitaḥ?
yo 'nvāsyata purā vīro vara|strībhir mahā|bhujaḥ
katham anvāsyate so 'dya śivābhiḥ patito mṛdhe?
yo 'stūyata purā hṛṣṭaiḥ sūta|māgadha|bandibhiḥ
so 'dya kravy'|âd|gaṇair ghorair vinadadbhir upāsyate.

Pāṇḍaveṣu ca nātheṣu Vṛṣṇi|vīreṣu vā vibho
Pāñcāleṣu ca vīreṣu hataḥ ken' âsy a|nāthavat?
78.10 a|tṛpta|darśanā putra darśanasya tav', ân|agha,
manda|bhāgyā gamiṣyāmi vyaktam adya Yama|kṣayam.
viśāl'|âkṣaṃ su|keś'|ântaṃ cāru|vākyaṃ su|gandhi ca
tava putra kadā bhūyo mukhaṃ drakṣyāmi nir|vraṇam?
dhig balaṃ Bhīmasenasya, dhik Pārthasya dhanuṣmatām,
dhig vīryaṃ Vṛṣṇi|vīrāṇāṃ, Pāñcālānāṃ ca dhig balam,
dhik Kekayāṃs tathā Cedīn Matsyāṃś c' âiv' âtha Sṛñjayān
ye tvāṃ raṇa|gataṃ vīraṃ na śekur abhirakṣitum.

"O child of my broken heart. You were as strong as your
father. O my little boy. How can you have met your end?
Will I have the strength to look into your gentle eyes as others now look upon you? To see the curl of your lip and your
sweet face dark as the blue lotus all caked in dust? A hero 78.5
fallen where he fought. A figure so beauteous beneath buckled mail, a brow and head and neck, arms and shoulders so
finely sculpted yet slick now with swordwounds. There you
lie like the watery moon before the gaze of eyes not mine.

Every pleasure was yours. The richest furs lay beneath
your cheek at night. Do you now bed down your arrowbro-
ken limbs in the mud? Your strong arms felt the soothing
touch of a nurse's gentle fingers. Is it now jackals that come
to tend you, mangled in the dirt? Bards and singers and poets serenaded you with their lays but now your lullaby will
be howled by dogs.

All the might of the Panchálas and Vrishnis and Pándavas to protect you in battle, yet you died alone. My spot-
less child. I will make my weary way to Death's withered 78.10
kingdom still hungry for a last sight of you. O son of mine
will I never again hear your dulcet voice or smell the hair
on your head or look into your deep eyes to see your face
free from the cruel gashes it now wears? Shame on mighty
Bhima·sena, on Partha's lords of the bow, on the brave Vrishni warriors and the great Panchála host. Shame on the
Kékayas and the Chedis and the Matsyas and Srínjayas. All
of you failed my son.

adya paśyāmi pṛthivīṃ śūnyām iva hata|tviṣam
Abhimanyum a|paśyantī śoka|vyākula|locanā.
78.15 svasrīyaṃ Vāsudevasya putraṃ Gāṇḍīva|dhanvanaḥ
kathaṃ tv” âtirathaṃ vīraṃ drakṣyāmy adya nipātitam?
ehy, ehi tṛṣito, vatsa, stanau pūrṇau pib' āśu me
aṅkam āruhya mandāyā hy a|tṛptāyāś ca darśane.
hā, vīra, dṛṣṭo naṣṭaś ca dhanaṃ svapna iv' âsi me.
aho hy a|nityaṃ mānuṣyaṃ jala|budbuda|cañcalam.
imāṃ te taruṇīṃ bhāryāṃ tav' ādhibhir abhiplutām,
kathaṃ saṃdhārayiṣyāmi vi|vatsām iva dhenukām?
aho hy a|kāle prasthānaṃ kṛtavān asi, putraka,
vihāya phala|kāle māṃ su|gṛddhāṃ tava darśane.
78.20 nūnaṃ gatiḥ kṛt'|ântasya prājñair api su|durvidā
yatra tvaṃ Keśave nāthe saṃgrāme '|nāthavadd hataḥ.
yajvanāṃ dāna|śīlānāṃ brāhmaṇānāṃ kṛt'|ātmanām,
carita|brahma|caryāṇāṃ puṇya|tīrth'|âvagāhinām,
kṛta|jñānāṃ vadānyānāṃ guru|śuśrūṣiṇām api
sahasra|dakṣiṇānāṃ ca yā gatis tām avāpnuhi.
yā gatir yudhyamānānāṃ śūrāṇām a|nivartinām
hatv” ârīn nihatānāṃ ca saṃgrāme tāṃ gatiṃ vraja.
go|sahasra|pradātṝṇāṃ kratu|dānāṃ ca yā gatiḥ
naiveśikaṃ c' âbhimataṃ dadatāṃ yā gatiḥ śubhā,
78.25 brāhmaṇebhyaḥ śaraṇyebhyo nidhiṃ nidadhatāṃ ca yā,
yā c' âpi nyasta|daṇḍānāṃ tāṃ gatiṃ vraja putraka.
brahma|caryeṇa yāṃ yānti munayaḥ saṃśita|vratāḥ
eka|patnyaś ca yāṃ yānti tāṃ gatiṃ vraja putraka.
rājñāṃ su|caritair yā ca gatir bhavati śāśvatī
catur|āśramiṇāṃ puṇyaiḥ pāvitānāṃ su|rakṣitaiḥ,

My eyes seek Abhimányu but do not find him. My tears
hide a world robbed of its lustre. You were Vasudéva's 78.15
nephew. You were born to Gandíva's keeper. How can I look upon your corpse? O my baby come to me come to me. My breasts are full, come drink your fill from me and lie in my lap so my eyes can at last consume you.

My strong boy. Though you are gone I can see you yet like some splendour in a dream. O this brief life of ours is as fleeting as a bubble in water. Your young wife's mate has been torn from her and she drowns in sorrow. How will I bear her up? O my son you have left too early. You have abandoned me in the summer of our lives and I am still so hungry to have you.

That you could die with Késhava to protect you shows 78.20
that even the wise cannot fathom the workings of fate. May you follow in the steps of the grandest sacrificers and the holiest hierophants, men who live lives of purity and defend the hallowed places, who know duty and generosity and the wisdom of elders and give away their treasure to their priests. Take the path of warriors brave and strong who die
only when their foes are dead. Take the path my son of kings 78.25
who open their coffers to the brahmins in their keep, the shining path of lords so magnanimous that after the rites are done and the herds of oxen gone they still give their priests whatever it is they want.

Take the path my son of the mendicant who lives by his dedication and vows alone and the woman who never undoes her own. Take the path to eternity of kings whose acts outlive them and whose every stage of life is marked by deep holiness and generosity without end, men of even temper

dīn'|ânukampinām yā ca satatam samvibhāginām
paiśunyāc ca nivṛttānāṃ tāṃ gatiṃ vraja putraka.
vratināṃ dharma|śīlānāṃ guru|śuśrūṣiṇām api
a|mogh'|âtithināṃ yā ca tāṃ gatiṃ vraja putraka.
78.30 kṛcchreṣu yā dhārayatām ātmānaṃ vyasaneṣu ca
gatiḥ śok'|âgni|dagdhānāṃ tāṃ gatiṃ vraja putraka.
mātā|pitroś ca śuśrūṣāṃ kalpayant' îha ye sadā
sva|dāra|niratānāṃ ca yā gatis tām avāpnuhi.
ṛtu|kāle svakāṃ bhāryāṃ gacchatāṃ yā manīṣinām
para|strībhyo nivṛttānāṃ tāṃ gatiṃ vraja putraka.
sāmnā ye sarva|bhūtāni paśyanti gata|matsarāḥ
n' âruṃ|tudānāṃ kṣamiṇāṃ yā gatis tām avāpnuhi.
madhu|māṃsa|nivṛttānāṃ madyād dambhāt tath" ânṛtāt
par'|ôpatāpa|tyaktānāṃ tāṃ gatiṃ vraja putraka.
78.35 hrīmantaḥ sarva|śāstra|jñā jñāna|tṛptā jit'|êndriyāḥ
yāṃ gatiṃ sādhavo yānti tāṃ gatiṃ vraja putraka.»
evaṃ vilapatīṃ dīnāṃ Subhadrāṃ śoka|karśitām
anvapadyata Pāñcālī Vairāṭī|sahitā tadā.
tāḥ prakāmaṃ ruditvā ca vilapya ca su|duḥkhitāḥ
unmattavat tadā rājan vi|saṃjñā nyapatan kṣitau.
s'|ôpacāras tu Kṛṣṇaś ca duḥkhitāṃ bhṛśa|duḥkhitaḥ
siktv" âmbhasā samāśvāsya tat tad uktvā hitaṃ vacaḥ,
vi|saṃjña|kalpāṃ rudatīṃ marma|viddhāṃ pravepatīm
bhaginīṃ Puṇḍarīkākṣa idaṃ vacanam abravīt.

who show compassion to those weaker than they. Take my son the path of men of their word who listen to counsel and who live as they ought and who open their homes to any that come to them. Take my son the path of those who 78.30
stand firm through calamity and misfortune though ablaze in the fire of grief.

May you follow in the steps of those who think only of the words and welfare of their mothers and fathers, who love only their own wives. Take my son the path of husbands who give their wives children and love most faithful. May you follow in the steps of all those patient and gentle folk who look upon the creatures of the world with mild eyes free of greed. Take my son the path of men who let pass another's unkindness without deceit or scorn just as they let pass mead and meat and wine. There live men of humility 78.35
who devote their lives to what is right and who through the satisfactions of wisdom tame the storms within them. Go where they go my son."

Subhádra sent up a tormented cry of despair and Dráupadi and Vairáti joined her ululation. O king they wailed like madwomen and when they could cry no more and all their strength had gone they sank down to their knees. Krishna and the servants were stricken at the sight. They sprinkled them with drops of water and tried to find the words to console them. But Subhádra was cut to the quick and she tottered and trembled and began to wail again. Lotuseye spoke then to his sister.

78.40 «Subhadre mā śucaḥ putraṃ. Pāñcāly āśvāsay' Ôttarām.
gato 'bhimanyuḥ prathitāṃ gatiṃ kṣatriya|puṃgavaḥ.
ye c' ânye 'pi kule santi puruṣā no var'|ânane
sarve te tāṃ gatiṃ yāntu hy Abhimanyor yaśasvinaḥ.
kuryāma tad vayaṃ karma kriyāsu suhṛdaś ca naḥ
kṛtavān yādṛśaṃ hy ekas tava putro mahā|rathaḥ.»
evam āśvāsya bhaginīṃ Draupadīm api c' Ôttarām
Pārthasy' âiva mahā|bāhuḥ pārśvam āgād ariṃ|damaḥ.
tato 'bhyanujñāya nṛpān Kṛṣṇo bandhūṃs tath" Ârjunam
viveś' ântaḥ|pure rājaṃs, te ca jagmur yath"|ālayam.

SAṂJAYA uvāca:

79.1 TATO 'RJUNASYA bhavanaṃ praviśy' â|pratimaṃ vibhuḥ
spṛṣṭv" âmbhaḥ Puṇḍarīkākṣaḥ sthaṇḍile śubha|lakṣaṇe
saṃtastāra śubhāṃ śayyāṃ darbhair vaiḍūrya|saṃnibhaiḥ.
tato mālyena vidhival lājair gandhaiḥ su|maṅgalaiḥ
alaṃ|cakāra tāṃ śayyāṃ parivāry' āyudh'|ôttamaiḥ.
tataḥ spṛṣṭ'|ôdake Pārthe vinītāḥ paricārakāḥ
darśayanto 'ntike cakrur naiśaṃ Traiyambakaṃ balim.
tataḥ prīta|manāḥ Pārtho gandha|mālyaiś ca Mādhavam
alaṃ|kṛty' ôpahāraṃ taṃ naiśaṃ tasmai nyavedayat.
79.5 smayamānas tu Govindaḥ
Phālgunaṃ pratyabhāṣata.

"Cease from your mourning Subhádra. Dráupadi find some words of solace for Úttara. Abhimányu has gone the celebrated way of the very greatest of warriors and I hope that all the men in our clan will follow in his glorious footsteps. May we and all those near to us strive to do things in our lives to match the great example of your son, and may our friends do things of the kind that this child born to you has done." 78.40

And so the great warrior and tamer of foes left his noble sister and went back to see Árjuna. The other kings were waiting for him. He took leave from his friends and they all retired to their beds, while Késhava went on o majesty up to Árjuna's tent.

SÁNJAYA spoke:

WHEN HE REACHED Árjuna's august pavilion, bounteous 79.1
Lotuseye walked out into open ground and found a rise that pleased him and sprinkled drops of water upon it. Then he covered the holy bank with grass that shimmered like cat's eyes and following the scriptures he decorated it with flowers, dry grain and blessed perfumes. Lastly he set out the ornate weapons of ritual. Partha arrived and was duly anointed and as he looked on, Krishna directed the priests in a night offering to the Three Eyed God.

At the rite's end Partha felt his heart lighten. He hung fragrant garlands around Mádhava's neck and gave the nightpiece* to his friend. Go·vinda smiled and spoke to the Red 79.5
Star Fighter.

«supyatāṃ, Pārtha, bhadraṃ te
kalyāṇāya. vrajāmy aham.»
sthāpayitvā tato dvāḥ|sthān
goptṝṃś c' ātt'|āyudhān narān
Dāruk'|ânugataḥ śrīmān
viveśa śibiraṃ svakam
śiśye ca śayane śubhre
bahu kṛtyaṃ vicintayan.
Pārthāya sarvaṃ bhagavān śoka|duḥkh'|âpahaṃ vidhim
vyadadhāt Puṇḍarīkākṣas tejo|dyuti|vivardhanam,
yogam āsthāya yukt'|ātmā sarveṣām īśvar'|ēśvaraḥ
śreyas|kāmaḥ pṛthu|yaśā Viṣṇur Jiṣṇu|priyaṃ|karaḥ.
na Pāṇḍavānāṃ śibire kaś cit suṣvāpa tāṃ niśām.
prajāgaraḥ sarva|janam hy āviveśa, viśāṃ pate.
79.10 «putra|śok'|âbhitaptena pratijñāto mah"|ātmanā
sahasā Sindhu|rājasya vadho Gāṇḍīva|dhanvanā.
tat kathaṃ nu mahā|bāhur Vāsaviḥ para|vīra|hā
pratijñāṃ sa|phalāṃ kuryād?» iti te samacintayan.
«kaṣṭaṃ h' îdaṃ vyavasitaṃ Pāṇḍavena mah"|ātmanā.
sa ca rājā mahā|vīryaḥ pārayatv Arjunaḥ sa tām.
putra|śok'|âbhitaptena pratijñā mahatī kṛtā
bhrātaraś c' âpi vikrāntā bahulāni balāni ca.
Dhṛtarāṣṭrasya putreṇa sarvaṃ tasmai niveditam.
79.15 sa hatvā Saindhavaṃ saṃkhye punar etu Dhanaṃjayaḥ
jitvā ripu|gaṇāṃś c' âiva pārayann Arjuno vratam.
śvo '|hatvā Sindhu|rājaṃ vai dhūma|ketuṃ pravekṣyati.
na hy asāv an|ṛtaṃ kartum alaṃ Pārtho Dhanaṃjayaḥ.
Dharma|putraḥ kathaṃ rājā bhaviṣyati mṛte 'rjune?

"O Partha. I think that we ought to get some sleep for good luck. I will go now."

He stationed armed guards before Árjuna's tent and left still aglow from the rite and went with Dáruka to his own encampment. When he arrived he sat down on his snow-white couch and thought of all that there was to do. Holy Pundaríkáksha settled into meditation. Deep in peaceful thought the emperor of all that is made a decision. Because he wanted to help his friend so dear to his heart fabled Vishnu resolved to do all he could to drive off Jishnu's sadness and pain and bathe him in splendour and glory.

O lord of these lands, no one in the Pándava camp could
sleep. They sat together in little groups wide awake through
the dark hours. They thought about how Árjuna had made 79.10
his sudden promise to slay the Sindhu king in the burning
heat of mourning. Gandíva was his bow and Indra his father
and no one doubted his prowess or fire. But would he make
good his oath?

"Great Pándava has set himself a difficult task. May King
Árjuna find the strength to see it through. His vow was
sworn in the fierce pain of loss. Our brothers may be brave
and our men may be many but Dhrita·rashtra's son will do
everything to keep Jayad·ratha safe. May Dhanan·jaya ride 79.15
into battle and cull his foes and kill Sáindhava and thus
make good his vow. Dhanan·jaya cannot break a promise
and if tomorrow the Sindhu king still lives then Partha will
step through the fire's smoky veil. What will Dharma's son
do when Árjuna is gone? His hopes live only in his brother.
If ever we have done or given or poured out a thing for the

tasmin hi vijayaḥ kṛtsnaḥ Pāṇḍavena samāhitaḥ.
yadi no 'sti kṛtaṃ kiṃ cid, yadi dattaṃ, hutaṃ yadi,
phalena tasya sarvasya Savyasācī jayatv arīn.»
evaṃ kathayatāṃ teṣāṃ jayam āśaṃsatāṃ prabho
kṛcchreṇa mahatā rājan rajanī vyatyavartata.
79.20 tasyāṃ rajanyāṃ madhye tu pratibuddho Janārdanaḥ.
smṛtvā pratijñāṃ Pārthasya Dārukaṃ pratyabhāṣata.
«Arjunena pratijñātam ārtena hata|bandhunā
‹Jayadrathaṃ vadhiṣyāmi śvo|bhūta› iti Dāruka.
tat tu Duryodhanaḥ śrutvā mantribhir mantrayiṣyati.
yathā Jayadrathaṃ Pārtho na hanyād iti saṃyuge
akṣauhiṇyo hi tāḥ sarvā rakṣiṣyanti Jayadratham.
Droṇaś ca saha putreṇa sarv'|âstra|vidhi|pāra|gaḥ
eko vīraḥ sahasr'|âkṣo Daitya|Dānava|darpa|hā.
79.25 so 'pi taṃ n' ôtsahet' ājau hantuṃ Droṇena rakṣitam,
so 'haṃ śvas tat kariṣyāmi yathā Kuntī|suto 'rjunaḥ
a|prāpte 'staṃ dina|kare haniṣyati Jayadratham.
na hi dārā na mitrāṇi jñātayo na ca bāndhavāḥ
kaś cid anyaḥ priyataraḥ Kuntī|putrān mam' Ârjunāt.
an|Arjunam imaṃ lokaṃ muhūrtam api, Dāruka,
udīkṣituṃ na śakto 'haṃ. bhavitā na ca tat tathā.
ahaṃ vijitya tān sarvān sahasā sa|haya|dvipān
Arjun'|ârthe haniṣyāmi sa|Karṇān sa|Suyodhanān.
śvo nirīkṣantu me vīryaṃ trayo lokā mah"|āhave
Dhanaṃjay'|ârthe samare parākrāntasya Dāruka.
79.30 śvo nar'|êndra|sahasrāṇi rāja|putra|śatāni ca
s'|âśva|dvipa|rathāny ājau vidraviṣyāmi Dāruka.
śvas tāṃ cakra|pramathitāṃ drakṣyase nṛ|pa|vāhinīm

gods then let it be that the Lefthanded Archer wins the day to come."

This was their talk o majesty and my lord they prayed for victory through an uneasy night. In the small hours Janár- 79.20
dana awoke and he thought again of Partha's vow and spoke of it to Dáruka.

"O Dáruka. It was in anguish at his son's death that Árjuna vowed to kill Jayad·ratha on the coming day. Duryódhana knows now that he made this promise and on the advice of his viziers will have his entire host protect Jayad·ratha to make sure that Partha fails.

Drona and his son are masters of the art of war. Drona is a single warrior with a hundred eyes, a tamer of demons and devils. Since even the son of Kunti cannot kill a man 79.25
in battle whom Drona preserves, tomorrow I will do all in my power to make certain that before the sun goes down Árjuna kills Jayad·ratha.

My wife, my friends, my kin and kind: none of them are as dear to me as Árjuna son of Kunti. O Dáruka a world without Árjuna would be dead to my eyes. This must never be. Let them all fall tomorrow, let their steeds fall, let Karna and Suyódhana fall for Árjuna's sake. O Dáruka tomorrow let the three worlds behold my power as I join this blood-bath at Dhanan·jaya's side. Tomorrow the greatest kings and 79.30
princes on earth will come teeming o Dáruka in steed car and howdah across the plain to meet us. And tomorrow you will see a whole army of kings crushed and buckled beneath our wheels as I ride into battle for Pandu's son. Tomorrow the gods and *gandhárvas*, the ghosts serpents and spirits and all the rest of the creatures of the world will know me as

mayā kruddhena samare Pāṇḍav'|ârthe nipātitām.
śvaḥ sa|devāḥ sa|gandharvāḥ piśāc'|ôraga|rākṣasāḥ
jñāsyanti lokāḥ sarve māṃ suhṛdaṃ Savyasācinaḥ.
yas taṃ dveṣṭi sa māṃ dveṣṭi, yas tam c' ânu sa mām anu
iti saṃkalpatāṃ buddhyā. śarīr'|ârdhaṃ mam' Ârjunaḥ.
yathā tvam me prabhātāyām asyāṃ niśi rath'|ôttamam
kalpayitvā yathā|śāstram ādāya vraja saṃyutaḥ.
79.35 gadāṃ Kaumodakīṃ divyāṃ śaktiṃ cakraṃ dhanuḥ śarān
āropya vai rathe, sūta, sarv'|ôpakaraṇāni ca
sthānaṃ ca kalpayitv" âtha rath'|ôpasthe dhvajasya me
Vainateyasya vīrasya samare ratha|śobhinaḥ,
chatraṃ jāmbūnadair jālair arka|jvalana|saprabhaiḥ
Viśvakarma|kṛtair divyair, aśvān api vibhūṣitān
Balāhakaṃ Meghapuṣpaṃ Śaivyaṃ Sugrīvam eva ca
yuktān vāji|varān yattaḥ kavacī tiṣṭha Dāruka.
Pāñcajanyasya nirghoṣam ārṣabheṇ' âiva pūritam
śrutvā ca bhairavaṃ nādam upeyās tvaṃ javena mām.
79.40 ek'|âhn" âham a|marṣaṃ ca sarva|duḥkhāni c' âiva ha
bhrātuḥ paitṛṣvaseyasya vyapaneṣyāmi Dāruka.
sarv'|ôpāyair yatiṣyāmi yathā Bībhatsur āhave
paśyatāṃ Dhārtarāṣṭrāṇāṃ haniṣyati Jayadratham.
yasya yasya ca Bībhatsur vadhe yatnaṃ kariṣyati
āśaṃse sārathe tatra bhavit" âsya dhruvo jayaḥ.»

DĀRUKA uvāca:

jaya eva dhruvas tasya. kuta eva parājayaḥ
yasya tvaṃ, puruṣa|vyāghra, sārathyam upajagmivān?
evaṃ c' âitat kariṣyāmi yathā māṃ anuśāsasi.
su|prabhātām imāṃ rātriṃ jayāya Vijayasya ha.

Savya·sachin's friend. Let them all understand that any who
hate him hate me and any who go with him go with me.
For Árjuna is truly a part of me.

My horseman. Go and deck our fine chariot as scripture
dictates and climb aboard and bring it forth at the break
of dawn. Set upon it my club Kaumódaki and my heav- 79.35
enly spear, my discus, bow and arrows and all the para-
phernalia of war. Fix in its bracket the pole atop which
the sign of mighty Vainatéya will dance above our enemies' heads, and open our parasol lined in nets of gold dazzling as the sun's fires and fashioned in heaven on Vishva·
karman's anvil. Cloak and bridle our swift steeds Thunderclap, Cloudflower, Lucky and Proudneck and o Dáruka belt
on your armour. When you hear the blare of Pancha·janya
wild as the bellow of a bull then come to me as quickly as
you can.

O Dáruka I can bear it no longer but in a single day I 79.40
will lift all suffering from the shoulders of the cousin born
to my father's sister. I will do all that I can to make sure that
the sons of Dhrita·rashtra can only watch as Árjuna takes
his revenge. If Bibhátsu decides that a man must die then
may I do my utmost to make it so."

DÁRUKA spoke:

O tiger in the forest of men. Árjuna's triumph is assured. For how can he be defeated if you ride beside him? I will do as you bid. As this night brightens so it crowns the Champion's glory.

SAMJAYA uvāca:

80.1 KUNTĪ|PUTRAS tu taṃ mantraṃ
smarann eva Dhanaṃjayaḥ
pratijñām ātmano rakṣan
mumoh' â|cintya|vikramaḥ.
taṃ tu śokena saṃtaptaṃ svapne kapi|vara|dhvajam
āsasāda mahā|tejā dhyāyantaṃ garuḍa|dhvajaḥ.
pratyutthānaṃ ca Kṛṣṇasya sarv'|âvastho Dhanaṃjayaḥ
na lopayati dharm'|ātmā bhaktyā premṇā ca sarvadā.
pratyutthāya ca Govindaṃ sa tasmā āsanaṃ dadau
na c' āsane svayaṃ buddhiṃ Bībhatsur vyadadhāt tadā.
80.5 tataḥ Kṛṣṇo mahā|tejā jānan Pārthasya niścayam
Kuntī|putram idaṃ vākyam āsīnaḥ sthitam abravīt.
«mā viṣāde manaḥ Pārtha kṛthāḥ. kālo hi dur|jayaḥ.
kālaḥ sarvāṇi bhūtāni niyacchati pare vidhau.
kim|arthaṃ ca viṣādas te? tad brūhi dvipadāṃ vara.
na śocyaṃ viduṣāṃ śreṣṭha śokaḥ kārya|vināśanaḥ.
yat tu kāryaṃ bhavet kāryaṃ karmaṇā tat samācara.
hīna|ceṣṭasya yaḥ śokaḥ sa hi śatrur Dhanaṃjaya.
śocan nandayate śatrūn karśayaty api bāndhavān
kṣīyate ca naras tasmān. na tvaṃ śocitum arhasi.»
80.10 ity ukto Vāsudevena Bībhatsur a|parājitaḥ
ābabhāṣe tadā vidvān idaṃ vacanam arthavat.
«mayā pratijñā mahatī Jayadratha|vadhe kṛtā
śvo 'smi hantā dur|ātmānaṃ putra|ghnam iti, Keśava.
mat|pratijñā|vighāt'|ârthaṃ Dhārtarāṣṭraiḥ kil' Âcyuta
pṛṣṭhataḥ Saindhavaḥ kāryaḥ sarvair gupto mahā|rathaiḥ.
daśa c' âikā ca tāḥ Kṛṣṇa akṣauhiṇyaḥ su|durjayāḥ

SÁNJAYA spoke:

DHANAN·JAYA SON of Kunti thought over his resolution 80.1
and though his courage did not falter he wondered if he could keep his word. He fell into a sleep hot with nightmares. Into the monkeymarked warrior's dream stepped the blazing champion marked with the bird. Dhanan·jaya never failed to welcome a friend with warmth and humility, and he waved the Herdsman in and offered him a seat although
he could not be sure that a seat was there. But vastsplen- 80.5
doured Krishna sat down. He knew what Partha was thinking and he spoke to Kunti's son of his design.

"O son of Pritha stay clear of despair. You cannot defeat time because time binds all living things to an ordinance far beyond them. Of they that walk on two legs few stand as tall as you. Tell me then: what is the point of despair? O best of men the wise do not feel sorrow because sorrow undoes him who suffers from it. If there is something that must be done then you must act to bring it to pass. Dhanan·jaya the sorrow that robs you of the ability to act is the only true enemy. Banish your troubles. A man in despair cheers his foes and starves his friends and for this reason he will not last long."

Bibhátsu was indeed unbowed and he understood and in 80.10
reply he addressed the matter of Vasudéva's words.

"Késhava my promise to kill Jayad·ratha was not made lightly. O Áchyuta I said that when the day dawns I will be the one to requite that vile childmurderer. Now all of Duryódhana's warriors will be watching Sáindhava's back because you know that they would like nothing more than for me to break my promise. Krishna he has eleven undefeated

hat'|âvaśeṣās tatr' êmā hanta Mādhava saṃkhyayā.
tābhiḥ parivṛtaḥ saṃkhye sarvaiś c' âiva mahā|rathaiḥ
kathaṃ śakyeta saṃdraṣṭuṃ dur|ātmā, Kṛṣṇa, Saindhavaḥ?
80.15 pratijñā|pāraṇaṃ c' âpi na bhaviṣyati Keśava
pratijñāyāṃ ca hīnāyāṃ kathaṃ jīvati mad|vidhaḥ?
duḥkh'|ôpāyasya me vīra vikāṅkṣā parivartate.
drutaṃ ca yāti savitā tata etad bravīmy aham.»
śoka|sthānaṃ tu tac chrutvā
Pārthasya dvija|ketanaḥ
saṃspṛśy' âmbhas tataḥ Kṛṣṇaḥ
prāṅmukhaḥ samavasthitaḥ.
idaṃ vākyaṃ mahā|tejā babhāṣe puṣkar'|ēkṣaṇaḥ
hit'|ârthaṃ Pāṇḍu|putrasya Saindhavasya vadhe dhṛtaḥ
«Pārtha, Pāśupataṃ nāma param'|âstraṃ sanātanam
yena sarvān mṛdhe Daityāñ jaghne devo Maheśvaraḥ.
80.20 yadi tad viditaṃ te 'dya śvo hant" âsi Jayadratham.
ath' ājñātaṃ prapadyasva manasā vṛṣabha|dhvajam.
taṃ devaṃ manasā dhyātvā joṣam āsva Dhanaṃjaya.
tatas tasya prasādāt tvaṃ bhaktaḥ prāpsyasi tan mahat.»
tataḥ Kṛṣṇa|vacaḥ śrutvā saṃspṛśy' âmbho Dhanaṃjayaḥ
bhūmāv āsīna ek'|âgro jagāma manasā Bhavam.
tataḥ praṇihito brāhme muhūrte śubha|lakṣaṇe
ātmānam Arjuno 'paśyad gagane saha|Keśavam.
puṇyaṃ Himavataḥ pādaṃ maṇimantaṃ ca parvatam
jyotirbhiś ca samākīrṇaṃ siddha|cāraṇa|sevitam.
80.25 vāyu|vega|gatiḥ Pārthaḥ khaṃ bheje saha|Keśavaḥ
Keśavena gṛhītaḥ sa dakṣiṇe vibhunā bhuje.

legions at his command and in all o Mádhava that makes a lot of men. I ask you Krishna: how will I even be able to catch a glimpse of the wicked king when they bury him behind their chariots? O Késhava my promise will be broken 80.15
and when my promise is broken how can a man such as I still live? O mighty one my hopes are mired in doubt. I am telling you this because whatever we may wish the sun will rise and tomorrow will surely come."

The glorious warrior marked by the bird listened to Partha's fears. He stood and faced towards the east and he let fall some drops of water from his hand. He was certain that Sáindhava had to die for Árjuna's sake. Krishna turned his lotus eyes towards his friend and spoke.

"O son of Pritha. There is a weapon eternal and divine called the Arrow of the Beast Lord and with it the Great God killed all of Diti's children. If you attain it then tomor- 80.20
row you will slay Jayad·ratha. Now that I have told you of it seek within yourself the god marked by the bull. Be silent when you have fixed him in your mind's eye. Honour him well and by his grace o Dhanan·jaya this great weapon will become yours."

Dhanan·jaya listened to Krishna. He dropped water on the ground and sat down and focussed his mind on Bhava. Árjuna concentrated on the blessed hour before dawn, and he saw himself and Késhava hanging in space. He saw the beautiful foothills of Hímavat below and then its sparkling peak thronged with saints and the bards of the sky. Great 80.25
Késhava took Árjuna by the arm and they flew through the air as if treading the courses of the wind.

prekṣamāṇo bahūn bhāvāñ jagām' âdbhuta|darśanān.
udīcyāṃ diśi dharm"|ātmā so 'paśyac chveta|parvatam.
Kuberasya vihāre ca Nalinīṃ padma|bhūṣitām,
saric|chreṣṭhāṃ ca tāṃ Gaṅgāṃ vīkṣamāṇo bah'|ûdakām,
sadā|puṣpa|phalair vṛkṣair upetāṃ sphaṭik'|ôpalām,
siṃha|vyāghra|samākīrṇāṃ nānā|mṛga|samākulām
puṇy'|āśramavatīṃ ramyāṃ manojñ'|âṇḍaja|sevitām,
Mandarasya pradeśāṃś ca kiṃnar'|ôdgīta|nāditān,
80.30 hema|rūpya|mayaiḥ śṛṅgair nān"|oṣadhi|vidīpitān
tathā mandāra|vṛkṣaiś ca puṣpitair upaśobhitān.

snigdh'|âñjana|cay'|ākāraṃ samprāptaḥ Kāla|parvatam
Brahmatuṅgaṃ nadīś c' ânyās tathā janapadān api,
Sutuṅgaṃ śata|śṛṅgaṃ ca Śaryāti|vanam eva ca
puṇyam Aśvaśiraḥ|sthānaṃ sthānam Ātharvaṇasya ca,
Vṛṣadaṃśaṃ ca śail'|êndraṃ Mahāmandaram eva ca
apsarobhiḥ samākīrṇaṃ kiṃnaraiś c' âiva śobhitam.
tasmin śaile vrajan Pārthaḥ sa|Kṛṣṇaḥ samavaikśata
śubhaiḥ prasravaṇair juṣṭāṃ hema|dhātu|vibhūṣitām,
80.35 candra|raśmi|prakāś'|âṅgīṃ pṛthivīṃ pura|mālinīm
samudrāṃś c' âdbhut'|ākārān apaśyad bahul'|ākarān.

viyad dyāṃ pṛthivīṃ c' âiva tathā Viṣṇu|padaṃ vrajan
vismitaḥ saha Kṛṣṇena kṣipto bāṇa iv' âbhyagāt.

Árjuna gazed at the visions spread around him and came
upon things yet more wondrous. Carried north in his pure
heart he saw a snowcovered peak and he saw the Nálini
flowing between banks of lotuses through Kubéra's plea-
suregardens. He saw the broad channel of the Ganges, the
greatest river of them all. On its shores lions and tigers
prowled across crystalline rocks, and deer darted beneath
fruittrees in eternal blossom clumped in inviting groves that
rang with birdsong. The tones of the strange horsehead
singers filled his ears as he crossed the gleaming carpets of 80.30
wild growth broken with golden ridges and moved among
the blossoming thornapples that covered the foothills of
Mándara.

Árjuna passed Mount Kala that glinted like a rock of
kohl and Brahma·tunga and its unnamed rivers and lands,
and he passed the hundred peaks of Sutúnga and the forest of Sharyáti, the holy grounds of Ashva·shiras and the
Athárvanas, and the great mountain Vrisha·dansha. At last
he came to Maha·mándara where the *ápsaras*es dwell and
which rang too with the songs of the horseheaded bards.
They paused on its peak and Partha and Krishna looked 80.35
down and by the light of the moon saw the whole of the
wondrous earth lying before them spangled in gold and
streaming with pale cascades, its cities like the flowers of
garlands strung between the million lustrous faces of its
lakes.

Árjuna was in awe. Like an arrow from a bow's string he and Krishna flew further out across the earth and up through the air and higher and higher into the heavens.

graha|nakṣatra|somānāṃ sūry'|âgnyoś ca sama|tviṣam
apaśyata tadā Pārtho jvalantam iva parvatam.
samāsādya tu taṃ śailaṃ śail'|âgre samavasthitam
tapo|nityaṃ mah"|ātmānam apaśyad vṛṣabha|dhvajam.
sahasram iva sūryāṇāṃ dīpyamānaṃ sva|tejasā
śūlinaṃ jaṭilaṃ gauraṃ valkal'|âjina|vāsasam
80.40 nayanānāṃ sahasraiś ca vicitr'|âṅgaṃ mah"|âujasam,
Pārvatyā sahitaṃ devaṃ bhūta|saṃghaiś ca bhāsvaraiḥ,
gīta|vāditra|saṃnādair hāsya|lāsya|samanvitam
valgit'|āsphoṭit'|ôtkruṣṭaiḥ puṇyair gandhaiś ca sevitam,
stūyamānaṃ stavair divyair ṛṣibhir brahma|vādibhiḥ
goptāraṃ sarva|bhūtānām iṣv|āsa|dharam a|cyutam.
Vāsudevas tu taṃ dṛṣṭvā jagāma śirasā kṣitim
Pārthena saha dharm'|ātmā gṛṇan brahma sanātanam
lok'|ādiṃ viśva|karmāṇam
a|jam īśānam a|vyayam,
manasaḥ paramāṃ, yoniṃ,
khaṃ, vāyuṃ, jyotiṣāṃ nidhim,
80.45 sraṣṭāraṃ vāri|dhārāṇāṃ, bhuvaś ca prakṛtiṃ parām,
deva|dānava|yakṣāṇāṃ mānavānāṃ ca sādhanam,
yogānāṃ ca paraṃ dhāma, dṛṣṭaṃ brahma|vidāṃ nidhim,
car'|âcarasya sraṣṭāraṃ pratihartāram eva ca,
kāla|kopaṃ mah"|ātmānaṃ, śakra|sūrya|guṇ'|ôdayam
vavande taṃ tadā Kṛṣṇo vāṅ|mano|buddhi|karmabhiḥ.

Partha spied a peak like a dancing flame dazzling as the light of the fire and sun and of the moon and the planets and the stars. They lighted on its highest reaches and as he planted his feet Árjuna saw before him the great everburning god marked by the bull.

The god was lit up by his own fire as if by a thousand 80.40
suns. He had lank and matted hair and a thousand eyes and a red body huge and magnificent and wrapped in bark and deerskin. In one hand he held a spear. Párvati his consort was there with him and a great crowd of bright creatures showered him in laughter and mirth and shimmering clamour and the chords of their lutes and the harmonies of their songs. The air bore gentle fragrances and the syllables of the chants of heaven's priests intoned the glory of the great and eternal ward of creatures: the god who bears the bow.

Vasudéva saw him and knowing what was right he bowed down to the ground and he and Partha spoke deathless praise to the origin and creator and unborn unencompassed lord of all creatures, the matrix of the soul, the abyss, the
wind, the store of lights, the spring of rivers, the air and 80.45
the ether, the end of gods and demons and spirits and men, the true cause, the open book of the keepers of secrets, the maker and taker of all that moves and all that is still, the fierce rage of time, the rising heart of the mighty sun. In word and thought and sense and deed Krishna showed his reverence. Like those wise enough to seek the deepest essence of creation he and Árjuna stood now before the refuge and everlasting nature of things. Árjuna too displayed a great adoration of Bhava for he understood that in

yaṃ prapadyanti vidvāṃsaḥ sūkṣm'|âdhyātma|pad'|âiṣiṇaḥ
tam a|jaṃ kāraṇ'|ātmānaṃ jagmatuḥ śaraṇaṃ Bhavam.
Arjunaś c' âpi taṃ devaṃ bhūyo bhūyo 'py avandata
jñātvā taṃ sarva|bhūt'|ādiṃ bhūta|bhavya|bhav'|ôdbhavam.
80.50 tatas tāv āgatau dṛṣṭvā Nara|Nārāyaṇāv ubhau
su|prasanna|manāḥ Śarvaḥ provāca prahasann iva.
«svāgataṃ vāṃ nara|śreṣṭhāv. uttiṣṭhetāṃ gataklamau.
kiṃ ca vām īpsitaṃ vīrau manasaḥ? kṣipram ucyatām.
yena kāryeṇa samprāptau yuvāṃ tat sādhayāmi kim.
vriyatām ātmanaḥ śreyas. tat sarvaṃ pradadāni vām.»
tatas tad|vacanaṃ śrutvā pratyutthāya kṛt'|âñjalī
Vāsudev'|Ârjunau Śarvaṃ tuṣṭuvāte mahā|matī
bhaktyā stavena divyena mah'|ātmānam a|ninditau.

KṚṢṆ'|ÂRJUNĀV ūcatuḥ:

namo Bhavāya, Śarvāya, Rudrāya vara|dāya ca,
paśūnāṃ pataye nityam, ugrāya ca Kapardine
80.55 Mahādevāya bhīmāya, Try|ambakāya ca, Śāntaye,
Īśānāya, Makha|ghnāya, namo 'stv, Andhaka|ghātine,
Kumāra|gurave tubhyaṃ, Nīla|grīvāya vedhase
Pinākine, Haviṣyāya Satyāya, Vibhave sadā
vilohitāya dhūmrāya Vyādhāy' ân|aparājite,
Nitya|nīla|śikhaṇḍāya, Śūline, Divya|cakṣuṣe,
Hotre, Potre, Tri|netrāya, Vyādhāya, Vasu|retase,
Acintyāy' Âmbikā|bhartre, Sarva|deva|stutāya ca
Vṛṣa|dhvajāya, Muṇḍāya, Jaṭine, Brahma|cāriṇe,
Tapyamānāya salile, Brahmaṇyāy' Âjitāya ca,

him was summed the past and present and future of all the creatures to which he had given form.

The God Who Kills With Arrows looked upon Nara and Naráyana with delight. A smile was on his lips when he spoke to them. 80.50

"Welcome o greatest of the race of men. Stand up and be at ease and may your weary limbs be rested. Tell me what your great souls want from me. Whatever you have come for I will make yours. Choose what you desire and I will give it to you."

Vasudéva and Árjuna heard Sharva's words and they rose to their feet with their hands still high, and once more the great and virtuous pair celebrated the mighty god with words of celestial devotion.

KRISHNA and ÁRJUNA spoke:

Glory to Bhava, the God Who Kills With Arrows, Rudra the giver, eternal and fearsome lord of the flock, the Wearer of Braids, mighty Maha·deva, the Three Eyed God, Peace- 80.55
bringer and Lord. Glory to the Violator of the Sacrifice, to the Blind Demon's Killer, to Skanda's Teacher, the Swallower of Poison, the Creator, to Falling Dust, the Hallowed Truth, the Vastness, the dark smoke crimson Hunter, the Unconquered, the Wearer of the Deathless Blue Crest, the Spearbearer, the Visionary, the Priest and the Slaughterer, He Who Gazes With Three Eyes, the Tormentor, the Quicksilver Seedcarrier, the Inconceivable, the consort of Ámbika, He Whom the Gods Praise, the Bearer of the Bull's Mark, the Shorn God, the God With Twisted Hair, the Mendicant, the One Who Burns in the Sea, The Surging

Viśv'|ātmane, Viśva|sṛje, viśvam āvṛtya tiṣṭhate.
80.60 namo namas te Sevyāya, bhūtānāṃ Prabhave sadā,
Brahma|vaktrāya, Śarvāya, Śaṃkarāya, Śivāya ca.
namo 'stu vācām pataye, prajānāṃ pataye namaḥ,
namo viśvasya pataye, mahatāṃ pataye namaḥ,
namaḥ Sahasra|śirase, Sahasra|bhuja|mṛtyave,
Sahasra|netra|pādāya namo 'saṃkhyeya|karmaṇe,
namo Hiraṇya|varṇāya, Hiraṇya|kavacāya ca
Bhakt'|ânukampine nityaṃ. sidhyatāṃ no varaḥ prabho.

SAṂJAYA uvāca:

evaṃ stutvā Mahādevaṃ Vāsudevaḥ sah'|Ârjunaḥ
prasādayām āsa Bhavaṃ tadā hy astr'|ôpalabdhaye.

81.1 TATO PĀRTHAḤ prasann'|ātmā prāñjalir vṛṣabha|dhvajam
dadarś' ôtphulla|nayanaḥ samastaṃ tejasāṃ nidhim.
taṃ c' ôpahāraṃ sva|kṛtaṃ naiśaṃ naityakam ātmanā
dadarśa Tryambak'|âbhyāśe Vāsudeva|niveditam.
tato 'bhipūjya manasā Kṛṣṇaṃ Śarvaṃ ca Pāṇḍavaḥ
«icchāmy ahaṃ divyam astram» ity abhāṣata Śaṃkaram.
tataḥ Pārthasya vijñāya var'|ârthe vacanaṃ tadā
Vāsudev'|Ārjunau devaḥ smayamāno 'bhyabhāṣata.
81.5 «svāgataṃ vāṃ, nara|śreṣṭhau. vijñātaṃ manas" ēpsitam.
yena kāmena samprāptau bhavadbhyāṃ taṃ dadāmy aham.
saro 'mṛtamayaṃ divyam abhyāśe, śatru|sūdanau.
tatra me tad dhanur divyaṃ śaraś ca nihitaḥ purā
yena dev'|ârayaḥ sarve mayā yudhi nipātitāḥ.
tata ānīyatāṃ Kṛṣṇau sa|śaraṃ dhanur uttamam.»

One, the Holy, the Unbeaten, the One Soul, the One Creator who ends the world yet remains.

Glory o glory to the Saviour of Things, the Eternal Be- 80.60
ing, the Holy Voice, to Sharva, to Shánkara, to Shiva. Glory to the lord of voices and the lord of creatures, glory to the lord of the universe, the lord of the mighty, the Hundredheaded God, to Thousandarmed Death, to the God with a Thousand Eyes and Legs, the Seething One, the Golden, the Goldmailed, the Ever Merciful. May you grant us our wish o great one.*

SÁNJAYA spoke:

Thus did Vasudéva and Árjuna sing the praise of Maha·deva and thus they prevailed upon him. And Bhava chose to give them the weapon they had come for.

WITH HIS HANDS still cupped in homage Partha looked 81.1
wideeyed into the deep furnace of all flame that is the deity marked by the bull. He saw somewhere within the Three Eyed God the delicate nightpiece that he had give to Vasudéva in the rite earlier that evening. Pandu's son filled his mind with reverence for Krishna and Sharva and asked Shánkara for the holy arrow. The god heard him and spoke to Vasudéva and Árjuna about the gift they desired.

"I know what you great and deadly warriors have come 81.5
for so be at peace. I will give you the thing you seek. Near to us there is pool full of nectar where long ago I sunk a magic bow and arrow. These were the weapons with which I battled and cast down all the enemies of the gods. O Dark Ones go and raise from the depths that great bow and its dart."

tath" êty uktvā tu tau vīrau sarva|pāriṣadaiḥ saha
prasthitau tat saro divyaṃ divy'|āścarya|śatair yutam
nirdiṣṭaṃ yad vṛṣ'|âṅkena puṇyaṃ sarv'|ârtha|sādhakam
tau jagmatur a|sambhrāntau Nara|Nārāyaṇāv ṛṣī.

81.10 tatas tau tat saro gatvā sūrya|maṇḍala|saṃnibham
nāgam antar|jale ghoraṃ dadṛśāte 'rjun'|Âcyutau.
dvitīyaṃ c' âparaṃ nāgaṃ sahasra|śirasaṃ varam
vamantaṃ vipulāṃ jvālāṃ dadṛśāte 'gni|varcasam.
tataḥ Kṛṣṇaś ca Pārthaś ca saṃspṛśy' âmbhaḥ kṛt'|âñjalī
tau nāgāv upatasthāte namasyantau Vṛṣadhvajam.

gṛṇantau veda|vidvāṃsau tad brahma śata|Rudriyam
a|prameyaṃ praṇamantau gatvā sarv'|ātmanā Bhavam.
tatas tau Rudra|māhātmyādd hitvā rūpaṃ mah"|ôragau
dhanur bāṇaś ca śatru|ghnaṃ tad dvaṃdvaṃ samapadyata.
81.15 tau taj jagṛhatuḥ prītau dhanur bāṇaṃ ca su|prabham
jahratuś ca mah"|ātmānau dadatuś ca mah"|ātmane.

tataḥ pārśvād Vṛṣāṅkasya brahma|cārī nyavartata
piṅg'|âkṣas tapasaḥ kṣetraṃ balavān nīla|lohitaḥ.
sa tad gṛhya dhanuḥ|śreṣṭhaṃ tasthau sthānaṃ samāhitaḥ.
vicakarṣ' âtha vidhivat sa|śaraṃ dhanur uttamam.
tasya maurvīṃ ca muṣṭiṃ ca sthānaṃ c' ālakṣya Pāṇḍavaḥ
śrutvā mantraṃ Bhava|proktaṃ jagrāh' â|cintya|vikramaḥ.
sa sarasy eva taṃ bāṇaṃ mumoc' âtibalaḥ prabhuḥ
cakāra ca punar vīras tasmin sarasi tad dhanuḥ.

Nara and Naráyana nodded, and the deity's retinue pointed the way to the heavenly lake that held the miraculous bow. The two wise heroes went straight to the blessed and pretty place where the god marked by the bull had told them all of their hopes would be fulfilled. The lake's sur- 81.10
face glittered like the sun. Árjuna and Áchyuta saw a terrifying dragon moving in its depths and coiling around it they saw another that was even more beautiful and terrible and that spewed from its thousand heads long tongues of bright flame. Krishna and Partha sprinkled holy water on the lake and cupping their hands they kneeled before the serpents and prayed to Sharva.

They prayed with all their knowledge of the Veda and venerated the immeasurable vault of the hundred storm gods and so with their being entire they came again before Bhava. And Rudra's shapeshifting power worked on the dragons and one became the bow and one became its lethal dart. In awe they picked up the bow and the won- 81.15
drous arrow and took them back to the great god to whom the items belonged.

From out of Rudra's side stepped a man with tawny eyes clad all in white. He stood like a great sheet of flame and with a dark purple hand took the fine bow and planted his feet and notched the arrow and drew back the string. It was clear that he knew the bow's secrets and Pandu's son whose courage never fails studied the man's fist and stance and heard the words Bhava then mumbled. The man's mighty fingers opened and the arrow flew towards the lake and then with a great swing he threw the bow after it and back to where it had come.

81.20 tataḥ prītaṃ Bhavaṃ jñātvā smṛtimān Arjunas tadā
varam āraṇyake dattaṃ darśanaṃ Śaṃkarasya ca
manasā cintayām āsa «tan me sampadyatām» iti.
tasya tan matam ājñāya prītaḥ prādād varaṃ Bhavaḥ
tac ca Pāśupataṃ ghoraṃ pratijñāyāś ca pāraṇam.
tataḥ Pāśupataṃ divyam avāpya punar īśvarāt
saṃhṛṣṭa|romā durdharṣaḥ kṛtaṃ kāryam amanyata.
vavandatuś ca saṃhṛṣṭau śirobhyāṃ taṃ Maheśvaram.
anujñātau kṣaṇe tasmin Bhaven' Ârjuna|Keśavau
prāptau sva|śibiraṃ vīrau mudā paramayā yutau.
81.25 tathā Bhaven' ânumatau mah"|âsura|nighātinā
Indra|Viṣṇū yathā prītau Jambhasya vadha|kāṅkṣiṇau.

SAṂJAYA uvāca:

82.1 TAYOḤ SAṂVADATOR evaṃ Kṛṣṇa|Dārukayos tadā
s" âtyagād rajanī, rājann, atha rāj" ânvabudhyata.
paṭhanti pāṇi|svanikā māgadhā madhu|parkikāḥ
vaitālikāś ca sūtāś ca tuṣṭuvuḥ puruṣa'|rṣabham.
nartakāś c' âpy anṛtyanta jagur gītāni gāyakāḥ
Kuru|vaṃśa|stav'|ârthāni madhuraṃ rakta|kaṇṭhinaḥ.
mṛdaṅgā jharjharā bheryaḥ paṇav'|ānaka|gomukhāḥ
āḍambarāś ca śaṅkhāś ca dundubhyaś ca mahā|svanāḥ,
82.5 evam etāni sarvāṇi tath" ānyāny api Bhārata
vādayanti su|saṃhṛṣṭāḥ kuśalāḥ sādhu|śikṣitāḥ.
sa megha|svana|nirghoṣo mahān śabdo 'spṛśad divam,
pārthiva|pravaraṃ suptaṃ Yudhiṣṭhiram abodhayat.

Árjuna knew that Bhava was pleased and he held in his memory the vision of Shánkara and the secret that the holy man born of his side had revealed. He pondered it and wished to himself that he too could master it. Bhava heard his thoughts and was satisfied and gave to Árjuna the gift. So it was that Árjuna received for a second time the gift of the Pashu·pata. 81.20

The Pashu·pata so deadly and divine would make good the hardy warrior's word. He thought once more on what he had to do and a thrill went through him. Árjuna and Késhava bowed their heads to the Great God and he gave them his leave and the two heroes returned to their beds with bliss in their bones. They had found favour with Bhava 81.25
the killer of the archdemons just as Indra and Vishnu had once found favour with him when they had gone to him to find a way to overthrow Jambha.

SÁNJAYA spoke:

O MAJESTY. KRISHNA and Dáruka spoke and the night 82.1
passed and the Pandu king began to surface from his slumber. The heralds clapped and chanted the hour and made their offerings of honey, and the bards and poets sent up praises to the bull of their herd. The dancers began to dance and in tones rich and sweet the singers sung songs to the Kuru dynasty. Then came the rumble of drums kettles tambours and tabla and across it came the blare of the horns.
The chorus swelled and o Bhárata all the bards played with 82.5
keen skill born of years of dedication and study. The great sound spread like thunder across the sky and roused Yudhi·shthira from his dreams.

pratibuddhaḥ sukhaṃ supto mah'|ārhe śayan'|ôttame
utthāy' âvaśya|kāry'|ârthaṃ yayau snāna|gṛhaṃ nṛ|paḥ.
tataḥ śukl'|âmbarāḥ snātās taruṇāḥ śatam aṣṭa ca
snāpakāḥ kāñcanaiḥ kumbhaiḥ pūrṇaiḥ samupatasthire.
bhadr'|âsaneṣ' ûpaviṣṭaḥ paridhāy' âmbaraṃ laghu
sasnau candana|saṃyuktaiḥ pānīyair abhimantritaiḥ.
82.10 utsāditaḥ kaṣāyeṇa balavadbhiḥ su|śikṣitaiḥ,
āplutaḥ s'|âdhivāsena jalena su|sugandhinā.
rāja|haṃsa|nibhaṃ prāpya uṣṇīṣaṃ śithil'|ârpitam
jala|kṣaya|nimittaṃ vai veṣṭayām āsa mūrdhani.
hariṇā candanen' âṅgam upalipya mahā|bhujaḥ
sragvī c' â|kliṣṭa|vasanaḥ prāṅ|mukhaḥ prāñjaliḥ sthitaḥ,
jajāpa japyaṃ Kaunteyaḥ satāṃ mārgam anuṣṭhitaḥ
tatr' âgni|śaraṇaṃ dīptaṃ praviveśa vinītavat.
samidbhiḥ sa|pavitrābhir agnim āhutibhis tathā
mantra|pūtābhir arcitvā niścakrāma gṛhāt tataḥ.
82.15 dvitīyāṃ puruṣa|vyāghraḥ kakṣyāṃ nirgamya pārthivaḥ
tato veda|vido vṛddhān apaśyad brāhmaṇa'|rṣabhān
dāntān veda|vrata|snātān snātān avabhṛtheṣu ca
sahasr'|ânucarān saurān sahasraṃ c' âṣṭa c' âparān.
akṣataiḥ sumanobhiś ca vācayitvā mahā|bhujaḥ
tān dvijān madhu|sarpirbhyāṃ phala|śreṣṭhaiḥ su|maṅgalaiḥ
prādāt kāñcanam ek'|âikaṃ niṣkaṃ viprāya Pāṇḍavaḥ,
alaṃkṛtaṃ c' âśva|śataṃ vāsāṃs' îṣṭāś ca dakṣiṇāḥ.
tathā gāḥ kapilā dogdhrīḥ sa|vatsāḥ Pāṇḍu|nandanaḥ
hema|śṛṅgā raupya|khurā dattvā cakre pradakṣiṇam.

The king rose from his royal bed well rested and ready
for all that the day would hold for him. He made his way
to the bathhouse where a hundred and eight young slaves
dressed in white who had risen and abluted before him
stood ready with golden buckets full to the brim. Wrapped
in light robes the king sat on the warm stone and washed
in holy sandalwater. Strong and skillfull arms rubbed his 82.10
limbs with decoctions and he was doused in pailfulls sweet
with the loveliest perfumes. He took a turban the colour of
flamingo feathers and bound it loosely around his head to
protect him from the rain. Anointed in yellow sandal and
clad in fresh robes and garlands Kunti's mighty son cupped
his hands and faced towards the east to chant the hymn that
would keep him on the sainted path. Then he went calmly
to the chamber where the fire burned.

He picked up some kindling and leaves and whispered
a hymn across them and dropped them into the fire and
turned to leave. He went out into the precinct and there 82.15
the great king met with the greatest of the Veda's old masters. The sunworshippers had washed for their vows and for
sacrifice and a thousand and eight priests and thousands of
helpers were all waiting to greet their king. Pandu's son had
the twiceborn chant the immortal prayers and then he gave
them honey and butter and ripe and sweetsmelling fruit. To
each of the seers he gave gold coins and robes and a hundred horses all caparisoned and other kinds of precious payment. Pandu's joy gave them red cows for milking and their
calves with horns of gold and hooves of silver. He bowed to
his priests and handed them talismans and golden charms 82.20

82.20 svastikān vardhamānāṃś ca nandy|āvartāṃś ca kāñcanān
mālyaṃ ca jala|kumbhāṃś ca jvalitaṃ ca hut'|âśanam
pūrṇāny akṣata|pātrāṇi rucakā rocanās tathā
sv|alaṃkṛtāḥ śubhāḥ kanyā dadhi sarpir madh' ûdakam
maṅgalyān pakṣiṇaś c' âiva yac c' ânyad api pūjitam.
dṛṣṭvā spṛṣṭvā ca Kaunteyo bāhyāṃ kakṣyām tato 'gamat.
tatas tasyāṃ mahā|bāhos tiṣṭhataḥ paricārakāḥ
sauvarṇaṃ sarvato|bhadraṃ muktā|vaiḍūrya|maṇḍitam
parārdhy'|āstaraṇ'|āstīrṇaṃ s'|ôttara|cchadam ṛddhimat
Viśvakarma|kṛtaṃ divyam upajahrur var'|āsanam.
82.25 tatra tasy' ôpaviṣṭasya bhūṣaṇāni mah"|ātmanaḥ
upajahrur mah"|ârhāṇi preṣyāḥ śubhrāṇi sarvaśaḥ.
mukt"|ābharaṇa|veṣasya Kaunteyasya mah"|ātmanaḥ
rūpam āsīn, mahā|rāja, dviṣatāṃ śoka|vardhanam.
pāṇḍaraiś candra|ramy'|ābhair hema|daṇḍaiś ca cāmaraiḥ
dodhūyamānaiḥ śuśubhe vidyudbhir iva toyadaḥ
saṃstūyamānaḥ sūtaiś ca vandyamānaś ca bandibhiḥ
upagīyamāno gandharvair āste sma Kurunandanaḥ.
tato muhūrtād āsīt tu syandanānāṃ svano mahān
nemi|ghoṣaś ca rathināṃ khura|ghoṣaś ca vājinām.
82.30 hrādena gaja|ghaṇṭānāṃ śaṅkhānāṃ ninadena ca
narāṇāṃ pada|śabdaiś ca kampat" îva sma medinī.
tataḥ śuddh'|ântam āsādya jānubhyāṃ bhū|tale sthitaḥ
śirasā vandanīyaṃ tam abhivādya jan'|ēśvaram
kuṇḍalī baddha|nistriṃśaḥ saṃnaddha|kavaco yuvā
abhipraṇamya śirasā dvāḥ|stho Dharm'|ātmajāya vai
nyavedayadd Hṛṣīkeśam upayāntaṃ mah"|ātmane.

for good luck and wreaths and jugs and sacred fire, holy urns full of elixir, burnished rings and virgins dressed in silk, and milk, ghee and honeywater, lucky birds and other auspicious things. He turned to the idol and sprinkled some drops of water and then he departed the temenos.

Back in his pavilion his slaves were waiting for him and they brought forth his shimmering sedan richly studded with pearls and crystal by the heavenly hand of Vishva·karman and they covered it in the finest fabrics and in pillows from farflung places and set its perfect bulk upon the
ground. The great king sat down and his helpers brought 82.25
forth his royal ornaments flashing in their hands. O majesty. Draped in pearls the mighty son of Kunti was a vision to strike his foes dead. With his gold wands and plumes white as jasmine blossom or the soft light of the moon he was like a raincloud edged in lightning. Kuru·nándana sat in state, as the bards canted his praise and the lutists played his glory and the *gandhárvas* sung out his honour. Then came the great sound of chariots moving, the trundle of wheels
and clop of horsehooves, the jangle of elephants' bells and 82.30
the blare of trumpets. The ground seemed to shake beneath the pounding feet of men. A young fighter armoured and earringed and with a sword sheathed at his hip came into the king's sanctum and kneeled on the ground and bowed down low before his venerable lord. He stood up in the doorway and lowered his head once again to Dharma's son and announced to his majesty that Hrishi·kesha had come. The great king welcomed Mádhava courteously and called for water and cushions to be brought out for his esteemed

so 'bravīt puruṣa|vyāghraḥ svāgaten' âiva Mādhavam
«arghyaṃ c' âiv' āsanaṃ c' âsmai dīyatāṃ param'|ârcitam.»
tataḥ praveśya Vārṣṇeyam upaveśya var'|āsane
pūjayām āsa vidhivad dharma|rājo Yudhiṣṭhiraḥ.

SAMJAYA uvāca:

83.1 TATO YUDHIṢṬHIRO rājā pratinandya Janārdanam
uvāca parama|prītaḥ Kaunteyo Devakī|sutam.
«sukhena rajanī vyuṣṭā kaccit te Madhusūdana?
kaccij jñānāni sarvāṇi prasannāni tav' Âcyuta?»
Vāsudevo 'pi tad|yuktaṃ paryapṛcchad Yudhiṣṭhiram.
tataś ca prakṛtīḥ kṣattā nyavedayad upasthitāḥ.
anujñātaś ca rājñā sa prāveśayata taṃ janam,
Virāṭaṃ Bhīmasenaṃ ca, Dhṛṣṭadyumnaṃ ca, Sātyakim,
Cedi|paṃ, Dhṛṣṭaketuṃ ca, Drupadaṃ ca mahā|ratham,
83.5 Śikhaṇḍinaṃ Yamau c' âiva, Cekitānaṃ sa|Kekayam,
Yuyutsuṃ c' âiva Kauravyaṃ, Pāñcālyaṃ c' Ôttamaujasam,
Yudhāmanyuṃ Subāhuṃ ca Draupadeyāṃś ca sarvaśaḥ.
ete c' ânye ca bahavaḥ kṣatriyāḥ kṣatriya'|rṣabham
upatasthur mah"|ātmānaṃ viviśuś c' āsane śubhe.
ekasminn āsane vīrāv upaviṣṭau mahā|balau
Kṛṣṇaś ca Yuyudhānaś ca mah"|ātmānau mahā|dyutī.
tato Yudhiṣṭhiras teṣāṃ śṛṇvatāṃ Madhusūdanam
abravīt Puṇḍarīkākṣam sambhāṣya madhuraṃ vacaḥ.
«ekaṃ tvāṃ vayam āśritya Sahasrākṣam iv' âmarāḥ
prārthayāmo jayaṃ yuddhe śāśvatāni sukhāni ca.
83.10 tvaṃ hi rājya|vināśaṃ ca dviṣadbhiś ca nirākriyām
kleśāṃś ca vividhān Kṛṣṇa sarvāṃs tān api veda naḥ.

guest. Varshnéya was led to the couch and invited to sit. And the righteous king gave him his blessing.

SÁNJAYA spoke:

WHEN KING Yudhi·shthira son of Kunti had made Dé- 83.1
vaki's son comfortable, he spoke to him with joyous words.

"O Madhu·súdana a new day brightens. How is it with you? Are you refreshed, Áchyuta?"

Vasudéva returned the king's pleasantries and while they spoke the doorkeeper announced the arrival of the king's vassals. The king told the man to fetch them. In came Virá- ta, Bhima·sena, Dhrishta·dyumna and Sátyaki, the Chedi
king, Dhrishta·ketu and mighty Drúpada, Shikhándin and 83.5
the Twins, Chekitána and Kékaya, Yuyútsu the Káurava and Uttamáujas the Panchála, Yudha·manyu and Subáhu and the five Draupadéyas and all the rest of the other warriors. They bowed before the grand throne of their lord, and took their place on the soft cushions at his feet. The mighty and resplendent pair Krishna and Yuyudhána and sat side by side on a single seat. They all fell silent and Yudhi·shthira spoke to lotuseyed Madhu·súdana. His words were rich and sweet.

"When they needed help the deathless gods sought out their thousandeyed champion. So it was that in hope of winning through war our longevity we came o Krishna to
you. Krishna, you know all about the destruction of our 83.10
kingdom, our expulsion at our enemies' hands, and all our sundry other sorrows.

tvayi, sarv'|ēśa, sarveṣām asmākaṃ bhakta|vatsala,
sukham āyattam atyarthaṃ yātrā ca Madhusūdana.
sa tathā kuru, Vārṣṇeya, yathā tvayi mano mama
Arjunasya yathā satyā pratijñā syāc cikīrṣitā.
sa bhavāṃs tārayatv asmād duḥkh'|â|marṣa|mah"|ârṇavāt
pāraṃ titīrṣatām adya. plavo no bhava, Mādhava.
na hi tat kurute saṃkhye rathī ripu|vadh'|ôdyataḥ
yathā vai kurute, Kṛṣṇa, sārathir yatnam āsthitaḥ.
83.15 yath" âiva sarvāsv āpatsu pāsi Vṛṣṇīñ Janārdana
tath" âiv' âsmān mahā|bāho vṛjinā trātum arhasi.
tvam a|gādhe 'plave magnān Pāṇḍavān Kuru|sāgare
samuddhara plavo bhūtvā, śaṃkha|cakra|gadā|dhara.
namaste deva|dev'|ēśa sanātana viśātana
Viṣṇo Jiṣṇo, Hare Kṛṣṇa, Vaikuṇṭha puruṣ'|ôttama.
Nāradas tvāṃ samācakhyau purāṇam ṛṣi|sattamam
vara|daṃ śārṅgiṇaṃ śreṣṭhaṃ. tat satyaṃ kuru Mādhava.
ity uktaḥ Puṇḍarīkākṣo dharma|rājena saṃsadi
toya|megha|svano vāgmī pratyuvāca Yudhiṣṭhiram.

KṚṢṆA uvāca:

83.20 s'|âmareṣv api lokeṣu sarveṣu na tathā|vidhaḥ
śar'|âsana|dharaḥ kaś cid yathā Pārtho Dhanaṃjayaḥ.
vīryavān astra|sampannaḥ parākrānto mahā|balaḥ
yuddha|śauṇḍaḥ sad" â|marṣī tejasvī paramo nṛṇām
sa yuvā vṛṣabha|skandho dīrgha|bāhur mahā|balaḥ
siṃha'|ṛṣabha|gatiḥ śrīmān dviṣatas te haniṣyati.

O lord of all that is. Care for us who love you so for in you o Madhu·súdana lie our high and desperate hopes. Make good the faith I have in you Varshnéya, and make sure that Árjuna's promise comes to pass, as it must. A sea lashed with suffering and pain lies all around us my friend, and we raise our eyes to distant shores. Mádhava, be the raft to take us there. Such is the task not of the warrior, fixed on his enemies' overthrow. No: such is the task of the driver,
who bears the warrior up. As come what may you shield 83.15
the Vrishnis with your mighty reach o Stirrer of Men save us even so from our woes. We are far from land and the Kurus want to swallow us into their depths. So take your club, discus and conch and raise us high. Glory to you o Vishnu the Conquering Sun, o Hara the Dark, o Vaikúntha, greatest of all who have lived, eternal destroyer and god of gods. Nárada named you the wisest man the world has ever known. He called you a giver of gifts, the grand master of the horned bow. Mádhava make good his claim."

The lotuseyed Krishna listened with the others to what the righteous king had said. His reply was full of wit and thunder.

KRISHNA spoke:

Put a bow and arrow in the hands of a god and he could 83.20
not do what Dhanan·jaya son of Pritha can do. The man is strong and brave and a master of the craft of war and none can quench the wild blaze of his battlefrenzy. He has vigour and power and reach, the shoulders of an ox and the speed of a lion. His many blessings will lay low your foes. I will clear the way for Árjuna son of Kunti to burn like a

aham ca tat kariṣyāmi yathā Kuntī|suto 'rjunaḥ
Dhārtarāṣṭrasya sainyāni dhakṣyaty agnir iv' ôtthitaḥ.
adya taṃ pāpa|karmāṇaṃ kṣudraṃ Saubhadra|ghātinam
a|punar|darśanaṃ mārgam iṣubhiḥ kṣepsyate 'rjunaḥ.
83.25 tasy' âdya gṛdhrāḥ śyenāś ca vaṇḍa|gomāyavas tathā
bhakṣayiṣyanti māṃsāni ye c' ânye puruṣ'|âdakāḥ.
yady asya devā goptāraḥ s'|Êndrāḥ sarve Yudhiṣṭhira
rāja|dhānīṃ Yamasy' âdya hataḥ prāpsyati saṃkule.
nihatya Saindhavaṃ Jiṣṇur adya tvām upayāsyati.
vi|śoko vi|jvaro rājan bhava bhūti|puras|kṛtaḥ.

SAṂJAYA uvāca:

84.1 TATHĀ SAṂVADATĀṂ teṣāṃ prādur āsīd Dhanaṃjayaḥ
didṛkṣur Bharata|śreṣṭhaṃ rājānaṃ sa|suhṛd|gaṇam.
taṃ niviṣṭaṃ śubhāṃ kakṣām abhivandy' âgrataḥ sthitam
samutthāy' Ârjunaṃ premṇā sasvaje Pāṇḍava'|rṣabhaḥ.
mūrdhni c' âinam upāghrāya pariṣvajya ca bāhunā
āśiṣaḥ paramāḥ procya smayamāno 'bhyabhāṣata.
«vyaktam Arjuna saṃgrāme dhruvas te vijayo mahān,
yādṛg|rūpā ca te chāyā prasannaś ca Janārdanaḥ.»
84.5 tam abravīt tato Jiṣṇur mahad āścaryam uttamam
«dṛṣṭavān asmi bhadraṃ te Keśavasya prasāda|jam.»
tatas tat kathayām āsa yathā|dṛṣṭaṃ Dhanaṃjayaḥ
āśvāsan'|ârthaṃ suhṛdāṃ Tryambakena samāgamam.

kindled fire through the serried rows of Duryódhana's men. Today Árjuna's arrows will send Saubhádra's vile and savage murderer down the path along which none return. Vultures 83.25
and jackals, bandylegged hyenas croaking like frogs and any other beasts that like the taste of human flesh will savage the man's carcass. Let Indra bring his army entire here to save him and o Yudhi·shthira still he will go down in the fray to lodge at Death's palace. Rest assured o king that when Jishnu rises to slay Sáindhava he will return to you. O king quell the fever and fire within you.

SÁNJAYA spoke:

AS THE COUNSEL went on Dhanan·jaya arrived and he 84.1
was keen to see the Bharata sovereign and all his assembled friends. He came into the enclosure and stepped through its bright interior to the front of the throng and when the bull of the Pándavas saw his brother he stood up and clasped his hand warmly and then embraced him and kissed him on the head. Yudhi·shthira was full of benedictions and he smiled as he spoke.

"Árjuna your lustre and glory assure us that today you will prevail. Victory cannot be in doubt when the Stirrer of Men rides with you."

Then the Conquering Sun told them of the night's 84.5
wonders.

"O brother I have already seen what is born of Késhava's grace."

And so to hearten his friends Dhanan·jaya told them all about his encounter with the Three Eyed God. Amazed at

tataḥ śirobhir avaniṃ spṛṣṭvā sarve ca vismitāḥ
namas|kṛtya Vṛṣāṅkāya sādhu sādhv ity ath' âbruvan.
anujñātās tataḥ sarve suhṛdo dharma|sūnunā
tvaramāṇāḥ su|saṃrabdhā hṛṣṭā yuddhāya niryayuḥ.
abhivādya tu rājānaṃ Yuyudhān'|Âcyut'|Ârjunāḥ
hṛṣṭā viniryayus te vai Yudhiṣṭhira|niveśanāt.
84.10 rathen' âikena dur|dharṣau Yuyudhāna|Janārdanau
jagmatuḥ sahitau vīrāv Arjunasya niveśanam.
tatra gatvā Hṛṣīkeśaḥ kalpayām āsa sūtavat
rathaṃ ratha|varasy' âjau vānara'|rṣabha|lakṣaṇam.
sa megha|sama|nirghoṣas tapta|kāñcana|suprabhaḥ
babhau ratha|varaḥ kḷptaḥ śiśur divasa|kṛd yathā.
tataḥ puruṣa|śārdūlaḥ sajjaṃ sajja|puraḥ|saraḥ
kṛt'|āhnikāya Pārthāya nyavedayata taṃ ratham.
taṃ tu loka|varaḥ puṃsāṃ kirīṭī hema|varma|bhṛt
cāpa|bāṇa|dharo vāhaṃ pradakṣiṇam avartata.
84.15 tapo|vidyā|vayo|vṛddhaiḥ kriyāvadbhir jit'|êndriyaiḥ
stūyamāno jay'|āśīrbhir āruroha mahā|ratham
jaitraiḥ sāṃgrāmikair mantraiḥ pūrvam eva rath'|ôttamam
abhimantritam arciṣmān udayaṃ bhās|karo yathā.
sa rathe rathināṃ śreṣṭhaḥ kāñcane kāñcan'|āvṛtaḥ
vibabhau vi|malo 'rciṣmān Merāv iva divā|karaḥ.
anvāruruhatuḥ Pārthaṃ Yuyudhāna|Janārdanau
Śaryāter yajñam āyāntaṃ rath'|êndraṃ devam Aśvinau.
atha jagrāha Govindo raśmīn raśmi|bhṛtāṃ varaḥ

his tale they bowed low to the ground and giving thanks and praise to the deity marked by the bull they muttered his praise. All of Árjuna's companions were now thrilled to the marrow and with the king's leave they hastened to prepare for battle. Yuyudhána, Áchyuta and Árjuna felt the same excitement, and bidding Yudhi·shthira farewell they
left his tent. Yuyudhána and Janárdana boarded a single 84.10
car and the two heroes followed Árjuna back to his camp. When Hrishi·kesha got there he went to prepare the monkey totem and he set it above the car that he was to drive for the greatest carwarrior of them all. With the sound of thunder at its wheels the chariot rolled forth. It shone heraldic with the light of heathammered gold, like the newborn sun that makes the day. The tiger Krishna stacked the car with its battle gear and buckled on his own. He brought the chariot before Pritha's son as the warrior was completing his morning prayers.

Árjuna wore his crown and golden cuirass and hefting his parasol and quiver the best of the men of this world
stood for a moment before his car for good luck. Priests 84.15
who had disavowed the temptations of this world for the power and scouring heat of ascesis and wisdom began the victory songs, and to their strains Árjuna climbed aboard the car's great finewrought bulk, now enchanted with battle mantras to make safe its return. Árjuna was like a blazing orb mounting the sky. Dressed in gold he stood upon gold. Like the sun brilliant above Meru, the greatest of his kind stepped upon the car all blazing with light. And as the Horse Gods bound for the sacrifice once followed Indra onto his chariot, Yuyudhána and Janárdana climbed

Mātalir Vāsavasy' êva Vṛtraṃ hantuṃ prayāsyataḥ.
84.20 sa tābhyāṃ sahitaḥ Pārtho ratha|pravaram āsthitaḥ
sahito Budha|Śukrābhyāṃ tamo nighnan yathā śaśī.
Saindhavasya vadhaṃ prepsuḥ prayātaḥ śatru|pūga|hā
sah'|Âmbupati|Mitrābhyāṃ yath" Êndras Tārakāmaye.

tato vāditra|nirghoṣair māṅgalyaiś ca stavaiḥ śubhaiḥ
prayāntam Arjunaṃ vīraṃ māgadhāś c' âiva tuṣṭuvuḥ.
sa|jay'|âśīḥ sa|puṇy'|âhaḥ sūta|māgadha|niḥsvanaḥ
yukto vāditra|ghoṣeṇa teṣāṃ rati|karo 'bhavat.
tam anuprayato vāyuḥ puṇya|gandha|vahaḥ śubhaḥ
vavau saṃharṣayan Pārthaṃ dviṣataś c' âpi śoṣayan.
84.25 tatas tasmin kṣaṇe, rājan, vividhāni śubhāni ca
prādur āsan nimittāni vijayāya bahūni ca
Pāṇḍavānāṃ tvadīyānāṃ viparītāni, māriṣa.
dṛṣṭv' Ârjuno nimittāni vijayāya pradakṣiṇam
Yuyudhānaṃ mah"|êṣv|āsam idaṃ vacanam abravīt.

«Yuyudhān' âdya yuddhe me dṛśyate vijayo dhruvaḥ
yathā h' îmāni liṅgāni dṛśyante Śini|puṃgava.
so 'haṃ tatra gamiṣyāmi yatra Saindhavako nṛ|paḥ
yiyāsur Yama|lokāya mama vīryaṃ pratīkṣate.
yathā paramakaṃ kṛtyaṃ Saindhavasya vadho mama
tath" âiva su|mahat kṛtyaṃ dharma|rājasya rakṣaṇam.
84.30 sa tvam adya mahā|bāho rājānaṃ paripālaya.
yath" âiva hi mayā guptas tvayā gupto bhavet tathā.
na paśyāmi ca taṃ loke yas tvāṃ yuddhe parājayet
Vāsudeva|samaṃ saṃkhye svayam apy amar'|ēśvaraḥ.

aboard after Pritha's son. Like Vásava's driver Mátali when he readied the horses to hunt down Vritra, the Herdsman took the reins that his hands knew so well. The two war- 84.20
riors stood alongside Pritha's son in his high car like Mercury and Venus conjunct with the gloomslaying moon. As Váruna and Mitra had gone with Indra to fetch Brihas·pati's starry bride, so it was that the Sindhu king's nemesis set out to hunt him down.*

Plucking chords the bards hymned mighty Árjuna's illustrious departure, and their songs merged with the dulcet blessings and prayers the poets and heralds extolled. A warm and sweetsmelling wind arose then and it soothed Pritha's son but blew harsh and dry upon his foes. And o majesty 84.25
the signs that came to cheer the Pándavas were many and just so many o king were the signs that came to blight the hopes of your sons. Árjuna saw that the omens were out for him and he turned to the mighty bowman Yuyudhána and spoke.

"Yuyudhána these portents betoken my success. O bull of the Shinis I will go now to find the Sindhu king. When he sees me coming for him he will make all haste for Death's kingdom. Sáindhava's end weighs upon me but so too does the safety of the righteous king. With your strong arms keep 84.30
my brother safe and guard him today as I have guarded him before. You are Vasudéva's equal and I see none in earth or in heaven who could better you in battle. You are a bull in the herd of men. I trust in you as I trust in mighty Pradyúmna and this alone means I can battle Sáindhava confident that the king will be safe. Sátvata I need no one to watch my back. I ask only that you with all your might make deadly

tvayi c' âhaṃ parāśvastaḥ Pradyumne vā mahā|rathe
śaknuyāṃ Saindhavaṃ hantum an|apekṣo, nara'|rṣabha.
mayy apekṣā na kartavyā kathaṃ cid api Sātvata.
rājany eva parā guptiḥ kāryā sarv'|ātmanā tvayā.
na hi yatra mahā|bāhur Vāsudevo vyavasthitaḥ
kiṃ cid vyāpadyate tatra yatr' âham api ca dhruvam.»
84.35 evam uktas tu Pārthena Sātyakiḥ para|vīra|hā
tath" êty uktv" âgamat tatra yatra rājā Yudhiṣṭhiraḥ.

sure the king is safe. Nothing can go wrong if Vasudéva is at my side and at my side he will assuredly be."

Sátyaki scourge of heroes heard Partha's wishes and as- 84.35
sented and went to find Yudhi·shthira.

85–109
THE DEATH OF JAYAD·RATHA

DHṚTARĀṢṬRA uvāca:

85.1 ŚVO|BHŪTE KIM akārṣus te duḥkha|śoka|samanvitāḥ
Abhimanyau hate tatra? ke v" âyudhyanta māmakāḥ?
jānantas tasya karmāṇi Kuravaḥ Savyasācinaḥ
kathaṃ tat kilbiṣaṃ kṛtvā nir|bhayā, brūhi, māmakāḥ?
putra|śok'|âbhisaṃtaptaṃ kruddhaṃ mṛtyum iv' ântakam
āyāntaṃ puruṣa|vyāghraṃ kathaṃ dadṛśur āhave?
kapi|rāja|dhvajaṃ saṃkhye vidhunvānaṃ mahad dhanuḥ
dṛṣṭvā putra|paridyūnaṃ kim akurvata māmakāḥ?
85.5 kiṃ nu, Saṃjaya, saṃgrāme vṛttaṃ Duryodhanaṃ prati
paridevo mahān adya śruto me n' âbhinandanam?
babhūvur ye mano|grāhyāḥ śabdāḥ śruti|sukh'|āvahāḥ
na śrūyante 'dya te sarve Saindhavasya niveśane.
stuvatāṃ n' âdya śrūyante putrāṇāṃ śibire mama
sūta|māgadha|saṃghānāṃ nartakānāṃ ca sarvaśaḥ.
śabdena nādit" âbhīkṣṇam abhavad yatra me śrutiḥ
dīnānām adya taṃ śabdaṃ na śṛṇomi samīritam.
niveśane satya|dhṛteḥ Somadattasya, Saṃjaya,
āsīno 'haṃ purā tāta śabdam aśrauṣam uttamam.
85.10 tad adya puṇya|hīno 'ham ārta|svara|nināditam
niveśanaṃ hat'|ôtsāhaṃ putrāṇāṃ mama lakṣaye.
Viviṃśater Durmukhasya, Citrasena|Vikarṇayoḥ
anyeṣāṃ ca sutānāṃ me na tathā śrūyate dhvaniḥ.
brāhmaṇāḥ kṣatriyā vaiśyā yaṃ śiṣyāḥ paryupāsate
Droṇa|putraṃ mah"|êṣv|āsaṃ putrāṇāṃ me parāyaṇam,
vitaṇḍ'|ālāpa|saṃlāpair druta|vāditra|vāditaiḥ
gītaiś ca vividhair iṣṭai ramate yo divā|niśam

DHRITA·RASHTRA spoke:

THEN HOW DID they fare that day, with Abhimányu's 85.1
death so fresh a wound in their hearts? Who among
us went to meet them? The Kurus know well what Savya·
sachin can do. Could they wrong him so terribly yet still
dare to face him? Tell me. When the Pándava tiger rode
aflame with sorrow for his son and crazed as death that ends
all things did my children stand their ground? What did
they do when they saw beneath the effigy of the monkey
king his great bow shaking and the grave cast of his visage?
Did they weep for Duryódhana so sure to meet his end? 85.5

O Sánjaya thus ends any happiness my son might once
have brought me. All the merry music so sweet to the ear
that once stirred from Sáindhava's camp I hear no more.
The sounds of dancing and the songs of the bards and poets that once rose across the tents of my children I hear
no more. Even the howls of mourning that not long ago
echoed and echoed across these parts no longer strike my
ears. O Sánjaya I used to sit and listen to the melodies that
rose from where the just King Soma·datta had pitched his
tent but my boy now all hope is gone. It will not be long 85.10
before cries of despair ring among the broken pavilions of
my sons.

The voices of Vivínshati and Dúrmukha, of Chitra·sena and Vikárna and my other children have all fallen silent now. I remember how men of every ilk used to come from far around to seek the wisdom of Drona's son, a true master of the bow. He was so devoted to my children. Day and night he would sit with the Kurus and Pándavas and Sát-vatas who had gathered around him and talk and argue and

upāsyamāno bahubhiḥ Kuru|Pāṇḍava|Sātvataiḥ,
sūta tasya gṛhe śabdho n' âdya Drauṇer yathā purā.
85.15 Droṇaputraṃ mah''|êṣv|āsaṃ gāyanā nartakāś ca ye
atyartham upatiṣṭhanti teṣāṃ na śrūyate dhvaniḥ.
Vind'|Ânuvindayoḥ sāyaṃ śibire yo mahā|dhvaniḥ
śrūyate so 'dya na tathā, Kekayānāṃ ca veśmasu.
nityaṃ pramuditānāṃ ca tāla|gīta|svano mahān
nṛtyatāṃ śrūyate tāta gaṇānāṃ so 'dya na dhvaniḥ.
sapta|tantūn vitanvānā yājakā yam upāsate
Saumadattiṃ śruta|nidhiṃ teṣāṃ na śrūyate dhvaniḥ.
jyā|ghoṣo brahma|ghoṣaś ca tomar'|âsi|ratha|dhvaniḥ
Droṇasy' āsīd a|virato gṛhe: taṃ na śṛṇomy aham.
85.20 nānā|deśa|samutthānāṃ gītānāṃ yo 'bhavat svanaḥ
vāditra|nāditānāṃ ca so 'dya na śrūyate mahān.
yadā prabhṛty Upaplavyāc chāntim icchañ Janārdanaḥ
āgataḥ sarva|bhūtānām anukamp'|ârtham Acyutaḥ,
tato 'ham abruvaṃ, sūta, mandaṃ Duryodhanaṃ tadā.
«Vāsudevena tīrthena putra saṃśāmya Pāṇḍavaiḥ.
kāla|prāptam ahaṃ manye. mā tvaṃ, Duryodhan', âtigāḥ.
śamaṃ ced yācamānaṃ tvaṃ pratyākhyāsyasi Keśavam
hit'|ârtham abhijalpantaṃ na tav' âsti raṇe jayaḥ.»
pratyācaṣṭa sa Dāśārham ṛṣabhaṃ sarva|dhanvinām
anuneyāni jalpantam a|nayān n' ânvapadyata.
85.25 tato Duḥśāsanasy' âiva Karṇasya ca mataṃ dvayoḥ
anvavartata māṃ hitvā kṛṣṭaḥ kālena dur|matiḥ.

joke with them, regaling them in rhyme and song. His fingers were so nimble on the strings of a harp. But o driver
in the house of Drauni all is not as it was. The mirth of the 85.15
dancers and singers that once thronged where the great Ashvattháman had pitched his camp now are heard no more.

At evening I would cock my ear to hear the rich tones of Vinda and Anuvínda but now they have fallen silent. Silent too are the dwellings of the Kékayas. The happy noise of people dancing, of songs and claps echoed through the long nights but now my son there is only silence. Holy men planning the seventhreaded rites would come to tap the wells of wisdom in Saumadátti but no more do I hear their chants. Among Drona's tents the bow's whisper and the crash of lance sword and car would sound above the drone of incantation in concert neverending: now their strains are heard
no more. Silent now are all the voices that lifted in song 85.20
above these places and silent now the instruments that accompanied them.

O driver. When Janárdana the Unfallen came from Upaplávya to bring peace and to avert the sufferings of the world I tried to shake Duryódhana from his stupor. Son make peace with the Pándavas, I said. Do so through Vasudéva's intervention. He has come as their minister. I fear that time has caught up with you, Duryódhana. Do not try to outrun it. If you spurn Késhava's offer of peace and scorn his mercies then you do so at your peril. Instead of appeasing the bull of the Dashárha archers he spurned him and he knew not the forces he was tempting. Foolishly he
ignored me. Drawn by a darker fate he followed Karna and 85.25
Duhshásana instead.

na hy ahaṃ dyūtam icchāmi. Viduro na praśaṃsati.
Saindhavo n' êcchati dyūtaṃ. Bhīṣmo na dyūtam icchati.
Śalyo Bhūriśravāś c' âiva Purumitro Jayas tathā,
Aśvatthāmā, Kṛpo, Droṇo dyūtaṃ n' êcchanti, Saṃjaya.
eteṣāṃ matam ādāya yadi varteta putrakaḥ,
sa|jñāti|mitraḥ sa|suhṛc ciraṃ jīved an|āmayaḥ.
ślakṣṇā madhura|sambhāṣā jñāti|bandu|priyaṃ|vadāḥ,
kulīnāḥ sammatāḥ prājñāḥ sukhaṃ prāpsyanti Pāṇḍavāḥ.
85.30 dharm'|āpekṣī naro nityaṃ sarvatra labhate sukham
pretya|bhāve ca kalyāṇaṃ prasādaṃ pratipadyate.
arhanty ardhaṃ pṛthivyās te bhoktuṃ sāmarthya|sādhanāḥ,
teṣām api samudr'|ântā pitṛ|paitāmahī mahī.

niyujyamānāḥ sthāsyanti Pāṇḍavā dharma|vartmani.
santi no jñātayas, tāta, yeṣāṃ śroṣyanti Pāṇḍavāḥ.
Śalyasya, Somadattasya, Bhīṣmasya ca mah"|ātmanaḥ,
Droṇasy' âtha Vikarṇasya, Bāhlīkasya Kṛpasya ca
anyeṣāṃ c' âiva vṛddhānāṃ Bharatānāṃ mah"|ātmanām
tvad|arthaṃ bruvatāṃ tāta kariṣyanti vaco hitam.
85.35 kaṃ vā tvaṃ manyase teṣāṃ yas tān brūyād ato 'nyathā?
Kṛṣṇo na dharmaṃ saṃjahyāt. sarve te hi tad|anvayāḥ.
may' âpi c' ôktās te vīrā vacanaṃ dharma|saṃhitam
n' ânyathā prakariṣyanti dharm'|ātmāno hi Pāṇḍavāḥ.
ity ahaṃ vilapan sūta bahuśaḥ putram uktavān

I did not want the dice game to go ahead.* Vídura was against it. Sáindhava did not believe the game should happen. Nor did Bhishma. Shalya and Bhuri·shravas, Puru·mitra and Jaya, Ashvattháman, Kripa and Drona: they were all of the same mind, Sánjaya. None of them thought the game should go ahead. If only my son had listened to his brothers or to his father or to any of the people that cared about him he might have lived a long and happy life. The Pándavas speak openly to one another. They hold the thoughts of their kith and kin close. Their actions are mea- 85.30
sured and thoughtful and they work together as all of their kind should. Because of this they will prosper. A man who considers what is just before he acts will in the end find happiness in this life and heaven's grace in the next. The Pándavas know the value of unity. It is only right that they should enjoy half of this seabounded land* that our forefathers bequeathed to us.

The Pándavas follow those that guide them and they do not stray from the path they follow. Our own kinsmen had their trust: Shalya, Soma·datta, mighty Bhishma and Drona and Vikárna, Bahlíka and Kripa and the other great and wise men of the Bharata clan. I told my son that the Pándavas would have listened to these men if he had let them argue his case. Do you think any of Pándavas would 85.35
transgress the word of an elder? Krishna would have shown justice and the rest would have followed his lead. I too could have pleaded with them in the name of fairness. The Pándavas live by the principle of order. They would have listened to reason. O driver again and again I berated my fool-

na ca me śrutavān mūḍho. manye kālasya paryayam.
Vṛkodar'|Ârjunau yatra Vṛṣṇi|vīraś ca Sātyakiḥ,
Uttamaujāś ca Pāñcālyo Yudhāmanyuś ca dur|jayaḥ,
Dhṛṣṭadyumnaś ca dur|dharṣaḥ Śikhaṇḍī c' â|parājitaḥ,
Aśmakāḥ Kaikeyāś c' âiva Kṣatradharmā ca Saumakiḥ,
85.40 Caidyaś ca Cekitānaś ca putraḥ Kāśyasya c' âbhibhuḥ,
Draupadeyā Virāṭaś ca Drupadaś ca mahā|rathaḥ,
Yamau ca puruṣa|vyāghrau mantrī ca Madhusūdanaḥ
ka etāñ jātu yudhyeta loke 'smin vai jijīviṣuḥ,
divyam astraṃ vikurvāṇān prasahed vā parān mama
anyo Duryodhanāt, Karṇāc Chakuneś c' âpi Saubalāt?
Duḥśāsana|caturthānāṃ n' ânyaṃ paśyāmi pañcamam.
yeṣām abhīṣu|hastaḥ syād Viṣvakseno rathe sthitaḥ
saṃnaddhaś c' Ârjuno yoddhā teṣāṃ n' âsti parājayaḥ.
teṣām atha vilāpānāṃ
n' âyaṃ Duryodhanaḥ smaret.
hatau hi puruṣa|vyāghrau
Bhīṣma|Droṇau tvam āttha vai.
85.45 teṣāṃ Vidura|vākyānāṃ muktānāṃ dīrgha|darśanāt
dṛṣṭv" êmāṃ phala|nirvṛttiṃ manye śocanti putrakāḥ.
senāṃ dṛṣṭv" âbhibhūtāṃ me Śaineyen' Ârjunena ca
śūnyān dṛṣṭvā rath'|ôpasthān manye śocanti putrakāḥ.
him'|âtyaye yathā kakṣaṃ śuṣkaṃ vāt'|ērito mahān
agnir dahet tathā senāṃ māmikāṃ sa Dhanaṃjayaḥ.
ācakṣva mama tat sarvaṃ, kuśalo hy asi, Saṃjaya,
yad upāyāta sāy'|âhne kṛtvā Pārthasya kilbiṣam

ish son but perhaps because we live in the last days he simply did not hear me.

Now Dogbelly and Árjuna, Sátyaki the Vrishni champion, Uttamáujas the Panchála and fearsome Yudha·manyu,
deadly Dhrishta·dyumna and indomitable Shikhándin, the
Áshmakas and Kaikéyas and Kshatra·dharman son of Sómaka, Chekitána of Chedi and the great prince of Kashi, 85.40
the sons of Dráupadi and Viráta and the mighty warrior
Drúpada, the tigerlike twins and the magus Madhu·súdana
all fight together in a single army. Who in this world could
stand a wisp of a hope against them? None but Duryódhana, Karna, and Shákuni son of Súbala could resist the
immortal weapons our enemies wield. These three warriors
and Duhshásana: only they. But if Árjuna has buckled on
his breastplate and Vishvak·sena holds his horses' reins then
I fear the Pándavas cannot be stopped. And let us not forget that they are in mourning. Duryódhana has no idea of
what their sorrow will drive them to.

You say that the tigers Bhishma and Drona are no more
in this world. I see the sooth that Vídura spoke now yield 85.45
its truth. I can imagine how my sons are suffering. I see
my army overturned by Shainéya and Árjuna and I see gaps
among the chariots where men should be and I can imagine
how my sons are suffering. As at the end of the cold season a
rising wind drives a fire through a dry wood so Dhanan·jaya
rolls through the rows of my men. Tell me all that happened
Sánjaya. After Abhimányu was slain and the sun rose on
Partha's misery how did you feel, my son? When the bearer
of Gandíva came to take revenge for so great a crime there

Abhimanyau hate, tāta, katham āsīn mano hi vaḥ?
na jātu tasya karmāṇi yudhi Gāṇḍīva|dhanvanaḥ
apakṛtya mahat tāta soḍhuṃ śakṣyanti māmakāḥ.
85.50 kiṃ nu Duryodhanaḥ kṛtyaṃ Karṇaḥ kṛtyaṃ kim abravīt
Duḥśāsanaḥ Saubalaś ca teṣām evaṃ|gateṣv api
sarveṣāṃ samavetānāṃ putrāṇāṃ mama Saṃjaya?
yad vṛttaṃ tāta saṃgrāme mandasy' âpanayair bhṛśam
lobh'|ânugasya dur|buddheḥ krodhena vikṛt'|ātmanaḥ
rājya|kāmasya mūḍhasya rāg'|ôpahata|cetasaḥ
dur|nītaṃ vā su|nītaṃ vā. tan mam' ācakṣva Saṃjaya.

SAṂJAYA uvāca:

86.1 HANTA TE sampravakṣyāmi sarvaṃ pratyakṣa|darśivān.
śuśrūṣasva sthiro bhūtvā, tava hy apanayo mahān.
gat'|ôdake setu|bandho yādṛk tādṛg ayaṃ tava
vilāpo niṣ|phalo rājan. mā śuco Bharata'|rṣabha.
an|atikramaṇīyo 'yaṃ kṛtāntasy' âdbhuto vidhiḥ.
mā śuco, Bharata|śreṣṭha. diṣṭam etat purātanam.
yadi tvaṃ hi purā dyūtāt Kuntī|putraṃ Yudhiṣṭhiram
nivartayethāḥ putrāṃś ca na tvāṃ vyasanam āvrajet.
86.5 yuddha|kāle punaḥ prāpte tad" âiva bhavatā yadi
nivartitāḥ syuḥ saṃrabdhā na tvāṃ vyasanam āvrajet.
Duryodhanaṃ c' â|vidheyaṃ badhnīt' êti purā yadi
Kurūn acodayiṣyas tvaṃ na tvāṃ vyasanam āvrajet.
na te buddhi|vyabhīcāram upalapsyanti Pāṇḍavāḥ
Pāñcālā Vṛṣṇayaḥ sarve ye c' ânye 'pi nar'|âdhipāḥ.
sa kṛtvā pitṛ|karma tvaṃ putraṃ saṃsthāpya sat|pathe
vartethā yadi dharmeṇa na tvāṃ vyasanam āvrajet.

could have been no way for my men to survive it. O Sánjaya 85.50
what did Duryódhana, what did Karna and Duhshásana and Sáubala tell the rest of my children to do in the face of such calamity? All the stupidities of my foolish children had their origin in Duryódhana's rage, in his ill judgment and troubled soul. After all the rash and foolish mistakes his avarice and his wild twisted misguided lust for power had wrung from him could Duryódhana find some sense in the fevered obsessions that had beset him? Or did it all end in disaster? Tell me Sánjaya.

SÁNJAYA spoke:

I WILL TELL you the whole of what I saw. Listen now if 86.1
you can to the story of your downfall.

O majesty your lamentations are as pointless as a bridge across a dry gully and for this reason o bull of the Bharatas I say to you do not beweep your fate. When a thing is done it has passed beyond us and it will not be revoked. O best of the Bharatas do not bewail what was ordained long ago. If in a time now gone you had forbidden the dice game your sons played against Kunti's heir then this calamity would not
have come to pass. O majesty even if on the very eve of war 86.5
you had doused their passions this calamity would not have come to pass. If in a time now gone you had restrained your lawless son and leashed the Kurus then this calamity would not have come to pass. The Pándavas will not forgive your lapses of judgment nor will the Panchálas nor the Vrishnis nor any of the regents who fight beside them. If you had been true to your forefathers and had set your son on the right path and if you had not erred from it yourself this

tvaṃ tu prājñatamo loke hitvā dharmaṃ sanātanam
Duryodhanasya Karṇasya Śakuneś c' ânvagā matam.
86.10 tat te vilapitaṃ sarvaṃ mayā rājan niśāmitam
arthe niviśamānasya viṣa|miśraṃ yathā madhu.
n' âmanyata tadā Kṛṣṇo
rājānaṃ Pāṇḍavaṃ purā
na Bhīṣmaṃ n' âiva ca Droṇaṃ
yathā tvāṃ manyate 'cyutaḥ.
ajānat sa yadā tu tvāṃ rāja|dharmād adhaś cyutam
tadā prabhṛti Kṛṣṇas tvāṃ na tathā bahu manyate.
paruṣāṇy ucyamānāṃś ca yathā Pārthān upekṣase
tasy' ânubandhaḥ prāptas tvāṃ putrāṇāṃ rājya|kāmukam.
pitṛ|paitāmahaṃ rājyam apavṛttaṃ tad" ân|agha
atha Pārthair jitāṃ kṛtsnāṃ pṛthivīṃ pratyapadyathāḥ.
86.15 Pāṇḍunā nirjitaṃ rājyaṃ Kauravāṇāṃ yaśas tathā
tataś c' âpy adhikaṃ bhūyaḥ Pāṇḍavair dharma|cāribhiḥ.
teṣāṃ tat tādṛśaṃ karma tvām āsādya su|niṣphalam
yat pitryād bhraṃśitā rājyāt tvay" êh' āmiṣa|gṛddhinā.
yat punar yuddha|kāle tvaṃ putrān garhayase nṛ|pa
bahudhā vyāharan doṣān, na tad ady' ôpapadyate.
na hi rakṣanti rājāno yudhyanto jīvitaṃ raṇe
camūṃ vigāhya Pārthānāṃ yudhyante kṣatriya'|rṣabhāḥ.
yāṃ tu Kṛṣṇ'|Ârjunau senāṃ yāṃ Sātyaki|Vṛkodarau
rakṣeran, ko nu tāṃ yudhyec camūm anyatra Kauravaiḥ?
86.20 yeṣāṃ yoddhā Guḍākeśo yeṣāṃ mantrī Janārdanaḥ
yeṣāṃ ca Sātyakir goptā yeṣāṃ goptā Vṛkodaraḥ,
ko hi tān viṣahed yoddhuṃ martya|dharmā dhanur|dharaḥ
anyatra Kauraveyebhyo ye vā teṣāṃ pad'|ânugāḥ?
yāvat tu śakyate kartum anta|raktair jan'|âdhipaiḥ

calamity would not have come to pass. Despite your deep wisdom you broke forever what binds the world and let Duryódhana and Karna and Shákuni pull it apart.

O king there is honey in your imprecations but I taste the 86.10
bitter tang of gall in them too. In times past Áchyuta did not hold Bhishma or Drona or even the Pándava king in the high regard in which he held you. But when Krishna saw how little you valued the honour of kings he knew you were not to be trusted. He realised that you set little store upon the Parthas' grievances because you wanted the kingdom for your children. O sinless one when you made that choice you ransomed your ancestral legacy and took from the Parthas
the broad earth that they had made their own. Even then 86.15
the virtue of Pandu's heir enriched the land and burnished the Kaurávyas' renown. Now that war is upon us again you blame your children for your own vainglory and for the evils you visited upon the Pándavas yourself because in your greed you could not bear to let your father's kingdom go.

I tell you o majesty that to prate of your sorrows is not enough. It will not save the lives of the warrior bulls who fight deep in the Pándava horde. Would any but the sons of Kuru even consider meeting an army when Krishna and Árjuna, Sátyaki and Dogbelly are its protectors? Guda·kesha is 86.20
their champion and Janárdana their vizier and at one flank rides Dogbelly and at the other Sátyaki. What creature of mortal stock would take a bow and try to stop them, except the Káuravas and their kind? Indeed there stand leaders of men among the sons of Kuru so besotted with death or devoted to the warrior's calling that they were brave enough to try. Listen now and I will take you to the very thick of the

kṣatra|dharma|rataiḥ śūrais tāvat kurvanti Kauravāḥ.
yathā tu puruṣa|vyāghrair yuddhaṃ parama|saṃkaṭam
Kurūṇāṃ Pāṇḍavaiḥ sārdhaṃ tat sarvaṃ śṛṇu tattvataḥ.

SAMJAYA uvāca:

87.1 TASYĀṂ NIŚĀYĀṂ vyuṣṭāyāṃ
Droṇaḥ śastra|bhṛtāṃ varaḥ
svāny anīkāni sarvāṇi
prākrāmad vyūhituṃ tataḥ.
śūrāṇāṃ garjatāṃ rājan saṃkruddhānām a|marṣiṇām
śrūyante sma giraś citrāḥ paras|para|vadh'|âiṣiṇām.
visphārya ca dhanūṃṣy anye jyāḥ pare parimṛjya ca
viniḥśvasantaḥ prākrośan «kv' êdānīṃ sa Dhanaṃjayaḥ?»
vi|kośān su|tsarūn anye kṛta|dhārān samāhitān
pītān ākāśa|saṃkāśān asīn ke cic ca cikṣipuḥ.
87.5 carantas tv asi|mārgāṃś ca dhanur|mārgāṃś ca śikṣayā
saṃgrāma|manasaḥ śūrā dṛśyante sma sahasraśaḥ.
sa|ghaṇṭāś candan'|ādigdhāḥ svarṇa|vajra|vibhūṣitāḥ
samutkṣipya gadāś c' ânye paryapṛcchanta Pāṇḍavam.
anye bala|mad'|ônmattāḥ parighair bāhu|śālinaḥ
cakruḥ sambādham ākāśam ucchrit'|êndra|dhvaj'|ôpamaiḥ.
nānā|praharaṇaiś c' ânye vicitra|srag|alaṃ|kṛtāḥ
saṃgrāma|manasaḥ śūrās tatra tatra vyavasthitāḥ.
«kv' Ârjunaḥ? kva sa Govindaḥ? kva ca mānī Vṛkodaraḥ?
kva ca te suhṛdas teṣām?» āhvayante raṇe tadā.
87.10 tataḥ śaṅkham upādhmāya tvarayan vājinaḥ svayam
itas tatas tān racayan Droṇaś carati vegitaḥ
teṣv anīkeṣu sarveṣu sthiteṣv āhava|nandiṣu
Bhāradvājo mahā|rāja Jayadratham ath' âbravīt.

fighting where the tigers of Kuru met the tigers of Pandu in war.

SÁNJAYA spoke:

As THE DARK of the night turned to day Drona best of 87.1
all who swing the sword came forth to muster his host. O
majesty the men were wild and impatient and eager to ride
out and their voices were loud in the dawn. They rubbed
down their bowstrings and flexed their bows. Where then
is Dhanan·jaya? they snorted. Swords with fine hilts and
sharp edges were drawn from sheaths and danced bright
in the shimmering air. Everywhere they seemed ready to 87.5
fight and their bows and blades cut perfect circles out of the
space around them. They had bathed in sandal and with
bells on their clothes and rings and torcs of diamonds and
gold on their arms they hefted maces and called aloud for
Pandu's son. They were wild with battlelust and the clubs
they swung with strength and skill filled the air as clouds fill
the sky to mark the storm god's coming. Dotted with gay
flora around their necks they fell into rank and hefted their
weapons and fixed on the battle before them. Where's Árjuna? And proud Dogbelly and the Herdsman? And where
are their friends? As Drona's soldiers called to their foes we 87.10
heard the blare of a horn and the crack of a whip and their
leader came darting through the host to range his men. In
their heated midst Bharad·vaja's son found Jayad·ratha and
o majesty these were the words that he said.

«tvaṃ c' âiva Saumadattiś ca Karṇaś c' âiva mahā|rathaḥ
Aśvatthāmā ca Śalyaś ca Vṛṣasenaḥ Kṛpas tathā
śataṃ c' âśva|sahasrāṇāṃ rathānām ayutāni ṣaṭ
dvi|radānāṃ prabhinnānāṃ sahasrāṇi catur|daśa
padātīnāṃ sahasrāṇi daṃśitāny eka|viṃśatiḥ
gavyūtiṣu tri|mātrāsu mām an|āsādya tiṣṭhata.
87.15 tatra|sthaṃ tvāṃ na saṃsoḍhuṃ śaktā devāḥ sa|Vāsavāḥ
kiṃ punaḥ Pāṇḍavāḥ sarve. samāśvasihi Saindhava.»
evam uktaḥ samāśvastaḥ Sindhu|rājo Jayadrathaḥ
samprāyāt saha Gāndhārair vṛtas taiś ca mahā|rathaiḥ
varmibhiḥ sādibhir yattaiḥ prāsa|pāṇibhir āsthitaiḥ.
cāmar'|āpīḍinaḥ sarve jāmbūnada|vibhūṣitāḥ
Jayadrathasya rāj'|êndra hayāḥ sādhu|pravāhinaḥ
te c' âiva sapta|sāhasrās tri|sāhasrāś ca Saindhavāḥ.
mattānām suvirūḍhānāṃ hasty|ārohair viśāradaiḥ
nāgānāṃ bhīma|rūpāṇāṃ varmiṇāṃ raudra|karmiṇām
adhyardhena sahasreṇa putro Durmarṣaṇas tava
agrataḥ sarva|sainyānāṃ yodhyamāno vyavasthitaḥ.
87.20 tato Duḥśāsanaś c' âiva Vikarṇaś ca tav' ātma|jau
Sindhu|rāj'|ârtha|siddhy|artham agr'|ānīke vyavasthitau.
dīrgho dvā|daśa gav|yūtiḥ paśc'|ârdhe pañca vistṛtaḥ
vyūhas tu cakra|śakaṭo Bhāradvājena nirmitaḥ.
nānā|nṛ|patibhir vīrais tatra tatra vyavasthitaiḥ
rath'|âśva|gaja|patty|oghair Droṇena vihitaḥ svayam.
paśc'|ârdhe tasya padmasya garbha|vyūhaḥ su|durbhidaḥ

"Keep clear of me. Take Saumadátti and mighty Karna and Ashvattháman, Shalya, Vrisha·sena and Kripa, and take a hundred companies of horsemen and six legions of cars and fourteen thousand elephants wild with the season and twentyone thousand fighters all clad in mail and withdraw with them three leagues hence. Sáindhava take heart. Even 87.15
Indra and his gods could not reach you there so how much less the sons of Pandu?"

Jayad·ratha king of the Sindhus took heart at Drona's words and he wheeled away among the great chariots of Gandhára and the spearbearers belted and ready that rode upon them. Now a full seven thousand Gandhára horsemen had joined the three thousand from Sindhu and o majesty at their very centre behind quickdrawing steeds that wore chaplets and chowries and caparisons of rivergold rode King Jayad·ratha. At the head of the armies ranged for the fray was your own son Durmárshana and at his back an elephant herd numbering one thousand and one half more and each of those beasts was wellgroomed and clad in armour and mighty of figure and wild and violent and bridled by a skilled rider. Alongside Durmárshana went his 87.20
brothers Duhshásana and Vikárna. The three of them rode at the very van with weapons drawn, steeled to protect the Sindhu king.

Drona son of Bharad·vaja had laid out his troops in the shape of an arum lily* twelve leagues deep and five leagues wide and he had shaped it so that the army's mightiest were stationed all throughout its long lines of cars horses elephants and men. The bulb at the lily's base was hardest to

sūcī|padmasya madhya|stho gūḍho vyūhaḥ kṛtaḥ punaḥ.
evam etaṃ mahā|vyūhaṃ vyūhya Droṇo vyavasthitaḥ.
sūcī|mukhe mah"|êṣv|āsaḥ Kṛtavarmā vyavasthitaḥ.
87.25 an|antaraṃ ca Kāmbojo Jalasaṃdhaś ca māriṣa
Duryodhanaś ca Karṇaś ca tad|anantaram eva ca.
tataḥ śata|sahasrāṇi yodhānām a|nivartinām
vyavasthitāni sarvāṇi śakaṭe mukha|rakṣiṇām.
teṣāṃ ca pṛṣṭhato rājā balena mahatā vṛtaḥ
Jayadrathas tato, rājan, sūcī|pārśve vyavasthitaḥ.
śakaṭasya tu rāj'|êndra Bhāradvājo mukhe sthitaḥ.
anu tasy' âbhavad Bhojo, jugop' âinaṃ tataḥ svayam.
śveta|varm'|âmbar'|ôṣṇīṣo vyūḍh'|ôrasko mahā|bhujaḥ
dhanur visphārayan Droṇas tasthau kruddha iv' ântakaḥ.
87.30 patākinaṃ śoṇa|hayaṃ vedī|kṛṣṇ'|âjina|dhvajam
Droṇasya ratham ālokya prahṛṣṭāḥ Kuravo 'bhavan.
siddha|cāraṇa|saṃghānāṃ vismayaḥ su|mahān abhūt
Droṇena vihitaṃ dṛṣṭvā vyūhaṃ kṣubdh'|ârṇav'|ôpamam.
sa|śaila|sāgara|vanāṃ nānā|jana|pad'|ākulām
grased vyūhaḥ kṣitiṃ sarvām iti bhūtāni menire.

bahu|ratha|manuj'|âśva|patti|nāgaṃ
pratibhaya|niḥsvanam adbhut'|ânurūpam
a|hita|hṛdaya|bhedanaṃ mahad vai
śakaṭam avekṣya kṛtaṃ nananda rājā.

breach and there in the spadix a secret cohort was hidden away.

With his array complete Drona went to take up his own position. Hefting his bow at the spadix's tip stood Krita·varman and o father shoulder to shoulder with him were 87.25
Jala·sandha of Kambója and Karna and Duryódhana. In all there were one hundred thousand brave soldiers protecting the edge of the spathe and o majesty behind that great ring at the base of the flower's needle stood their ward King Jayad·ratha. Placed at the tip of the spathe with Bhoja watching his back was Bharad·vaja's son. White was the armour about his broad shoulders and white his robes and white the turban he wore on his head, and as his bow thrummed in his mighty grip he seemed none but Death come to bear us all away. To see his red horses and the sign 87.30
of the black antelope and pedestal atop his car filled Kuru hearts with wild joy. The saints and holy ones of heaven looked down upon Drona's array rippling like the sea and they too were amazed. They thought his army might devour the whole of the stony earth, all of its seas and all of its trees and all of the tribes that make their home upon it.

Upon cars, kings, men, beasts and horses,
In tumult and dazzling splendour,
Upon the blade that would pierce his haters' hearts,
The king's gaze fell, and he was pleased.

SAMJAYA uvāca:

88.1 TATO VYŪḌHEṢV anīkeṣu samutkṛṣṭeṣu, māriṣa,
tāḍyamānāsu bherīṣu mṛdaṅgeṣu nadatsu ca
anīkānāṃ ca saṃhrāde vāditrāṇāṃ ca niḥsvane
pradhmāpiteṣu śaṅkheṣu saṃnāde loma|harṣaṇe
abhihārayatsu śanakair Bharateṣu yuyutsuṣu
raudre muhūrte samprāpte Savyasācī vyadṛśyata.
balānāṃ vāyasānāṃ ca purastāt Savyasācinaḥ
bahulāni sahasrāṇi prākrīḍaṃs tatra, Bhārata.
88.5 mṛgāś ca ghora|saṃnādāḥ śivāś c' âśiva|darśanāḥ
dakṣiṇena prayātānām asmākaṃ prāṇadaṃs tathā.
sa|nirghātā jvalantyaś ca petur ulkāḥ sahasraśaḥ
cacāla ca mahī kṛtsnā bhaye ghore samutthite.
viṣvag vātāḥ sa|nirghātā rūkṣāḥ śarkara|karṣiṇaḥ
vavur āyāti Kaunteye saṃgrāme samupasthite.
Nākulis ca Śatānīko Dhṛṣṭadyumnaś ca Pārṣataḥ
Pāṇḍavānām anīkāni prājñau tau vyūhatus tadā.
tato ratha|sahasreṇa dvi|radānāṃ śatena ca
tribhir aśva|sahasraiś ca padātīnāṃ śataiḥ śataiḥ
88.10 adhyardha|mātre dhanuṣāṃ sahasre tanayas tava
agrataḥ sarva|sainyānāṃ sthitvā Durmarṣaṇo 'bravīt.
«adya Gāṇḍīva|dhanvānaṃ
tapantaṃ yuddha|dur|madam
aham āvārayiṣyāmi
vel" êva makar'|ālayam.
adya paśyantu saṃgrāme Dhanaṃjayam a|marṣaṇam
viṣaktam api durdharṣam aśma|kūṭam iv' âśmani.
tiṣṭhadhvaṃ rathino yūyaṃ saṃgrāmam abhikāṅkṣiṇaḥ.
yudhyāmi saṃhatān etān yaśo mānaṃ ca vardhayan.»

SÁNJAYA spoke:

O MAJESTY. As drumrolls and cymbalcrashes and clari- 88.1
oncalls and trumpetblasts rose in a ghastly crescendo above the closepacked Bharata lines full of men edging forward hungry for battle the Lefthanded Archer appeared before them, a vision sudden and doomsome. O Bhárata. Crows wheeled above his head and packs of jackals prowled before him and there were deer moaning strangely and bark- 88.5
ing hyenas that traced evil circles in the dust. We turned against their omens but terror welled within us.

The skies were lit up by a storm of burning and crackling stars and the earth shook beneath our feet and the four winds whipped up the grit of the plain in dry and scorching dustdevils. Kauntéya's host stood ready to attack as down through the Pándava ranks went Nákula's son Shataníka and Dhrishta·dyumna son of Pándava making final adjustments to their array. Meanwhile at the head of a hundred
elephants and a thousand chariots, fifteen hundred archers 88.10
and double that number of horses and hundreds upon hundreds of soldiers your own boy Durmárshana drew up his car and spoke.

"Though he burns berserk and carries Gandíva in his hands he will break upon me like the sea upon the shore. Behold the blow of Dhanan·jaya so deadly and proud crack like a hammer against a stone. Warriors hot for the fight stand your ground. I go now to hew glory and fame from the dense press before me."

evam bruvan mahā|rāja mah"|ātmā sa mahā|matiḥ
mah"|êṣv|āsair vṛto rājan mah"|êṣv|āso vyavasthitaḥ.
88.15 tato 'ntaka iva kruddhaḥ, sa|vajra iva Vāsavaḥ,
daṇḍa|pāṇir iv' â|sahyo mṛtyuḥ kālena coditaḥ,
śūla|pāṇir iv' â|kṣobhyo Varuṇaḥ pāśavān iva,
yug'|ânt'|âgnir iv' ârciṣmān pradhakṣyan vai punaḥ prajāḥ
krodh'|âmarṣa|bal'|ôddhūto Nivātakavac'|ântakaḥ
jayo jetā sthitaḥ satye pārayiṣyan mahā|vratam,
āmukta|kavacaḥ khaḍgī jāmbūnada|kirīṭa|bhṛt
śubhra|māly'|âmbara|dharaḥ sv|aṅgadaś cāru|kuṇḍalaḥ
ratha|pravaram āsthāya Naro Nārāyaṇ'|ânugaḥ
vidhunvan Gāṇḍivaṃ saṃkhye babhau sūrya iv' ôditaḥ.
88.20 so 'gr'|ânīkasya mahata iṣu|pāte Dhanaṃjayaḥ
vyavasthāpya rathaṃ, rājañ, śaṅkhaṃ dadhmau pratāpavān.
atha Kṛṣṇo 'py a|sambhrāntaḥ Pārthena saha, māriṣa,
prādhmāpayat Pāñcajanyaṃ śaṅkha|pravaram ojasā.
tayoḥ śaṅkha|praṇādena tava sainye viśāṃ pate
āsan saṃhṛṣṭa|romāṇaḥ kampitā gata|cetasaḥ.
yathā trasyanti bhūtāni sarvāṇy aśani|niḥsvanāt
tathā śaṅkha|praṇādena vitresus tava sainikāḥ,
prasusruvuḥ śakṛn|mūtraṃ vāhanāni ca sarvaśaḥ.
evaṃ sa|vāhanaṃ sarvam āvignam abhavad balam.
88.25 sīdanti sma narā rājañ śaṅkha|śabdena māriṣa
vi|saṃjñāś c' âbhavan ke cit ke cid rājan vitatrasuḥ.
tataḥ kapir mahā|nādaṃ saha bhūtair dhvaj'|ālayaiḥ
akarod vyādit'|âsyaś ca bhīṣayaṃs tava sainikān.

O majesty even in that grand company of great archers
your son's words were bold and brazen. But furious as the 88.15
Destroyer, like Indra holding his thunderbolt or like time's ministrant sceptred Death whom none can oppose, like Váruna rudely awoken and bearing his spear to his flock, like the great fire at the end of the age that burns us all away the destroyer of the Niváta·kávachas stood with Naráyana at his side in his supernal car, wild with might and rage and hate and soon to add to his towering store of triumphs the fulfillment of his mighty oath, and clad in pearled armour with his sword and diadem of gold and his bright robes and garlands and glittering torcs and rings and with Gandíva in his hand Nara shone then across the plain like the risen sun.

O king. In the broad path of arrows at the van of his 88.20
horde, Dhanan·jaya drew to a halt and blazed. O majesty, he blew into his great conch and as he did Krishna lifted Pancha·janya and with all his breath added its note to the sound.

O lord of men the drone from those two shells shook through the lines of your soldiers and their hair stood on end as a witless horror took hold of them. The sound was like the roll of thunder that brings fear to all mortal things and all about us the animals pissed and shat in terror and
a tremor passed through the whole of the host. My lord 88.25
every man felt his knees go weak and his thoughts dissolve as above the susurrus of the other spirits in the standards we heard a gruesome hoot from the monkey's muzzle.*

tataḥ śaṅkhāś ca bheryaś ca mṛdaṅgāś c' ānakaiḥ saha
punar ev' âbhyahanyanta tava sainya|praharṣaṇāḥ
nānā|vāditra|saṃhrādaiḥ kṣveḍit'|āsphoṭit'|ākulaiḥ
siṃha|nādaiḥ samutkṛṣṭaiḥ samāhūtair mahā|rathaiḥ.
tasmiṃs tu tumule śabde bhīrūṇāṃ bhaya|vardhane
atīva hṛṣṭo Dāśārham abravīt Pākaśāsaniḥ.

ARJUNA uvāca:

89.1 CODAY' ÂŚVĀN, Hṛṣīkeśa, yatra Durmarṣaṇaḥ sthitaḥ.
etad bhittvā gaj'|ânīkaṃ pravekṣyāmy ari|vāhinīm.

SAṂJAYA uvāca:

evam ukto mahā|bāhuḥ Keśavaḥ Savyasācinā
acodayadd hayāṃs tatra yatra Durmarṣaṇaḥ sthitaḥ.
sa samprahāras tumulaḥ sampravṛttaḥ su|dāruṇaḥ
ekasya ca bahūnāṃ ca ratha|nāga|nara|kṣayaḥ.
tataḥ sāyaka|varṣeṇa parjanya iva vṛṣṭimān,
parān avākirat Pārthaḥ parvatān iva nīradaḥ.
89.5 te c' âpi rathinaḥ sarve tvaritāḥ kṛta|hastavat
avākiran bāṇa|jālais tataḥ Kṛṣṇa|Dhanaṃjayau.
tataḥ kruddho mahā|bāhur vāryamāṇaḥ parair yudhi
śirāṃsi rathināṃ Pārthaḥ kāyebhyo 'pāharac charaiḥ.
udbhrānta|nayanair vaktraiḥ
saṃdaṣṭ'|âuṣṭha|puṭaiḥ śubhaiḥ
sa|kuṇḍala|śiras|trāṇair
vasudhā samakīryata.
puṇḍarīka|vanān' îva vidhvastāni samantataḥ
vinikīrṇāni yodhānāṃ vadanāni cakāśire.
tapanīya|tanu|trāṇāḥ saṃsiktā rudhireṇa ca
saṃsaktā iva iṣyante megha|saṃghāḥ sa|vidyutaḥ.

Nonetheless your men were mighty warriors and to fire their blood they blew trumpets and hit drums and gongs and chimes and struck up their own orchestra of war in a chorus of battlecries and handclaps and roars. As our answer deathly and drear rung in his ears the Guardian's Son turned to Dashárha. When he spoke there was glee in his voice.

ÁRJUNA spoke:

DRIVE THE HORSES for Durmárshana, Hrishi·kesha. I 89.1
will break into their host through his elephant line.

SÁNJAYA spoke:

As soon as the Lefthanded Archer had spoken Késhava
tugged hard on the reins and drove their steeds for Durmárshana. Between that lone chariot and our assembled host
a battle ghast and wild began and it would be the last for
many a car, beast and man. Arrows were in Partha like water. He pelted his foes like a mountain storm. With skill and 89.5
speed our warriors wove a net of darts across the heads of
Krishna and Dhanan·jaya but even as they parried him they
merely fueled his wrath and the next volley from Partha's
bow took their heads from their necks.

Suddenly the earth was full of skulls still wearing helms
on their crowns and rings in their ears, eyes rolling in their
sockets or eyelids and lips screwed shut. He lopped off heads
like lotus flowers and strewed them all about. It was as if the
heavens had stirred and opened and dropped them upon
the ground all awelter in blood and still cheekpieced in
heated gold. Men fell with the thud of palmyras grown too 89.10
old to stand. Here lay a trunk and an arm that yet held

89.10 śirasāṃ patatāṃ rājañ śabdo 'bhūd vasudhā|tale
kālena paripakvānāṃ tālānāṃ patatām iva.
tataḥ kabandhaṃ kiṃ cit tu dhanur ālambya tiṣṭhati
kiṃ cit khaḍgaṃ viniṣkṛṣya bhujen' ôdyamya tiṣṭhati.
patitāni na jānanti śirāṃsi puruṣa'|ṛṣabhāḥ
a|mṛṣyamāṇāḥ saṃgrāme Kaunteyaṃ jaya|gṛddhinaḥ.
hayānām uttam'|âṅgaiś ca hasti|hastaiś ca medinī
bāhubhiś ca śirobhiś ca vīrāṇāṃ samakīryata.

ayaṃ Pārthaḥ kutaḥ Pārtha eṣa Pārtha iti prabho
tava sainyeṣu yodhānāṃ Pārtha|bhūtam iv' âbhavat.
89.15 anyo|'nyam api c' âjaghnur ātmānam api c' âpare
Pārtha|bhūtam amanyanta jagat kālena mohitāḥ.
niṣṭanantaḥ sa|rudhirā vi|saṃjñā gāḍha|vedanāḥ
śayānā bahavo vīrāḥ kīrtayantaḥ sva|bāndhavān.
sa|bhindipālāḥ sa|prāsāḥ sa|śakty|ṛṣṭi|paraśvadhāḥ
sa|nirvyūhāḥ sa|nistriṃśāḥ sa|śar'|âsana|tomarāḥ
sa|bāṇa|varm'|ābharaṇāḥ sa|gadāḥ s'|âṅgadā raṇe
mahā|bhujaga|saṃkāśā bāhavaḥ parigh'|ôpamāḥ
udveṣṭanti viceṣṭanti saṃveṣṭanti ca sarvaśaḥ,
vegaṃ kurvanti saṃrabdhā nikṛttāḥ param'|êṣubhiḥ
89.20 yo yaḥ sma samare Pārthaṃ pratisaṃrabhate naraḥ,
tasya tasy' ântako bāṇaḥ śarīram upasarpati.

nṛtyato ratha|mārgeṣu dhanur vyāyacchatas tathā
na kaś cit tatra Pārthasya dadṛśe 'ntaram aṇv api.
yattasya ghaṭamānasya kṣipraṃ vikṣipataḥ śarān
lāghavāt Pāṇḍu|putrasya vyasmayanta pare janāḥ.
hastinaṃ hasti|yantāram aśvam āśvikam eva ca
abhinat Phalguno bāṇai rathinaṃ ca sa|sārathim.
āvartamānam āvṛttaṃ yudhyamānaṃ ca Pāṇḍavaḥ
pramukhe tiṣṭhamānaṃ ca na kiṃ cin na nihanti saḥ.

a bow, there a sword a hand had drawn and raised high. Yet the warrior bulls that still lived were so keen to fight Kaun-téya they barely noticed as their brothers' severed heads fell about them and joined the huge piles of horses and trunks of elephants that already lay caked in dust.

Here was Partha and there was Partha and then he was gone. O king they called aloud while Pritha's son like a
thing ethereal went racing among them. They blundered 89.15
and swung as Partha's ghost went past and struck one other and struck themselves. Time had tipped up their minds. Roaring and bloodsoaked and raving and bellowing man upon man went to ground. Each called out for a friend to save him. Slings and spears, pikes, lances and flails, swords and the crests of helmets, arrows and darts and javelins and fletchings and greaves and chains and torcs were held in the lifeless fingers of severed hands or tangled with severed arms that writhed on the ground like snakes. All about men shuddered and twisted and stumbled and jerked in spasms
as those fine shafts went through them. Any that did get 89.20
close enough to Pritha's son felt the bite of an arrow come to bear his life away.

Partha danced in a blur where the cars were and we could not comprehend how quickly his fingers fended as they plucked the strings of his raised bow. Elephant from driver, horse from rider, car from carwarrior the Red Star Fighter sundered with his shafts. Whether it flew or turned or thought to stand its ground Pándava stove it in two.
The sun rising into the sky drives away the dark of night 89.25
and thus radiant with feathered arrows Árjuna drove back the elephant line. Its beasts lay broken among us like the

89.25 yath" ôdayan vai gagane sūryo hanti mahat tamaḥ
tath" Ârjuno gaj'|ânīkam avadhīt kaṅka|patribhiḥ.
hastibhiḥ patitair bhinnais tava sainyam adṛśyata
anta|kāle yathā bhūmir vyavakīrṇā mahī|dharaiḥ.
yathā madhyaṃ|dine sūryo duṣ|prekṣyaḥ prāṇibhiḥ sadā
tathā Dhanaṃjayaḥ kruddho duṣ|prekṣyo yudhi śatrubhiḥ.
tat tathā tava putrasya sainyaṃ yudhi, paraṃ|tapa,
prabhagnaṃ drutam āvignam atīva śarapīḍitam.
Māruten' eva mahatā megh'|ânīkaṃ vyadīryatā
prakālyamānaṃ tat sainyaṃ n' âśakat prativīkṣitum.
89.30 pratodaiś cāpa|koṭībhir huṃ|kāraiḥ sādhu|vāhitaiḥ
kaśā|pārṣṇy|abhighātaiś ca vāgbhir ugrābhir eva ca
codayanto hayāṃs tūrṇaṃ palāyante sma tāvakāḥ
sādino rathinaś c' âiva pattayaś c' Ârjun'|ârditāḥ.
pārṣṇy|aṅguṣṭh'|âṅkuśair nāgāṃś codayantas tathā pare,
śaraiḥ sammohitāś c' ânye tam ev' âbhimukhā yayau
tava yodhā hat'|ôtsāhā vibhrānta|manasas tadā.

DHṚTARĀṢṬRA uvāca:

90.1 TASMIN PRABHAGNE sainy' âgre vadhyamāne Kirīṭinā
ke tu tatra raṇe vīrāḥ pratyudīyur Dhanaṃjayam?
āho svic chakaṭa|vyūhaṃ praviṣṭā mogha|niścayāḥ
Droṇam āśritya tiṣṭhantaṃ prākāram akutobhayam?

SAṂJAYA uvāca:

tath' Ârjunena sambhagne tasmiṃs tava bale, 'n|agha,
hata|vīre hat'|ôtsāhe palāyana|kṛta|kṣaṇe
Pāka|śāsanin" âbhīkṣṇaṃ vadhyamāne śar'|ôttamaiḥ
na tatra kaś cit saṃgrāme śaśāk' Ârjunam īkṣitum.
90.5 tatas tava suto, rājan, dṛṣṭvā sainyaṃ tathā|gatam
Duḥśāsano bhṛśaṃ kruddho yuddhāy' Ârjunam abhyagāt.
sa kāñcana|vicitreṇa kavacena samāvṛtaḥ

canted panorama of the world at its end. And just as from the meridian sun we turn our eyes so did Dhanan·jaya's foes avert their gaze from the full light of his fury.

O burner of foes, his arrows had crushed torn beaten and ruined a legion of your son's men, and like cumulus shredded by the great god of the wind his damaged line
had lost its shape. With whips and bowlimbs and gees and 89.30
curses and the gouge of spur and goad riders and drivers and soldiers all forced the horses back to make good their escape. With hooks heels and thumbs the elephantriders drove their steeds on while others now fond from the arrows that fell around them found themselves somehow advancing again to meet their foe, their sanity like their strength all gone.

DHRITA·RASHTRA spoke:

SO THE LINE failed before the Crowned Warrior. Did any 90.1
of our fighters rise again against Dhanan·jaya? Or did they all retreat in despair back through the array to where Drona their defender still held his head up high?

SÁNJAYA spoke:

O pure one. When your frontline lay shattered and spent, its men dead and defences down still the arrows flew from Árjuna's bow and through their haze no pitiful soul could even discern the vague shape of the Guardian's Son. All anyone could see was ruin.

Duhshásana looked around him and he was seized by 90.5
fury at what he saw. O majesty your bold son was zoned in whitehot courage and his armour sparkled gold and gold

jāmbūnada|śiras|trāṇaḥ śūras tīvra|parākramaḥ
nāg'|ânīkena mahatā grasann iva mahīm imām
Duḥśāsano mahā|rāja Savyasācinam āvṛṇot.
hrādena gaja|ghaṇṭānāṃ śaṅkhānāṃ ninadena ca
jy"|ākṣepa|ninadaiś c' âiva virāveṇa ca dantinām
bhūr diśaś c' ântarikṣaṃ ca śabden' āsīt samāvṛtam.
sa muhūrtaṃ pratibhayo dāruṇaḥ samapadyata.
90.10 tān dṛṣṭvā patatas tūrṇam aṅkuśair abhicoditān
vyālamba|hastān saṃrabdhān sa|pakṣān iva parvatān
siṃha|nādena mahatā nara|siṃho Dhanaṃjayaḥ
gaj'|ânīkam a|mitrāṇām abhito vyadhamac charaiḥ.
mah"|ōrmiṇam iv' ôddhūtaṃ śvasanena mah"|ârṇavam
Kirīṭī tad gaj'|ānīkaṃ prāviśan makaro yathā.
kāṣṭh'|âtīta iv' âdityaḥ pratapan sa yuga|kṣaye
dadṛśe dikṣu sarvāsu Pārthaḥ para|puraṃ|jayaḥ.
khura|śabdena c' âśvānāṃ nemi|ghoṣeṇa tena ca
tena c' ôtkruṣṭa|śabdena jyā|ninādena tena ca
90.15 nānā|vāditra|śabdena Pāñcajanya|svanena ca
Devadattasya ghoṣeṇa Gāṇḍīva|ninadena ca
manda|vegā narā nāgā babhūvus te vi|cetasaḥ
śarair āśīviṣa|sparśair nirbhinnāḥ Savyasācinā.
te gajā vi|śikhais tīkṣṇair yudhi Gāṇḍīva|coditaiḥ
an|eka|śata|sāhasraiḥ sarv'|âṅgeṣu samarpitāḥ
ārāvaṃ paramaṃ kṛtvā vadhyamānāḥ Kirīṭinā
nipetur a|niśaṃ bhūmau chinna|pakṣā iv' âdrayaḥ.
apare danta|veṣṭeṣu kumbheṣu ca kaṭeṣu ca
śaraiḥ samarpitā nāgāḥ krauñcavad vyanadan muhuḥ.
90.20 gaja|skandha|gatānāṃ ca puruṣāṇāṃ Kirīṭinā
chidyante c' ôttam'|âṅgāni bhallaiḥ saṃnata|parvabhiḥ.
sa|kuṇḍalānāṃ patatāṃ śirasāṃ dharaṇī|tale

was the helm upon his head, and as if swallowing up the ground he swept his great phalanx of elephants across the face of the plain towards Savya·sachin. The din of jangling and horns and the buzz of bowstrings and the clack of tusks rose to fill the earth air and sky in a gyre of awesome sound.

Driven to a gallop by their drivers with their heads down 90.10
and their blood up Duhshásana's elephants tore across the battlefield like the winged mountains of old. But a lion stood waiting and watching. With a lion's roar Dhanan·jaya sent up his arrows as his foes came nearer and like a fish leaping into a foaming sea lashed by the wind he disappeared as the elephant line swept over him. And once again all around us and unencompassed we saw Partha destroyer of cities rise like a doomsday sun. Cutting across the clop of horsehooves and keen of chariotwheels and bowt-
wangs and hollers and thump of drums came the drones of 90.15
Deva·datta and Pancha·janya and Gandíva's endless whisper. Men lost their courage and elephants bolted as the Left-handed Archer's venomhot darts began once again to bite.

There were hundreds then thousands of them flying sharp and deadly from Gandíva's string and they sunk deep into the hides of our steeds. Elephants bellowed beneath Kirítin's blows or screeched like birds and toppled one after another to earth like the mountaingods when their wings were clipped, shafts piercing their temples and skulls and even
the gums between their teeth. The strong men who rode 90.20
upon their shoulders Kirítin cut through with heavy and knotless arrows and like an offering of lotuses cast their heads still beringed in clusters to earth. Men covered in blood and wounds and with their armour gone and the

padmānām iva saṃghātaiḥ Pārthaś cakre nivedanam.
yantra|baddhā vi|kavacā vraṇ'|ārtā rudhir'|ôkṣitāḥ
bhramatsu yudhi nāgeṣu manuṣyā vilalambire.
ke cid ekena bāṇena su|muktena su|patriṇā
dvau trayaś ca vinirbhinnā nipetur dharaṇī|tale.
atividdhāś ca nārācair vamanto rudhiraṃ mukhaiḥ
s'|ārohā nyapatan bhūmau drumavanta iv' â|calāḥ.
90.25 maurvīṃ dhvajaṃ dhanuś c' âiva yugām īṣāṃ tath" âiva ca
rathināṃ kuṭṭayām āsa bhallaiḥ saṃnata|parvabhiḥ.
na saṃdadhan na c' ākarṣan na vimuñcan na c' ôdvahan
maṇḍalen' âiva dhanuṣā nṛtyan Pārthaḥ sma dṛśyate.
atividdhāś ca nārācair vamanto rudhiraṃ mukhaiḥ
muhūrtān nyapatann anye vāraṇā vasudhā|tale.
utthitāny a|gaṇeyāni kabandhāni samantataḥ
adṛśyanta mahā|rāja tasmin parama|saṃkule.
sa|cāpāḥ s'|âṅguli|trāṇāḥ sa|khaḍgāḥ s'|âṅgadā raṇe
adṛśyanta bhujāś chinnā hem'|ābharaṇa|bhūṣitāḥ.
90.30 s'|ûpaskarair adhiṣṭhānair īṣā|daṇḍaka|bandhuraiḥ
cakrair vimathitair akṣair bhagnaiś ca bahudhā yugaiḥ
carma|cāpa|dharaiś c' âiva vyavakīrṇais tatas tataḥ
sragbhir ābharaṇair vastraiḥ patitaiś ca mahā|dhvajaiḥ
nihatair vāraṇair aśvaiḥ kṣatriyaiś ca nipātitaiḥ
adṛśyata mahī tatra dāruṇa|pratidarśanā.
evaṃ Duḥśāsana|balaṃ vadhyamānaṃ Kirīṭinā
samprādravan mahā|rāja vyathitaṃ saha|nāyakam.
tato Duḥśāsanas trastaḥ sah'|ânīkaḥ śar'|ârditaḥ
Droṇaṃ trātāram ākāṅkṣañ śakaṭa|vyūham abhyagāt.

reins fallen from lifeless hands hung in the stirrups as their halfdead steeds wandered away across the plain. A single arrow from Árjuna's skilled hands would send two or three of them crashing dead to the earth, and down they came vomiting blood and they came to rest on the ground covered in shafts like hills covered in trees. His whittled darts 90.25
broke the axles and yokes, the poles and the chariots and broke the bows men held and cut through their bowstrings as Partha danced on with a hoop in his hand. So fast was he that we did not see him notch, draw, loose or even reach for another shaft.

O majesty down to the earth they came again with blood pouring from their mouths and after this second bout of slaughter the carcasses could no more be counted. There were pieces of arms still clasped in torcs and ornaments of gold and hands yet holding bows and swords with bow-plectrums on their thumbs. How many carved planks were 90.30
pulled from the cars, how many were the crossshafts and poles and wings and buckled wheels and snapped axles and yokes, shields and bows and garlands and neckchains and bits of clothes and flags torn in great strips and dead elephants and dead horses and fallen fighters. How grim a horror to behold.

O majesty so it was that beaten down and blasted by the Crowned Warrior and his arrows Duhshásana's legion withered away and with it went their commander, harrowed back with the tatters of his force to seek safety in the rear of Drona's arum array.

SAMJAYA uvāca:

91.1 DUḤŚĀSANA|BALAṂ hatvā Savyasācī mahā|rathaḥ
Sindhu|rājaṃ parīpsan vai Droṇ'|ânīkam upādravat.
sa tu Droṇaṃ samāsādya vyūhasya pramukhe sthitam
kṛt'|âñjalir idaṃ vākyaṃ Kṛṣṇasy' ânumate 'bravīt.
«śivena dhyāhi māṃ, brahman, svasti c' âiva vadasva me.
bhavat|prasādād icchāmi praveṣṭuṃ dur|bhidāṃ camūm.
bhavān pitṛ|samo mahyaṃ dharma|rāja|samo 'pi ca
tathā Kṛṣṇa|samaś c' âiva. satyam etad bravīmi te.
91.5 Aśvatthāmā yathā tāta rakṣaṇīyas tvay" ânagha,
tath" âham api te rakṣyaḥ sad" âiva dvija|sattama.
tava prasādād iccheyaṃ Sindhu|rājānam āhave
nihantuṃ dvipadāṃ śreṣṭha pratijñāṃ rakṣa me vibho.»

SAMJAYA uvāca:

evam uktas tad" Ācāryaḥ pratyuvāca smayann iva.
«mām a|jitvā na, Bībhatso, śakyo jetuṃ Jayadrathaḥ.»
etāvad uktvā taṃ Droṇaḥ śara|vrātair avākirat
sa|rath'|âśva|dhvajaṃ tīkṣṇaiḥ prahasan vai sa|sārathim.
tato 'rjunaḥ śara|vrātān Droṇasy' āvārya sāyakaiḥ
Droṇam abhyadravad bāṇair ghora|rūpair mahattaraiḥ.
91.10 vivyādha ca raṇe Droṇam anumānya, viśāṃ pate,
kṣatra|dharmaṃ samāsthāya navabhiḥ sāyakaiḥ punaḥ.
tasy' êṣūn iṣubhiś chittvā Droṇo vivyādha tāv ubhau
viṣ'|âgni|jvalita|prakhyair iṣubhiḥ Kṛṣṇa|Pāṇḍavau.
iyeṣa Pāṇḍavas tasya bāṇaiś chettuṃ śar'|âsanam.
tasya cintayatas tv evaṃ Phālgunasya mah"|ātmanaḥ
Droṇaḥ śarair a|sambhrānto jyāṃ cicched' âśu vīryavān,

SÁNJAYA spoke:

WITH DUHSHÁSANA'sforce in ruins behind him the Left-handed Archer came in his great car to seek out the Sindhu king all the way up to Drona's own line. He drew to a halt before Drona's company and with a glance at Krishna raised his hands in respect and spoke to the brahmin. 91.1

"O holy one. In thought and word may you treat me kindly. I ask leave to step across your sturdy line. Your honour, my word is as good as the word of my father or of my brother or of Krishna. You have no peer among the twice- 91.5
born and no sin to blemish you and o father I entreat you to look upon me as you look upon Ashvattháman your son. With your leave o best of men I will put the Sindhu king to death. Master. Help me keep my word."

SÁNJAYA spoke:

The Teacher smiled a little when he answered.

"Jayad·ratha will not be yours Bibhátsu, unless you take him from me."

Drona's words trailed into laughter and onto Árjuna's steeds standard car and driver he scattered a cruel arrow rain. With his own darts Árjuna cut through it and then sent at Drona a volley deadlier still. O majesty, he called 91.10
to Drona to forgive his trespass for cleaving to the warrior code and then another nine arrows flew from his bow. Shaft for shaft Drona cut them from the air and with darts hot as venom or fire he struck at Krishna and Pándava. Árjuna tried desperately to break Drona's bow but even as the thought came into his mind his mighty opponent cut through Gandíva's string then covered the great Phálguna's

vivyādha ca hayān asya dhvajaṃ sārathim eva ca
Arjunaṃ ca śarair vīraḥ smayamāno 'bhyavākirat.
etasminn antare Pārthaḥ sa|jyaṃ kṛtvā mahad dhanuḥ
viśeṣayiṣyann Acāryaṃ sarv'|âstra|viduṣāṃ varaḥ
mumoca ṣaṭ|śatān bāṇān gṛhītv" âikam iva drutam.
91.15 punaḥ sapta|śatān anyān sahasraṃ c' â|nivartināṃ
cikṣep' âyutaśaś c' ânyāṃs. te 'ghnan Droṇasya tāṃ camūm.
taiḥ saṃyag astair balinā kṛtinā citra|yodhinā
manuṣya|vāji|mātaṅgā viddhāḥ petur gat'|âsavaḥ.
vi|sūt'|âśva|dhvajāḥ petuḥ saṃchinn'|āyudha|jīvitāḥ
rathino ratha|mukhyebhyaḥ sahasā śara|pīḍitāḥ.
cūrṇit'|ākṣipta|dagdhānāṃ vajr'|ânila|hutāśanaiḥ
tulya|rūpā gajāḥ petur giry|agr'|âmbuda|veśmanām.
petur aśva|sahasrāṇi prahatāny Arjun'|êṣubhiḥ
haṃsā Himavataḥ pṛṣṭhe vāri|viprahatā iva.
91.20 rath'|âśva|dvipa|patty|oghāḥ salil'|âughā iv' âdbhutāḥ
yug'|ânt'|āditya|raśmy|ābhaiḥ Pāṇḍav'|âstra|śarair hatāḥ.

tam Pāṇḍav'|āditya|śar'|âṃśu|jālaṃ
Kuru|pravīrān yudhi niṣṭapantam
sa Droṇa|meghaḥ śara|vṛṣṭi|vegaiḥ
prācchādayan megha iv' ârka|raśmīn.

ath' âtyarthaṃ vimṛṣṭena dviṣatām asu|bhojinā
ājaghne vakṣasi Droṇo nārācena Dhanaṃjayam.
sa vihvalita|sarv'|âṅgaḥ kṣiti|kampe yath" â|calaḥ
dhairyam ālambya Bībhatsur Droṇaṃ vivyādha pattribhiḥ.

horses standard and driver in arrows, smiling all the while as he sowed his stalks upon him. In an instant Pritha's son had another bow strung and striving to undo his teacher with his own weaponmastery as if with a single swipe of his arm he sent six hundred arrows up into the sky, then seven hun- 91.15
dred more and then a thousand and more again in flocks too numerous to count. Down they came onto Drona's line. His men stood firm but as those arrows wrought from Árjuna's subtle and dazzling fingerwork descended upon them the elephants horses and men below fell dead.

Darts streaked across them and down from their great cars came the carwarriors with their drivers steeds and standards, with their bows and bodies all broken. Down came elephants like cloudy mountain palaces shattered, toppled or burned by lightning wind or fire. Down came the horses beneath Árjuna's arrows in thousands upon thousands like flocks of geese struck by falling snow. Arrows radiated from 91.20
Pándava like the beams of the doomsday sun and they pierced the surging ocean of cars and horses and elephants and men.

Then the shafts latticed from the Pandu orb
To scorch the Kuru champions
The streaming arrows of Drona's cloud
Eclipsed, as a storm smothers sunbeams.

With an iron shaft polished to a gleam to snatch the life of what it struck Drona hit Dhanan·jaya in the chest. A shudder went through his body as a tremor shakes a crag. Bibhátsu gathered himself up and sent back at Drona his

Droṇas tu pañcabhir bāṇair Vāsudevam atāḍayat
Arjunaṃ ca tri|saptatyā dhvajaṃ c' âsya tribhiḥ śaraiḥ.
91.25 viśeṣayiṣyañ śiṣyaṃ ca Droṇo, rājan, parākramī
a|dṛśyam Arjunaṃ cakre nimeṣāc chara|vṛṣṭibhiḥ.
prasaktān patato 'drākṣma Bhāradvājasya sāyakān
maṇḍalī|kṛtam ev' âsya dhanuś c' âdṛśyat' âdbhutam.
te 'bhyayuḥ samare rājan Vāsudeva|Dhanaṃjayau
Droṇa|sṛṣṭāḥ su|bahavaḥ kaṅka|pattra|paricchadāḥ.
tad dṛṣṭvā tādṛśaṃ yuddhaṃ Droṇa|Pāṇḍavayos tadā
Vāsudevo mahā|buddhiḥ kāryavattām acintayat.
tato 'bravīd Vāsudevo Dhanaṃjayam idaṃ vacaḥ.
«Pārtha Pārtha mahā|bāho, na naḥ kāl'|âtyayo bhavet.
91.30 Droṇam utsṛjya gacchāmaḥ kṛtyam etan mahattaram.»
Pārthaś c' âpy abravīt Kṛṣṇaṃ, «yath" êṣṭam iti Keśava.»
tataḥ pradakṣiṇaṃ kṛtvā Droṇaṃ prāyān mahā|bhujam.
parivṛttaś ca Bībhatsur agacchad visṛjañ śarān.
tato 'bravīt svayaṃ Droṇaḥ «kv' êdaṃ Pāṇḍava gamyate?
nanu nāma raṇe śatrum a|jitvā na nivartase.»

ARJUNA uvāca:

gurur bhavān na me śatruḥ. śiṣyaḥ putra|samo 'smi te.
na c' âsti sa pumāl̃ loke yas tvāṃ yudhi parājayet.

SAMJAYA uvāca:

evaṃ bruvāṇo Bībhatsur Jayadratha|vadh'|ôtsukaḥ
tvarā|yukto mahā|bāhus tvat|sainyaṃ samupādravat.
91.35 taṃ cakra|rakṣau Pāñcālyau Yudhāmany'|Ûttamaujasau

own feathered darts. Drona found Vasudéva with five of his arrows and Árjuna with a full seventythree, shredding his
pennants with three more. Now o king it was bold Drona's 91.25
turn to outdo his acolyte and in an eye's blink Árjuna vanished in a rain of reeds. We watched Bharadvája's shafts flow to their target as his bow blurred into a circle. He aimed at Vasudéva and Dhanan·jaya and arrows dressed in heronfeathers flew from his fingers in numbers my king that we could no longer count.

Vasudéva saw what was happening between Drona and Pandu's son and realising what might be its end he called across to Dhanan·jaya.

"Partha. Partha let these moments not be our last. Loosen 91.30
your hold on Drona and let us return to our greater task."

Partha demurred to Krishna and turned to his great opponent's left as a sign of respect before he and his friend rode on. But as the car swung about in the shower of arrows and Bibhátsu took his leave, Drona demanded that he stop.

"What is this o son of Pandu? In battle you leave an opponent only when he is dead."

ÁRJUNA spoke:

O master you are not my opponent. I am your pupil. Look upon me as your son. There is there is no man on earth who could beat you in battle.

SÁNJAYA spoke:

Saying these words Bibhátsu swerved away with all speed
towards the rest of our host to find and slay Jayad·ratha, and 91.35
as his great car made its way onward the mighty Panchála fighters Yudha·manyu and Uttamáujas followed on to guard

anvayātāṃ mah"|ātmānau viśantaṃ tāvakaṃ balam.
tato Jayo mahā|rāja Kṛtavarmā ca, Sātvataḥ,
Kāmbojaś ca, Śrutāyuś ca, Dhanaṃjayam avārayan.
teṣāṃ daśa sahasrāṇi rathānām anuyāyinām
Abhīṣāhāḥ, Śūrasenāḥ, Śibayo 'tha Vasātayaḥ,
Māvellakā, Lalitthāś ca, Kekayā, Madrakās tathā,
Nārāyaṇāś ca, Gopālāḥ, Kāmbojānāṃ ca ye gaṇāḥ,
Karṇena vijitāḥ pūrvaṃ saṃgrāme śūra|sammatāḥ,
Bhāradvājaṃ puras|kṛtya hṛṣṭ'|ātmāno 'rjunaṃ prati
91.40 putra|śok'|âbhisaṃtaptaṃ kruddhaṃ mṛtyum iv' ântakam
tyajantaṃ tumule prāṇān saṃnaddhaṃ citra|yodhinam
gāhamānam anīkāni mātaṅgam iva yūthapam
mah"|êṣv|āsaṃ parākrāntaṃ nara|vyāghram avārayan.
tataḥ pravavṛte yuddhaṃ tumulaṃ loma|harṣaṇam
anyo|'nyaṃ vai prārthayatāṃ yodhānām Arjunasya ca.
Jayadratha|vadha|prepsum āyāntaṃ puruṣa'|rṣabham
nyavārayanta sahitāḥ kriyā vyādhim iv' ôtthitam.

SAṂJAYA uvāca:

92.1 SAṂNIRUDDHAS TU taiḥ Pārtho mahā|bala|parākramaḥ
drutaṃ samanuyātaś ca Droṇena rathināṃ varaḥ
kirann iṣu|gaṇāṃs tikṣṇān sa raśmīn iva bhās|karaḥ
tāpayām āsa tat sainyaṃ dehaṃ vyādhi|gaṇo yathā.
aśvo viddho dhvajaś chinnaḥ s'|ārohaḥ pātito gajaḥ
chatrāṇi cāpa|viddhāni rathāś cakrair vinā kṛtāḥ.
vidrutāni ca sainyāni śar'|ārtāni samantataḥ.
ity āsīt tumulaṃ yuddhaṃ. na prājñāyata kiṃ cana.
92.5 teṣām saṃyacchatāṃ saṃkhye paras|param a|jihma|gaiḥ

its wheels. And o majesty Jaya and Krita·varman, Sátvata, Kambója and Shrutáyus stood before Dhanan·jaya, and behind them were the Abhisháhas, the Shura·senas, the Shibis and Vasátis, the Mavéllakas, Lalítthas, the Kékayas and Mádrakas, the Naráyanas and Go·palas and a company of Kambójas, ten thousand chariotwarriors from the lands that Karna had conquered, all of whom had sworn fealty to Drona. Their hearts hammered as Árjuna approached.
And steeled and still burning with a father's sorrow and a 91.40
rage akin to death that ends all things the bold and mighty archer so illustrious to whom life was a mere toy to be cast into war's chaos crashed like a wild elephant through their ranks. They dug in their heels to hold him back. With a noise to chill the blood a new battle began between Árjuna and the Kuru elect as each sought the other's doom. Fixed on Jayad·ratha's death above all else their bull tore through our men like a plague and they drew tight together in hope of a cure.

SÁNJAYA spoke:

THEY HELD HIM briefly. But even as Drona best of all 92.1
warriors bore down upon him again, Partha so brave and bold sent forth his arrows hot as the sun's rays to blast the horde that stood before him. He was like a disease in the organs of our army. His bow eviscerated horses, tattered flags, brought down riders and elephants, pierced parasols and chopped the wheels from chariots. Everywhere you looked there were arrows and the army frayed and burst and dim
chaos and noise engulfed it. O majesty we fought back with 92.5

Arjuno dhvajinīṃ rājann abhīkṣṇaṃ samakampayat.
satyāṃ cikīrṣamāṇas tu pratijñāṃ satya|saṃgaraḥ
abhyadravad ratha|śreṣṭhaṃ śoṇ'|âśvaṃ śveta|vāhanaḥ.
taṃ Droṇaḥ pañca|viṃśatyā marma|bhidbhir a|jihma|gaiḥ
ante|vāsinam Acāryo mah"|êṣv|āsaṃ samārpayat.
taṃ tūrṇam iva Bībhatsuḥ sarva|śastra|bhṛtāṃ varaḥ
abhyadhāvad iṣūn asyann iṣu|vega|vighātakān.
tasy' âśu|kṣiptān bhallān hi bhallaiḥ saṃnata|parvabhiḥ
pratyavidhyad a|mey'|ātmā Brahm'|âstraṃ samudīrayan.
92.10 tad adbhutam apaśyāma Droṇasy' ācāryakaṃ yudhi
yatamāno yuvā n' âinaṃ pratyavidhyad yad Arjunaḥ.
kṣarann iva mahā|megho vāri|dhārāḥ sahasraśaḥ
Droṇa|meghaḥ Pārtha|śailaṃ vavarṣa śara|vṛṣṭibhiḥ.
Arjunaḥ śara|varṣaṃ tad Brahm'|âstreṇ' âiva, māriṣa,
pratijagrāha tejasvī bāṇān bāṇair niśātayan.
Droṇas tu pañca|viṃśatyā śveta|vāhanam ārdayat
Vāsudevaṃ ca saptatyā bāhvor urasi c' âśu|gaiḥ.
Pārthas tu prahasan dhīmān Ācāryaṃ sa|śar'|âughiṇam
visṛjantaṃ śitān bāṇān avārayata taṃ yudhi.
92.15 atha tau vadhyamānau tu Droṇena ratha|sattamau
avarjayetāṃ dur|dharṣaṃ yug'|ânt'|âgnim iv' ôtthitam.
varjayan niśitān bāṇān Droṇa|cāpa|viniḥsṛtān
kirīṭa|mālī Kaunteyo Bhoj'|ânīkaṃ vyaśātayat.
so 'ntarā Kṛtavarmāṇaṃ Kāmbojaṃ ca Sudakṣiṇam
abhyayād varjayan Droṇaṃ Mainākam iva parvatam.

arrows of our own but Árjuna's strikes rippled right through our bannered host.

His pact was with the truth alone and he had to make good his word. One wellfashioned car stood in his path. White steeds closed on red and as his adept came nearer the Teacher plied Árjuna with five and twenty shafts flying true and biting deep. Bibhátsu best of bowmen did not break his pace and deftly deflected Drona's shafts in a burst of his own but then Drona raised from his fathomless soul Heaven's Attack and bolt for whittled bolt he matched his foe's quick fingerwork. Drona's trick was the act of a true master and 92.10
we watched in awe as Árjuna strove like a novice to find an answer.

O father. Though a thousand streams poured from Drona's nimbus and his arrows rained down upon Partha's peak, somehow Árjuna's brilliance shone through the storm of Heaven's Attack and o father he began to cut Drona's arrows from the sky. Five and twenty of Drona's shafts found Árjuna behind his white steeds and seven struck Vasudéva in his chest, arms and hands, but all the while Partha kept his cool. He smiled grimly and stood firm as the sharp shafts clustered from the Teacher's bow.

Drona's blaze that day was as hot as the fire kindled at the 92.15
end of time, and the two heroes chose not to get too close. Dodging the sharp shafts falling from Drona's bow the diademed son of Kunti turned to face the Bhojas instead. As if skirting the feet of a mountain god, Árjuna circled wide towards Krita·varman and Sudákshina the Kambója.

tato Bhojo nara|vyāghro dur|dharṣaṃ Kuru|sattamam
avidhyat tūrṇam a|vyagro daśabhiḥ kaṅka|patribhiḥ.
tam Arjunaḥ śaten' ājau rājan vivyādha patriṇāṃ,
punaś c' ânyais tribhir bāṇair mohayann iva Sātvatam.
92.20 Bhojas tu prahasan Pārthaṃ Vāsudevaṃ ca Mādhavam
ek'|âikaṃ pañca|viṃśatyā sāyakānāṃ samārpayat.
tasy' Ârjuno dhanuś chittvā vivyādh' âinaṃ tri|saptabhiḥ
śarair agni|śikh"|ākāraiḥ kruddh'|āśīviṣa|saṃnibhaiḥ.
ath' ânyad dhanur ādāya Kṛtavarmā mahā|rathaḥ
pañcabhiḥ sāyakais tūrṇaṃ vivyādh' ôrasi Bhārata.
punaś ca niśitair bāṇaiḥ Pārthaṃ vivyādha pañcabhiḥ.
taṃ Pārtho navabhir bāṇair ājaghāna stan'|ântare.
dṛṣṭvā viṣaktaṃ Kaunteyaṃ Kṛtavarma|rathaṃ prati
cintayām āsa Vārṣṇeyo «na naḥ kāl'|âtyayo bhavet.»
92.25 tataḥ Kṛṣṇo 'bravīt Pārthaṃ «Kṛtavarmaṇi mā dayām
kuru. sambandhakaṃ hitvā pramathy' âinaṃ viśātaya.»
tataḥ sa Kṛtavarmāṇaṃ mohayitv" Ârjunaḥ śaraiḥ
abhyagāj javanair aśvaiḥ Kāmbojānām anīkinīm.
a|marṣitas tu Hārdikyaḥ praviṣṭe śveta|vāhane
vidhunvan sa|śaraṃ cāpaṃ Pāñcālyābhyāṃ samāgataḥ.
cakra|rakṣau tu Pāñcālyāv Arjunasya pad'|ânugau
paryavārayad āyāntau Kṛtavarmā rath'|êṣubhiḥ.
tāv avidhyat tato Bhojaḥ Kṛtavarmā śitaiḥ śaraiḥ
tribhir eva Yudhāmanyuṃ caturbhiś c' Ôttamaujasam.
92.30 tāv apy enaṃ vividhatur daśabhir daśabhiḥ śaraiḥ
tribhir eva Yudhāmanyur Uttamaujās tribhis tathā

The tiger Krita·varman saw him coming and levelled his aim. Ten arrows carried on feathers from herons' wings he loosed at his foe, but Árjuna answered with a hundred of his own and o majesty with a flourish as if for Krishna's sake he touched off his volley with a final three. Bhoja grinned 92.20
and in turn struck both Pritha's son and Mádhava son of Vasu·deva. But when five and twenty arrows had left Bhoja's fingers, Árjuna broke the bow he held and struck back with seventythree quarrels hot as the blue of the flame and deadly as writhing snakes. O Bhárata the great Krita·varman did not pause and swept up another bow and pierced Partha five times in the chest, then found him with five more whetted shafts. His foe struck him back in the trunk with nine.

Krishna the Vrishni watched as Kunti's son toiled against Krita·varman and anxious that they not lose time he turned 92.25
to Árjuna and spoke. "Have no pity for Krita·varman. I tell you now that the bonds you made with him you must break. Cut him down."

Árjuna spread a veil of arrows across Krita·varman and drove his swift steeds at the Kambója line. The white horses flew past Hrídika's son and the two Panchálas followed on. As the Panchála wheelguards came near to him Krita·varman now wild with anger notched an arrow and strove with car and bow to break their path. With three sharp shafts the Bhoja found Yudha·manyu and then Uttamáujas with four, then back came ten and ten again and three 92.30
from Yudha·manyu and three from Uttamáujas splintering through Krita·varman's bow and pole. But Hrídika's son was the very shape of rage and grabbing another bow and

saṃcicchidatur apy asya dhvajaṃ kārmukam eva ca.
ath' ânyad dhanur ādāya Hārdikyaḥ krodha|mūrchitaḥ
kṛtvā vi|dhanuṣau vīrau śara|varṣair avākirat.
tāv anye dhanuṣī sa|jye kṛtvā Bhojaṃ vijaghnatuḥ.
ten' ântareṇa Bībhatsur viveś' â|mitra|vāhinīm.
na lebhāte tu tau dvāraṃ vāritau Kṛtavarmaṇā
Dhārtarāṣṭreṣv anīkeṣu yatamānau nara'|rṣabhau.
anīkāny ardayan yuddhe tvaritaḥ śveta|vāhanaḥ
n' āvadhīt Kṛtavarmāṇaṃ prāptam apy ari|sūdanaḥ.
92.35 taṃ dṛṣṭvā tu tathā yāntaṃ śūro rājā Śrutāyudhaḥ
abhyadravat su|saṃkruddho vidhunvāno mahad dhanuḥ.
sa Pārthaṃ tribhir ānarchat saptatyā ca Janārdanam
kṣurapreṇa su|tīkṣṇena Pārtha|ketum atāḍayat.
tato 'rjuno navatyā tu śarāṇāṃ nata|parvaṇām
ājaghāna bhṛśaṃ kruddhas tottrair iva mahā|dvipam.
sa tan na mamṛṣe, rājan, Pāṇḍaveyasya vikramam
ath' âinaṃ sapta|saptatyā nārācānāṃ samārpayat.
tasy' Ârjuno dhanuś chittvā śar'|āvāpaṃ nikṛtya ca
ājaghān' ôrasi kruddhaḥ saptabhir nata|parvabhiḥ.
92.40 ath' ânyad dhanur ādāya sa rājā krodha|mūrchitaḥ
Vāsaviṃ navabhir bāṇair bāhvor urasi c' ârpayat.
tato 'rjunaḥ smayann eva Śrutāyudham ariṃ|damaḥ
śarair an|eka|sāhasraiḥ pīḍayām āsa, Bhārata.
aśvāṃś c' âsy' âvadhīt tūrṇaṃ sārathiṃ ca mahā|rathaḥ
vivyādha c' âinaṃ saptatyā nārācānāṃ mahā|balaḥ.
hat'|âśvaṃ ratham utsṛjya sa tu rājā Śrutāyudhaḥ
abhyadravad raṇe Pārthaṃ gadām udyamya vīryavān.

scattering his showery arrows he knocked his foe's weapons from their hands. Two new bows were strung and while his wheelguards fought back against Bhoja, Bibhátsu took his chance and plunged on into the enemy line. Locked in combat with Krita·varman the two Panchála bulls could not get through the door Árjuna had opened into Duryódhana's host and it shut tight once again. So it was that as he raced on and ravaged the troops before him the deadly warrior of the white horses did not finish Krita·varman though he had had him in his grasp.

Bold King Shrutáyudha was the next to mark Árjuna's 92.35
approach. Drawing his bow he rode out to meet him. He found Partha with three of his shafts and Janárdana with seven and with a razorsharp bolt tore a hole in their flag. Anger flared in Árjuna and he sent back ninety knotless arrows of his own. They were like whips on an elephant's back and Shrutáyudha bristled beneath them and seventyseven irons flew from his bow in answer. But then his fierce adversary broke Shrutáyudha's bow in two and cut down his quivers and studded his chest with seven wellmade shafts.
Rage came upon the king and picking up another bow he 92.40
harrowed Indra's son with nine arrows in his hands and ribs.

O Bhárata. The great tamer of foes merely smiled. Down on Shrutáyudha mighty Árjuna brought arrows in myriad and soon the king's steeds were dead and his driver was dead and he wore seven iron bolts in his breast. But bold King Shrutáyudha was a brave fighter, and he leapt from his horseless car and swinging his mace above his head lunged at Pritha's son.

Varuṇasy' ātma|jo vīraḥ sa tu rājā Śrutāyudhaḥ
Parṇāśā jananī yasya śīta|toyā mahā|nadī.
92.45 tasya māt" âbravīd rājan Varuṇaṃ putra|kāraṇāt.
«a|vadhyo 'yaṃ bhavel loke śatrūṇāṃ tanayo mama.»
Varuṇas tv abravīt prīto. «dadāmy asmai varaṃ hitam
divyam astraṃ, sutas te 'yaṃ yen' â|vadhyo bhaviṣyati.
n' âsti c' âpy amaratvaṃ vai manuṣyasya kathaṃ cana.
sarveṇ' âvaśya|martavyaṃ jātena saritāṃ vare.
dur|dharṣas tv eṣa śatrūṇāṃ raṇeṣu bhavitā sadā
astrasy' âsya prabhāvād vai. vyetu te mānaso jvaraḥ.»
ity uktvā Varuṇaḥ prādād gadāṃ mantra|puras|kṛtām
yām āsādya dur|ādharṣaḥ sarva|loke Śrutāyudhaḥ,
92.50 uvāca c' âinaṃ bhagavān punar eva jal'|ēśvaraḥ.
«a|yudhyati na moktavyā. sā tvayy eva pated iti.
hanyād eṣā pratīpaṃ hi prayoktāram api, prabho.»
na c' âkarot sa tad|vākyaṃ prāpte kāle Śrutāyudhaḥ.
sa tayā vīra|ghātinyā Janārdanam atāḍayat.
pratijagrāha tāṃ Kṛṣṇaḥ pīnen' âṃsena vīryavān.
n' âkampayata Śauriṃ sā Vindhyaṃ girim iv' ânilaḥ.
pratyudyāntī tam ev' âiṣā kṛty" êva dur|adhiṣṭhitā
jaghāna c' āsthitaṃ vīraṃ Śrutāyudham a|marṣaṇam.
hatvā Śrutāyudhaṃ vīraṃ dharaṇīm anvapadyata.

The bold king Shrutáyudha son of Váruna had been born to the river Parnásha whose waters flow deep and cold. O 92.45
majesty his mother had loved her child and she had gone before Váruna and addressed him.

"May my son be invincible before his foes."

Váruna was pleased with her and these were the words that he said.

"There is a weapon of heaven and if armed with it your son will be truly invincible. I will give it to him. O wonder of flowing water no man can ever hope for immortality, for death cannot be transgressed by any that are born. But let your mind be at peace. With this weapon in his hand your son will win any battle he fights."

With these words Váruna bestowed upon Shrutáyudha an enchanted mace that did indeed make him a match for
any man, though the holy lord of waters had a warning for 92.50
him.

"Hear me my good son. Never swing this mace at an unarmed man lest it recoil upon you. For it can strike down the man that wields it."

When the fatal moment came Shrutáyudha forgot his father's words. He swung the mace at the Stirrer of Hearts and Krishna took its deadly bulk on his brawny shoulder. The wind cannot move Mount Vindhya and that blow did not move Shauri. But black magic seemed to bounce the mace back and it cracked against Shrutáyudha and knocked the wild and mighty hero dead and then followed him down to the earth.

92.55 gadāṃ nivartitāṃ dṛṣṭvā nihataṃ ca Śrutāyudham
hāhā|kāro mahāṃs tatra sainyānāṃ samajāyata
sven' âstreṇa hataṃ dṛṣṭvā Śrutāyudham ariṃdamam.
a|yudhyamānāya tataḥ Keśavāya nar'|âdhipa
kṣiptā Śrutāyudhen' âtha, tasmāt tam avadhīd gadā.
yath" ôktaṃ Varuṇen' ājau tathā sa nidhanaṃ gataḥ
vy|asuś c' âpy apatad bhūmau prekṣatāṃ sarva|dhanvinām.
patamānas tu sa babhau Parṇāśāyāḥ priyaḥ sutaḥ
sa bhagna iva vātena bahu|śākho vanas|patiḥ.
tataḥ sarvāṇi sainyāni senā|mukhyāś ca sarvaśaḥ
prādravanta hataṃ dṛṣṭvā Śrutāyudham ariṃ|damam.
92.60 tataḥ Kāmboja|rājasya putraḥ śūraḥ Sudakṣiṇaḥ
abhyayāj javanair aśvaiḥ Phalgunaṃ śatru|sūdanam.
tasya Pārthaḥ śarān sapta preṣayām āsa, Bhārata.
te taṃ śūraṃ vinirbhidya prāviśan dharaṇī|talam.
so 'tividdhaḥ śarais tīkṣṇair Gāṇḍīva|preṣitair mṛdhe
Arjunaṃ prativivyādha daśabhiḥ kaṅka|patribhiḥ.
Vāsudevaṃ tribhir viddhvā punaḥ Pārthaṃ ca pañcabhiḥ
tasya Pārtho dhanuś chittvā ketuṃ ciccheda māriṣa.
bhallābhyāṃ bhṛśa|tīkṣṇābhyāṃ taṃ ca vivyādha Pāṇḍavaḥ.
sa tu Pārthaṃ tribhir viddhvā siṃha|nādam ath' ânadat.
92.65 sarva|pāraśavīṃ c' âiva śaktiṃ śūraḥ Sudakṣiṇaḥ
sa|ghaṇṭāṃ prāhiṇod ghorāṃ kruddho Gāṇḍīva|dhanvane.
sā jvalantī mah"|ôlk" êva tam āsādya mahā|ratham
sa|visphuliṅgā nirbhidya nipapāta mahī|tale.

The soldiers who saw the weapon twist and strike its master cried out in disbelief to see one so feared as Shrutáyudha die at his own hand. Késhava had not been armed and for that o lord of men Shrutáyudha's own weapon had slain its wielder. So it was that Shrutáyudha met the fate in battle against which Váruna had warned him. As he fell down dead his fellow archers looked on. The son so dear to the river Parnásha and once so feared by his foes lay now upon the earth like a broadbranching tree uprooted by the wind, and all the men who had fought with him in the van backed away in terror at the sight. 92.55

On rode the Red Star Fighter to quell other foes. It 92.60
was Sudákshina the great scion of the Kambója king who next brought his swift horses to meet him. O Bhárata, Pritha's son struck first with seven arrows and they went right through Sudákshina and slid into the ground. Wounded by Gandíva's sharp shafts Sudákshina hit back at Árjuna with ten arrows fletched in heronfeathers. He found Vasudéva with three and sent at Partha five more but then o father it was Partha's turn again. He cut Sudákshina's bow in two and sliced apart his standard. Pierced through with two bolts sharpened to a hiss Sudákshina roared out at Pandu's
son and found him with three more darts and then hurled 92.65
with all his might a huge length of solid iron right at his foe as he raised up Gandíva. Blazing like a falling star it crashed upon the great warrior and with a spark it broke in two and each piece thumped to earth.

śaktyā tv abhihato gāḍhaṃ mūrchay" ābhipariplutaḥ,
samāśvāsya mahā|tejāḥ sṛkkaṇī parilelihan,
taṃ catur|daśabhiḥ Pārtho nārācaiḥ kaṅka|patribhiḥ
s'|âśva|dhvaja|dhanuḥ|sūtaṃ vivyādh' â|cintya|vikramaḥ.
rathaṃ c' ânyaiḥ su|bahubhiś cakre viśakalaṃ śaraiḥ.
92.70 Sudakṣiṇaṃ taṃ Kāmbojaṃ mogha|saṃkalpa|vikramam
bibheda hṛdi bāṇena pṛthu|dhāreṇa Pāṇḍavaḥ.
sa bhinna|varmā srast'|âṅgaḥ prabhraṣṭa|mukuṭ'|âṅgadaḥ,
papāt' âbhimukhaḥ śūro yantra|mukta iva dhvajaḥ.
gireḥ śikhara|jaḥ śrīmān su|śākhaḥ su|pratiṣṭhitaḥ
nirbhagna iva vātena karṇikāro him'|âtyaye,
śete sma nihato bhūmau Kāmboj'|āstaraṇ'|ôcitaḥ
mah"|ârh'|ābharaṇ'|ôpetaḥ sānumān iva parvataḥ,
su|darśanīyas tāmr'|âkṣaḥ karṇinā sa Sudakṣiṇaḥ
putraḥ Kāmboja|rājasya Pārthena vinipātitaḥ.
92.75 dhārayann agni|saṃkāśāṃ śirasā kāñcanīṃ srajam
aśobhata mahā|bāhur vy|asur bhūmau nipātitaḥ.
tataḥ sarvāṇi sainyāni vyadravanta sutasya te
hataṃ Śrutāyudhaṃ dṛṣṭvā Kāmbojaṃ ca Sudakṣiṇam.

SAṂJAYA uvāca:

93.1 HATE SUDAKṢIṆE, rājan, vīre c' âiva Śrutāyudhe
javen' âbhyadravan Pārthaṃ kupitāḥ sainikās tava.
Abhīṣāhāḥ Śūrasenāḥ Śibayo 'tha Vasātayaḥ
abhyavarṣaṃs tato, rājañ, śara|varṣair Dhanaṃjayam.
teṣāṃ ṣaṣṭi|śatān anyān prāmathnāt Pāṇḍavaḥ śaraiḥ.

Árjuna's head swam at the pike's heavy blow. He crowed in pain and his tongue lolled in his mouth. But his fierce glory would not be darkened. With fourteen arrows flying on feathers from herons' wings he struck at his foe's horse, flag and bow and the man that drove his steeds and 92.70
then with a brace more splintered his car and with a single broadflanged shaft the son of Pandu pierced Sudákshina's heart. The Kambója's mind blurred and his muscles buckled. With his armour torn open and his limbs spasmodic and his crown and his bracelets ripped away, the great warrior toppled forward like a flagpole wrenched from its socket.

Like a flame of the forest once so sturdy leafy and bright plucked from a mountaintop by a storm at the year's turning, down came Sudákshina son of the Kambója king when Partha's hooked arrow found its mark. He laid his handsome coppereyed head not on the silks of Kambója he once had known but on the rough earth beneath him. There he came to rest crested in jewels like a mountain ridged in trees. With his limbs splayed lifeless and the chaplet gold 92.75
as fire upon his head how beautiful he looked then. First Shrutáyudha and now Sudákshina: your son's men ran for their lives at the sight.

SÁNJAYA spoke:

"O MAJESTY WHEN their champions Sudákshina and 93.1
Shrutáyudha had fallen your men swarmed in fury at Pritha's son. O king the Abhisháhas, the Shura·senas, the Shibis and Vasátis brought a storm of arrows down upon Dhanan·jaya's head. But with his own shafts the Pándava swept a hundred

te sma bhītāḥ palāyante vyāghrāt kṣudra|mṛgā iva.
te nivṛttāḥ punaḥ Pārthaṃ sarvataḥ paryavārayan
raṇe sapatnān nighnantaṃ jigīṣantaṃ parān yudhi.
93.5 teṣām āpatatāṃ tūrṇaṃ Gāṇḍīva|preṣitaiḥ śaraiḥ
śirāṃsi pātayām āsa bāhūṃś c' âiva Dhanaṃjayaḥ.
śirobhiḥ patitais tatra bhūmir āsīn nir|antarā
abhra|cchāy" êva c' âiv' āsīd dhvāṅkṣa|gṛdhra|balair yudhi.
teṣu t' ûtsādyamāneṣu krodh'|āmarṣa|samanvitau
Śrutāyuś c' Âcyutāyuś ca Dhanaṃjayam ayudhyatām.
balinau spardhinau vīrau kula|jau bāhu|śālinau
tāv enaṃ śara|varṣāṇi savya|dakṣiṇam asyatām.
tvarā|yuktau mahā|rāja prārthayānau mahad yaśaḥ
Arjunasya vadha|prepsū putr'|ârthe tava dhanvinau.
93.10 tāv Arjunaṃ sahasreṇa patriṇāṃ nata|parvaṇām
pūrayām āsatuḥ kruddhau taḍāgaṃ jaladau yathā.
Śrutāyuś ca tataḥ kruddhas tomareṇa Dhanaṃjayam
ājaghāna ratha|śreṣṭhaḥ pītena niśitena ca.
so 'tividdho balavatā śatruṇā śatru|karśanaḥ
jagāma paramaṃ mohaṃ mohayan Keśavaṃ raṇe.
etasminn eva kāle tu so 'cyutāyur mahā|rathaḥ
śūlena bhṛśa|tīkṣṇena tāḍayām āsa Pāṇḍavam.
kṣate kṣāraṃ sa hi dadau Pāṇḍavasya mah"|ātmanaḥ.
Pārtho 'pi bhṛśa|saṃviddho dhvaja|yaṣṭiṃ samāśritaḥ.
93.15 tataḥ sarvasya sainyasya tāvakasya viśāṃ pate
siṃha|nādo mahān āsīdd hataṃ matvā Dhanaṃjayam.

and sixty of them clean away. They vanished in terror like
fawns before a tiger. Some regrouped and pressed in around
Pritha's son but he was eager to meet them and once more
Dhanan·jaya struck down his foes with abandon. With ar- 93.5
rows from Gandíva's string he sliced heads and arms from
their dying trunks before they could hit the ground. Little
of the earth could still be glimpsed through its freight of
severed heads and as the flocks of crows and vultures passed
above us a shadow fell across the plain.

From the dwindling horde two found their mettle and
rose to face Dhanan·jaya. Shrutáyus and Achyutáyus were
mighty heroes both and both were sprung from noble stock
and keen to show their skill and speed. Arrows streamed
from their hands. O king of kings great and vaunting glory
they sought and wild with battlelust they had strung their
bows to seek your son's profit and Árjuna's demise. Like 93.10
clouds filling a lake they poured madly onto Árjuna a thousand finewrought and feathered shafts. Madder still the
great Shrutáyus slung a rosewood spear honed to a hiss at
Dhanan·jaya with all his might. It struck home. He had
pierced his own nemesis to the quick. Árjuna's head swam
suddenly, and Késhava's head swam to see him so. Before
Árjuna could recover bold Achyutáyus sent at him a honed
and deadly arrow and it bit deep. The great son of Pandu
and Pritha shuddered and fell against the pole of his flag. O 93.15
king a huge cheer went up among us when we saw Dhanan·
jaya swoon.

Kṛṣṇaś ca bhṛśa|saṃtapto dṛṣṭvā Pārthaṃ vicetanam
āśvāsayat su|hṛdyābhir vāgbhis tatra Dhanaṃjayam.
tatas tau rathināṃ śreṣṭhau labdha|lakṣau Dhanaṃjayam
Vāsudevaṃ ca Vārṣṇeyaṃ śara|varṣaiḥ samantataḥ,
sa|cakra|kūbara|rathaṃ s'|âśva|dhvaja|patākinam
a|dṛśyaṃ cakratur yuddhe. tad adbhutam iv' âbhavat.
pratyāśvastas tu Bībhatsuḥ śanakair iva Bhārata
preta|rāja|puraṃ prāpya punaḥ pratyāgato yathā,
93.20 saṃchannaṃ śara|jālena rathaṃ dṛṣṭvā sa|Keśavam
śatrū c' âbhimukhau dṛṣṭvā dīpyamānāv iv' ânalau,
prāduś cakre tataḥ Pārthaḥ Śākram astraṃ mahā|rathaḥ.
tasmād āsan sahasrāṇi śarāṇāṃ nata|parvaṇām.
te jaghnus tau mah"|êṣv|āsau. tābhyāṃ muktāś ca sāyakāḥ
vicerur ākāśa|gatāḥ Pārtha|bāṇa|vidāritāḥ.
pratihatya śarāṃs tūrṇaṃ śara|vegena Pāṇḍavaḥ
pratasthe tatra tatr' âiva yodhayan vai mahā|rathān.
tau ca Phalguna|bāṇ'|âughair vi|bāhu|śirasau kṛtau
vasudhām anvapadyetāṃ vāta|nunnāv iva drumau.
93.25 Śrutāyuṣaś ca nidhanaṃ vadhaś c' âiv' Âcyutāyuṣaḥ
loka|vismāpanam abhūt samudrasy' êva śoṣaṇam.
tayoḥ pad'|ânugān hatvā punaḥ pañcāśataṃ rathān
pratyagād Bhāratīṃ senāṃ nighnan Pārtho varān varān.
Śrutāyuṣaṃ ca nihataṃ prekṣya c' âiv' Âcyutāyuṣam
Niyutāyuś ca saṃkruddho Dīrghāyuś c' âiva, Bhārata,
putrau tayor nara|śreṣṭhau Kaunteyaṃ pratijagmatuḥ

Krishna was witless with shock and gabbling in his ear tried desperately to revive Dhanan·jaya. Their assailants realised the prize was in their grasp and with another gout of arrows they covered Dhanan·jaya and Vasudéva the Vrishni. Only moments later we watched in wonder as the wheels and base of their car and their horse, flag and banner were all crosshatched from sight. But o Bhárata, as if on his return journey from the place where the ghost king reigns, Bibhátsu the mighty son of Pritha them came with a jolt back to consciousness. He glanced first at Késhava standing 93.20
with him in their car bound in that lattice of wood, and second at his two foes wild as balefires. And then he brought forth Shakra's Bolt.

A thousand arrows flew, and then a thousand and a thousand more. As Partha's shafts slammed into them the two bowmen sent their own volleys up in to the sky to frustrate a second wave. But with a pulse of darts Pándava struck back and soon reached the very ground from which they fought. The Red Star Fighter's deluge broke through and took with it the heads and arms of his foes. Down they went to earth like trees in a gale.

To see Shrutáyus go down and to see Achyutáyus drop so 93.25
suddenly dead was as strange as seeing the ocean melt into sand. Leaving in his wake their decimated guard and fifty dead charioteers who had ridden with them Partha rode on into the Bhárata host cutting down warrior upon warrior as he came. Shrutáyus and Achyutáyus's sons had watched their fathers die and now the very horror of the sight drove Niyutáyus and Dirgháyus forth to fight Kauntéya themselves. O Bhárata, they were fine archers. They scattered

kirantau vividhān bāṇān pitṛ|vyasana|karśitau.
tāv Arjuno muhūrtena śaraiḥ saṃnata|parvabhiḥ
preṣayat parama|kruddho Yamasya sadanaṃ prati.
93.30 loḍayantam anīkāni dvipaṃ padma|saro yathā
n' âśaknuvan vārayituṃ Pārthaṃ kṣatriya|puṃgavāḥ.
Aṅgās tu gaja|vāreṇa Pāṇḍavaṃ paryavārayan
kruddhāḥ sahasraśo, rājañ, śikṣitā hasti|sādinaḥ
Duryodhana|samādiṣṭāḥ kuñjaraiḥ parvat'|ôpamaiḥ
prācyāś ca dākṣiṇātyāś ca Kaliṅga|pramukhā nṛ|pāḥ.
teṣām āpatatāṃ śīghraṃ Gāṇḍīva|preṣitaiḥ śaraiḥ
nicakarta śirāṃsy ugro bāhūn api su|bhūṣaṇān.
taiḥ śirobhir mahī kīrṇā bāhubhiś ca sah'|âṅgadaiḥ
babhau kanaka|pāṣāṇā bhuja|gair iva saṃvṛtā.
93.35 bāhavo viśikhaiś chinnāḥ śirāṃsy unmathitāni ca
patamānāny adṛśyanta drumebhya iva pakṣiṇaḥ.
śaraiḥ sahasraśo viddhā dvipāḥ prasruta|śoṇitāḥ
adṛśyant' âdrayaḥ Kāle gairik'|âmbu|sravā iva.
nihatāḥ śerate sm' ânye Bībhatsor niśitaiḥ śaraiḥ
gaja|pṛṣṭha|gatā mlecchā nānā|vikṛta|darśanāḥ
nānā|veṣa|dharā, rājan, nānā|śastr'|âugha|saṃvṛtāḥ
rudhireṇ' ânulipt'|âṅgā bhānti citraiḥ śarair hatāḥ.
śoṇitaṃ nirvamanti sma dvipāḥ Pārtha|śar'|āhatāḥ
sahasraśaś chinna|gātrāḥ s'|ārohāḥ sa|pad'|ânugāḥ.
93.40 cukruśuś ca nipetuś ca babhramuś c' âpare diśaḥ
bhṛśaṃ trastāś ca bahavaḥ svānena mamṛdur gajāḥ.

their myriad shafts before them. But Árjuna's blood was up and with darts of knotless wood he drove them down to where Yama dwells. Like an elephant splashing through a 93.30
lily pond Partha went through and over our men and even the strongest could not stop him.

O majesty. He came to the riders of Anga, fierce and hardened warriors who strove to hold Árjuna back with a wall of elephants a thousand strong.

With them atop beasts tall as mountains rode the high kings of Kalínga and the men of the east and the south that had allied to Duryódhana. But they could not halt Árjuna's violent progress and they soon gave way beneath Gandíva's shafts. Off came arms still bangled in torcs and off came heads and their heads were yellow stones and their gilded arms were snakes strewn far across the plain. Like so many 93.35
birds fluttering from the trees severed hands and heads came down to the earth. Elephants quilled in a thousand arrows and slick with blood lay like the rocks on Kala when the rains make the red chalk run. Warriors from distant lands clad in strange garb and bristling with weird blades toppled from their howdahs in flashes of colour as their broken bodies veined in scarlet and studded with the Despiser's whittled arrows rolled and came to rest. Some elephants though torn through by Partha's shafts still carried their riders and they vomited blood onto the heads of the soldiers teeming around their gashed legs, while others moved and fell and 93.40
stumbled everywhere you looked in a welter of terror and stools and the blare from their trunks.

s'|ântar'|āyudhinaś c' âiva dvipāṃs tīkṣṇa|viṣ'|ôpamāḥ
vidanty asura|māyāṃ ye su|ghorā ghora|cakṣuṣaḥ
Yavanāḥ Pāradāś c' âiva Śakāś ca saha Bāhlikaiḥ
kāka|varṇā dur|ācārāḥ strī|lolāḥ kalaha|priyāḥ.
Drāvihās tatra yudhyante satta|mātaṅga|vikramāḥ
go|yoni|prabhavā mlecchāḥ kāla|kalpāḥ prahāriṇaḥ.
Dārv'|Âtisārā Daradāḥ Puṇḍrāś c' âiva sahasraśaḥ
te na śakyāḥ sma saṃkhyātuṃ vrātāḥ śata|sahasraśaḥ.
93.45 abhyavarṣanta te sarve Pāṇḍavaṃ niśitaiḥ śaraiḥ
avākiraṃś ca te mlecchā nānā|yuddha|viśāradāḥ.
teṣām api sasarj' āśu śara|vṛṣṭiṃ Dhanaṃjayaḥ.
sṛṣṭis tathā|vidhā hy āsīc chalabhānām iv' āyatiḥ.
abhra|cchāyām iva śaraiḥ sainye kṛtvā Dhanaṃjayaḥ
muṇḍ'|ârdha|muṇḍāñ jaṭilān a|śucīñ jaṭil'|ānanān
mlecchān aśātayat sarvān sametān astra|tejasā.
śaraiś ca śataśo viddhās te saṃghā giri|cāriṇaḥ
prādravanta raṇe bhītā giri|gahvara|vāsinaḥ.
gaj'|âśva|sādi|mlecchānāṃ patitānāṃ śataiḥ śaraiḥ
bakāḥ kaṅkā vṛkā bhūmāv apiban rudhiraṃ mudā.
93.50 patty|aśva|ratha|nāgaiś ca pracchanna|kṛta|saṃkramām
śara|varṣa|plavāṃ ghorāṃ keśa|śaivala|śādvalām
prāvartayan nadīm ugrāṃ śoṇit'|âugha|taraṅgiṇīm
chinn'|âṅgulī|kṣudra|matsyāṃ yug'|ânte kāla|saṃnibhām
prakarod gaja|sambādhāṃ nadīm uttara|śoṇitām
dehebhyo rāja|putrāṇāṃ nāg'|âśva|ratha|sādinām.

Behind the elephants there were men deadly as poison who knew the diabolic ways and they had fearful faces and fearful eyes. They were the Yávanas and the Páradas, the Shakas and Bahlíkas, crowcoloured and lustful men of rough tricks and quick tempers. Fighting with them were the uncouth and deadly warriors called the Drávihas, people born of cows and strong as wild elephants. The Wooden Ones and the Muck Men were next, and the Dáradas and the Pundras added their number to the countless hundreds of thousands that made up the barbarian ranks. From 93.45
behind their panoplies they sent up whittled arrows that poured down upon Pándava. But Dhanan·jaya sent forth his own arrow swarms. And they came streaming down like locusts.

The men looked up. Heads shaven or halfshaven or dangling matted locks or thick and dirty beards looked up and the shadow from Dhanan·jaya's arrows fell across them. Then they felt the dark splendour of Árjuna's attack. Arrow after arrow struck the knots of cavedwellers and mountainmen and they fled in fear from the fray as soldier rider horse and beast crashed over and the crows and vultures and dogs of that place rushed in to drink fitfully of their blood. Soon the arrow rain that fell swelled about those creatures 93.50
a ghastly river of swirling gore verdant with hair flowing in the chasms between the carcasses of man and beast, horse and car, and shoaled with fingers no longer fixed to hands. It was a prodigy from the world's end and its crimson waters ran between the banks of elephants and the bodies of princes fallen from steeds or cars or palanquins. As after a

yathā sthalaṃ ca nimnaṃ ca na syād varṣati vāsave
tath" āsīt pṛthivī sarvā śoṇitena pariplutā.
ṣaṭ|sahasrān hayān vīrān punar daśa|śatān varān
prāhiṇon mṛtyu|lokāya kṣatriyān kṣatriya'|rṣabhaḥ.
93.55 śaraiḥ sahasraśo viddhā vidhivat kalpitā dvipāḥ
śerate bhūmim āsādya śailā vajra|hatā iva.
sa|vāji|ratha|mātaṅgān nighnan vyacarad Arjunaḥ
prabhinna iva mātaṅgo mṛdnan nala|vanaṃ yathā.
bhūri|druma|latā|gulmaṃ śuṣk'|êndhana|tṛṇ'|ôlapam
nirdahed analo 'raṇyaṃ yathā vāyu|samīritaḥ,
sen"|āraṇyaṃ tava tathā Kṛṣṇ'|ânila|samīritaḥ
śar'|ârcir adahat kruddhaḥ Pāṇḍav'|âgnir Dhanaṃjayaḥ.
śūnyān kurvan rath'|ôpasthān mānavaiḥ saṃstaran mahīm
prānṛtyad iva sambādhe cāpa|hasto Dhanaṃjayaḥ.
93.60 vajra|kalpaiḥ śarair bhūmiṃ kurvann uttara|śoṇitām
prāviśad Bhāratīṃ senāṃ saṃkruddho vai Dhanaṃjayaḥ.
taṃ Śrutāyus tath" Āmbaṣṭho vrajamānaṃ nyavārayat.
tasy' Ârjunaḥ śarais tīkṣṇaiḥ kaṅka|patra|paricchadaiḥ
nyapātayadd hayāñ śīghraṃ yatamānasya māriṣa.
dhanuś c' âsy' âparaiś chittvā śaraiḥ Pārtho vicakrame.
Ambaṣṭhas tu gadāṃ gṛhya krodha|paryākul'|ēkṣaṇaḥ
āsasāda raṇe Pārthaṃ Keśavaṃ ca mahā|ratham.
tataḥ sampraharan vīro gadām udyamya Bhārata
ratham āvārya gadayā Keśavaṃ samatāḍayat.

great rain the contours of the land change so it was that a blood tide washed across the whole of the plain.

Six thousand stallions and a thousand of the best of men the bull of the warrior caste sent to Death's domain that
day. The horses fell in their finery riddled with a thousand 93.55
shafts and lay still as stones struck from a mountain in a storm. As a wild elephant tramples a brake of reeds Árjuna rampaged through beast car and horse, and as a fire raised by a wind licks at the dry twigs and grass of a wood thick with trees and creepers and shrubs and then spreads quickly through it so the army became the forest and Krishna the wind to raise him, with Dhanan·jaya son of Pandu the raging fire and his arrows the flames. He emptied cars of drivers and strewed them across the earth and bow in
hand danced where they died. As the lightning of his ar- 93.60
rows raged overhead he drenched the earth in blood and tore horribly through the Bharata horde.

On he came and Shrutáyus of Ambáshtha* rode up and tried to stop him but o father in the blink of an eye Árjuna son of Pritha loosed biting darts fletched in heronfeathers and brought down the man's steeds and knocked the bow and arrows from his hands. Partha and great Késhava swerved on their way but Ambáshtha swept up a club and tried to block their path. Anger flashed in his eyes. Boldly he rode close and clashed with their car and o Bharata he raised his club high and swung it at Késhava.

93.65 gadayā tāḍitaṃ dṛṣṭvā Keśavaṃ para|vīra|hā
Arjuno 'tha bhṛśaṃ kruddhaḥ so 'mbaṣṭhaṃ prati Bhārata.
tataḥ śarair hema|puṅkhaiḥ sa|gadaṃ rathināṃ varam
chādayām āsa samare meghaḥ sūryam iv' ôditam.
ath' âparaiḥ śaraiś c' âpi gadāṃ tasya mah"|ātmanaḥ
acūrṇayat tadā Pārthas: tad adbhutam iv' âbhavat.
atha tāṃ patitāṃ dṛṣṭvā gṛhy' ânyāṃ ca mahā|gadām
Arjunaṃ Vāsudevaṃ ca punaḥ punar atāḍayat.
tasy' Ârjunaḥ kṣuraprābhyāṃ sa|gadāv udyatau bhujau
cicched' Êndra|dhvaj'|ākārau śiraś c' ânyena patriṇā.
93.70 sa papāta hato rājan vasudhām anunādayan
Indra|dhvaja iv' ôtsṛṣṭo yantra|nirmukta|bandhanaḥ.
rath'|ânīk'|āvagāḍhaś ca vāraṇ'|âśva|śatair vṛtaḥ
adṛśyata tadā Pārtho ghanaiḥ sūrya iv' āvṛtaḥ.

SAMJAYA uvāca:

94.1 TATAḤ PRAVIṢṬE Kaunteye Sindhu|rāja|jighāṃsayā
Droṇ'|ânīkaṃ vinirbhidya Bhoj'|ânīkaṃ ca dus|taram
Kāmbojasya ca dāyāde hate, rājan, Sudakṣiṇe
Śrutāyudhe ca vikrānte nihate Savyasācinā
vipradruteṣv anīkeṣu vidhvasteṣu samantataḥ
prabhagnaṃ sva|balaṃ dṛṣṭvā putras te Droṇam abhyayāt.
tvarann eka|rathen' âiva
sametya Droṇam abravīt.
«gataḥ sa puruṣa|vyāghraḥ
pramathy' êmāṃ mahā|camūm.
94.5 atra buddhyā samīkṣasva. kiṃ nu kāryam anantaram

Árjuna scourge of heroes saw Ambáshtha lunge and rage 93.65
overtook him. With arrows whose fletchings were flecked
in gold he hid weapon and warrior both, as a cloud occludes
the sun. Partha used his darts to whittle to splinters the
great man's club in a feat of dizzying skill. Ambáshtha took
up another heftier mace and once more swung at his foe,
but then with two razorlike darts Árjuna sliced away his
arms thick as Indra's staves with the club still held in his
hands, and with a third feathered shaft cut right through
the warrior's neck. Gurgling he crashed to earth o king like 93.70
the pole of a god's car shaken from its lock. And there was
Partha, deep in the chariot throng, bound in the knots of
horses and beasts, like the sun bound thickly in cloud.

SÁNJAYA spoke:

ON RODE KUNTI's son keen to spill the blood of the 94.1
Sindhu king. He broke through the sturdy defense Drona
and Bhoja had built. O king. Sudákshina heir of Kambója
lay dead by his left hand and dead too was bold Shrutáyudha. All about us our line had been mangled or blasted
open. Your son looked upon the ranks of his army all shattered by a single car and made haste for Drona. He drew
up before him and spoke.

"A tiger has been here. He has shredded a great herd of
our men. Bear this thought close and tell me: what do I 94.5
do now to put an end to this bloodbath? You are our only

Arjunasya vighātāya dāruṇe 'smiñ jana|kṣaye?
yathā sa puruṣa|vyāghro na hanyeta Jayadrathaḥ
tathā vidhatsva, bhadraṃ te. tvaṃ hi naḥ paramā gatiḥ.
asau Dhanaṃjay'|âgnir hi kopa|māruta|coditaḥ
senā|kakṣaṃ dahati me vahniḥ kakṣam iv' ôtthitaḥ.
atikrānte hi Kaunteye bhittvā sainyaṃ, paraṃ|tapa,
Jayadrathasya goptāraḥ saṃśayaṃ paramaṃ gatāḥ.
sthirā buddhir nar'|êndrāṇām āsīd, brahma|vidāṃ vara:
n' âtikramiṣyati Droṇaṃ jātu jīvan Dhanaṃjayaḥ.
94.10 yo 'sau Pārtho vyatikrānto miṣatas te mahā|dyute
sarvaṃ hy ady' āturaṃ manye. n' êdam asti balaṃ mama.
jānāmi tvāṃ mahā|bhāga Pāṇḍavānāṃ hite ratam.
tathā muhyāmi ca brahman kāryavattāṃ vicintayan.
yathā|śakti ca te brahman vartaye vṛttim uttamām
prīṇāmi ca yathā|śakti: tac ca tvaṃ n' âvabudhyase.
asmān na tvaṃ sadā bhaktān icchasy a|mita|vikrama.
Pāṇḍavān satataṃ prīṇāsy asmākaṃ vipriye ratān.
asmān ev' ôpajīvaṃs tvam asmākaṃ vipriye rataḥ.
na hy ahaṃ tvāṃ vijānāmi madhu|digdham iva kṣuram.
94.15 n' âdāsyac ced varaṃ mahyaṃ bhavān Pāṇḍava|nigrahe
n' âvārayiṣyaṃ gacchantam ahaṃ Sindhu|patiṃ gṛhān.
mayā tv āśaṃsamānena tvattas trāṇam a|buddhinā
āśvāsitaḥ Sindhu|patir, mohād dattaś ca mṛtyave.
Yama|daṃṣṭr'|ântaraṃ prāpto mucyet' âpi hi mānavaḥ,
n' Ârjunasya vaśaṃ prāpto mucyet' âjau Jayadrathaḥ.
sa tathā kuru, śoṇ'|âśva, yathā mucyeta Saindhavaḥ.
mama c' ārta|pralāpānāṃ mā krudhaḥ. pāhi Saindhavam.»

hope. All I ask is that you protect our own tiger from the ravages of theirs. Fanned by the tempests in his heart the fire Dhanan·jaya has burnt down our edge like a blaze rising through the scrub. O nemesis. Now that Kunti's son has broken through and rides deep among us Jayad·ratha's guardians are no longer safe. O seer of seers none of our 94.10
champions ever dreamed that Dhanan·jaya son of Pritha would make it past Drona this side of death. And yet despite your great valour there you stand, blinking in his dust.

What is this perversion? My army is no longer my own. I know full well that you would like nothing better than to see Pandu's children win. Try as I might o priest I cannot grasp the sense in this. I do all that I can o priest to see you live as fine a life as you do. I care for you more than you know. And yet despite my endless devotion you despise me. It is the Pándavas whom you adore and who bask in your limitless favour as they plot to destroy me. And you plot with them even as you take food at my table.

Your words are sweet as honey but I have not looked close. There are thorns in the jar.* If you had not given 94.15
me your unimpeachable word that you would capture the Pandu king then I would not have stopped Jayad·ratha from abandoning us for home. In my forlorn hope that you would protect us I persuaded the Sindhu king to stay and so with a false promise delivered him up to death. A man might be snatched from Yama's jaws, but nothing will save Jayad·ratha if Árjuna gets hold of him. O warrior of the red horses, do what you can to save Sáindhava. Forgive me my ravings. Protect the Sindhu king."

DROṆA uvāca:

n' âbhyasūyāmi te vākyam. Aśvatthāmn" âsi me samaḥ.
satyaṃ tu te pravakṣyāmi. taj juṣasva, viśāṃ pate.
94.20 sārathiḥ pravaraḥ Kṛṣṇaḥ śīghrāś c' âsya hay'|ôttamāḥ
alpaṃ ca vivaraṃ kṛtvā tūrṇaṃ yāti Dhanaṃjayaḥ.
kiṃ nu paśyasi bāṇ'|âughān krośa|mātre Kirīṭinaḥ
paścād rathasya patitān kṣiptāñ śīghraṃ hi gacchataḥ.
na c' âhaṃ śīghra|yāne 'dya samartho vayas" ânvitaḥ,
senā|mukhe ca Pārthānām etad balam upasthitam.
Yudhiṣṭhiraś ca me grāhyo miṣatāṃ sarva|dhanvinām.
evaṃ mayā pratijñātaṃ kṣatra|madhye, mahā|bhuja.
Dhanaṃjayena c' ôtsṛṣṭo vartate pramukhe, nṛ|pa.
tasmād vyūha|mukhaṃ hitvā n' âhaṃ yāsyāmi Phālgunam.
94.25 tuly'|âbhijana|karmāṇaṃ śatrum ekaṃ sahāyavān
gatvā yodhaya: mā bhais tvaṃ. tvaṃ hy asya jagataḥ patiḥ.
rājā śūraḥ kṛtī dakṣo netuṃ para|puraṃ|jayaḥ
vīra, svayaṃ prayāhy atra yatra Pārtho Dhanaṃjayaḥ.

DURYODHANA uvāca:

kathaṃ tvām apy atikrāntaḥ sarva|śastra|bhṛtāṃ varam
Dhanaṃjayo mayā śakya Ācārya pratibādhitum?
api śakyo raṇe jetuṃ vajra|hastaḥ puraṃ|daraḥ?
n' Ârjunaḥ samare śakyo jetuṃ para|puraṃ|jayaḥ,
yena Bhojaś ca Hārdikyo bhavāṃś ca tri|daś'|ôpamaḥ

DRONA spoke:

You will not provoke me. You are as much my son as is Ashvattháman. I will speak to you plainly now and o lord of men take heart from what I say.

Krishna is a fine charioteer and his horses are the fastest 94.20
there are and this is why Dhanan·jaya has escaped us. But he leaves only a light wound behind him. Look at the arrows that lie scattered in Kirítin's wake. They span a distance no wider than a man's call. He makes his rapid escape only because the years when I had his speed and energy are long gone. Meanwhile we are ready to meet Partha's main attack. Great king recall the promise I made with all royalty as my witness that no matter who bears a bow to protect him Yudhi·shthira will be mine. He goes in their van without Dhanan·jaya to protect him. My work o majesty is here at the frontline and the Red Star Fighter is not my concern.
Your foe is alone. In deed and blood you are his equal and 94.25
Árjuna has no friends at his side. Go forth to fight him and have no fear in your heart for you hold in your hand this unruly sphere entire. You are a king and warrior and whole cities cower at your feet. You have the skill and main to lead your men. Go boldly forth to fight Pritha's son.

DURYÓDHANA spoke:

You are our teacher and the grand master of all the weapons of war and still you could not stop Dhanan·jaya. Yet you say that I can match him? Can any defeat the god that razes cities with his thunderbolt? No fortress could withstand Árjuna and no man can better him in battle. Bhoja son of Hrídika was burnt up by him. Godlike though you are you

astra|pratāpena jitau Śrutāyuś ca nibarhitaḥ
94.30 Sudakṣiṇaś ca nihataḥ sa ca rājā Śrutāyudhaḥ
Śrutāyuś c' Âcyutāyuś ca mlecchāś c' âyutaśo hatāḥ.
taṃ kathaṃ Pāṇḍavaṃ yuddhe dahantam iva pāvakam
pratiyotsyāmi dur|dharṣaṃ tam ahaṃ śastra|kovidam?
kṣamaṃ ca manyase yuddhaṃ mama ten' âdya saṃyuge.
paravān asmi bhavati. preṣyavad rakṣa mad|yaśaḥ.

DROṆA uvāca:

satyaṃ vadasi, Kauravya: dur|ādharṣo Dhanaṃjayaḥ.
ahaṃ tu tat kariṣyāmi yath" âinaṃ prasahiṣyasi.
adbhutaṃ c' âdya paśyantu loke sarva|dhanur|dharāḥ
viṣaktaṃ tvayi Kaunteyaṃ Vāsudevasya paśyataḥ.
94.35 eṣa te kavacaṃ, rājaṃs, tathā badhnāmi kāñcanam
yathā na bāṇā n' âstrāṇi prahariṣyanti te raṇe.
yadi tvāṃ s'|âsura|surāḥ sa|yakṣ'|ôraga|rākṣasāḥ
yodhayanti trayo lokāḥ sa|narā, n' âsti te bhayam.
na Kṛṣṇo na ca Kaunteyo na c' ânyaḥ śastra|bhṛd raṇe
śarān arpayituṃ kaś cit kavace tava śakṣyati.
sa tvaṃ kavacam āsthāya kruddham adya raṇe 'rjunam
tvaramāṇaḥ svayaṃ yāhi. na tv" âsau visahiṣyate.

SAṂJAYA uvāca:

evam uktvā tvaran Droṇaḥ
spṛṣṭv" âmbho varma bhāsvaram
ābabandh' âdbhutatamaṃ
japan mantraṃ yathā|vidhi
94.40 raṇe tasmin su|mahati vijayāya sutasya te
visismāpayiṣur lokān vidyayā brahma|vittamaḥ.

too felt the heat of his attack. Shrutáyus is no more and 94.30
Sudákshina lies slain and the kings Shrutáyudha, Shrutáyus and Achyutáyus and their thousandstrong barbarian horde are all dead by Pándava's hand. He burns like fire through the fray. How could I even get close to the flash of his blade? You say that this is a contest that I should fight. Well I am here to serve you. But defend my honour as a master ought.

DRONA spoke:

O son of Kuru. What you say is true: Dhanan·jaya is dangerous. All the same, I will ensure that you are a match for him. Let every warrior in the world look upon this wonder. Kunti's son will grind to a halt before you and Vasudéva will not be able to do a thing to help him.

Majesty behold. I give you armour of gold that neither 94.35
arrow nor blade can break. The gods and demons, the spirits serpents and ghosts, all the men and all the creatures that fill the triple world may rise against you and still you will have nothing to fear. Whether Krishna or Kauntéya or any third beside that bears a blade, none that live will pierce this plate. Buckle it on and it will withstand the force of Árjuna's fury. Then make haste to find him, for the battle will be an even one.

SÁNJAYA spoke:

Drona finished speaking and with a flourish brought forth a finetooled cuirass splendid as the sun and sprinkling
water across it he muttered secret enchantments and bound 94.40
it close upon Duryódhana's back. The wise seer sought to enchant us all with his arcana and bring victory to your son in the great strife to come.

DROṆA uvāca:

karotu svasti te Brahma Brahmā c' âpi dvi|jātayaḥ
sarīsṛpāś ca ye śreṣṭhās, tebhyas te svasti Bhārata.
Yayātir Nahuṣaś c' âiva, Dhundhumāro Bhagīrathaḥ
tubhyaṃ rāja'|rṣayaḥ sarve svasti kurvantu te sadā.
svasti te 'stv eka|pādebhyo bahu|pādebhya eva ca
svasty astv a|pādakebhyaś ca nityaṃ tava mahā|raṇe.
Svāhā Svadhā Śacī c' âiva svasti kurvantu te sadā.
Lakṣmīr Arundhatī c' âiva kurutāṃ svasti te 'n|agha.
94.45 Asito Devalaś c' âiva, Viśvāmitras tath" Âṅgirāḥ,
Vasiṣṭhaḥ Kaśyapaś c' âiva svasti kurvantu te nṛ|pa.
Dhātā Vidhātā Lokeśo diśaś ca sa|dig|īśvarāḥ
svasti te 'dya prayacchantu Kārttikeyaś ca ṣaṇ|mukhaḥ.
vivasvān bhagavān svasti karotu tava sarvaśaḥ
dig|gajāś c' âiva catvāraḥ kṣitiś ca gaganaṃ grahāḥ.
adhastād dharaṇīṃ yo 'sau sadā dhārayate nṛ|pa
s'|ōṣaś ca pannaga|śreṣṭhaḥ svasti tubhyaṃ prayacchatu.

Gāndhāre yudhi vikramya nirjitāḥ sura|sattamāḥ
purā Vṛtreṇa Daityena bhinna|dehāḥ sahasraśaḥ.
94.50 hṛta|tejo|balāḥ sarve tadā s'|Êndrā div'|âukasaḥ
Brahmāṇaṃ śaraṇaṃ jagmur Vṛtrād bhītā mah"|âsurāt.

DEVĀ ūcuḥ:

pramarditānāṃ Vṛtreṇa devānāṃ, deva|sattama,
gatir bhava sura|śreṣṭha trāhi no mahato bhayāt.

DRONA spoke:

O scion of Bharata the blessing of the Spirit and Creator upon you. The blessing of the twiceborn and of all the good snakes of the earth upon you. The eternal blessing of Yayáti and Náhusha, of Dhundhu·mara and Bhagi·ratha and all the philosopher kings upon you. May all that lives and all that runs scuttles and slithers bless you without end in the great battle to come. May Svaha, Svadha and Shachi lay their blessing upon you. May Lakshmi and
Arúndhati lay their blessing upon your pure soul. The bless- 94.45
ing of Ásita Dévala, of Vishva·mitra and Ángiras, Vasíshtha and Káshyapa upon this king. May Dhatri and Vidhátri and Lokésha and the quarters of the air and they that guard them and sixheaded Karttikéya bestow their blessing upon you. The eternal blessing of the holy sun upon you and of the planets and of the sky and of the spaces above us and of the earth below and of the four elephants that bear it up. O king may the great Serpent deep underground that ever shapes the fertile earth bestow his blessing upon you.

Long ago Vritra child of Diti invaded Gandhára and cast down the great gods in legion. He left them battered and
afraid, with their strength and splendour gone. So Indra 94.50
led the sky's denizens to Brahma and they begged him to protect them from the archdemon.

THE GODS spoke:

O lord of our kind. Vritra has crushed us. Show us the way o god of gods and banish this fear from our hearts.

atha pārśve sthitaṃ Viṣṇuṃ Śakr'|ādīṃś ca sur'|ôttamān
prāha tathyam idaṃ vākyaṃ viṣaṇṇān sura|sattamān.
«rakṣyā me satataṃ devāḥ sah'|Êndrāḥ sa|dvijātayaḥ.
Tvaṣṭuḥ su|durdharaṃ tejo yena Vṛtro vinirmitaḥ.
Tvaṣṭrā purā tapas taptvā varṣ'|âyuta|śataṃ tadā
Vṛtro vinirmito, devāḥ, prāpy' ânujñāṃ Maheśvarāt.
94.55 sa tasy' âiva prasādād vo hanyād eva ripur balī.
n' â|gatvā Śaṃkara|sthānaṃ bhagavān dṛśyate Haraḥ.
dṛṣṭvā jeṣyatha Vṛtraṃ taṃ. kṣipraṃ gacchata Mandaram
yatr' āste tapasāṃ yonir Dakṣa|yajña|vināśanaḥ,
pinākī sarva|bhūt'|ēśo Bhaga|netra|nipātanaḥ.»
te gatvā sahitā devā Brahmaṇā saha Mandaram
apaśyaṃs tejasāṃ rāśiṃ sūrya|koṭi|sama|prabham.
so 'bravīt: «svāgataṃ devā. brūta kiṃ karavāṇy aham.
a|moghaṃ darśanaṃ mahyaṃ: kāma|prāptir ato 'stu vaḥ.»
evam uktās tu te sarve pratyūcus taṃ div'|âukasaḥ.
«tejo hṛtaṃ no Vṛtreṇa. gatir bhava div'|âukasām.
94.60 mūrtīr īkṣasva no, deva, prahārair jarjarī|kṛtāḥ.
śaraṇaṃ tvāṃ prapannāḥ sma. gatir bhava Maheśvara.»

ŚARVA uvāca:

viditaṃ vo yathā, devāḥ kṛty" êyaṃ su|mahā|balā
Tvaṣṭus tejo|bhavā ghorā dur|nivāry" â|kṛt'|ātmabhiḥ.

Brahma then made a promise to Shakra and Vishnu and the rest of the great celestials as they stood in sorrow before him.

"I am the deathless haven of Indra and of the gods and of the twiceborn that go with them. Vritra is made of Tvashtri's adamantine heat. O gods, in an olden age Tvashtri burned in meditation for a thousand summers and thus with Mahéshvara's leave Vritra came to be. It is because Mahéshvara 94.55
has willed it that your adversary has the power to destroy you. You must visit Hara's hallowed ground to seek an audience with him, and when you have done so Vritra will be finished. Go now to Mándara and seek the vault of fire. Go to where the ghost king dwells. Go to the god who bears the trident, the god who burned out Bhaga's eyes and left Daksha's rite in ruins."

Off to Mándara went Brahma and the gods and there they found the core of flame, bright as ten million suns. These were the words that they heard.

"Welcome gods. Tell me what I can do. This mighty vision cannot go dark: all you desire will be so."

The celestials replied in concert to his words.

"Vritra has robbed us of our light. Have mercy on heav-
en's sons. See o god: our shapes are tattered from his blows. 94.60
We have come to seek your protection and we ask o Mahéshvara that you keep us safe."

SHARVA spoke:

O gods you know full well that powerful magic spawned this creature. He is built of Tvashtri's heat and even the

avaśyaṃ tu mayā kāryaṃ sāhyaṃ sarva|div'|âukasām.
mam' êdaṃ gātra|jaṃ Śakra kavacaṃ gṛhya bhāsvaram
badhān' ânena mantreṇa mānasena sur'|ēśvara
vadhāy' âsura|sukhyasya Vṛtrasya sura|ghātinaḥ.

DROṆA uvāca:

ity uktvā vara|daḥ prādād varma tan mantram eva ca.
sa tena varmaṇā guptaḥ prāyād Vṛtra|camūṃ prati.
94.65 nānā|vidhaiś ca śastr'|âughaiḥ pātyamānair mahā|raṇe
na saṃdhiḥ śakyate bhettuṃ varma|bandhasya tasya tu.
tato jaghāna samare Vṛtraṃ deva|patiḥ svayam.
taṃ ca mantramayaṃ bandhaṃ varma c' Âṅgirase dadau
Aṅgirāḥ prāha putrasya mantra|jñasya Bṛhaspateḥ.
Bṛhaspatir ath' ôvāca Agniveśyāya dhīmate.
Agniveśyo mama prādāt tena badhnāmi varma te
tav' âdya deha|rakṣ"|ârthaṃ mantreṇa nṛpa|sattama.

SAṂJAYA uvāca:

evam uktvā tato Droṇas tava putraṃ mahā|dyutim
punar eva vacaḥ prāha śanair ācārya|puṃgavaḥ.
94.70 «brahma|sūtreṇa badhnāmi kavacaṃ tava, pārthiva,
Hiraṇyagarbheṇa yathā baddhaṃ Viṣṇoḥ purā raṇe.
yathā ca Brahmaṇā baddhaṃ saṃgrāme Tārakāmaye
Śakrasya kavacaṃ divyaṃ tathā badhnāmy ahaṃ tava.»

rarest of souls stand little hope before him. I cannot grant the celestials a simple triumph. This armour splendid as the sun is made of my body: take it o Shakra and bind it with this silent incantation that you o lord of the gods might bring low the scourge of your kind and treasure of the demons whom we know as Vritra.

DRONA spoke:

And so the Giver handed him the armour and the mantra and clad within them he marched against Vritra's host.
Many many blades fell upon him in the war that followed 94.65
but none could breach a single joint or ligature in his suit, and thus the king of the gods brought Vritra down in combat. It was to Ángiras that Indra passed the plate and so too the mantra to bind it. Ángiras passed the mantra to Brihas·pati his son who was already steeped in such arts: he told it to brilliant Agni·veshya and Agni·veshya passed it on to me. O king of kings with its power I bind now this armour to you so that during what is to come your body will in no way be harmed.

SÁNJAYA spoke:

Drona paused for a moment. Then to stir your son's courage even more the venerable Instructor spoke again.
"King. I bind this armour upon you with sacred thread 94.70
as Brahma born in gold once bound Vishnu as he prepared for war. As Brahma once bound Shakra's magic armour in the battle for Táraka so do I bind this plate upon you now."

baddhvā tu kavacaṃ tasya mantreṇa vidhi|pūrvakam
preṣayām āsa rājānaṃ yuddhāya mahate dvijaḥ.
sa saṃnaddho mahā|bāhur Ācāryeṇa mah'|ātmanā
rathānāṃ ca sahasreṇa Trigartānāṃ prahāriṇām
tathā danti|sahasreṇa mattānāṃ vīrya|śālinām
aśvānām niyuten' âiva tath" ânyaiś ca mahā|rathaiḥ,
94.75 vṛtaḥ prāyān mahā|bāhur Arjunasya rathaṃ prati
nānā|vāditra|ghoṣeṇa yathā Vairocanis tathā.
tataḥ śabdo mahān āsīt sainyānāṃ tava Bhārata
a|gādhaṃ prasthitaṃ dṛṣṭvā samudram iva Kauravam.

SAMJAYA uvāca:

95.1 PRAVIṢṬAYOR, mahā|rāja, Pārtha|Vārṣṇeyayo raṇe
Duryodhane prayāte ca pṛṣṭhataḥ puruṣa'|ṛṣabhe,
javen' âbhyadravan Droṇaṃ mahatā niḥsvanena ca
Pāṇḍavāḥ Somakaiḥ sārdhaṃ. tato yuddham avartata.
tad yuddham abhavat tīvraṃ tumulaṃ loma|harṣaṇam
Kurūṇāṃ Pāṇḍavānāṃ ca vyūhasya purato 'dbhutam.
rājan kadā cin n' âsmābhir dṛṣṭaṃ tādṛṅ na ca śrutam
yādṛṅ madhya|gate sūrye yuddham āsīd viśāṃ pate.
95.5 Dhṛṣṭadyumna|mukhāḥ Pārthā vyūḍh'|ânīkāḥ prahāriṇaḥ
Droṇasya sainyaṃ te sarve śara|varṣair avākiran.
vayaṃ Droṇaṃ puras|kṛtya sarva|śastra|bhṛtāṃ varam
Pārṣata|pramukhān Pārthān abhyavarṣāma sāyakaiḥ.
mahā|meghāv iv' ôdīrṇau miśra|vātau him'|âtyaye
sen"|âgre pracakāśete rucire ratha|bhūṣite.
sametya tu mahā|sene cakratur vegam uttamam
Jāhnavī|Yamune nadyau prāvṛṣ' îv' ôlbaṇ'|ôdake.

Thus the priest sent forth the king to the great battle that awaited him, well clad in armour and secret enchantments. Girt by the great Instructor and by a thousand Tri·garta cars and a thousand mighty elephants wild with the season and by horses and warriors in multitudes seething ring upon ring, the hardy king set forth for Árjuna while the drums 94.75
and flutes sang to him as once they had sung for Vairóchani. O Bhárata the great chorus rolled through the lines of the army as if the men bid your son a safe voyage far across the deep of the sea.

SÁNJAYA spoke:

O MAJESTY. So it was that Duryódhana bull in the herd 95.1
of men rode on into the breach left by Partha and Varshnéya. Meanwhile with hammering hooves the Pándavas and Sómakas came stampeding towards Drona. In the van between Pándava and Kuru a new battle began, and its heat and noise and bloodiness were beyond imagining. O king of these lands I can liken nothing to the sound and fury of the battle that opened out across the plain beneath the noon sun that day. The Partha warriors under Dhrishta· 95.5
dyumna's command loosed their bows and down the arrows rained on Drona's host. Best of all who bear blades, the brahmin gave the sign and our own darts streamed onto the sons of Príshata and Pritha. Crusted in cars the edges of the two armies were like vast cloudbanks churned by gales as the cold season closes, and as the Ganges and Yámuna swollen with monsoon rain plunge into each other where their courses cross so the two armies merged and roiled.

nānā|śastra|puro|vāto dvip'|âśva|ratha|saṃvṛtaḥ
gadā|vidyun mahā|raudraḥ saṃgrāma|jalado mahān
95.10 Bhāradvāj'|ânil'|ôddhūtaḥ śara|dhārā|sahasravān
abhyavarṣan mahā|sainyaḥ Pāṇḍu|sen"|âgnim uddhatam.
samudram iva gharm'|ânte viśan ghoro mah"|ânilaḥ
vyakṣobhayad anīkāni Pāṇḍavānāṃ dvij'|ôttamaḥ.
te 'pi sarva|prayatnena Droṇam eva samādravan
bibhitsanto mahā|setuṃ vāry|oghāḥ prabalā iva.
vārayām āsa tān Droṇo jal'|âugham a|calo yathā
Pāṇḍavān samare kruddhān Pāñcālāṃś ca sa|Kekayān.
ath' âpare vai rājānaḥ parivṛtya samantataḥ
mahā|balā raṇe śūrāḥ Pāñcālān anvavārayan.
95.15 tato raṇe nara|vyāghraḥ Pārṣataḥ Pāṇḍavaiḥ saha
saṃjaghān' â|sakṛd Droṇaṃ bibhitsur ari|vāhinīm.
yath" âiva śara|varṣāṇi Droṇo varṣati Pārṣate
tath" âiva śara|varṣāṇi Dhṛṣṭadyumno 'py avarṣata.
sa|nistriṃśa|puro|vātaḥ śakti|prāsa'|ṛṣṭi|saṃvṛtaḥ
jyā|vidyuc cāpa|saṃhrādo Dhṛṣṭadyumna|balāhakaḥ
śara|dhār"|âśma|varṣāṇi vyasṛjat sarvato|diśam.
nighnan ratha|var'|âśv'|âughān plāvayām āsa vāhinīm.
yaṃ yam ārcchac charair Droṇaḥ
Pāṇḍavānāṃ ratha|vrajam
tatas tataḥ śarair Droṇam
apākarṣata Pārṣataḥ.
95.20 tathā tu yatamānasya Droṇasya yudhi, Bhārata,
Dhṛṣṭadyumnaṃ samāsādya tridhā sainyam abhidyata.
Bhojam eke 'bhyavartanta Jalasaṃdham tath" âpare
Pāṇḍavair hanyamānāś ca Droṇam ev' âpare yayuḥ.

We swung our blades and our maces flashed like bolts of lightning. The great noisome storm of men and beasts and cars whipped up by Bharadvája's winds rolled in and 95.10
it poured down its thousand drops of rain upon the billowing fire of Pandu's men. The great brahmin shook the Pándava lines like a fierce gale upon the ocean when the hot days are ending, and like huge and malevolent waves breaking across a mighty span the Pándavas, Panchálas and Kékayas gathered and crashed into Drona. Drona stood still as stone in their boiling waters as other of his kings bold and strong seethed about the Panchálas and for a moment held them in check. Then hatred flared in the tiger Párshata and 95.15
he brought the Pándava pack back at Drona with sudden force. As the arrows streamed from Drona's bow Dhrishta·dyumna matched each with one of his own. Thrumming and strumming bow and string and raising the winds with his knives the storm Dhrishta·dyumna bristled with blades and spears and staves and burst with a hail of arrows from every quarter of the sky. They poured into our lines and struck hard our fine cars and all the teams that drew them.

Drona sent his arrows coursing through the Pándava horde yet each time Párshata found him with his own and repelled him. O Bhárata. Drona began to struggle then, and 95.20
as he did our army broke on Dhrishta·dyumna and split in three. Some went with Bhoja, some with Jala·sandha and some were driven back by the Pándavas to where Drona fought. The great man rallied his troops but mighty Dhrishta·dyumna shook them once more. Your defenders stood

samghaṭṭayati sainyāni Droṇas tu rathinām varaḥ.
vyadhamac c' âpi tāny asya Dhṛṣṭadyumno mahā|rathaḥ.
Dhārtarāṣṭrās tathā|bhūtā vadhyante Pāṇḍu|Sṛñjayaiḥ
a|gopāḥ paśavo 'raṇye bahubhiḥ śvāpadair iva.
kālaḥ sma grasate yodhān Dhṛṣṭadyumnena mohitān
saṃgrāme tumule tasminn, iti saṃmenire janāḥ.
95.25 ku|nṛpasya yathā rāṣṭraṃ dur|bhikṣa|vyādhi|taskaraiḥ
drāvyate, tadvad āpannā Pāṇḍavais tava vāhinī.
arka|raśmi|vimiśreṣu śastreṣu kavaceṣu ca
cakṣūṃṣi pratyahanyanta sainyena rajasā tathā.
tridhā|bhūteṣu sainyeṣu vadhyamāneṣu Pāṇḍavaiḥ
a|marṣitas tato Droṇaḥ Pāñcālān vyadhamac charaiḥ.
mṛdnatas tāny anīkāni nighnataś c' âpi sāyakaiḥ
babhūva rūpaṃ Droṇasya kāl'|âgner iva dīpyataḥ.
rathaṃ nāgaṃ hayaṃ c' âpi pattinaś ca viśāṃ pate
ek'|âiken' êṣuṇā saṃkhye nirbibheda mahā|rathaḥ.
95.30 Pāṇḍavānāṃ tu sainyeṣu n' âsti kaś cit sa Bhārata
dadhāra yo raṇe bāṇān Droṇa|cāpa|cyutāñ prabho.
tat pacyamānam arkeṇa Droṇa|sāyaka|tāpitam
babhrāma Pārṣataṃ sainyaṃ tatra tatr' âiva Bhārata.
tath" âiva Pārṣaten' âpi kālyamānaṃ balaṃ tava
abhavat sarvato dīptaṃ śuṣkaṃ vanam iv' âgninā.
vadhyamāneṣu sainyeṣu Droṇa|Pārṣata|sāyakaiḥ
tyaktvā prāṇān paraṃ śaktyā yudhyante sarvato|mukhāḥ.

divided and they had as little chance before the Pandus
and Srínjayas as a shepherdless flock beset by jackals in the
wilderness. Men said that in the din and crash of that battle Dhrishta·dyumna had come to stun the prey for Time's
feast. As the land of a weak king falls victim to death, plague 95.25
or banditry, so were we riddled by the Pándava attack and
began to give way, our eyes blind from the dust of combat
and the flash of the sun's rays bouncing back at us from the
surface of sword and shield.

Drona saw his army split in three and battered by the
Pándavas and he would not brook it. Now his arrows found
the Panchálas and he ground and crushed them beneath
his shafts. Drona flared like the fire that blazes at the age's
end as he cut down car, elephant, horse and man and o
majesty his mastery was such that he felled each with but a
single shaft. Wise scion of Bharata I tell you that none in the 95.30
Pándava host could escape the arrows that fluttered from
Drona's fingers through the fray. O Bhárata now it was the
turn of Párshata's army to fade, beaten down by the sun's
rays and scorched by Drona's darts, even as Párshata had
put us all to the torch like a brushwood forest consumed by
flame. Whether ravaged by Drona or Dhrishta·dyumna we
all turned our backs on life and drove ourselves onward to
fight with all the strength we could muster.

tāvakānāṃ pareṣāṃ ca yudhyatāṃ, Bharata'|rṣabha,
n' āsīt kaś cin, mahā|rāja, yo 'tyākṣīt saṃyugaṃ bhayāt.
95.35 Bhīmasenaṃ tu Kaunteyaṃ sodaryāḥ paryavārayan
Viviṃśatiś Citraseno Vikarṇaś ca mahā|rathaḥ.
Vind'|Ânuvindāv Āvantyau Kṣemadhūrtiś ca vīryavān
trayāṇāṃ tava putrāṇāṃ traya ev' ânuyāyinaḥ.
Bāhlīka|rājas tejasvī kula|putro mahā|rathaḥ
saha|senaḥ sah'|âmātyo Draupadeyān avārayat.
Śaibyo Govāsano rājā yodhair daśa|śat'|āvaraiḥ
Kāśyasy' Âbhibhuvaḥ putraṃ parākrāntam avārayat.
Ajātaśatruṃ Kaunteyaṃ jvalantam iva pāvakam
Madrāṇām īśvaraḥ Śalyo rājā rājānam āvṛṇot.
95.40 Duḥśāsanas tv avasthāpya svam anīkam a|marṣaṇaḥ
Sātyakiṃ prayayau kruddhaḥ śūro ratha|varaṃ yudhi.
svaken' âham anīkena saṃnaddhaḥ kavac'|āvṛtaḥ
catuḥ|śatair mah"|êṣv|āsaiś Cekitānam avārayam.
Śakunis tu sah'|ânīko Mādrī|putram avārayat
Gāndhārakaiḥ sapta|śataiś cāpa|śakty|asi|pāṇibhiḥ.
Vind'|Ânuvindāv Āvantyau
Virāṭaṃ Matsyam ārcchatām
prāṇāṃs tyaktvā mah"|êṣv|āsau
mitr'|ârthe 'bhyudyat'|āyudhau.
Śikhaṇḍinaṃ Yājñaseniṃ rundhānam a|parājitam
Bāhlīkaḥ pratisaṃyattaḥ parākrāntam avārayat.
95.45 Dhṛṣṭadyumnaṃ ca Pāñcālyaṃ
krūraiḥ sārdhaṃ Prabhadrakaiḥ
Āvantyaḥ saha Sauvīraiḥ
kruddha|rūpam avārayat.

O bull of the Bharatas. There was not one man that hour
on either side who fled the field in fear. The brothers Vivín- 95.35
shati, Chitra·sena and bold Vikárna went to meet Bhima·
sena son of Kunti. With your three sons went their three
companions Vinda and Anuvínda and mighty Kshema·
dhurti. It was the highborn and valiant king of Bahlíka
who came against the Draupadéyas, phalanx and friends in
his fiery wake. Just shy of ten thousand men followed Go·
vásana the Shibi chieftain as he drove his car at the brave
heir of Ábhibhu lord of Kashi. King met king when Shalya
lord of the Madras crossed the dancing flame that was Ajáta·
shatru son of Kunti. Duhshásana brought his legions in 95.40
might and wrath upon the champion Sátyaki, while mailed
and ready to fight I rallied my own bowmen four hundred
strong and made for Chekitána.

Seven hundred Gandháras bearing swords and spears and
bows Shákuni led against Madri's son, and the great Avánti
archers Vinda and Anuvínda set aside their lives for their
friend's cause and raising their bows wheeled away to face
Viráta the Matsya king. Bahlíka steeled himself as down
upon him bore Shikhándin the matchless son of Yajnya·
sena whom none have yet bettered, and Dhrishta·dyumna 95.45
lord of Panchála was fury incarnate when he brought his
cruel Prabhádrakas to meet the myrmidons of Avántya.
The nightwalker Ghatótkacha so fell and foul turned his

Ghaṭotkacaṃ tathā śūraṃ rākṣasaṃ krūra|karmiṇam
Alāyudho 'dravat tūrṇaṃ kruddham āyāntam āhave.
Alambuṣaṃ rākṣas'|êndraṃ Kuntibhojo mahā|rathaḥ
sainyena mahatā yuktaḥ krūra|rūpam avārayat.
  Saindhavaḥ pṛṣṭhatas tv āsīt sarva|sainyasya Bhārata
rakṣitaḥ param'|êṣv|āsaiḥ Kṛpa|prabhṛtibhī rathaiḥ.
tasy' âstāṃ cakra|rakṣau dvau Saindhavasya bṛhattamau
Drauṇir dakṣiṇato, rājan, Sūta|putraś ca vāmataḥ.
95.50 pṛṣṭha|gopās tu tasy' āsan Saumadatti|puro|gamāḥ
Kṛpaś ca Vṛṣasenaś ca Śalaḥ Śalyaś ca dur|jayaḥ.
nītimanto mah"|êṣv|āsāḥ sarve yuddha|viśāradāḥ
Saindhavasya vidhāy' âivaṃ rakṣāṃ yuyudhire tataḥ.

SAMJAYA uvāca:

96.1 RĀJAN, SAMGRĀMAM āścaryaṃ śṛṇu kīrtayato mama
Kurūṇāṃ Pāṇḍavānāṃ ca yathā yuddham avartata.
  Bhāradvājaṃ samāsādya vyūhasya pramukhe sthitam
ayodhayan raṇe Pārthā Droṇ'|ânīkaṃ bibhitsavaḥ.
rakṣamāṇaḥ svakaṃ vyūhaṃ Droṇo 'pi saha sainikaiḥ
ayodhayad raṇe Pārthān prārthayāno mahad yaśaḥ.
Vind'|Ânuvindāv Āvantyau Virāṭaṃ daśabhiḥ śaraiḥ
ājaghnatuḥ su|saṃkruddhau tava putra|hit'|âiṣiṇau.
96.5 Virāṭaś ca mahā|rāja tāv ubhau samare sthitau
parākrāntau parākramya yodhayām āsa s'|ânugau.
teṣāṃ yuddhaṃ samabhavad
    dāruṇaṃ śoṇit'|ôdakam
siṃhasya dvipa|mukhyābhyāṃ
    prabhinnābhyāṃ yathā vane.
  Bāhlīkaṃ rabhasaṃ yuddhe Yājñasenir mahā|balaḥ
ājaghne viśikhais tīkṣṇair ghorair marm'|âsthi|bhedibhiḥ.
Bāhlīko Yājñasenim tu hema|puṅkhaiḥ śilā|śitaiḥ

frenzy on Aláyudha, and the demon king Alámbusha had no mercy in his heart when he met the great legion under bold Kunti·bhoja's command.

O Bhárata hidden behind all these men by the cars of Kripa's crack troops stood Sáindhava. Protecting his wheels, my king, were men without peer, Drauni watching the right and the Horseman's Son the left. Watching his back were 95.50
Saumadátti and Kripa, Vrisha·sena, Shala and hardy Shalya, all of them lords of the bow steeped in their craft and fighting with a solitary aim in mind: that Sáindhava would be kept from harm.

SÁNJAYA spoke:

WONDROUS WERE the battles that day fought between 96.1
Kuru and Pándava. Hear me now my king and I will tell you of them.

Eager to break Drona's line the Parthas clove for Bharad·vaja's son, and bracing his troops to meet them Drona stood firm at the head of his host ready to make good his renown. Vinda and Anuvínda the scions of Avánti loosed their bows for your son's cause and ten of their arrows found Viráta. Viráta o majesty was made of the same stern stuff and he 96.5
rode out to meet the brothers and their men where they tarried in the fray. As when a lion leaps at wild elephants near the jungle's edge his counterattack was a bloody and savage one.

With sharp and deadly shafts biting to the bone the great son of Yajnya·sena struck Bahlíka, but with zeal and fervour Bahlíka struck back at Shikhándin with nine knotless darts each honed to a hiss and fletched in feathers flecked gold.

ājaghāna bhṛśaṃ kruddho navabhir nata|parvabhiḥ.
tad yuddham abhavad ghoraṃ śara|śakti|samākulam
bhīrūṇāṃ trāsa|jananaṃ śūrāṇāṃ harṣa|vardhanam.
96.10 tābhyāṃ tatra śarair muktair antarikṣaṃ diśas tathā
abhavat saṃvṛtaṃ sarvaṃ, na prājñāyata kiṃ cana.
Śaibyo Govāsano yuddhe Kāśya|putraṃ mahā|ratham
sa|sainyo yodhayām āsa gajaḥ pratigajaṃ yathā.
Bāhlīka|rājaḥ saṃkruddho Draupadeyān mahā|rathān
manaḥ pañc' êndriyāṇ' îva śuśubhe yodhayan raṇe.
ayodhayaṃs te subhṛśaṃ taṃ śar'|âughaiḥ samantataḥ
indriy'|ârthā yathā dehaṃ śaśvad, dehavatāṃ vara.
Vārṣṇeyaṃ Sātyakiṃ yuddhe putro Duḥśāsanas tava
ājaghne sāyakais tīkṣṇair navabhir nata|parvabhiḥ.
96.15 so 'tividdho balavatā mah"|êṣv|āsena dhanvinā
īṣan mūrchāṃ jagām' āśu Sātyakiḥ satya|vikramaḥ.
samāśvastas tu Vārṣṇeyas tava putraṃ mahā|ratham
vivyādha daśabhis tūrṇaṃ sāyakaiḥ kaṅka|patribhiḥ.
tāv anyo|'nyaṃ dṛḍhaṃ viddhāv anyonya|śara|pīḍitau
rejatuḥ samare, rājan, puṣpitāv iva kiṃśukau.
Alambuṣas tu saṃkruddhaḥ Kuntibhoja|śar'|ârditaḥ
aśobhata bhṛśaṃ lakṣmyā puṣp"|āḍhya iva kiṃśukaḥ.
Kuntibhojaṃ tato rakṣo viddhvā bahubhir āyasaiḥ
anadad bhairavaṃ nādaṃ vāhinyāḥ pramukhe tava.
96.20 tatas tau samare śūrau yodhayantau paras|param
dadṛśuḥ sarva|sainyāni Śakra|Jambhau yathā purā.
Śakuniṃ rabhasaṃ yuddhe kṛta|vairaṃ ca, Bhārata,
Mādrī|putrau su|saṃrabdhau śaraiś c' ârdayatāṃ bhṛśam.
tumulaḥ sa, mahā|rāja, prāvartata jana|kṣayaḥ
tvayā saṃjanito 'tyarthaṃ Karṇena ca vivardhitaḥ.

To watch their fearful fight thicken with spears and bolts
did chill the blood and quicken the pulse of any whose mettle was made for it. Their arrows aflight packed the air and 96.10
sky and soon were all we could see of them.

I watched Go·vásana scion of Shibi swing his guard towards Kashi's bold son like a bull swerving for its rival
and then there again went King Bahlíka, and this time he
made for the Draupadéyas' high cars and thrust himself between them like the soul blazing through the senses. And o
majesty as the things of the world glance across us all peas-
ant to king without surcease so arrows from their five bows
rained down upon him.*

Nine arrows knotless and sharp from the bow of your
own boy Duhshásana found Sátyaki, and such were their 96.15
power and accuracy that the massive Vrishni felt his vision
mist for a moment. Then he gathered himself and struck
back at your rugged son with ten quick shafts borne on vul-
ture's plumes. Deep went each of their quarrels and each
studded by the other stood tall o king as a flame of the forest in flower. Like forest's flame too right in the van of the
host Alámbusha burst with bright wounds made by Kunti·
bhoja's bow, and from the ogre's gruesome jaws there came
a terrible furious roar. With a flock of his own darts he
answered his foe. They fought ferociously, like Shakra and 96.20
Jambha in battles of yore.

O Bhárata. With wild energy the Madri twins aimed
their volleys at Shákuni and he rounded on them, rancour
and hate in his eyes. So went the bloody dissolution of
men that you o majesty began and that Karna had brought
to hideous fruition. Now the fire that passion had kindled

rakṣitas tava putraiś ca krodha|mūlo hut"|āśanaḥ
ya imāṃ pṛthivīṃ, rājan, dagdhuṃ sarvāṃ samudyataḥ.
Śakuniḥ Pāṇḍu|putrābhyāṃ kṛtaḥ sa vimukhaḥ śaraiḥ
na sma jānāti kartavyaṃ yuddhe kiṃ cit parākramam.
96.25 vimukhaṃ c' âinam ālokya Mādrī|putrau mahā|rathau
vavarṣatuḥ punar bāṇair yathā meghau mahā|girim.
sa vadhyamāno bahubhiḥ śaraiḥ saṃnata|parvabhiḥ
samprāyāj javanair aśvair Droṇ'|ânīkāya Saubalaḥ.
Ghaṭotkacas tathā śūraṃ rākṣasaṃ tam Alāyudham
abhyayād rabhasaṃ yuddhe vegam āsthāya madhyamam.
tayor yuddhaṃ mahā|rāja citra|rūpam iv' âbhavat
yādṛśaṃ hi purā vṛttaṃ Rāma|Rāvaṇayor mṛdhe.
tato Yudhiṣṭhiro rājā Madra|rājānam āhave
viddhvā pañcāśatā bāṇaiḥ punar vivyādha saptabhiḥ.
96.30 tataḥ pravavṛte yuddhaṃ tayor atyadbhutaṃ nṛ|pa
yathā pūrvaṃ mahad yuddhaṃ Śambar'|âmararājayoḥ.
Viviṃśatiś Citraseno Vikarṇaś ca tav' ātma|jaḥ
ayodhayan Bhīmasenaṃ mahatyā senayā vṛtāḥ.

SAṂJAYA uvāca:

97.1 TATHĀ TASMIN pravṛtte tu saṃgrāme loma|harṣaṇe
Kauraveyāṃs tridhā|bhūtān Pāṇḍavāḥ samupādravan.
Jalasaṃdhaṃ mahā|bāhuṃ Bhīmaseno 'bhyavartata,
Yudhiṣṭhiraḥ sah'|ânīkaḥ Kṛtavarmāṇam āhave.
kiraṃs tu śara|varṣāṇi rocamāna iv' âṃśumān
Dhṛṣṭadyumno, mahā|rāja, Droṇam abhyadravad raṇe.
tataḥ pravavṛte yuddhaṃ tvaratāṃ sarva|dhanvinām
Kurūṇāṃ Pāṇḍavānāṃ ca saṃkruddhānāṃ paras|param.

and that you my king and your children had stoked flared ever higher to burn to ash the whole of this flowery sphere. Down the sons of Pandu drove Shákuni and he could do
nothing to fight back. Madri's twins glanced from their high 96.25
cars at his sufferings and like clouds on a mountaintop they poured their shafts upon his head. As knotless darts rained unremitting upon Súbala's son he drove his swift steeds back for Drona's line.

Wading through the middle course of the fighting Ghatótkacha made for Aláyudha torrid and dire and majesty they met in a melée that harked back to Rávana and Rama and their clash of long ago. Across the plain King Yudhi·shthira pierced the Madra king with fifty of his shafts then
pierced him again with seven more. O lord they battled on 96.30
in a spectacle like to the duel Shámbara and the immortal sire fought in a time now past. And I saw your sons square up to Bhima·sena: Vivínshati, Chitra·sena and Vikárna all ranged the broad lines of their troops for the fight.

SÁNJAYA spoke:

ON WENT THESE shuddersome battles as the Pándavas 97.1
crashed among the Káurava's thricesplit lines. Bhima·sena found brawny Jala·sandha in the fray and Yudhi·shthira abreast his troops found Krita·varman and streaming with arrows and shining like a sun Dhrishta·dyumna rushed at Drona. Káurava met Pándava and no archer paused in his battlefrenzy.

97.5 samkṣaye tu tathā|bhūte vartamāne mahā|bhaye
dvaṃdvī|bhūteṣu sainyeṣu yudhyamāneṣv a|bhītavat,
Droṇaḥ Pāñcāla|putreṇa balī balavatā saha
yad akṣipat pṛṣatk'|âughāṃs: tad adbhutam iv' âbhavat.
puṇḍarīka|vanān' îva vidhvastāni samantataḥ
cakrāte Droṇa|Pāñcālyau nṛṇāṃ śīrṣāṇy an|ekaśaḥ
vinikīrṇāni vīrāṇām anīkeṣu samantataḥ.
vastr'|ābharaṇa|śastrāṇi dhvaja|varm'|āyudhāni ca
tapanīya|tanu|trāṇāḥ saṃsiktā rudhireṇa ca
saṃsaktā iva dṛśyante megha|saṃghāḥ sa|vidyutaḥ.
kuñjar'|âśva|narān anye pātayanti sma patribhiḥ
tāla|mātrāṇi cāpāni vikarṣanto mahā|rathāḥ.
97.10 asi|carmāṇi cāpāni śirāṃsi kavacāni ca
viprakīryanta śūrāṇāṃ samprahāre mah"|ātmanām.
utthitāny a|gaṇeyāni kabandhāni samantataḥ
adṛśyanta, mahā|rāja, tasmin parama|saṃkule.
gṛdhrāḥ kaṅkā balāḥ śyenā vāyasā jambukās tathā
bahuśaḥ piśit'|āśāś ca tatr' âdṛśyanta māriṣa
bhakṣayantaś ca māṃsāni pibantaś c' âpi śoṇitam
vilumpantaś ca keśāṃś ca majjāś ca bahudhā nṛ|pa
ākarṣantaḥ śarīrāṇi śarīr'|âvayavāṃs tathā
nar'|âśva|gaja|saṃghānāṃ śirāṃsi ca tatas tataḥ.
97.15 kṛt'|âstrā raṇa|dīkṣābhir dīkṣitā raṇa|śālinaḥ
raṇe jayaṃ prārthayanto bhṛśaṃ yuyudhire tadā.
asi|mārgān bahu|vidhān viceruḥ sainikā raṇe.
ṛṣṭibhiḥ śaktibhiḥ prāsaiḥ śūla|tomara|paṭṭiśaiḥ,
gadābhiḥ parighaiś c' ânyair āyudhaiś ca bhujair api
anyo|'nyaṃ jaghnire kruddhā yuddha|raṅga|gatā narāḥ.
rathino rathibhiḥ sārdham aśv'|ārohāś ca sādibhiḥ
mātaṅgā vara|mātaṅgaiḥ padātāś ca padātibhiḥ,

All was mayhem and madness yet still the riven clans 97.5
fought on without fear. Drona's flocking darts found the Panchála prince and it was a fine display as they matched might for might. Down the rows of soldiers they sliced off the heads of men, scattering them like dead flowers all across the plain. Like lightning in mingled cloud blood streaked blades and amulets and cloaks, flags, finery and scimitars, and breastplates of beaten gold.

Bows tall as trees twanged in the hands of other warriors
and feathered shafts felled man and beast, and then down 97.10
those bows were dashed, and swords and armour and mail and heads as the battle of heroes raged on. All through the great melée my king I saw the trunks of men still standing. I could not count them. Vultures herons and crows swept above us and dogs and jackals and hyenas moved in packs with other drinkers of blood, and o father all around they chewed on flesh, lapped blood, tore hair and crunched bone between their teeth. From the carcasses of men and steeds piled high they dragged away bodies, limbs and heads.

But the hands of these men were made for weapons and 97.15
war's delirium was what they knew and they were steeped in its rites and dreamed of its glory and so they struggled on. Swords were swung and spears and staves and javelins and pikes and lances and tridents traced crisscrossing lines through the air as jubilant in the playhouse of battle they struck each other with mace or club or some other bludgeon or failing those used their fists: chariot against chariot and horseman against rider and elephant against elephant and soldier against soldier. First they yelled at each other

kṣībā iv' ânye c' ônmattā raṅgeṣv iva ca cāraṇāḥ
uccukruśur ath' ânyo|'nyaṃ jaghnur anyo|'nyam eva ca.
97.20 vartamāne tathā yuddhe nir|maryāde, viśāṃ pate,
Dhṛṣṭadyumno hayān aśvair Droṇasya vyatyamiśrayat.
te hayā sādhv aśobhanta miśritā vāta|raṃhasaḥ
pārāvata|sa|varṇāś ca rakta|śoṇāś ca saṃyuge.
pārāvata|sa|varṇās te rakta|śoṇa|vimiśritāḥ
hayāḥ śuśubhire rājan meghā iva sa|vidyutaḥ.
Dhṛṣṭadyumnas tu saṃprekṣya Droṇam abhyāśam āgatam
asi|carm' ādade vīro dhanur utsṛjya Bhārata.
cikīrṣur duṣ|karaṃ karma Pārṣataḥ para|vīra|hā
īṣayā samatikramya Droṇasya ratham āviśat.
97.25 atiṣṭhad yuga|madhye sa yuga|saṃnahaneṣu ca
jaghān' ârdheṣu c' âśvānāṃ. tat sainyāny abhyapūjayan.
khaḍgena caratas tasya śoṇ'|âśvān adhitiṣṭhataḥ
na dadarś' ântaraṃ Droṇas. tad adbhutam iv' âbhavat.
yathā śyenasya patanaṃ vaneṣv āmiṣa|gṛddhinaḥ
tath" âiv' âsīd abhīsāras tasya Droṇaṃ jighāṃsataḥ.
tataḥ śara|śaten' âsya śata|candraṃ samākṣipat
Droṇo Drupada|putrasya khaḍgaṃ ca daśabhiḥ śaraiḥ.
hayāṃś c' âiva catuḥ|ṣaṣṭyā śarāṇāṃ jaghnivān balī
dhvajaṃ chatraṃ ca bhallābhyāṃ tathā tau pārṣṇi|sārathī.
97.30 ath' âsmai tvarito bāṇam aparaṃ jīvit'|ântakam
ākarṇa|pūrṇaṃ cikṣepa vajraṃ vajra|dharo yathā.
taṃ catur|daśabhis tīkṣṇair bāṇaiś ciccheda Sātyakiḥ
grastam ācārya|mukhyena Dhṛṣṭadyumnaṃ vyamocayat.
siṃhen' êva mṛgaṃ grastaṃ nara|siṃhena māriṣa
Droṇena mocayām āsa Pāñcālyaṃ Śini|puṃgavaḥ.

and then they lashed out and all of them mummed mad or drunk like actors upon a stage.

O lord of men. As the chaos overtook us Dhrishta·dyum- 97.20
na tangled his steeds with Drona's horses and still racing like the wind their teams bloodred and dovegrey painted wild splendour upon the plain. Bloodred and dovegrey: think o king of the colour and lustre of stormclouds. O Bhárata, bold Dhrishta·dyumna son of Príshata and scourge of foes saw how close Drona had come and he cast aside his bow and swept up a sword and shield, and o Bhárata he saw how he might risk a daring trick and dodging the brahmin's
bow stepped upon his car. Planting his feet on the ropes of 97.25
the yoke's harness he struck at the horses flanks to cheer his men and stood up on their rustcoloured backs, hefting his sword. Drona gaped in confusion and disbelief as Párshata swooped upon him like a hawk over the jungle hungry for its prey.

A moment passed, and as Drúpada's son brought up his sword Drona clattered an arrow against it for each of the hundred moons damasked on its blade. Ten more struck against it, then a hail of four and sixty hit Dhrishta·dyumna's steeds pole and parasol before the great brahmin found
with two iron darts the men who guarded his wheels. A 97.30
shaft glinted pristine and lethal as Indra's thunderbolt in his fingers, but as Drona's hand came back to his ear Sátyaki cut the dart from his grasp in a volley of fourteen arrows. Though Drona had held him in his teeth as a lion holds a deer it was the bull of the Shinis o father who knocked Dhrishta·dyumna from the Teacher's jaws.

Sātyakiṃ prekṣya goptāraṃ Pāñcālyaṃ ca mah"|āhave
śarāṇāṃ tvarito Droṇaḥ ṣaḍ|viṃśatyā samarpayat.
tato Droṇaṃ Śineḥ pautro grasantam iva Sṛñjayān
pratyavidhyac chitair bāṇaiḥ ṣaḍ|viṃśatyā stan'|ântare.
97.35 tataḥ sarve rathās tūrṇaṃ Pāñcālyā jaya|gṛddhinaḥ
Sātvat'|âbhisṛte Droṇe Dhṛṣṭadyumnam avākṣipan

DHṚTARĀṢṬRA uvāca:

98.1 BĀṆE TASMIN nikṛtte tu Dhṛṣṭadyumne ca mokṣite
tena Vṛṣṇi|pravīreṇa Yuyudhānena, Saṃjaya,
a|marṣito mah"|êṣv|āsaḥ sarva|śastra|bhṛtāṃ varaḥ
nara|vyāghre Śineḥ pautre Droṇaḥ kim akarod yudhi?

SAṂJAYA uvāca:

sa pradrutaḥ krodha|viṣo vyādit'|āsya|śar'|âsanaḥ,
tīkṣṇa|dhār"|êṣu|daśanaḥ śita|nārāca|daṃṣṭravān
saṃrambh'|â|marṣa|tāmr'|âkṣo mah"|ôraga iva śvasan,
nara|vīra|praṇuditaiḥ śoṇair aśvair mahā|javaiḥ
98.5 utpatadbhir iv' ākāśaṃ kramadbhir iva sarvataḥ
rukma|puṅkhāñ śarān asyan Yuyudhānam upādravat.
śara|pāta|mahā|varṣaṃ ratha|ghoṣa|balāhakam
kārmuk'|ākarṣa|vikṣepaṃ nārāca|bahu|vidyutam
śakti|khaḍg'|âśani|dharaṃ krodha|vega|samutthitam
Droṇa|megham an|āvāryaṃ haya|māruta|coditam
dṛṣṭv" aîv' âbhipatantaṃ taṃ śūraḥ para|puraṃ|jayaḥ
uvāca sūtaṃ Śaineyaḥ prahasan yuddha|dur|madaḥ.

Drona swung round and saw the Panchála's protector and ravening now for the Srínjayas he let fly across the gulf between them six and twenty shafts. But Shini's grandson answered him arrow for honed arrow and they all lodged
fast in Drona's chest. Drona had turned on the Sátvata, and 97.35
the disappointed Panchála warriors all jeered at Dhrishta·dyumna for forfeiting their prize.

DHRITA·RASHTRA spoke:

98.1 AMONG THOSE who bear the bow or blade none could overmaster Drona. Yet the Vrishni champion Yuyudhána broke his arrow and snatched Dhrishta·dyumna from his grasp. Tell me Sánjaya. How did our tiger fight back against Shini's grandson?

SÁNJAYA spoke:

His eyes flushed to copper in passion and fury, and he arched wide his maw lined with whittled wooden teeth and sharp iron fangs all dipped in anger's poison and hissing like a serpent darted forward. Out flew arrows fletched in feathers flecked gold as the hero's driver cracked his whip
and as if the ground could not keep them and they would 98.5
take to the air his red chargers made for Yuyudhána. Carried by their wind the car thundered on bearing an arrowfall twisted from Drona's fury and flashing with iron and horizoned in the curve of his bow. The storm bore spears and swords in its clouds and it would not be outrun. But Shini's mighty grandson had conquered cities. He watched its course through wardrunk eyes and smiled and spoke to his driver.

«etaṃ vai brāhmaṇaṃ śūraṃ sva|karmaṇy an|avasthitam
āśrayaṃ Dhārtarāṣṭrasya rājño duḥkha|bhay'|âpaham,
98.10 śīghraṃ prajavitair aśvaiḥ pratyudyāhi prahṛṣṭavat
ācāryaṃ rāja|putrāṇāṃ satataṃ śūra|māninam.»
tato rajata|saṃkāśā Mādhavasya hay'|ôttamāḥ
Droṇasy' âbhimukhāḥ śīghram agacchan vāta|raṃhasaḥ.
tatas tau Droṇa|Śaineyau yuyudhāte paraṃ|tapau.
śarair an|eka|sāhasrais tāḍayan tau paras|param
iṣu|jāl'|āvṛtaṃ vyoma cakratuḥ puruṣa'|rṣabhau.
pūrayām āsatur vīrāv ubhau daśa|diśaḥ śaraiḥ
meghāv iv' ātap'|âpāye dhārābhir itar'|êtaram.
98.15 na sma sūryas tadā bhāti na vavau ca samīraṇaḥ.
iṣu|jāl'|āvṛtaṃ ghoram andha|kāram an|antaram
an|ādhṛṣyam iv' ânyeṣāṃ śūrāṇām abhavat tadā.
andha|kārī|kṛte loke Droṇa|Śaineyayoḥ śaraiḥ
tayoḥ śīghr'|âstra|viduṣor Droṇa|Sātvatayos tadā
n' ântaraṃ śara|vṛṣṭīnāṃ dadṛśe nara|siṃhayoḥ.
iṣūṇāṃ saṃnipātena śabdo dhār"|âbhighāta|jaḥ
śuśruve Śakra|muktānām aśanīnām iva svanaḥ.
nārācair vyapaviddhānāṃ śarāṇāṃ rūpam ābabhau
āśīviṣa|vidaṣṭānāṃ sarpāṇām iva Bhārata.
98.20 tayor jyā|tala|nirghoṣaḥ śuśruve yuddha|śauṇḍayoḥ
ajasraṃ śaila|śṛṅgāṇāṃ vajreṇ' āhanyatām iva.
ubhayos tau rathau, rājaṃs, te c' âśvās tau ca sārathī
rukma|puṅkhaiḥ śaraiś channāś citra|rūpā babhus tadā.
nir|malānām a|jihmānāṃ nārācānāṃ, viśāṃ pate,
nirmukt'|āśīviṣ'|ābhānāṃ sampāto 'bhūt su|dāruṇaḥ.

"Here comes the pious knight. The king's saviour. He has left his grimoires at home* to deliver Dhrita·rashtra's boy
from all his sorrows and fears. Spur on our happy steeds and 98.10
make haste. This princeling's tutor dreams he might make himself a hero."

Mádhava's fine ivory steeds flew like the wind and soon he was close by Drona. Drona and Shainéya put each other to the torch. They were great enemies and arrows flew from them in thousands upon thousands as each sought to undo the other. Weaving nets of wood across the sky the two champions let fly a huge mass of arrows. They filled all the ten reaches of the sky with biting rain like the clouds of the
hot season passing. Soon the sun was gone and the wind 98.15
fell and a heavy darkness woven from wood hung dismal and impenetrable above our heads. Drona and Shainéya's arrows had put out the world's light. Such was their sheer dexterity that Drona and Sátvata darkened all of heaven's fires with reeds.

The shafts clattered against each other and the sound was like Shakra rattling his thunderbolts. Iron bit through wood
like a pantophagy of snakes and o Bhárata the bowstrings 98.20
whipped against their frenzied arms like the endless echoing thunder of the mountaintops. Between the glinting feathers of the arrowfletchings we saw fragments of their cars steeds and drivers as the deluge of lethally honed and polished darts fell o king like a rain of cobras to the earth.

ubhayoḥ patite chatre tath" âiva patitau dhvajau
ubhau rudhira|sikt'|âṅgāv ubhau ca vijay'|âiṣiṇau,
sravadbhiḥ śoṇitaṃ gātraiḥ prasrutāv iva vāraṇau
anyo|'nyam abhyavidhyetāṃ jīvit'|ânta|karaiḥ śaraiḥ.
98.25 garjit'|ôtkruṣṭa|saṃnādāḥ śaṅkha|dundubhi|niḥsvanāḥ
upāraman mahā|rāja vyājahāra na kaś cana.
tūṣṇīṃ|bhūtāny anīkāni, yodhā yuddhād upāraman.
dadarśa dvairathaṃ tābhyāṃ jāta|kautūhalo janaḥ.
rathino hasti|yantāro hay'|ārohāḥ padātayaḥ
avaikṣant' â|calair netraiḥ parivārya ratha'|rṣabhau.
hasty|anīkāny atiṣṭhanta tath" ânīkāni vājinām
tath" âiva ratha|vāhinyaḥ prativyūhya vyavasthitāḥ.
muktā|vidruma|citraiś ca maṇi|kāñcana|bhūṣitaiḥ
dhvajair ābharaṇaiś citraiḥ kavacaiś ca hiraṇmayaiḥ,
98.30 vaijayantī|patākābhiḥ paristom'|âṅga|kambalaiḥ
vi|malair niśitaiḥ śastrair hayānāṃ ca prakīrṇakaiḥ,
jāta|rūpa|mayībhiś ca rājatībhiś ca mūrdhasu
gajānāṃ kumbha|mālābhir danta|veṣṭaiś ca Bhārata,
sa|balākāḥ sa|kha|dyotāḥ s'|âirāvata|śata|hradāḥ
adṛśyant' ôṣṇa|paryāye meghānām iva vāgurāḥ.
apaśyann asmadīyāś ca te ca Yaudhiṣṭhirāḥ sthitāḥ
tad yuddhaṃ Yuyudhānasya Droṇasya ca mah"|ātmanaḥ.
vimān'|âgra|gatā devā Brahma|Soma|puro|gamāḥ
siddha|cāraṇa|saṃghāś ca vidyā|dhara|mah"|ôragāḥ
98.35 gata|pratyāgat'|ākṣepaiś citrair astra|vighātibhiḥ
vividhair vismayaṃ jagmus tayoḥ puruṣa|siṃhayoḥ.
hasta|lāghavam astreṣu darśayantau mahā|balau

O lord of men. Down came their parasols and down came their banners, but bloodsoaked and battlehungry as elephants in musth they raised limbs streaming red and each notched yet another arrow to end the other's life. Neither 98.25
drum nor horn was heard and the warcries and hollers fell away. Swordpoints dropped and soldiers settled back into their lines as we all turned in wonder to watch the duelling cars. In chariot and howdah and saddle and all across the plain men stood staring, eyes fixed on the bulls of their herd. O Bhárata. The elephantlines were still and the cavalry arrayed and the chariots in their wide ranges unmoving. They stood there crusted in pearl, coral and chains of gemstones and gold, in armour and ornaments bright and 98.30
burnished, with flags, oriflammes and banners and doublets and cuirasses, their swordblades all polished and gleaming, the chowries about the horses' heads plated with gold and silver and the urns looped around the elephants' tusks braided with flowers. To look upon them was like looking out upon a sky of breaking weather when the hot season ends and the cranes and fireflies fill the air and rainbows arch with a hundred colours through the cloud.

Whether yours or Yudhi·shthira's every man stood and watched the battle between Yuyudhána and great Drona. Even Brahma and Soma and the gods in their heavenly cars, the saints and singers, the fairies and the serpents were 98.35
awestruck at the intricate patterns the two men made and unmade with their lightfingered hands to loose their arrows. Our hale champions Drona and Sátyaki dazzled in space with the lightness of their fingers and continued to trade their attacks. Then o glorious king with his stout feathered

anyo|'nyam abhividhyetāṃ śarais tau Droṇa|Sātyakī.
tato Droṇasya Dāśārhaḥ śarāṃś ciccheda saṃyuge
patribhiḥ su|dṛḍhair āśu dhanuś c' âiva mahā|dyute.
nimeṣ'|ântara|mātreṇa Bhāradvājo 'paraṃ dhanuḥ
sa|jyaṃ cakāra. tad api cicched' âsya ca Sātyakiḥ.
tatas tvaran punar Droṇo dhanur|hasto vyatiṣṭhata
sa|jyaṃ sa|jyaṃ dhanuś c' âsya ciccheda nava sapta ca.
98.40 tato 'sya saṃyuge Droṇo dṛṣṭvā karm' âtimānuṣam
Yuyudhānasya, rāj'|êndra, manas" âitad acintayat:
«etad astra|balaṃ Rāme Kārtavīrye Dhanaṃjaye
Bhīṣme ca puruṣa|vyāghre yad idaṃ Sātvatāṃ vare.»
taṃ c' âsya manasā Droṇaḥ pūjayām āsa vikramam
lāghavaṃ Vāsavasy' êva samprekṣya dvija|sattamaḥ.
tutoṣ' âstra|vidāṃ śreṣṭhas tathā devāḥ sa|Vāsavāḥ
na tām ālokayām āsur laghutāṃ śīghra|cāriṇaḥ.
devāś ca Yuyudhānasya gandharvāś ca viśāṃ pate
siddha|cāraṇa|saṃghāś ca vidur Droṇasya karma tat.
98.45 tato 'nyad dhanur ādāya Droṇaḥ kṣatriya|mardanaḥ
astrair astra|vidāṃ śreṣṭho yodhayām āsa Bhārata.
tasy' âstrāṇy astra|māyābhiḥ pratihatya sa Sātyakiḥ
jaghāna niśitair bāṇais. tad adbhutam iv' âbhavat.
tasy' âtimānuṣaṃ karma dṛṣṭv" ânyair a|samaṃ raṇe
yuktaṃ yogena yoga|jñās tāvakāḥ samapūjayan.
yad astram asyati Droṇas tad ev' âsyati Sātyakiḥ
tam Ācāryo 'tha sambhrānto 'yodhayac chatru|tāpanaḥ.
tataḥ kruddho mahā|rāja dhanur|vedasya pāra|gaḥ
vadhāya Yuyudhānasya divyam astram udairayat.
98.50 tad Āgneyaṃ mahā|ghoraṃ ripu|ghnam upalakṣya saḥ
divyam astraṃ mah"|êṣv|āso Vāruṇaṃ samudairayat.

shafts the Dashárha splintered Drona's darts and bow even as he worked them. In an eye's blink Bharadvája had another in his hands yet Sátyaki broke it in two as soon as it was strung. Drona stood firm and at once took another but every bow he strung Sátyaki broke until sixteen had passed through his hands. It was a superhuman trick and o king 98.40
of kings Drona marvelled at his foe and remarked to himself how this genius of Sátvata rivalled Rama, Karta·virya, Dhanan·jaya and even the tiger Bhishma in his bowcraft. With silent awe the great brahmin thought Yuyudhána deft as Indra, and though none knew the archer's secrets deeply as he neither Drona nor Indra nor any of the gods had witnessed a quickness like the kind they saw from Sátyaki that day. And majesty the gods and *gandhárva*s and the saints and singers sensed the grace of Drona's thought.

Drona was a destroyer of kings and master archer him- 98.45
self and o Bhárata he swept up yet another bow and fought on. Sátyaki still worked his wonders and meeting Drona's darts with the magic of his own his sharp shafts found their target. We too knew of his discipline and we watched his technique so peerless and diabolic with the reverence that was its due. Flight for flight Sátyaki matched Drona and for a moment the Teacher faltered and his fire dimmed. But then o king delving deep into the lore of the bow Drona brought forth a sorcerous attack intending to finish off his foe. It was the Arrow of Fire that slays all and spares none. 98.50
Yet Yuyudhána knew it, and in his turn invoked the magical Arrow of Water.

hāhā|kāro mahān āsīd dṛṣṭvā divy'|âstra|dhāriṇau.
na vicerus tad" ākāśe bhūtāny ākāśa|gāny api.
astre te Vāruṇ'|Āgneye tābhyāṃ bāṇa|samāhite
tad yāvad abhyapadyetāṃ vyāvartad atha bhāskaraḥ.
tato Yudhiṣṭhiro rājā Bhīmasenaś ca Pāṇḍavaḥ
Nakulaḥ Sahadevaś ca paryarakṣanta Sātyakim.
Dhṛṣṭadyumna|mukhaiḥ sārdhaṃ Virāṭaś ca sa|Kekayaḥ
Matsyāḥ Śālveya|senāś ca Droṇam ājagmur añjasā.
98.55 Duḥśāsanaṃ puras|kṛtya rāja|putrāḥ sahasraśaḥ
Droṇam abhyupapadyanta sapatnaiḥ parivāritam.
tato yuddham abhūd rājaṃs teṣāṃ tava ca dhanvināṃ
rajasā saṃvṛte loke śara|jāla|samāvṛte.
sarvam āvignam abhavan, na prājñāyata kiṃ cana,
sainyena rajasā dhvaste nir|maryādam avartata.

SAṂJAYA uvāca:

99.1 VIVARTAMĀNE TV āditye tatr' âsta|śikharaṃ prati
rajasā kīryamāṇe ca mandī|bhūte divā|kare
tiṣṭhatāṃ yudhyamānānāṃ punar āvartatām api
bhajyatāṃ jayatāṃ c' âiva jagāma tad ahaḥ śanaiḥ.
tathā teṣu viṣakteṣu sainyeṣu jaya|gṛddhiṣu
Arjuno Vāsudevaś ca Saindhavāy' âiva jagmatuḥ.
ratha|mārga|pramāṇaṃ tu Kaunteyo niśitaiḥ śaraiḥ
cakāra tatra panthānaṃ yayau yena Janārdanaḥ.
99.5 yatra yatra ratho yāti Pāṇḍavasya mah"|ātmanaḥ
tatra tatr' âiva dīryante senās tava viśāṃ pate.
ratha|śikṣāṃ tu Dāśārho darśayām āsa vīryavān
uttam'|ādhama|madhyāni maṇḍalāni vidarśayan.
te tu nām'|âṅkitāḥ pītāḥ kāla|jvalana|saṃnibhāḥ
snāyu|naddhāḥ su|parvāṇaḥ pṛthavo dīrgha|gāminaḥ,
vaiṇavāś c' āyasāś c' ôgrā grasanto vividhān arīn

We saw what they were doing and a cry went up. The two of them charged their missiles. The birds came to roost. The Arrows of Water and Fire took to flight and the very sun in the sky winked out. King Yudhi·shthira and Bhima·sena son of Pandu, Nákula and Saha·deva rushed in around Sátyaki as Viráta and the Kékayas and Dhrishta·dyumna and the Matsyas and Shalvéya brought their men against
Drona. As his enemies closed in Duhshásana gave the sign 98.55
and a horde of princes swept to Drona's side. O king with heels and hooves driving the dust into the air our archers met theirs once again in a world choked in fog and overwoven with wood, and through all that was lost and obscure we passed ever deeper into chaos.

SÁNJAYA spoke:

DOWN ROLLED THE sun behind the western peak and the 99.1
sky's orb shone dusty and wan on figures that stood and fought or turned and ran. On victor and victim alike the day began to fade.

Through packed and battlehungry lines Árjuna and Vasudéva came for the Sindhu king. Kauntéya's sharp shafts carved out a path wide as their chariot's axle and down
along it Janárdana drove. O lord of men the army split 99.5
before the great Pándava's car as Dashárha showed off his might and skill and traced out circles within circles across the plain.

Each of Árjuna's finetooled arrows had been stitched with sinew, sharpened to a hiss and etched with his name and now in bamboo and iron they flew flashing like doom's fire far from his hands and fell. Thirstily they drank down the

rudhiraṃ patagaiḥ sārdhaṃ prāṇināṃ papur āhave.
ratha|sthito 'grataḥ krośaṃ yān asyaty Arjunaḥ śarān
rathe krośam atikrānte tasya te ghnanti śātravān.
99.10 Tārkṣya|māruta|raṃhobhir vājibhir dhura|vāhibhiḥ
tath" âgacchadd Hṛṣīkeśaḥ kṛtsnaṃ vismāpayañ jagat.
na tathā gacchati rathas tapanasya viśāṃ pate
n' Êndrasya ca na Rudrasya n' âpi Vaiśravaṇasya ca
n' ânyasya samare rājan gata|pūrvas tathā rathaḥ
yathā yayāv Arjunasya mano|'bhiprāya|śīghra|gaḥ.
praviśya tu raṇe, rājan, Keśavaḥ para|vīra|hā
senā|madhye hayāṃs tūrṇaṃ codayām āsa Bhārata.
tatas tasya rath'|âughasya madhyaṃ prāpya hay'|ôttamāḥ
kṛcchreṇa ratham ūhus taṃ kṣut|pipāsā|samānvitāḥ.
99.15 kṣatāś ca bahubhiḥ śastrair yuddha|śauṇḍair an|ekaśaḥ
maṇḍalāni vicitrāṇi vicerus te muhur muhuḥ.
hatānāṃ vāji|nāgānāṃ rathānāṃ ca naraiḥ saha
upariṣṭād atikrāntāḥ śail'|ābhānāṃ sahasraśaḥ.
etasminn antare vīrāv Āvantyau bhrātarau, nṛ|pa,
saha|senau samārchetāṃ Pāṇḍavaṃ klānta|vāhanam.
tāv Arjunaṃ catuḥ|ṣaṣṭyā saptatyā ca Janārdanam
śarāṇāṃ ca śatair aśvān avidhyetāṃ mud"|ânvitau.
tāv Arjuno, mahā|rāja, navabhir nata|parvabhiḥ
ājaghāna raṇe kruddho marma|jño marma|bhedibhiḥ.
99.20 tatas tau tu śar'|âugheṇa Bībhatsuṃ saha|Keśavam
ācchādayetāṃ saṃrabdhau siṃha|nādaṃ ca cakratuḥ.
tayos tu dhanuṣī citre bhallābhyāṃ śveta|vāhanaḥ
ciccheda samare tūrṇaṃ dhvajau ca kanak'|ôjjvalau.
ath' ânyad|dhanuṣī rājan pragṛhya samare tadā
Pāṇḍavaṃ bhṛśa|saṃkruddhāv ardayām āsatuḥ śaraiḥ.
tayos tu bhṛśa|saṃkruddhaḥ śarābhyāṃ Pāṇḍu|nandanaḥ

blood of bird and beast as the battle raged on. A league from
the prow of his car he sent them and a league thence they
found his foes.

How Hrishi·kesha drove his yoked steeds fleet as a god 99.10
of the birds or winds none could fully attest. O lord of men
neither the sun's hot chariot nor the car that bore Indra or
Rudra or Kubéra or any other before them had ever moved
like Árjuna's moved then. My king quick as thought or sense
they went as vengeful Késhava drove them on unrelenting
further and further into the host. And o Bhárata when they 99.15
reached its heart and thirst and hunger and injury made
heavy their burden still they drew a tremendous arc through
the myriad drunken blades and coming from behind them
trampled down a thousand cars elephants horses and men
like so many stones beneath their hooves.

O lord of men. As the Pándava's horses began to slow
the bold brothers of Avánti swung their line to face him.
Four and sixty shafts struck Árjuna and seven Janárdana and
hundreds more their steeds. Rage rose up in Árjuna and o
majesty nine were the notchless darts he sent deftly through
the joints in their chainmail. The brothers roared in fury 99.20
and hid Bibhátsu and Késhava in a heap of arrows but with
twin barbed shafts the warrior of the white horses broke the
bright bows in their hands and sliced through their fluttering flags. But o king the battle was not at an end. Two more
bows were in their hands and the brothers cut into Pándava
with their shafts. Anger flashed in Dhanan·jaya. Once more
the joy of the Pandus split their bows with his darts. Then
with glittering shafts honed on the stone he harrowed their

dhanuṣī cicchide tūrṇaṃ bhūya eva Dhanaṃjayaḥ.
tath" ânyair vi|śikhais tūrṇaṃ rukma|puṅkhaiḥ śilā|śitaiḥ
jaghān' âśvāṃs tathā sūtau pārṣṇī ca sa|pad'|ânugau.
99.25 jyeṣṭhasya ca śiraḥ kāyāt kṣurapreṇa nyakṛntata.
sa papāta hataḥ pṛthvyāṃ vāta|rugṇa iva drumaḥ.

Vindaṃ tu nihataṃ dṛṣṭvā hy Anuvindaḥ pratāpavān
hat'|âśvaṃ ratham utsṛjya gadāṃ gṛhya mahā|balaḥ
abhyavartata saṃgrāme bhrātur vadham anusmaran
gadayā rathināṃ śreṣṭho nṛtyann iva mahā|rathaḥ.
Anuvindas tu gadayā lalāṭe Madhusūdanam
spṛṣṭvā n' âkampayat kruddho Mainākam iva parvatam.
tasy' Ârjunaḥ śaraiḥ ṣaḍbhir grīvāṃ pādau bhujau śiraḥ
nicakarta. sa saṃchinnaḥ papāt' âdri|cayo yathā.

99.30 tatas tau nihatau dṛṣṭvā tayo, rājan, pad'|ânugāḥ
abhyadravanta saṃkruddhāḥ kirantaḥ śataśaḥ śarān.
tān Arjunaḥ śarais tūrṇaṃ nihatya, Bharata'|rṣabha,
vyarocata yathā vahnir dāvaṃ dagdhvā him'|âtyaye.
tayoḥ senām atikrāmya kṛcchrād iva Dhanaṃjayaḥ
vibabhau jala|daṃ hitvā divā|kara iv' ôditaḥ.
taṃ dṛṣṭvā Kuravas trastāḥ prahṛṣṭāś c' âbhavan punaḥ
abhyavartanta Pārthaṃ ca samantād Bharata'|rṣabha.
śrāntaṃ c' âinaṃ samālakṣya jñātvā dūre ca Saindhavam
siṃha|nādena mahatā sarvataḥ paryavārayan.

99.35 tāṃs tu dṛṣṭvā su|saṃrabdhān utsmayan puruṣa'|rṣabhaḥ
śanakair iva Dāśārham Arjuno vākyam abravīt.

horses and drivers, flankriders and followers and next with a 99.25
single razorlike dart cut the older brother's head clean away, and it fell down to earth like a shrub wrenched from its roots by the wind.

Anuvínda looked at his dead brother and he burned with anguish and rage. Grabbing a club he leapt from the unhorsed wreck of his car back into the fray. The great warrior hefted his mace and livid with his brother's death landed a ferocious blow on Madhu·súdana's brow. Krishna stood solid as Mount Mainága, as six arrows from Árjuna's bow sliced into Anuvínda's neck feet arms and head and he fell to pieces like a heap of broken stone.

O king. When their soldiers saw the brothers fall they 99.30
hotly redoubled their attack and poured their volleys on Árjuna but o bull of the Bháratas he smashed them all down with arrows of his own. Árjuna shone bright as a forest fire at the cold season's turning. He seemed to rise through what remained of the brothers' men like a dawn sun rising through the mist. O bull of the Bharatas fear and delight coursed through the Kurus in equal measure and they pressed in upon Partha from all around, encircling him in a noisome ring. They could see him tiring and knew that Sáindhava was still a safe distance away in the rear.

The taurine warrior smiled to see them come ravening 99.35
towards him. When Árjuna turned to Dashárha and spoke there was no concern in his voice.

«śar'|ârditāś ca glānāś ca hayā, dūre ca Saindhavaḥ.
kim ih' ân|antaraṃ kāryaṃ jyāyiṣṭhaṃ tava rocate?
brūhi Kṛṣṇa yathā|tattvaṃ. tvaṃ hi prājñatamaḥ sadā.
bhavan|netrā raṇe śatrūn vijeṣyant' îha Pāṇḍavāḥ.
mama tv an|antaraṃ kṛtyaṃ yad vai, tat tvaṃ nibodha me:
hayān vimucya hi sukhaṃ vi|śalyān kuru Mādhava.»
evam uktas tu Pārthena
Keśavaḥ pratyuvāca tam.
«mam' âpy etan mataṃ, Pārtha,
yad idaṃ te prabhāṣitam.»

ARJUNA uvāca:

99.40 aham āvārayiṣyāmi sarva|sainyāni, Keśava.
tvam apy atra yathā|nyāyaṃ kuru kāryam an|antaram.

SAMJAYA uvāca:

so 'vatīrya rath'|ôpasthād a|sambhrānto Dhanaṃjayaḥ
Gāṇḍīvaṃ dhanur ādāya tasthau girir iv' â|calaḥ.
tam abhyadhāvan krośantaḥ kṣatriyā jaya|kāṅkṣiṇaḥ,
idaṃ chidram iti jñātvā dharaṇī|sthaṃ Dhanaṃjayam.
tam ekaṃ ratha|vaṃśena mahatā paryavārayan
vikarṣantaś ca cāpāni visṛjantaś ca sāyakān.
śastrāṇi ca vicitrāṇi kruddhās tatra vyadarśayan
chādayantaḥ śaraiḥ Pārthaṃ meghā iva divā|karam.
99.45 abhyadravanta vegena kṣatriyāḥ kṣatriya'|rṣabham
ratha|siṃhaṃ rath'|ôdārāḥ siṃhaṃ mattā iva dvipāḥ.
tatra Pārthasya bhujayor mahad balam adṛśyata
yat kruddho bahulāḥ senāḥ sarvataḥ samavārayat.
astrair astrāṇi saṃvārya dviṣatāṃ sarvato vibhuḥ
iṣubhir bahubhis tūrṇaṃ sarvān eva samāvṛṇot.
tatr' ântarikṣe bāṇānāṃ pragāḍhānāṃ viśāṃ pate

"The horses are wounded and tired and Sáindhava is some way hence. What course should we take? Share with me your wisdom, Krishna. You lead the sons of Pandu on the path to victory. O Mádhava tell me what to do. One thing is certain: you must unyoke the horses and let them rest."

Késhava heard Partha and replied.

"Son of Pritha you speak my very thoughts."

ÁRJUNA spoke:

I will hold back this horde, Késhava. Do whatever you 99.40
must.

SÁNJAYA spoke:

Dhanan·jaya stepped from the box and raised the bow Gandíva and planted his feet. He stood solid as a mountain. Thinking Dhanan·jaya mad to take to the ground his enemies roared and rode out to steal their prize. Back came bowstrings and out flew arrows as the circle of chariots drew in tighter around the lone warrior. Blades flashed and shook and keenly they wrapped him in arrows like clouds around
the sun. As they hurtled towards Árjuna it was like a herd 99.45
of elephants crazed by the season stampeding a lion. Once more we saw what fierce strength lay in Partha. With his vast reach he held the whole mass of men back, matching his foes' arrows with arrows of his own and somehow blanketing them once more beneath his shafts.

O king the air was so thick with arrows they drilled a brilliant fire from the sky. Blood sprayed and the archers

saṃgharṣeṇa mah"|ârciṣmān pāvakaḥ samajāyata.
tatra tatra mah"|êṣv|āsaiḥ śvasadbhiḥ śoṇit'|ôkṣitaiḥ
hayair nāgaiś ca sambhinnair nadadbhiś c' âri|karśanaiḥ
99.50 saṃrabdhaiś cāribhir vīraiḥ prārthayadbhir jayaṃ mṛdhe
eka|sthair bahubhiḥ kruddhair ūṣm" êva samajāyata.
śar'|ōrmiṇaṃ dhvaj'|āvartaṃ nāga|nakraṃ dur|atyayam
padāti|matsya|kalilaṃ śaṅkha|dundubhi|niḥsvanam,
a|saṃkhyeyam a|pāraṃ ca rath'|ōrmiṇam atīva ca
uṣṇīṣa|kamaṭhaṃ chatra|patākā|phena|mālinam,
raṇa|sāgaram akṣobhyaṃ mātaṅg'|āṅga|śilā|citam
velā|bhūtas tadā Pārthaḥ patribhiḥ samavārayat.
tato Janārdanaḥ saṃkhye priyaṃ puruṣa|sattamam
a|sambhrānto mahā|bāhur Arjunaṃ vākyam abravīt.
99.55 «uda|pānam ih' âśvānāṃ n' âlam asti raṇe, 'rjuna.
parīpsante jalaṃ c' ême peyaṃ, na tv avagāhanam.»
«idam ast'» îty a|sambhrānto bruvann astreṇa medinīm
abhihaty' Ârjunaś cakre vāji|pānaṃ saraḥ śubham.
haṃsa|kāraṇḍav'|ākīrṇaṃ cakravāk'|ôpaśobhitam
su|vistīrṇaṃ prasann'|âmbhaḥ praphulla|vara|paṅkajam
kūrma|matsya|gaṇ'|ākīrṇam a|gādham ṛṣi|sevitam.
āgacchan Nārada|munir darśan'|ârthaṃ kṛtaṃ kṣaṇāt.
śara|vaṃśaṃ śara|sthūṇaṃ śar'|ācchādanam adbhutam
śara|veśm' âkarot Pārthas Tvaṣṭ" êv' ādbhuta|karma|kṛt.
99.60 tataḥ prahasya Govindaḥ «sādhu sādhv» ity ath' âbravīt
śara|veśmani Pārthena kṛte tasmin mah"|ātmanā.

SAMJAYA uvāca:

100.1 SALILE JANITE tasmin Kaunteyena mah"|ātmanā
nivārite dviṣat|sainye kṛte ca śara|veśmani,
Vāsudevo rathāt tūrṇam avatīrya mahā|dyutiḥ
mocayām āsa turagān vitunnān kaṅka|patribhiḥ.

hissed and horses and elephants neighed and trumpeted in the press and trampled each other, and as warriors crashed 99.50
and scrabbled wildly to beat each other down steam rose about the writhing mass. Banners whorled and arrows came in fordless currents that bore elephants like crocodiles and shoals of men and as it echoed with conch and drum the vast limitless ocean of battle churning with chariots and with turbans for tortoises and laced with the foam of parasol and oriflamme met the shore which was Partha and the gulls that were his darts.

Then mighty Janárdana spoke softly to his great friend.

"If only there were a spring here on the battlefield. Árjuna 99.55
the horses need water: not so much to bathe, but to drink."

Árjuna nodded mildly and striking the earth with an arrow he brought forth an oasis of fresh water for his steeds. Its broad and pellucid surface was adazzle with lotus in bloom and in its deep vault were turtles and fish. Wildfowl lighted upon it and ducks and geese adorned its banks. Seers sat at its edge and even holy Nárada came to linger before its beauty. Then Partha performed a second miracle and using arrows for its pillars, beams and roof he crafted a splendid caravanserai from his darts. The Herdsman smiled and 99.60
sung out praise for the place of reeds that mighty Partha had made.

SÁNJAYA spoke:

As KUNTI'S SON stirred that sea and kept his enemies 100.1
at bay, into the house of arrows Árjuna had built gloried Vasudéva stepped lightly from his station and passing his hands across the horses' backs frilled with arrowfletchings

a|dṛṣṭa|pūrvaṃ tad dṛṣṭvā sādhu|vādo mahān abhūt
siddha|cāraṇa|saṃghānāṃ sainikānāṃ ca sarvaśaḥ.
padātinaṃ tu Kaunteyaṃ yudhyamānaṃ mahā|rathāḥ
n' āśaknuvan vārayituṃ: tad adbhutam iv' âbhavat.
100.5 āpatatsu rath'|âugheṣu prabhūta|gaja|vājiṣu
n' âsambhramat tadā Pārthas: tad asya puruṣān ati.
vyasṛjanta śar'|âughāṃs te Pāṇḍavaṃ prati pārthivāḥ
na c' âvyathata dharm'|ātmā Vāsaviḥ para|vīra|hā.
sa tāni śara|jālāni gadāḥ prāsāṃś ca vīryavān
āgatān agrasat Pārthaḥ saritaḥ sāgaro yathā.
astra|vegena mahatā Pārtho bāhu|balena ca
sarveṣāṃ pārthiv'|êndrāṇām agrasat tāñ śar'|ôttamān.
sa Pārthaḥ pārthivān sarvān bhūmi|ṣṭho 'pi ratha|sthitān
eko nivārayām āsa lobhaḥ sarva|guṇān iva.
100.10 tat tu Pārthasya vikrāntaṃ Vāsudevasya c' ôbhayoḥ
apūjayan, mahā|rāja, Kauravā mahad adbhutam.
kim adbhutatamaṃ loke bhavit" âpy atha vā hy abhūt
yad aśvān Pārtha|Govindau mocayām āsatū raṇe?
bhayaṃ vipulam asmāsu tāv adhattāṃ nar'|ôttamau
tejo vidadhatuś c' ôgraṃ visrabdhau raṇa|mūrdhani.
atha smayan Hṛṣīkeśaḥ strī|madhya iva Bhārata
Arjunena kṛte saṃkhye śara|garbha|gṛhe tathā
upāvartayad a|vyagras tān aśvān puṣkar'|ēkṣaṇaḥ
miṣatāṃ sarva|sainyānāṃ tvadīyānāṃ viśāṃ pate.
100.15 teṣāṃ śramaṃ ca glāniṃ ca vepathuṃ ca pṛthu|vraṇāt
sarvaṃ vyapānudat Kṛṣṇaḥ kuśalo hy aśva|karmaṇi.
śalyān uddhṛtya pāṇibhyāṃ parimṛjya ca tān hayān

he untied his team. To see such things never seen before
the saints seers and *gandhárvas* joined with the soldiers
to whisper in wonder. What was happening defied belief.
Though he fought on foot none of the carwarriors could
drive back Pritha's superhuman son. Nor did he even wa- 100.5
ver as the chariots bunched in around him and the horses
and elephants teemed closer. The kings heaped their arrows
upon him but the puresouled Pándava born to Indra did
not flinch and fought back hard. As arrows clubs and spears
poured riverine towards him Pritha's mighty son swallowed
them up as the ocean swallows up rivers. With the might
of his arms and force of his arrows he engulfed every fashioned shaft that the bold kings of the earth let fly at him.

Passion works alone and the finer feelings cannot withstand it. The kings of the earth flew above the ground but
Pritha's son was rooted to it and he overturned every car
that reached him. O majesty. Despite themselves the Káu- 100.10
ravas were mesmerized by the pair's courage. Is there or was
there ever a spectacle as strange as Partha and Go·vinda sta-
bling their horses on the battlefield? We had felt the terror the great men had brought to the fray and witnessed
their wild and effortless splendour. Now as if strolling the
seraglio lotuseyed Hrishi·kesha had uncoupled his horses in
the sanctuary of reeds Árjuna had fashioned on the plain.
O lord of men and scion of Bharata all we could do was
blink in astonishment. Krishna used his equerry's skill to 100.15
salve the horses' distress and fatigue and tended to the broad
wounds in their trembling flanks, plucking out arrowheads
and washing them down. He let the horses breathe for a
moment and gave them water to drink. Only when slaked

upāvartya yathā|nyāyaṃ pāyayām āsa vāri saḥ.
sa tāl̐ labdh'|ôdakān snātāñ jagdh'|ânnān vigata|klamān
yojayām āsa saṃhṛṣṭaḥ punar eva rath'|ôttame.
sa taṃ ratha|varaṃ Śauriḥ sarva|śastra|bhṛtāṃ varaḥ
samāsthāya mahā|tejāḥ s'|Ârjunaḥ prayayau drutam.
rathaṃ ratha|varasy' ājau yuktaṃ labdh'|ôdakair hayaiḥ
dṛṣṭvā Kuru|bala|śreṣṭhāḥ punar vi|manaso 'bhavan.
100.20 viniḥśvasantas te, rājan, bhagna|daṃṣṭrā iv' ôragāḥ
«dhig aho dhig gataḥ Pārthaḥ Kṛṣṇaś c'» êty abruvan pṛthak.
sarva|kṣatrasya miṣato rathen' âikena daṃśitau
bālaḥ krīḍanaken' êva kad|arthī|kṛtya no balam
krośatāṃ yatamānānām a|saṃsaktau paraṃ|tapau
darśayitv" ātmano vīryaṃ prayātau sarva|rājasu.
tau prayātau punar dṛṣṭvā tad" ānye sainik" âbruvan.
«tvaradhvaṃ Kuravaḥ sarve vadhe Kṛṣṇa|Kirīṭinoḥ.
rathaṃ yuktvā hi Dāśārho miṣatāṃ sarva|dhanvinām
Jayadrathāya yāty eṣa kad|arthī|kṛtya no raṇe.»
100.25 tatra ke cin mitho rājan samabhāṣanta bhūmi|pāḥ
a|dṛṣṭa|pūrvaṃ saṃgrāme tad dṛṣṭvā mahad adbhutam.
«sarva|sainyāni rājā ca Dhṛtarāṣṭro 'tyayaṃ gataḥ
Duryodhan'|âparādhena kṣatraṃ kṛtsnā ca medinī
vilayaṃ samanuprāptā. tac ca rājā na budhyate.»
ity evaṃ kṣatriyās tatra bruvanty anye ca Bhārata.

and bathed, fed and rested, were they harnessed back to Partha's wellfashioned car. Shauri best of all that bear blades was also restored and climbing aboard the great chariot he and Árjuna sped off once more.

Even the Kuru champions stared in disbelief as the great
warrior's car set off for battle behind its watered steeds, and 100.20
whistling like fangless snakes they muttered their astonishment when Partha and Krishna were once again on the move. As our legions stood there blinking at the mailed figures atop their solitary car the army seemed a plaything in the wanton grip of a child. The fiery heroes barely seemed to notice our shouts and fumbles as they came once again to display their prowess among the kings. And men cried out at the sight.

"Kurus we must stop Krishna and Kirítin and be swift about it. Dashárha has readied his car while we bowmen stand and gape and now he disdains us and makes for Jayad·ratha."

And majesty the prodigy they had just witnessed moved 100.25
other of the chieftains to share other thoughts.

"Duryódhana's greed betakes all our warrior kind from vassal to king and all the rest of the earth to its doom. We cannot escape our fate. Disaster is upon us all and still our leader does not realise it."

O Bhárata there were yet other voices heard among the fighters.

«Sindhu|rājasya yat kṛtyaṃ gatasya Yama|sādanam
tat karotu vṛthā|dṛṣṭir Dhārtarāṣṭro 'n|upāya|vit.
tataḥ śīghrataraṃ prāyāt Pāṇḍavaḥ Saindhavaṃ prati
nivartamāne tigm'|âṃśau hṛṣṭaiḥ pīt'|ôdakair hayaiḥ.»
100.30 taṃ prayāntaṃ mahā|bāhuṃ sarva|śastra|bhṛtāṃ varam
n' âśaknuvan vārayituṃ yodhāḥ kruddham iv'ântakam.
vidrāvya tu tataḥ sainyaṃ Pāṇḍavaḥ śatru|tāpanaḥ
yathā mṛga|gaṇān siṃhaḥ Saindhav'|ârthe vyaloḍayat.
gāhamānas tv anīkāni tūrṇam aśvān acodayat
balāk'|ābhaṃ tu Dāśārhaḥ Pāñcajanyaṃ vyanādayat.
Kaunteyen' âgrataḥ sṛṣṭā nyapatan pṛṣṭhataḥ śarāḥ
tūrṇāt tūrṇataraṃ hy aśvāḥ prāvahan vāta|raṃhasaḥ,
tato nṛ|patayaḥ kruddhāḥ parivavrur Dhanañjayam
kṣatriyā bahavaś c' ânye Jayadratha|vadh'|âiṣiṇam.
100.35 sainyeṣu viprayāteṣu dhi|ṣṭhitaṃ puruṣa'|rṣabham
Duryodhano 'nvayāt Pārthaṃ tvaramāṇo mah"|āhave.
vāt'|ôddhūta|patākaṃ taṃ rathaṃ jala|da|niḥsvanam
ghoraṃ kapi|dhvajaṃ dṛṣṭvā viṣaṇṇā rathino 'bhavan.
divā|kare 'tha rajasā sarvataḥ saṃvṛte bhṛśam
śar'|ārtāś ca raṇe yodhāḥ śekuḥ Kṛṣṇau na vīkṣitum.

SAMJAYA uvāca:

101.1 SRAṂSANTA IVA majjānas tāvakānāṃ bhayān, nṛpa,
tau dṛṣṭvā samatikrāntau Vāsudeva|Dhanaṃjayau
sarve tu pratisaṃrabdhā hrīmantaḥ sattva|coditāḥ
sthirī|bhūtā mah"|ātmānaḥ pratyagacchan Dhanaṃjayam.
ye gatāḥ Pāṇḍavaṃ yuddhe roṣ'|âmarṣa|samanvitāḥ
te 'dy' âpi na nivartante sindhavaḥ sāgarād iva.
a|santas tu nyavartanta vedebhya iva nāstikāḥ
narakaṃ bhajamānās te pratyapadyanta kilbiṣam.

"If Sindhu is marked for Death's kingdom then may
Duryódhana's blindness and ill judgment send him there.
Faster now rides Pándava for Sáindhava, as his steeds are refreshed and their thirst is quenched and the sun's hot rays
are waning."

On came the best of all who bear blades wild as death 100.30
and none could stop his mighty progress. His foes were his
fuel. Like a lion before deer he scattered our line and made
his way towards the Sindhu king. As Pancha·janya's note
rang out Dashárha spurred his cranecoloured steeds on into
our host and fleet as the wind they galloped faster than before and with them came the arrows from Kauntéya's bow.
Jayad·ratha's death was in his eyes. The kings rode out fu- 100.35
riously with their serried fighters to try to counter Partha's
fixed and taurine will and as they converged to do battle
Duryódhana joined with them. The thunder of his car and
the grim shape of the monkey dancing in the wind chilled
the blood of all who rode out to meet him. The sun was
sunk in dust and all our fighters could see of the Krishnas
were the arrows they shook down upon us.

SÁNJAYA spoke:

O LORD OF men. Dread ran to the marrow of our bones 101.1
as we watched Vasudéva and Dhanan·jaya pass through
us. But great natures drove your children on. Their blood
coursed and their hearts drummed and they steeled themselves to meet Dhanan·jaya. Some men heedless and in-
temperate poured like rivers from the ocean to do battle
with Pandu's son, while others of a lesser constitution fled

101.5 tāv atītya rath'|ânīkaṃ vimuktau puruṣa'|rṣabhau
dadṛśāte yathā Rāhor āsyān muktau prabhā|karau.
matsyāv iva mahā|jālaṃ vidārya vigata|klamau
tathā Kṛṣṇāv adṛśyetāṃ senā|jālaṃ vidārya tat.
vimuktau śastra|sambādhād Droṇ'|ânīkāt su|durbhidāt
adṛśyetāṃ mah"|ātmānau kāla|sūryāv iv' ôditau.
astra|sambādha|nirmuktau vimuktau śastra|saṃkaṭāt
adṛśyetāṃ mah"|ātmānau śatru|sambādha|kāriṇau.
vimuktau jvalana|sparśān makar'|āsyāj jhaṣāv iva
vyakṣobhayetāṃ senāṃ tau samudraṃ makarāv iva.
101.10 tāvakās tava putrāś ca Droṇ'|ānīka|sthayos tayoḥ
«n' âitau tariṣyato Droṇam» iti cakrus tadā matim.
tau tu dṛṣṭvā vyatikrāntau Droṇ'|ânīkaṃ mahā|dyutī
n' āśaśaṃsur mahā|rāja Sindhu|rājasya jīvitam.
āśā balavatī rājan Sindhu|rājasya jīvite
Droṇa|Hārdikyayoḥ Kṛṣṇau na mokṣyete iti prabho.
tām āśāṃ viphalī|kṛtya saṃtīrṇau tau paraṃ|tapau
Droṇ'|ânīkaṃ mahā|rāja Bhoj'|ânīkaṃ ca dus|taram.
atha dṛṣṭvā vyatikrāntau jvalitāv iva pāvakau
nir|āśāḥ Sindhu|rājasya jīvitaṃ n' āśaśaṃsire.
101.15 mithaś ca samabhāṣetām a|bhītau bhaya|vardhanau
Jayadratha|vadhe vācas tās tāḥ Kṛṣṇa|Dhanaṃjayau.

like heretics from the true beliefs and thus chose the nether course of sin.

Like twin suns bursting from Rahu's mouth the Pandu 101.5
champions broke forth from the chariot line. Like fish flashing above the surface of a river the Dark Ones emerged through arrowy torrents. We saw the two heroes like black suns rising as they rolled clear of the hard jagged lines that Drona had drawn for them, and as they pulled away from the dense press of spear and sword we saw the two heroes pack those narrows ever tighter. As minnows spring forth from a pike's jaws when a flame is touched to its tail, so the two of them burst free then and broke the rippling surface of our host.

Your kith and kin had never dreamed that faced with 101.10
Drona's array the two of them could transgress its maker. But o majesty when they saw the Dark Ones blaze through Drona's formation they did not hold the Sindhu king as long for this world. There had been high hopes he would live, for highness they thought that Drona and Hardíkya could hold the Panchálas back. But o majesty these hopes did wither as Krishna and Árjuna scorched through Drona's array and on through the Bhoja horde. We watched them flicker like flame tearing athwart us and the Sindhu king's time in this world we knew grew short.

They were unafraid, for fear rode at their side. Krishna 101.15
and Dhanan·jaya spoke then of Jayad·ratha's death, and these were the words that they said.

«asau madhye kṛtaḥ ṣaḍbhir Dhārtarāṣṭrair mahā|rathaiḥ
cakṣur|viṣaya|samprāpto na me mokṣyati Saindhavaḥ.
yady asya samare goptā Śakro deva|gaṇaiḥ saha
tath" âpy enaṃ nihaṃsyāva iti Kṛṣṇāv abhāṣatām.»
iti Kṛṣṇau mahā|bāhū mithaḥ kathayatāṃ tadā
Sindhu|rājam avekṣantau tvat|putrā bahu cukruśuḥ.
atītya maru|dhanvānaṃ prayāntau tṛṣitau gajau
pītvā vāri samāśvastau, tath' âiv' āstām ariṃ|damau.
101.20 vyāghra|siṃha|gaj'|ākīrṇān atikramya ca parvatān
vaṇijāv iva dṛśyetāṃ hīna|mṛtyū jar'|âtigau.
tathā hi mukha|varṇo 'yam anayor iti menire
tāvakā vīkṣya muktau tau vikrośanti sma sarvaśaḥ.
Droṇād āśīviṣ'|ākārāj jvalitād iva pāvakāt
anyebhyaḥ pārthivebhyaś ca bhāsvantāv iva bhāskarau.
vimuktau sāgara|prakhyād Droṇ'|ânīkād ariṃdamau
adṛśyetāṃ mudā yuktau samuttīry' ârṇavaṃ yathā.
astr'|âughān mahato muktau Droṇa|Hārdikya|rakṣitān
rocamānāv adṛśyetām Indr'|âgnyoḥ sadṛśau raṇe.
101.25 udbhinna|rudhirau Kṛṣṇau Bhāradvājasya sāyakaiḥ
śitaiś citau vyarocetāṃ karṇikārair iv' â|calau.
Droṇa|grāha|hradān muktau śakty|āśīviṣa|saṃkaṭāt
ayaḥ|śar'|ôgra|makarāt kṣatriya|pravar'|âmbhasaḥ.
jyā|ghoṣa|tala|nirhrādād gadā|nistriṃśa|vidyutaḥ
Droṇ'|âstra|meghān nirmuktau sūry'|êndū timirād iva.
bāhubhyām iva saṃtīrṇau Sindhu|ṣaṣṭhāḥ samudra|gāḥ

"When through the six rings of Dhrita·rashtra's army we have made our way and our eyes light on Sáindhava he will not escape our grasp. Come Indra and his gang of gods to save him: still we will cast him down."

Such were the Dark Ones' words, and as the great warriors spoke these things and spied the Sindhu king up went
the cry from your children. Like elephants that had crossed
the curving desert* and now quenched their thirst at the
other side they reared up refreshed to take their vengeance.
Like travelers who had come through all the wild perils 101.20
of the mountains they looked like neither time nor death
could stay them.

As they shot towards them your men saw the strange
cast of their faces and all about a cry went up. Through
Drona's searing fire and through all the kings of the earth
the two of them burned yet brighter. They had crossed
the sea that was Drona's array and now they smiled like
sailors back on dry land. Splendid as Indra or Agni they
had slipped through the great ring of iron that Drona and
Hardíkya had tightly bound, and now bedewed in blood 101.25
let by Bharadvája's sharp shafts they shimmered like mountains decked in flame of the forest. They had climbed from
a lake swirling with mighty men and shoaled in deadly iron
where spears slid like watersnakes and the great beast Drona
lurked. With the shudder and snap of string against palm
and with sword and morning star flashing about them they
had broken like sun and moon from the cloudy dark Drona
cast. It was as if with only their arms to carry them they had
crossed the six rivers that lead to the ocean at the hot season's end, when their courses burst the banks and piscine

tap'|ânte saritaḥ pūrṇā mahā|grāha|samākulāḥ.
iti Kṛṣṇau mah"|êṣv|āsau praśastau loka|viśrutau
sarva|bhūtāny amanyanta Droṇ'|āstra|bala|vismayāt.
101.30 Jayadratham samīpa|stham avekṣantau jighāṃsayā
rurum nipāte lipsantau vyāghravat tāv atiṣṭhatām.
yathā hi mukha|varṇo 'yam anayor iti menire
tava yodhā, mahā|rāja, hatam eva Jayadratham.
lohit'|âkṣau mahā|bāhū saṃyuktau Kṛṣṇa|Pāṇḍavau
Sindhu|rājam abhiprekṣya hṛṣṭau vyanadatāṃ muhuḥ.
Śaurer abhīṣu|hastasya Pārthasya ca dhanuṣmataḥ
tayor āsīt prabhā rājan sūrya|pāvakayor iva.
harṣa eva tayor āsīd Droṇ'|ānīka|pramuktayoḥ
samīpe Saindhavaṃ dṛṣṭvā śyenayor āmiṣaṃ yathā.
101.35 tau tu Saindhavam ālokya vartamānam iv' ântike
sahasā petatuḥ kruddhau kṣipraṃ śyenāv iv' āmiṣam.
tau tu dṛṣṭvā vyatikrāntau Hṛṣīkeśa|Dhanaṃjayau
Sindhu|rājasya rakṣ"|ârthaṃ parākrāntaḥ sutas tava
Droṇen' ābaddha|kavaco rājā Duryodhanas tadā
yayāv eka|rathen' ājau haya|saṃskāra|vit prabho.
Kṛṣṇa|Pārthau mah"|êṣv|āsau vyatikramy' âtha te sutaḥ
agrataḥ Puṇḍarīkākṣaṃ pratīyāya, nar'|âdhipa.
tataḥ sarveṣu sainyeṣu vāditrāṇi prahṛṣṭavat
prāvādyanta vyatikrānte tava putre Dhanaṃjayam.
101.40 siṃha|nāda|ravāś c' āsañ śaṅkha|śabda|vimiśritāḥ
dṛṣṭvā Duryodhanaṃ tatra Kṛṣṇayoḥ pramukhe sthitam.
ye ca te Sindhu|rājasya goptāraḥ pāvak'|ôpamāḥ
te 'py ahṛṣyanta samare dṛṣṭvā putraṃ tava, prabho.
dṛṣṭvā Duryodhanaṃ Kṛṣṇo vyatikrāntaṃ sah'|ânugam
abravīd Arjunaṃ, rājan, prāpta|kālam idaṃ vacaḥ.

life surges across the lowlands. Such were the thoughts that
came to us when the Dark Ones so famed and fabled had
confounded Drona's iron and wood.

Now they wanted blood. They drew to a halt and watched 101.30
Jayad·ratha like tigers eager for their prey. O majesty. We
took one look at their faces and we knew Jayad·ratha was
already dead. Their eyes were red. They were ready. Their
arms flexed and then celebrant at the sight of the Sindhu
king they hollered a battlecry, and shining like the gods of
the fire and of the sun Shauri snapped the reins and Partha
raised his bow. When a hawk sees its prey it hovers and then
plunges: so it was that they cast their eyes from the edge of 101.35
Drona's array to where Sáindhava stood, and realising that
they had him they plunged.

Your son saw Hrishi·kesha and Dhanan·jaya cut across
the fray. Bound in Drona's armour it was King Duryódhana
o majesty who all alone drove out his wellbedight steeds to
try to protect the Sindhu king. O lord of men your boy
outpaced their great car and he wheeled ahead of Lotuseye. The instruments of war burst out a proud chord as
Duryódhana trumped Dhanan·jaya so. Men's roars mingled 101.40
with the blare of trumpets as your son took on the Dark
Ones. Majesty, the sentinels of the Sindhu king flared up
like fire to see him. O father. Krishna watched as Duryódhana streamed ahead of him with his men and he turned
to Árjuna and spoke. And he chose his words with care.

VĀSUDEVA uvāca:

102.1 DURYODHANAM atikrāntam etaṃ paśya, Dhanaṃjaya.
atyadbhutam imaṃ manye. n' âsty asya sadṛśo rathaḥ.
dūra|pātī mah"|êṣv|āsaḥ kṛt'|âstro yuddha|dur|madaḥ,
dṛḍh'|âstraś citra|yodhī ca Dhārtarāṣṭro mahā|balaḥ,
atyanta|sukha|saṃvṛddho mānitaś ca mahā|rathaiḥ,
kṛtī ca satataṃ Pārtha nityaṃ dveṣṭi ca Pāṇḍavān.
tena yuddham imaṃ manye prāpta|kālaṃ tav' ân|agha.
atra vo dyūtam āyattaṃ vijayāy' êtarāya vā.
102.5 atra krodha|viṣaṃ Pārtha vimuñca cira|sambhṛtam.
eṣa mūlam an|arthānāṃ Pāṇḍavānāṃ mahā|rathaḥ.
so 'yaṃ prāptas tav' ākṣepaṃ: paśya sāphalyam ātmanaḥ.
kathaṃ hi rājā rājy'|ârthī tvayā gaccheta saṃyugam?
diṣṭyā tv idānīṃ samprāpta eṣa te bāṇa|gocaram.
yath" âyaṃ jīvitaṃ jahyāt tathā kuru Dhanaṃjaya.
aiśvarya|mada|saṃmūḍho n' âiṣa duḥkham upeyivān
na ca te saṃyuge vīryaṃ jānāti, puruṣa'|rṣabha.
tvāṃ hi lokās trayaḥ Pārtha sa|sur'|âsura|mānuṣāḥ
n' ôtsahante raṇe jetuṃ. kim ut' âikaḥ Suyodhanaḥ?
102.10 sa diṣṭyā samanuprāptas tava, Pārtha, rath'|ântikam.
jahy enaṃ tvaṃ mahā|bāho yathā Vṛtraṃ Puraṃdaraḥ.
eṣa hy an|arthe satataṃ parākrāntas tav' ân|agha
nikṛtyā dharma|rājaṃ ca dyūte vañcitavān ayam.
bahūni su|nṛśaṃsāni kṛtāny etena māna|da
yuṣmāsu pāpa|matinā a|pāpeṣv eva nityadā.

VASUDÉVA spoke:

DHANAN·JAYA. See Duryódhana make his brazen ap- 102.1
proach. A marvel to behold for I swear there is no chariot
like to his. Dhrita·rashtra's mighty son is a colourful fighter.
His arrows are strong and farflying. His bow is stout and
his hand is deft. Battle is his liquor. He was born and bred
in opulence and his peers revere him. And his devious heart
has never harboured anything but contempt for Pandu's
line.

O sinless son of Pritha I think that the time is right for
this confrontation. The die is cast for you or for another.
At long last let from your veins the bitter poison that has 102.5
flowed in them for so long. This warlord is the root of all the
sufferings of Pandu's children. Now he stands before you
think of what you stand to gain in ridding yourself of him.
Will you brook a man that so covets your kingdom he has
crossed swords with you to make it his? Fate has brought
him within the reach of your arrows. Do what you must
to be free of him Dhanan·jaya. He is drunk on the wine of
power and has yet to come to grief but o bull in the herd of
men he does not comprehend your capability in combat.
Partha this triple world of men gods and demons could not
better you in battle. What of lone Suyódhana?

O Partha. Fate has brought him close to your car so raise 102.10
your two strong arms and strike him down as Puran·dara
struck down Vritra. It was he who though you did him no
wrong* loaded the dice and tricked the righteous king and
toiled without end to destroy you. Break the pride that visited so many endless evils upon your good selves. Be quick.

tam an|āryaṃ sadā kruddhaṃ puruṣaṃ kāma|rūpiṇam
āryāṃ yuddhe matiṃ kṛtvā jahi Pārth' â|vicārayan.
nikṛtyā rājya|haraṇaṃ vana|vāsaṃ ca Pāṇḍava
parikleśaṃ ca Kṛṣṇāyā hṛdi kṛtvā parākrama.
102.15 diṣṭy" âiṣa tava bāṇānāṃ go|care parivartate,
pratighātāya kāryasya diṣṭyā ca yatate 'grataḥ.
diṣṭyā jānāti saṃgrāme yoddhavyaṃ hi tvayā saha,
diṣṭyā ca sa|phalāḥ Pārtha sarve kāmā hy a|kāmitāḥ.
tasmāj jahi raṇe Pārtha Dhārtarāṣṭraṃ kul'|âdhamam
yath" Êndreṇa hataḥ pūrvaṃ Jambho dev'|âsure mṛdhe.
asmin hate tvayā sainyam a|nāthaṃ bhidyatām idam
vairasy' âsy' âstv avabhṛtho. mūlaṃ chindhi dur|ātmanām.

SAṂJAYA uvāca:

tam tath" êty abravīt Pārthaḥ, «kṛtya|rūpam idaṃ mama.
sarvam anyad an|ādṛtya gaccha yatra Suyodhanaḥ.
102.20 yen' âitad dīrgha|kālaṃ no bhuktaṃ rājyam a|kaṇṭakam
apy asya yudhi vikramya chindyāṃ mūrdhānam āhave.
api tasya hy an|arhāyāḥ parikleśasya Mādhava
Kṛṣṇāyāḥ śaknuyāṃ gantuṃ padaṃ keśa|pradharṣaṇe.»
ity evaṃ|vādinau Kṛṣṇau hṛṣṭau śvetān hay'|ôttamān
preṣayām āsatuḥ saṃkhye prepsantau taṃ nar'|âdhipam.
tayoḥ samīpaṃ samprāpya putras te Bharata'|rṣabha
na cakāra bhayaṃ prāpte bhaye mahati māriṣa

He is in thrall to gruesome lusts that have corrupted his noble blood.* Dignify him with a last battle and Partha strike him dead. It was he o son of Pandu who calumnied your inheritance and your years in the wilderness and whose wanton cruelty broke Krishná's heart. Step up to him. Fate 102.15
brings him just an arrow's flight away. It is fate that brings him into the path of your necessary revenge. Fate has made him fight you and o Partha fate will now decide whether all your hopes will prosper or fail. O Partha strike down Dhrita·rashtra's degenerate child as in the olden battle between gods and demons Indra struck down Jambha. With their leader dead at your feet his army will cave and all this enmity will be purged. Cut out its vile root.

SÁNJAYA spoke:

Pritha's son agreed with him and replied.

"What you say is true. Ignore the others and make for Suyódhana. He has for too long enjoyed our kingdom un- 102.20
challenged. May I beat him in battle and cut off his head and in so doing o Mádhava be avenged on they who took the blameless Krishná's hair in their fists."

Thrilled by these words the Dark Ones drove their pure white steeds straight for the king. O bull of the Bháratas they drew close to your son. Though there was terror in the air he seemed not to feel it. His vassals admired his courage.

tad asya kṣatriyās tatra sarva ev' âbhyapūjayan
yad Arjuna|Hṛṣīkeśau pratyudyātau nyavārayat.
102.25 tataḥ sarvasya sainyasya tāvakasya viśāṃ pate
mahā|nādo hy abhūt tatra dṛṣṭvā rājānam āhave.
tasmiñ jana|samunnāde pravṛtte bhairave sati
kad|arthī|kṛtya te putraḥ pratyamitram avārayat.
āvāritas tu Kaunteyas tava putreṇa dhanvinā
saṃrambham agamad bhūyaḥ sa ca tasmin paraṃ|tapaḥ.
tau dṛṣṭvā pratisaṃrabdhau Duryodhana|Dhanaṃjayau
abhyavaikṣanta rājāno bhīma|rūpāḥ samantataḥ.
dṛṣṭvā tu Pārthaṃ saṃrabdhaṃ Vāsudevaṃ ca māriṣa
prahasann eva putras te yoddhu|kāmaḥ samāhvayat.
102.30 tataḥ prahṛṣṭo Dāśārhaḥ Pāṇḍavaś ca Dhanaṃjayaḥ
vyakrośetāṃ mahā|nādaṃ dadhmatuś c' âmbuj'|ôttamau.
tau hṛṣṭa|rūpau samprekṣya Kauraveyās tu sarvaśaḥ
nir|āśāḥ samapadyanta putrasya tava jīvite.
śokam āpuḥ pare c' âiva Kuravaḥ sarva eva te
amanyanta ca putraṃ te Vaiśvānara|mukhe hutam.
tathā tu dṛṣṭvā yodhās te prahṛṣṭau Kṛṣṇa|Pāṇḍavau
hato rājā hato rāj" êty ūcire ca bhay'|ârditāḥ.
janasya saṃninādaṃ tu śrutvā Duryodhano 'bravīt.
«vyetu vo bhīr. ahaṃ Kṛṣṇau preṣayiṣyāmi mṛtyave.»
102.35 ity uktvā sainikān sarvāñ jay'|āpekṣī nar'|âdhipaḥ.
Pārtham ābhāṣya saṃrambhād idaṃ vacanam abravīt.

There he was, facing down Árjuna and Hrishi·kesha in full
flight. O lord a great cheer rose from your men when they 102.25
saw the figure of your son standing and waiting. The commotion grew loud in our ears but Duryódhana ignored it and stood with bow drawn to meet his foe. Kauntéya looked across at your boy and the fury in him raged ever higher. All around the fearsome fighters stood and watched as Duryódhana and Dhanan·jaya blazed at each other.

O majesty your son eyed Partha and Vasudéva as they tore towards him. He was keen to fight and with a mocking
smile on his lips he beckoned them closer. Dashárha reared 102.30
up and with a battlecry he and Dhanan·jaya son of Pandu put their polished seashells to their lips and blew.

Your other children watched the dauntless pair and they feared for their brother's life. Despair swept through the ranks. Krishna and Pándava were so inflamed it was as if Duryódhana had fallen into a furnace's mouth. Men muttered in terrified voices that their king was already dead. But Duryódhana heard their susurrus and he spoke.

"Have no fear. I will send the Dark Ones to hell."

Such were the words he called out to his soldiers for 102.35
the king believed he would win. Rashly he turned towards Pritha's son and shouted across to him.

«Pārtha, yac chikṣitaṃ te 'straṃ divyaṃ pārthivam eva ca
tad darśaya mayi kṣipraṃ yadi jāto 'si Pāṇḍunā.
yad balaṃ tava vīryaṃ ca Keśavasya tath" âiva ca
tat kuruṣva mayi kṣipraṃ. paśyāmas tava pauruṣam.
asmat|parokṣaṃ karmāṇi kṛtāni pravadanti te.
svāmi|sat|kāra|yuktāni yāni tān' îha darśaya.»

SAṂJAYA uvāca:

103.1 EVAM UKTV" Ârjunaṃ rājā tribhir marm'|âtigaiḥ śaraiḥ
abhyavidhyan mahā|vegaiś caturbhiś caturo hayān.
Vāsudevaṃ ca daśabhiḥ pratyavidhyat stan'|ântare
pratodaṃ c' âsya bhallena chittvā bhūmāv apātayat.
taṃ catur|daśabhiḥ Pārthaś citra|puṅkhaiḥ śilā|śitaiḥ
avidhyat tūrṇam a|vyagras te c' âbhraśyanta varmaṇi.
teṣāṃ naiṣphalyam ālokya punar nava ca pañca ca
prāhiṇon niśitān bāṇāṃs te c' âbhraśyanta varmaṇaḥ.
103.5 aṣṭā|viṃśati tān bāṇān astān vipreksya niṣphalān
abravīt para|vīra|ghnaḥ Kṛṣṇo 'rjunam idaṃ vacaḥ.
«a|dṛṣṭa|pūrvaṃ paśyāmi śilānām iva sarpaṇam.
tvayā sampreṣitāḥ Pārtha n' ârthaṃ kurvanti patriṇaḥ.
kaccid Gāṇḍīvataḥ prāṇās tath" âiva Bharata'|rṣabha
muṣṭiś ca te yathā|pūrvaṃ bhujayoś ca balaṃ tava?
na vā kaccid ayaṃ kālaḥ prāptaḥ syād adya paścimaḥ
tava c' âiv' âsya śatroś ca? tan mam' ācakṣva pṛcchataḥ.
vismayo me mahān Pārtha tava dṛṣṭvā śarān imān
vy|arthān nipatatān saṃkhye Duryodhana|rathaṃ prati.
103.10 vajr'|âśani|samā ghorāḥ para|kāy'|âvabhedinaḥ
śarāḥ kurvanti te n' ârthaṃ. Pārtha, k" âdya viḍambanā?

"Partha. If Pandu is indeed your father, show me now these weapons earthly and divine in which you have been schooled. Bring all your power and might to bear on me. Késhava too: let us see what stuff you are made of. People talk of the things you have done but I am not so sure. Show me what you learned at the feet of old men."

SÁNJAYA spoke:

So SAID THE king and with three arrows biting to the 103.1
bone he pierced Árjuna and sent four more whistling towards his four horses. Ten shafts thudded into Vasudéva's
chest and an iron dart snapped the whip from his hands
and cast it to the earth. Partha's son stayed calm. He shot
back fourteen finefiligreed arrows each honed to a hiss and
they hurtled through the air but when they struck Duryódhana's armour they glanced off without effect. Árjuna
saw them fall and followed them with nine then five sharp
shafts and they too glanced off the plate. When the twen- 103.5
tyeighth arrow had flown from Árjuna's bow and failed,
Krishna scourge of heroes turned to his friend and spoke.

"This o Partha is like stone melting. I have never seen
such a thing before. The arrows you shoot do not strike
home. Is Gandíva now a giver of life? O bull of the Bharatas
do your fingers and arms have their strength of old? It cannot be that the final hour has come for you and not for the
man you fight. Can it? Enlighten me Partha for I cannot 103.10
believe what I see. Your arrows hard and deadly as diamond
that have taken apart many a foe fly now across the fray
at Duryódhana's car and yet they do no damage. O son of
Pritha. What is this devilment?

ARJUNA uvāca:

Droṇen' âiṣā matiḥ Kṛṣṇa Dhārtarāṣṭre niveśitā.
a|bhedyā hi mam' âstrāṇām eṣā kavaca|dhāraṇā.
asminn antar|hitaṃ Kṛṣṇa trailokyam api varmaṇi.
eko Droṇo hi ved' âitad ahaṃ tasmāc ca sattamāt.
na śakyam etat kavacaṃ bāṇair bhettuṃ kathaṃ cana
api vajreṇa Govinda svayaṃ Maghavatā yudhi.
jānaṃs tvam api vai, Kṛṣṇa, māṃ vimohayase katham?
yad vṛttaṃ triṣu lokeṣu, yac ca Keśava vartate,
103.15 tathā bhaviṣyad yac c' âiva tat sarvaṃ viditaṃ tava.
na tv idaṃ veda vai kaś cid yathā tvaṃ Madhusūdana.
eṣa Duryodhanaḥ Kṛṣṇa Droṇena vihitām imām
tiṣṭhaty a|bhītavat saṃkhye bibhrat kavaca|dhāraṇām.
yat tv atra vihitaṃ kāryaṃ n' âiṣa tad vetti, Mādhava.
strīvad eṣa bibharty etāṃ yuktāṃ kavaca|dhāraṇām.
paśya bāhvoś ca me vīryaṃ dhanuṣaś ca, Janārdana.
parājayiṣye Kauravyaṃ kavacen' âpi rakṣitam.
idam Aṅgirase prādād dev'|ēśo varma bhāsvaram,
tasmād Bṛhaspatiḥ prāpa tataḥ prāpa Puraṃdaraḥ.
punar dadau sura|patir mahyaṃ varma sa|saṃgraham.
103.20 daivaṃ yady asya varm' âitad Brahmaṇā vā svayaṃ kṛtam,
n' âinaṃ gopsyati dur|buddhim adya bāṇa|hataṃ mayā.

SAMJAYA uvāca:

evam uktv" Ârjuno bāṇān abhimantrya vyakarṣayat.
vikṛṣyamāṇāṃs ten' âivaṃ dhanur|madhya|gatāñ śarān
tān asy' âstreṇa ciccheda Drauṇiḥ sarv'|âstra|ghātinā.

ÁRJUNA spoke:

Krishna this is Drona's work. He has bound Duryódhana in armour that my arrows cannot pierce. The secret of this cuirass o Krishna the great seer Drona gleaned alone from the hidden world and I from him. It cannot be pierced by any arrow Go·vinda, nor even by the thunderbolt that Mághavat yields. Why do you pretend not to know all this? Nothing transpires in any of the three realms without your knowledge, Krishna. O Késhava you know all that 103.15
will come to pass and none are better acquainted with life's mysteries Madhu·súdana than you.

Duryódhana waits unafraid to do battle with me clad in the armour that Drona has bound to his back. But see, Mádhava. He does not know what to do next. He stands there posing in his new costume like a girl in a dress. O Janárdana. Behold now the power in my arm and bow as I penetrate Kauravya's defence. This armour bright as the sun passed from the lord of the gods to Ángiras and from him to Brihas·pati and from Brihas·pati to Puran·dara. The king of heaven passed on this wondrous metal and so too
the spell to bind it. Though none but Brahma crafted this 103.20
celestial suit Duryódhana is foolish to think that it will be any use to him when my arrows have riddled it with holes.

SÁNJAYA spoke:

With these words Árjuna took a clutch of shafts and incanted across them and notched them on his bow. But as he drew them back on the string Drona's son splintered through all of them with a single shaft charmed to destroy

tān nikṛttān iṣūn dṛṣṭvā dūrato brahma|vādinā
nyavedayat Keśavāya vismitaḥ śveta|vāhanaḥ.
«n' âitad astraṃ mayā śakyaṃ
dviḥ prayoktuṃ Janārdana.
astraṃ mām eva hanyādd hi
hanyāc c' âpi balaṃ mama.»
103.25 tato Duryodhanaḥ Kṛṣṇau navabhir navabhiḥ śaraiḥ
avidhyata raṇe rājañ śarair āśīviṣ'|ôpamaiḥ.
bhūya ev' âbhyavarṣac ca samare Kṛṣṇa|Pāṇḍavau
śara|varṣeṇa mahatā. tato 'hṛṣyanta tāvakāḥ.
cakrur vāditra|ninadān siṃha|nāda|ravāṃs tathā.
tataḥ kruddho raṇe Pārthaḥ sṛkkiṇī parisaṃlihan
n' âpaśyac ca tato 'sy' âṅgaṃ yan na syād varma|rakṣitam.
tato 'sya niśitair bāṇaiḥ su|muktair antak'|ôpamaiḥ
hayāṃś cakāra nir|dehān ubhau ca pārṣṇi|sārathī.
103.30 dhanur asy' âcchinat tūrṇaṃ hast'|âvāpaṃ ca vīryavān,
rathaṃ ca śakalī|kartuṃ Savyasācī pracakrame.
Duryodhanaṃ ca bāṇābhyāṃ tīkṣṇābhyāṃ virathī|kṛtam
avidhyadd hasta|talayor ubhayor Arjunas tadā.
tam kṛcchrām āpadaṃ prāptaṃ dṛṣṭvā parama|dhanvinaḥ
samāpetuḥ parīpsanto Dhanaṃjaya|śar'|ârditam.
taṃ rathair bahu|sāhasraiḥ kalpitaiḥ kuñjarair hayaiḥ
padāty|oghaiś ca saṃrabdhaiḥ parivavrur Dhanaṃjayam.
atha n' Ârjuna|Govindau na ratho vā vyadṛśyata
astra|varṣeṇa mahatā jan'|âughaiś c' âpi saṃvṛtau.

all others. The warrior of the white horses could not believe that the priest had found his arrows at such a distance. His eyes widened and he spoke to Késhava.

"O Stirrer of Men I dare not use this spell twice. If I did it might destroy me or at the very least wound me to the quick."

Then with nine arrows and nine again swift and deadly 103.25
as poison Duryódhana struck at the Dark Ones. More did he rain down upon their heads and o majesty as our hearts leapt to see the storm he brewed the songs and sounds and roars of battle rose from our ranks.

Partha's tongue darted between his lips and his pulse quickened. He could not see a join in Duryódhana's armour. So with his sharp shafts aflight, like death he cut the heads from the bodies of his foe's horses and so too
the heads of his flankriders. A moment passed and Duryó- 103.30
dhana's bow was in splinters and his vambrace torn away and then with a great flurry the Lefthanded Archer carved his car too to pieces, and as the chariot collapsed around him Árjuna sent two biting arrows through the palms of Duryódhana's hands.

Our very best bowmen saw Dhanan·jaya's arrows cutting through Duryódhana and they all swept forward to save him from the terrible danger he was in. Thousands upon thousands of wellbedecked cars and elephants and horses and groups of furious warriors poured in around Dhanan·jaya. Soon neither Árjuna nor the Herdsman nor the chariot they rode in could any more be seen through the great cataract of arrows and swirl of men that engulfed it.

103.35 tato 'rjuno 'stra|vīryeṇa nijaghne tāṃ varūthinīm
tatra vy|aṅgī|kṛtāḥ petuḥ śataśo 'tha ratha|dvipāḥ.
te hatā hanyamānāś ca nyagṛhṇaṃs taṃ rath'|ôttamam.
sa ratha|stambhitas tasthau krośa|mātre samantataḥ.
tato 'rjunaṃ Vṛṣṇi|vīras
tvarito vākyam abravīt.
«dhanur visphāray' âtyartham.
ahaṃ dhmāsyāmi c' âmbu|jam.»
tato visphārya balavad Gāṇḍīvaṃ jaghnivān ripūn
mahatā śara|varṣeṇa tala|śabdena c' Ârjunaḥ.
Pāñcajanyaṃ ca balavān dadhmau tāreṇa Keśavaḥ
rajasā dhvasta|pakṣm'|ântaḥ prasvinna|vadano bhṛśam.
103.40 tasya śaṅkhasya nādena dhanuṣo niḥsvanena ca
niḥ|sattvāś ca sa|sattvāś ca kṣitau petus tadā janāḥ.
tair vimukto ratho reje vāyv|īrita iv' âmbu|daḥ.
Jayadrathasya goptāras tataḥ kṣubdhāḥ sah'|ânugāḥ.
te dṛṣṭvā sahasā Pārthaṃ goptāraḥ Saindhavasya tu
cakrur nādān mah"|êṣv|āsāḥ kampayanto vasuṃ|dharām.
bāṇa|śabda|ravāṃś c' ôgrān vimiśrāñ śaṅkha|niḥsvanaiḥ
prāduś cakrur mah"|ātmānaḥ siṃha|nāda|ravān api.
taṃ śrutvā ninadaṃ ghoraṃ tāvakānāṃ samutthitam
pradadhmatuḥ śaṃkha|varau Vāsudeva|Dhanaṃjayau.
103.45 tena śabdena mahatā pūrit" êva vasuṃ|dharā
sa|śailā s'|ârṇava|dvīpā sa|pātālā, viśāṃ pate.

Then Árjuna struck back. Down came his foes in their hundreds as he lopped off the limbs of beasts and wheels of cars with the sheer might of his arms. The dead and the dying crashed in upon his car and for a league in every direction there was nowhere it could go. The Vrishni chieftain glanced at Árjuna and spoke. 103.35

"Deafen them with the string of your bow while I sound my conch."

Árjuna plucked Gandíva's string hard and men fell dead from the sound and the storm that it brought. Blinking through dust and sweat Késhava raised Pancha·janya and
its keening note pealed above the fray. The seashell's echo 103.40
and the song of the bow knocked the men to their knees whether or not they yet lived. Now Árjuna's car stood all alone, like a lonely cloud driven on the wind.

For a moment Jayad·ratha's guard were too stunned to move. Then his sentinels raised their eyes and bows once more to Partha and raised a battlecry to shake the earth. It was a dire and animal sound that their great lungs made and it mixed with the clamour and clack of arrows and the conch's note. When Vasudéva and Dhanan·jaya heard the drear roar they lifted their hands and as one they breathed
deep and put their shells to their lips. O lord of men. The 103.45
sound they made filled the world, from the mountains and the rivers and the oceans to the caves beneath the earth.

sa śabdo Bharata|śreṣṭha vyāpya sarvā diśo daśa
pratisasvāna tatr' âiva Kuru|Pāṇḍavayor bale.
tāvakā rathinas tatra dṛṣṭvā Kṛṣṇa|Dhanaṃjayau
sambhramaṃ paramaṃ prāptās tvaramāṇā mahā|rathāḥ.
atha Kṛṣṇau mahā|bhāgau tāvakā vīkṣya daṃśitau
abhyadravanta saṃkruddhās: tad adbhutam iv' âbhavat.

SAMJAYA uvāca:

104.1 TĀVAKĀ HI samīkṣy' âiva Vṛṣṇy|Andhaka|Kur'|ûttamau
prāg atvarañ jighāṃsantas tath" âiva vijayaḥ parān,
suvarṇa|citrair vaiyāghraiḥ svanavadbhir mahā|rathaiḥ
dīpayanto diśaḥ sarvā jvaladbhir iva pāvakaiḥ,
rukma|pṛṣṭhaiś ca duṣ|prekṣyaiḥ kārmukaiḥ pṛthivī|pate
kūjadbhir a|tulān nādān kopitais turagair iva,
Bhūriśravāḥ, Śalaḥ, Karṇo, Vṛṣaseno, Jayadrathaḥ,
Kṛpaś ca, Madra|rājaś ca, Drauṇiś ca rathināṃ varaḥ.
104.5 te pibanta iv' ākāśam aśvair aṣṭau mahā|rathāḥ
vyarājayan daśa diśo vaiyāghrair hema|candrakaiḥ.
te daṃśitāḥ su|saṃrabdhā rathair megh'|âugha|niḥsvanaiḥ
samāvṛṇvan daśa diśaḥ Pārthasya niśitaiḥ śaraiḥ.
kulīnāś ca hayāś citrā vahantas tān mahā|rathān
vyaśobhanta tadā śīghrā dīpayanto diśo daśa.
ājāneyair mahā|vegair nānā|deśa|samutthitaiḥ
pārvatīyair nadī|jaiś ca saindhavaiś ca hay'|ôttamaiḥ
Kuru|yodha|varā rājaṃs tava putraṃ parīpsavaḥ
Dhanaṃjaya|rathaṃ śīghraṃ sarvataḥ samupādravan.

O best of the Bharatas that sound passed all across the sky and it echoed above the heads of Kuru and Pándava alike. As it did your mighty men seethed. They fixed their vision on Krishna and Dhanan·jaya. The frenzy was in them, and as the Dark Ones glittered illustrious before their eyes, they rushed forth to attack.

SÁNJAYA spoke:

OF ALL IN THE bloodline of Kuru, Ándhaka and Vri- 104.1
shni, this pair were the finest and locking their gaze upon
them your men raced ahead eager to bring them low. Fes-
tooned in the pelts of tigers their huge chariots screeched all
across the plain and shimmered like flickering fire. O lord
of the wide world their goldbacked bows hissed weird and
unearthly like the whinny of wild horses as Bhuri·shravas,
Shala, Karna, Vrisha·sena, Jayad·ratha, Kripa, the Madra
king and greatest of them all the son of Drona seemed 104.5
to drink up space with their steeds, eight mighty cars and eight mighty fighters blazing in the ten quarters all tiger-striped and patterned in mooncrescents of gold. Wheeling close they blotted Partha's horizon out in a slew of whetted shafts, and the glossy thoroughbreds that drew their great chariots streaked the plain with brightness where they went. Strongflanked and wellreared they were, exotic creatures sprung from hill riverplain and seashore and o king behind them the other Kuru champions swung wide and descended from every angle upon Dhanan·jaya's car to swipe back your son from his grasp.

104.10 te pragṛhya mahā|śaṅkhān dadhmuḥ puruṣa|sattamāḥ
pūrayanto divaṃ rājan pṛthivīṃ ca sa|sāgarām.
tath" âiva dadhmatuḥ śaṅkhau Vāsudeva|Dhanaṃjayau
pravarau sarva|devānāṃ sarva|śaṅkha|varau bhuvi
Devadattaṃ ca Kaunteyaḥ Pāñcajanyaṃ ca Keśavaḥ.
śabdas tu Devadattasya Dhanaṃjaya|samīritaḥ
pṛthivīṃ c' ântarikṣaṃ ca diśaś c' âiva samāvṛṇot.
tath" âiva Pāñcajanyo 'pi Vāsudeva|samīritaḥ
sarva|śabdān atikramya pūrayām āsa rodasī.
tasmiṃs tathā vartamāne dāruṇe nāda|saṃkule
bhīrūṇāṃ trāsa|janane śūrāṇāṃ harṣa|vardhane,
104.15 pravāditāsu bherīṣu jharjhareṣv ānakeṣu ca
mṛdaṅgeṣv api rāj'|êndra vādyamāneṣv an|ekaśaḥ
mahā|rathāḥ samāhūtā Duryodhana|hit'|âiṣiṇaḥ
a|mṛṣyamāṇās taṃ śabdaṃ kruddhāḥ parama|dhanvinaḥ,
nānā|deśyā mahī|pālāḥ sva|sainya|parirakṣiṇaḥ
a|marṣitā mahā|śaṅkhān dadhmur vīrā mahā|rathāḥ
kṛte pratikariṣyantaḥ Keśavasy' Ârjunasya ca.
babhūva tava tat sainyaṃ śaṅkha|śabda|samīritam
udvigna|ratha|nāg'|âśvam a|svastham iva vā, vibho.
tat praviddham iv' ākāśaṃ śūraiḥ śaṅkha|vināditam
babhūva bhṛśam udvignaṃ nirghātair iva nāditam.
104.20 sa śabdaḥ su|mahān, rājan, diśaḥ sarvā vyanādayat
trāsayām āsa tat|sainyaṃ yug'|ânta iva sambhṛtaḥ.
tato Duryodhano 'ṣṭau ca rājānas te mahā|rathāḥ
Jayadrathasya rakṣ'|ârthaṃ Pāṇḍavaṃ paryavārayan.
tato Drauṇis tri|saptatyā Vāsudevam atāḍayat
Arjunaṃ ca tribhir bhallair dhvajam aśvāṃś ca pañcabhiḥ.

The eight heroes raised their great shells and o majesty   104.10
land sea and sky rang with the sound. But Késhava held
Pancha·janya and Kauntéya Deva·datta and among neither gods nor men are there finer horns than these. From
Vasudéva and Dhanan·jaya came the answering note. As
Dhanan·jaya blew Deva·datta the sound filled up the earth
and the air and the deeper vault of heaven, and as Vasudéva
blew Pancha·janya nothing else could be heard as its drone
poured out across the domain of the living. The echoes
came dreadful and building one upon the other to shake
the timid and thrill the brave and o king of kings from all   104.15
around the beat of timpani and drum began to throb and
swell as the bold kings of the earth who had come from all
across its surface to draw their mighty bows to help Duryódhana and save their own demesnes were crazed by the
sound they heard and blew ever harder into their trumpets
to drown out the noise Késhava and Árjuna had made.

O lord. Down the avenues of horses elephants and cars
our heroes' counterpoint rumbled and everything began to
shake as if the earth could no longer hold itself together.
The blast seemed to tear the air itself and the howling shock
came upon us like a tornado. O king. What a din that was.   104.20
It shook through the sky so fearsomely we thought the end
of the world had come.

The circle of eight kings closed in around Pándava to finish the matter for Jayad·ratha. Duryódhana fell in alongside. With three and seventy arrows Drauni beat upon Vasudéva and with three barbed shafts he struck Árjuna and

tam Arjunaḥ pṛṣatkānāṃ śataiḥ ṣaḍbhir atāḍayat
atyartham iva saṃkruddhaḥ pratividdhe Janārdane.
Karṇaṃ sa daśabhir viddhvā Vṛṣasenaṃ tribhis tathā
Śalyasya sa|śaraṃ cāpaṃ muṣṭau ciccheda vīryavān.
104.25 gṛhītvā dhanur anyat tu Śalyo vivyādha Pāṇḍavam.
Bhūriśravās tribhir bāṇair hema|puṅkhaiḥ śilā|śitaiḥ
Karṇo dvā|triṃśatā c' âiva Vṛṣasenaś ca pañcabhiḥ,
Jayadrathas tri|saptatyā Kṛpaś ca daśabhiḥ śaraiḥ
Madra|rājaś ca daśabhir vivyadhuḥ Phalgunaṃ raṇe.
tataḥ śarāṇāṃ ṣaṣṭyā tu Drauṇiḥ Pārtham avākirat
Vāsudevaṃ ca viṃśatyā punaḥ Pārthaṃ ca pañcabhiḥ.
prahasaṃs tu nara|vyāghraḥ śvet'|âśvaḥ Kṛṣṇa|sārathiḥ
pratyavidhyat sa tān sarvān darśayan pāṇi|lāghavam.
104.30 Karṇaṃ dvā|daśabhir viddhvā Vṛṣasenaṃ tribhiḥ śaraiḥ
Śalyasya sa|śaraṃ cāpaṃ muṣṭi|deśe vyakṛntata.
Saumadattiṃ tribhir viddhvā Śalyaṃ ca daśabhiḥ śaraiḥ
śitair agni|śikh'|ākārair Drauṇiṃ vivyādha c' âṣṭabhiḥ.
Gautamaṃ pañca|viṃśatyā Saindhavaṃ ca śatena ha
punar Drauṇiṃ ca saptatyā śarāṇāṃ so 'bhyatāḍayat.
Bhūriśravās tu saṃkruddhaḥ pratodaṃ cicchide Hareḥ
Arjunaṃ ca tri|saptatyā bāṇānām ājaghāna ha.
tataḥ śara|śatais tīkṣṇais tān arīñ śveta|vāhanaḥ
pratyaṣedhad drutaṃ kruddho mahā|vāto ghanān iva.

with five his flag and steeds. Árjuna was furious to see Janárdana attacked and he hit back hard with six of his arrows. Then battering Karna with ten and Vrisha·sena with three
he knocked the bow and arrow from Shalya's fists. Shalya 104.25
swept up another and aimed at Pándava. Three stonewhetted arrows fletched in feathers flecked gold flew from Bhuri·shravas' bow as two and thirty came from Karna, five from Vrisha·sena and from Jayad·ratha seventythree more. Kripa found the Red Star Fighter with a flight of ten and ten more coursed from the fingers of the Madra king through the fray. Drauni followed and found Partha with six of his shafts, Vasudéva with twenty and then Partha once again with five.

The warrior of the white horses bridled by Krishna merely
smiled a tiger's smile. His fingers fluttered and he swept 104.30
their arrows to the ground. Striking Karna with twelve arrows of his own and Vrisha·sena with three he cut once again Shalya's bow and arrow from his grasp. With three arrows he found Saumadátti and Shalya with ten and then at Drauni he sent eight more hot as flame. He hit Sáindhava with a hundred arrows and Gáutama with twentyfive and then found Drauni again with seven more. But Bhuri·shravas sliced the reins from Hari's hands and with ferocious skill blasted Árjuna with seventythree of his shafts. Then with biting darts in their hundreds the warrior of the white horses came back at his foes in full fury, like a wind tearing through cloud.

DHṚTARĀṢṬRA uvāca:

105.1 DHVAJĀN BAHU|vidh'|ākārān bhrājamānān atiśriyā
Pārthānāṃ māmakānāṃ ca tān mam' ācakṣva Saṃjaya.

SAṂJAYA uvāca:

dhvajān bahu|vidh'|ākārāñ śṛṇu teṣāṃ mah"|ātmanām
rūpato varṇataś c' âiva nāmataś ca nibodha me.
teṣāṃ tu ratha|mukhyānāṃ ratheṣu vividhā dhvajāḥ
pratyadṛśyanta rāj'|êndra jvalitā iva pāvakāḥ.
kāñcanāḥ kāñcan'|āpīḍāḥ kāñcana|srag|alaṃkṛtāḥ
kāñcanān' îva śṛṅgāṇi kāñcanasya mahā|gireḥ.
105.5 an|eka|varṇā vividhā dhvajāḥ parama|śobhanāḥ
te dhvajāḥ saṃvṛtās teṣāṃ patākābhiḥ samantataḥ.
nānā|varṇa|virāgābhiḥ śuśubhuḥ sarvato vṛtāḥ
patākāś ca tatas tās tu śvasanena samīritāḥ.
nṛtyamānā vyadṛśyanta raṅga|madhye vilāsikāḥ
Indr'|āyudha|sa|varṇ'|ābhāḥ patākā Bharata'|rṣabha.
dodhūyamānā rathināṃ śobhayanti mahā|rathān
siṃha|lāṅgūlam ugr'|āsyaṃ dhvajaṃ vānara|lakṣaṇam
Dhanaṃjayasya saṃgrāme pratyadṛśyata bhairavam.
sa vānara|varo, rājan, patākābhir alaṃkṛtaḥ
105.10 trāsayām āsa tat sainyaṃ dhvajo Gāṇḍīva|dhanvanaḥ.
tath" âiva siṃha|lāṅgūlaṃ Droṇa|putrasya Bhārata
dhvaj'|âgraṃ samapaśyāma bāla|sūrya|sama|prabham,
kāñcanaṃ pavan'|ôddhūtaṃ Śakra|dhvaja|sama|prabham
nandanaṃ Kaurav'|êndrāṇāṃ
Drauṇer lakṣma samucchritam.
hasti|kakṣyā punar haimī
babhūv' Ādhirather dhvajaḥ

DHRITA·RASHTRA spoke:

I CAN ALMOST see the bright and various totems of Pritha's 105.1
children and my own flashing against the sky. Describe them to me Sánjaya.

SÁNJAYA spoke:

Bright and various those totems were, and mighty the men that bore them. Listen now and hear their names shapes and colours.

O king of kings like flickering flame the different blazes danced above the chariots of the champions. The poles were of gold and they were bound in gold bindings and hung with gold chains like peaks of gold on a golden mountain.
Each held an effigy that coruscated with a thousand colours, 105.5
blending and merging and darkening and brightening as it moved in the wind. O bull of the Bharatas these things glowed in all the colours of the rainbow and seemed to dance upon the painted field beneath them. The tail of a lion, a pair of fearsome jaws, the effigy of the monkey: they swayed in the breeze to sign the cars and the warriors that rode within them.

O king it was above the head of Dhanan·jaya that the shape of the monkey so fine and fearful trailed its pennants.
As sure as Dhanan·jaya's blaze sent panic through the ranks 105.10
so too o Bhárata did the lion's tail that marked Drona's son. We saw it shake atop his pole bright as a rainbow and rendered in shades of lapis lazuli and gold. Hoisted high Drauni's totem thrilled the hearts of the Káurava heroes, as did the golden tiger on Ádhirathi's pole for o majesty his goldwrought standard and chainbound staff seemed to

āhave khaṃ mahā|rāja dadṛśe pūrayann iva.
patākā kāñcanī sragvī dhvajaḥ Karṇasya saṃyuge
nṛtyat' îva rath'|ôpasthe śvasanena samīritaḥ.
ācāryasya tu Pāṇḍūnāṃ brāhmaṇasya tapasvinaḥ
105.15 go|vṛṣo Gautamasy' āsīt Kṛpasya su|pariṣkṛtaḥ.
sa tena bhrājate rājan go|vṛṣeṇa mahā|rathaḥ
tri|pura|ghna|ratho yadvad go|vṛṣeṇa virājatā.
mayūro Vṛṣasenasya kāñcano maṇi|ratnavān
vyāhariṣyann iv' âtiṣṭhat sen"|âgram upaśobhayan.
tena tasya ratho bhāti mayūreṇa mah"|ātmanaḥ,
yathā Skandasya rāj'|êndra mayūreṇa virājatā.
Madra|rājasya Śalyasya dhvaj'|âgre 'gni|śikhām iva
sauvarṇīṃ pratipaśyāma sītām a|pratimāṃ śubhām.
sā sītā bhrājate tasya ratham āsthāya māriṣa,
sarva|bīja|virūḍh" êva yathā sītā śriyā vṛtā.
105.20 varāhaḥ Sindhu|rājasya rājato 'bhivirājate
dhvaj'|âgre '|lohit'|ârk'|ābho hema|jāla|pariṣkṛtaḥ.
śuśubhe ketunā tena rājatena Jayadrathaḥ
yathā dev'|âsure yuddhe purā Pūṣā sma śobhate.
Saumadatteḥ punar yūpo yajña|śīlasya dhīmataḥ
dhvajaḥ sūrya iv' ābhāti somaś c' âtra pradṛśyate.
sa yūpaḥ kāñcano, rājan, Saumadatter virājate
rāja|sūye makha|śreṣṭhe yathā yūpaḥ samucchritaḥ.
Śalasya tu mahā|rāja rājato dvi|rado mahān
ketuḥ kāñcana|citr'|âṅgair mayūrair upaśobhitaḥ.
105.25 sa ketuḥ śobhayām āsa sainyaṃ te Bharata'|rṣabha
yathā śveto mahā|nāgo deva|rāja|camūṃ tathā.
nāgo maṇi|mayo rājño dhvajaḥ kanaka|saṃvṛtaḥ
kiṅkiṇī|śata|saṃhrādo bhrājaṃś citro rath'|ôttame.
vyabhrājata bhṛśaṃ rājan putras tava viśāṃ pate

fill the sky above the fray. The finest hand had made the 105.15
calf that in the breeze seemed to dance atop the pole of the Pandu teacher, the fiery priest Kripa son of Gótama. With that calf he rode resplendent as once had the Destroyer of the Triple City with the selfsame beast upon his car.

A golden peacock encrusted with jewels and gemstones was raised tall and lustrous above the van atop Vrisha·sena's pole, and o king the hero's car shone with the totem as once Skanda's had shone with the same. The pole of Shalya the Madra king seemed crested in flame for we saw there the slash of the wholesome furrow that none can mistake, and o father planted upon his car it was wondrous as the cleft that
sown with care will raise up any seed. Strung with nets of 105.20
gold the sign of the boar was a silver flash the colour of a pale bloodless sun that marked the Sindhu king. Jayad·ratha's car shone with its silver totem as Pushan's car had shone when the demons met the gods in war. Saumadátti was a wise man wellversed in ritual and his sign was the sacrificial stake. Though the colour of the moon it shone like the sun. O king the stake on Saumadátti's car flashed wondrous as any raised when a king is anointed for his throne.

O majesty a great elephant of silver graced Shala's chariot and it was ringed in peacocks fashioned from glittering
gold. His totem shone above us o bull of the Bharatas like 105.25
the great white serpent above the battalion of heaven's king. Above our own king's chariot flashed the snake made of jewels and it was decorated in gold and jangled with a circlet of a hundred little bells. O king and lord of this realm your son the bull of the Kurus blazed in the fray with that great effigy above him. Thus were the nine signs our band

dhvajena mahatā saṃkhye Kurūṇām ṛṣabhas tadā.
nav' âite tava vāhinyām ucchritāḥ parama|dhvajāḥ
vyadīpayaṃs te pṛtanāṃ yug'|ânt'|āditya|saṃnibhāḥ.
daśamas tv Arjunasy' āsīd eka eva mahā|kapiḥ
adīpyat' Ârjuno yena Himavān iva vahninā.
105.30 tataś citrāṇi śubhrāṇi su|mahānti mahā|rathāḥ
kārmukāṇy ādadus tūrṇam Arjun'|ârthe paraṃ|tapāḥ.
tath" âiva dhanur āyacchat Pārthaḥ śatru|vināśanaḥ
Gāṇḍīvaṃ divya|karmā tad rājan dur|mantrite tava.
tav' âparādhād rājāno nihatā bahudhā yudhi
nānā|digbhyaḥ samāhūtāḥ sa|hayāḥ sa|ratha|dvipāḥ.
teṣām āsīd vyatikṣepo garjatām itar'|êtaram
Duryodhana|mukhānāṃ ca Pāṇḍūnām ṛṣabhasya ca.
tatr' âdbhutaṃ paraṃ cakre Kaunteyaḥ Kṛṣṇa|sārathiḥ
yad eko bahubhiḥ sārdhaṃ samāgacchad a|bhītavat.
105.35 aśobhata mahā|bāhur Gāṇḍīvaṃ vikṣipan dhanuḥ
jigīṣus tān nara|vyāghrāñ jighāṃsuś ca Jayadratham.
tatr' Ârjuno nara|vyāghraḥ śarair muktaiḥ sahasraśaḥ
adṛśyāṃs tāvakān yodhān pracakre śatru|tāpanaḥ.
tatas te 'pi nara|vyāghrāḥ Pārthaṃ sarve mahā|rathāḥ
a|dṛśyaṃ samare cakruḥ sāyak'|âughaiḥ samantataḥ.
saṃvṛte nara|siṃhais tu Kurūṇām ṛṣabhe 'rjune
mahān āsīt samuddhūtas tasya sainyasya niḥsvanaḥ.

DHṚTARĀṢṬRA uvāca:

106.1 ARJUNE SAINDHAVAṂ prāpte Bhāradvājena saṃvṛtāḥ
Pāñcālāḥ Kurubhiḥ sārdhaṃ kim akurvata, Saṃjaya?

had raised and they burned in the host like suns at the end of time. And the tenth and final was Árjuna's great monkey. It flashed like fire set in mountain snow.

Come to burn their foe away the great fighters all drew 105.30
back their vast and arcing bows and aimed at Árjuna. Partha fabled in heaven also drew back his bow for it was with Gandíva that he would take revenge upon the wrongs o king you had done him. This war has seen the end of dynasties. So many came from across the earth with their horses and elephants and chariots and they have all have fallen in the name of your crime.

In sudden commotion the Pandu bull and Duryódhana's best called aloud to each other, and then with Krishna at his side the son of Kunti rode out alone against their group.
It was impossible to believe but he showed no fear. With 105.35
Gandíva taut in his strong arms he blazed on eager to trample the tigers who stood against him and keen to bring Jayad·ratha down. Árjuna the champion and furnace of foes let fly a thousand arrows and he hid his opponents beneath them. All the great tigers loosed their own bows and they too hid Partha in clouds of their darts. And as Árjuna the bull vanished beneath the Kurus' wild attack a great clamour rose from the ranks of our host.

DHRITA·RASHTRA spoke:

So WHILE ÁRJUNA came ever closer to Sáindhava how 106.1
were the Panchálas faring against the Kurus? Had Bharadvája overcome them, Sánjaya?

SAMJAYA uvāca:

apar'|âhṇe, mahā|rāja, saṃgrāme loma|harṣaṇe
Pāñcālānāṃ Kurūṇāṃ ca Droṇa|dyūtam avartata.
Pāñcālā hi jighāṃsanto Droṇaṃ saṃhṛṣṭa|cetasaḥ
abhyamuñcanta garjantaḥ śara|varṣāṇi māriṣa.
tatas tu tumulas teṣāṃ saṃgrāmo 'vartat' âdbhutaḥ
Pāñcālānāṃ Kurūṇāṃ ca ghoro dev'|âsur'|ôpamaḥ.
106.5 sarve Droṇa|rathaṃ prāpya Pāñcālāḥ Pāṇḍavaiḥ saha
tad anīkaṃ bibhitsanto mah"|âstrāṇi vyadarśayan.
Droṇasya ratha|paryantaṃ rathino ratham āsthitāḥ
kampayanto 'bhyavartanta vegam āsthāya madhyamam.
tam abhyagād Bṛhatkṣatraḥ Kekayānāṃ mahā|rathaḥ
pravapan niśitān bāṇān Mahendr'|âśani|saṃnibhān.
taṃ tu pratyudyayau śīghraṃ Kṣemadhūrtir mahā|yaśāḥ
vimuñcan niśitān bāṇāñ śataśo 'tha sahasraśaḥ.
Dhṛṣṭaketuś ca Cedīnām ṛṣabho 'tibal'|ôditaḥ
tvarito 'bhyadravad Droṇaṃ Mahendra iva Śambaram.
106.10 tam āpatantaṃ sahasā vyādit'|āsyam iv' ântakam
vīra|dhanvā mah"|êṣv|āsas tvaramāṇaḥ samabhyayāt.
Yudhiṣṭhiraṃ mahā|rājaṃ jigīṣuṃ samavasthitam
sah'|ânīkaṃ tato Droṇo nyavārayata vīryavān.

Nakulaṃ kuśalaṃ yuddhe parākrāntaṃ parākramī
abhyagacchat samāyāntaṃ Vikarṇas te sutaḥ prabho.
Sahadevaṃ tath" āyāntaṃ Durmukhaḥ śatru|karśanaḥ
śarair an|eka|sāhasraiḥ samavākirad āśu|gaiḥ.
Sātyakiṃ tu nara|vyāghraṃ Vyāghradattas tv avārayat
śaraiḥ su|niśitais tīkṣṇaiḥ kampayan vai muhur muhuḥ.
106.15 Draupadeyān nara|vyāghrān muñcataḥ sāyak'|ôttamān
saṃrabdhān rathinaḥ śreṣṭhān Saumadattir avārayat.
Bhīmasenaṃ tadā kruddhaṃ bhīma|rūpo bhayānakaḥ

SÁNJAYA spoke:

O majesty. The sun sank lower and the fighting grew crueller as the Panchálas and Kurus fought a contest for Drona. O father the Panchálas were mad for Drona's blood and they hollered and sent up arrows in storms. The battle when Panchála met Kuru was full of noise and splendour, and awesome as any that demon or god had ever fought.

The Panchálas and Pándavas pressed on for Drona with 106.5
quarrels in their hands and rancour in their hearts. As their chariots shook the earth and rolled on steadily towards Drona's car, Brihat·kshatra champion of the Kékayas swept ahead strewing about him arrows sharp as the Great God's lightning. Against him fabled Kshema·dhurti rode out and sent up a hundred then a thousand shafts before him. The vaunting bull of the Chedis Dhrishta·ketu rushed next at
Drona like Mahéndra at Shámbara, and as his quarry ca- 106.10
reered like widemawed Death across the plain the great archer brandished his heavy bow and made to cut across his track. But mighty Drona wheeled back around and headed for where the great king Yudhi·shthira stood bold and stern among his men.

O lord your son Vikárna raced off to match Nákula's warcraft blow for blow while Dúrmukha who grinds his foes sprinkled Saha·deva's moving car with a thousand quickflying shafts. Vyaghra·datta rode at Sátyaki, tiger at tiger,
pouring tracts of razorsharp darts upon him. Saumadátti 106.15
came to meet the wild beasts born to Dráupadi as they rode through the fray, and they sprayed their fine darts upon him as he came near their high cars. Rishya·shringa's bold, brutal and fearsome son cut across the fierce path of Bhima·

pratyavārayad āyāntam Ārṣyaśṛṅgir mahā|rathaḥ.
tayoḥ samabhavad yuddhaṃ nara|rākṣasayor mṛdhe
yādṛg eva purā vṛttaṃ Rāma|Rāvaṇayor nṛpa.
  tato Yudhiṣṭhiro Droṇaṃ navatyā nata|parvaṇām
ājaghne Bharata|śreṣṭhaḥ sarva|marmasu Bhārata.
taṃ Droṇaḥ pañca|viṃśatyā nijaghāna stan'|ântare
roṣito Bharata|śreṣṭha Kaunteyena yaśasvinā.
106.20 bhūya eva tu viṃśatyā sāyakānāṃ samācinot
s'|âśva|sūta|dhvajaṃ Droṇaḥ paśyatāṃ sarva|dhanvinām.
tāñ śarān Droṇa|muktāṃs tu śara|varṣeṇa Pāṇḍavaḥ
avārayata dharm'|ātmā darśayan pāṇi|lāghavam.
tato Droṇo bhṛśaṃ kruddho dharma|rājasya saṃyuge
ciccheda samare dhanvī dhanus tasya mah"|ātmanaḥ.
ath' âinaṃ chinna|dhanvānaṃ tvaramāṇo mahā|rathaḥ
śarair an|eka|sāhasraiḥ pūrayām āsa sarvataḥ.
a|dṛśyaṃ vīkṣya rājānaṃ Bhāradvājasya sāyakaiḥ
sarva|bhūtāny amanyanta hatam eva Yudhiṣṭhiram.
106.25 ke cic c' âinam amanyanta tath" âiva vi|mukhī|kṛtam,
hato rāj" êti rāj'|êndra brāhmaṇena mah"|ātmanā.
  sa kṛcchraṃ paramaṃ prāpto dharma|rājo Yudhiṣṭhiraḥ,
tyaktvā tat kārmukaṃ chinnaṃ Bhāradvājena saṃyuge
ādade 'nyad dhanur divyaṃ bhāsvaraṃ vegavattaram.
tatas tān sāyakāṃs tatra Droṇa|nunnān sahasraśaḥ
ciccheda samare vīras. tad adbhutam iv' âbhavat.
chittvā tu tāñ śarān rājan krodha|saṃrakta|locanaḥ
śaktiṃ jagrāha samare girīṇām api dāraṇīm.
svarṇa|daṇḍāṃ mahā|ghorāṃ aṣṭa|ghaṇṭāṃ bhay'|āvahām
samutkṣipya ca tāṃ hṛṣṭo nanāda balavad balī,
nādena sarva|bhūtāni trāsayann iva Bhārata.

sena, and like Rama and Rávana in a time now gone man clashed against demon.

O Bhárata it was Yudhi·shthira the finest of your line who was the first to strike. With nine knotless shafts he found the gaps in Drona's armour, before Drona struck him back in the chest with twentyfive. O best of the Bharatas
Kunti's fabled son had raised Drona's ire. We all watched as 106.20
he dropped another twenty of his darts on Yudhi·shthira's horses, flags and driver, but Pandu's good son showed us how light his fingers were as with a volley of his own he parried the arrows from Drona's bow. Drona's choler burst forth and he lifted his bow and broke the weapon that the righteous king held in his hands and as the great man stood there holding its stumps Drona poured upon him a fresh slew of darts. Yudhi·shthira vanished in Bharadvája's onslaught and everyone thought the king dead. O majesty 106.25
some even thought they saw his head fly from his shoulders, struck away by the great priest's hand.

Yet even as calamity threatened the righteous king, he dropped the bow Bharadvája had broken and picked up another spryer still and bright and holy as the sky. Then with miraculous force Yudhi·shthira cut down the thousand arrows that Drona had launched, and o lord as they fell about him his eyes burned a ferocious red. He grabbed a spear fit to cut stone. Its haft was of gold and its dreadful tip bristled with eight prongs and he hefted it and with a giddy
cry that made us all flinch o Bhárata he let it go. The spear 106.30
flew from the righteous king's hand across the battlefield and to see it fly we pitied poor Drona, for with the force

106.30 śaktim samudyatām dṛṣṭvā dharma|rājena saṃyuge
svasti Droṇāya sahasā sarva|bhūtāny ath' âbruvan.
sā rāja|bhuja|nirmuktā nirmukt'|ôraga|saṃnibhā
prajvālayantī gaganaṃ diśaḥ sa|pradiśas tathā
Droṇ'|ântikam anuprāptā dīpt'|āsyā pannagī yathā.

tām āpatantīṃ sahasā dṛṣṭvā Droṇo, viśāṃ pate,
prāduś cakre tato Brāhmam astram astra|vidāṃ varaḥ.
tad astraṃ bhasmasāt kṛtvā tāṃ śaktiṃ ghora|darśanām
jagāma syandanaṃ tūrṇaṃ Pāṇḍavasya yaśasvinaḥ.
tato Yudhiṣṭhiro rājā Droṇ'|âstraṃ tat samudyatam
aśāmayan mahā|prājño Brahm'|âstreṇ' âiva māriṣa.
106.35 viddhvā taṃ ca raṇe Droṇaṃ pañcabhir nata|parvabhiḥ
kṣurapreṇa su|tīkṣṇena cicched' âsya mahad dhanuḥ.
tad apāsya dhanuś chinnaṃ Droṇaḥ kṣatriya|mardanaḥ
gadāṃ cikṣepa sahasā Dharma|putrāya māriṣa.
tām āpatantīṃ sahasā gadāṃ dṛṣṭvā Yudhiṣṭhiraḥ
gadām ev' âgrahīt kruddhaś, cikṣepa ca paraṃ|tapaḥ.
te gade sahasā mukte samāsādya paras|param
saṃgharṣāt pāvakaṃ muktvā sameyātāṃ mahī|tale.

tato Droṇo bhṛśaṃ kruddho dharma|rājasya, māriṣa,
caturbhir niśitais tīkṣṇair hayāñ jaghne śar'|ôttamaiḥ.
106.40 cicched' âikena bhallena dhanuś c' êndra|dhvaj'|ôpamam
ketum ekena ciccheda Pāṇḍavaṃ c' ârdayat tribhiḥ.

hat'|âśvāt tu rathāt tūrṇam avaplutya Yudhiṣṭhiraḥ
tasthāv ūrdhva|bhujo rājā vy|āyudho Bharata'|rṣabha.
vi|rathaṃ taṃ samālokya vy|āyudhaṃ ca viśeṣataḥ
Droṇo vyamohayac chatrūn sarva|sainyāni vā vibho.
muñcaṃś c' êṣu|gaṇāṃs tīkṣṇāl̃ laghu|hasto dṛḍha|vrataḥ
abhidudrāva rājānaṃ siṃho mṛgam iv' ôlbaṇaḥ.

of the king's swing it flashed through space like a gleaming snake and out across the sky and then like a firebreathing serpentdemon hurtled on towards its target.

O lord of men. Drona watched it plummet and from his arsenal of secrets invoked Heaven's Attack. The spear's dreadful shaft turned to ash before it and it made its way on towards Pándava's splendid car. But Yudhi·shthira's wisdom was as deep, and invoking Heaven's Attack himself he stilled
Drona's missile o father with his own. With five knotless 106.35
darts he followed it and then with a single razorlike dart cut right through Drona's stout bow. Drona crusher of kings casually threw the wreck aside and father he grabbed a club and slung it with all his force at Dharma's son. Yudhi·shthira burner of foes eyed its arc and snatched up a club of his own and flung it violently into the air. The projectiles met in space and such was their velocity that they sparked before they fell and struck the earth.

Anger flashed in Drona. O lord, with four finefashioned shafts sharpened to a hiss he struck the righteous king's
horses. With a single barbed dart he splintered the king's 106.40
bow and with another he cut through his standardpole tall as Indra's, and then Pandu's son himself felt the bite of three more.

Yudhi·shthira dropped from the wreck of his car to the ground and o bull of the Bharatas he stood there among his dead horses holding up his empty hands. Friends and foes alike Drona held spellbound o king. Yudhi·shthira had no car and no weapon to fight with and sternvowed Drona fluttered his fingers and let down another mass of sharp shafts onto the king's head and raced upon him like a lion

tam abhidrutam ālokya Droṇen' â|mitra|ghātinā
hā h" êti sahasā śabdaḥ Pāṇḍūnāṃ samajāyata.
106.45 hato rājā, hato rājā Bhāradvājena, māriṣa
ity āsīt su|mahāñ śabdaḥ Pāṇḍu|sainyasya Bhārata.
tatas tvaritam āruhya Sahadeva|rathaṃ nṛ|paḥ
apāyāj javanair aśvaiḥ Kuntī|putro Yudhiṣṭhiraḥ.

SAMJAYA uvāca:

107.1 BṚHATKṢATRAM ath' āyāntaṃ Kaikeyaṃ dṛḍha|vikramam
Kṣemadhūrtir, mahā|rāja, vivyādh' ôrasi mārgaṇaiḥ.
Bṛhatkṣatras tu taṃ rājā navatyā nata|parvaṇām
ājaghne tvarito rājan Droṇ'|ânīka|bibhitsayā.
Kṣemadhūrtis tu saṃkruddhaḥ Kaikeyasya mah"|ātmanaḥ
dhanuś ciccheda bhallena pītena niśitena ha.
ath' âinaṃ chinna|dhanvānaṃ śareṇ' ānata|parvaṇā
vivyādha samare tūrṇaṃ pravaraṃ sarva|dhanvinām.
107.5 ath' ânyad dhanur ādāya Bṛhatkṣatro hasann iva
vy|aśva|sūta|rathaṃ cakre Kṣemadhūrtiṃ mahā|ratham.
tato 'pareṇa bhallena pītena niśitena ca
jahāra nṛ|pateḥ kāyāc chiro jvalita|kuṇḍalam.
tac chinnaṃ sahasā tasya śiraḥ kuñcita|mūrdha|jam
sa|kirīṭaṃ mahīṃ prāpya babhau jyotir iv' âmbarāt.
taṃ nihatya raṇe hṛṣṭo Bṛhatkṣatro mahā|rathaḥ
sahas" âbhyapatat sainyaṃ tāvakaṃ Pārtha|kāraṇāt.

Dhṛṣṭaketum ath' āyāntaṃ Droṇa|hetoḥ parākramī
Vīradhanvā mah"|êṣv|āso vārayām āsa Bhārata.
107.10 tau paras|param āsādya śara|daṃṣṭrau tarasvinau
śarair an|eka|sāhasrair anyo|'nyam abhijaghnatuḥ.
tāv ubhau nara|śārdūlau yuyudhāte paras|param

at a deer. As Drona fell upon his prey the Pándavas let out a cry. Bharadvája's hand came down and they yelled o lord that their king was dead. But at that very moment Saha·deva's car swept past and Yudhi·shthira son of Kunti leapt aboard and its fleet steeds bore them both away. 106.45

SÁNJAYA spoke:

107.1 O MAJESTY. As Brihat·kshatra the unbending scion of Kékaya rode past, Kshema·dhurti struck him in the chest with his darts. King Brihat·kshatra's riposte was quick for he was keen to find passage through Drona's line. He hit back with nine knotless shafts. Rage swept through Kshema·dhurti. He took a whetted rosewood bolt and sent it splintering through the great Kékaya's bow, and as the mighty archer stood there with the broken bow in his hands he was struck hard again with another wellwhittled shaft. Bri- 107.5
hat·kshatra just smiled and raised another bow. He felled Kshema·dhurti's driver and horses and cut his car to pieces and then with another whetted rosewood bolt he took the great man's head from his body. Its earrings flashed as with its crown and curls it was torn away and fell to settle on the earth. It glistered on the ground with heavenly light. Thrilled with his kill Brihat·kshatra rode his high car deeper into your horde to fight on for the sake of Pritha's sons.

For Drona's cause there was the great bowman Vira·dhanvan and he swung his car into Dhrishta·ketu's path.
O Bhárata they came together in a thousand arrows. Reeds 107.10
flashing in their maws the fiery pair fought like animals, like elephants mad with the season that out in the vast wastes

mahā|vane tīvra|madau vāraṇāv iva yūtha|pau.
giri|gahvaram āsādya śārdūlāv iva roṣitau
yuyudhāte mahā|vīryau paras|para|jighāṃsayā.
tad yuddham āsīt tumulaṃ prekṣaṇīyaṃ viśāṃ pate,
siddha|cāraṇa|saṃghānāṃ vismay'|âdbhuta|darśanam.
Vīradhanvā tataḥ kruddho Dhṛṣṭaketoḥ śar'|âsanam
dvi|dhā ciccheda bhallena prahasann iva Bhārata.
107.15 tad utsṛjya dhanuś chinnaṃ Cedi|rājo mahā|rathaḥ
śaktiṃ jagrāha vipulāṃ rukma|daṇḍām ayasmayīm.
tāṃ tu śaktiṃ mahā|vīryāṃ dorbhyām āyamya Bhārata
cikṣepa sahasā yatto Vīradhanva|rathaṃ prati.
tayā tu vīra|ghātinyā śaktyā tv abhihato bhṛśam
nirbhinna|hṛdayas tūrṇaṃ nipapāta rathān mahīm.
tasmin vinihate vīre Traigartānāṃ mahā|rathe
balaṃ te 'bhajyata vibho Pāṇḍaveyaiḥ samantataḥ.
Sahadeve tataḥ ṣaṣṭiṃ sāyakān Durmukho 'kṣipat
nanāda ca mahā|nādaṃ tarjayan Pāṇḍavaṃ raṇe.
107.20 Mādreyas tu tataḥ kruddho Durmukhaṃ ca śitaiḥ śaraiḥ
bhrātā bhrātaram āyāntaṃ vivyādha prahasann iva.
taṃ raṇe rabhasaṃ dṛṣṭvā Sahadevaṃ mahā|balam
Durmukho navabhir bāṇais tāḍayām āsa Bhārata.
Durmukhasya tu bhallena chittvā ketuṃ mahā|balaḥ
jaghāna caturo vāhāṃś caturbhir niśitaiḥ śaraiḥ.
ath' âpareṇa bhallena pītena niśitena ha
ciccheda sāratheḥ kāyāc chiro jvalita|kuṇḍalam.
kṣurapreṇa ca tīkṣṇena Kauravyasya mahad dhanuḥ
Sahadevo raṇe chittvā taṃ ca vivyādha pañcabhiḥ.
107.25 hat'|âśvaṃ tu rathaṃ tyaktvā Durmukho vi|manās tadā

battle for supremacy or like savage leopards coming upon each other somewhere up in a mountain cave. No love was lost between them. O lord of men their fight was so vicious and loud and spectacular that even the seers and saints of heaven were shocked to see it. At last with cruel glee Vira·dhanvan sent forth a barbed shaft and o Bhárata it split
Dhrishta·ketu's bow in two. The great Chedi king cast the 107.15
pieces aside and picked up a long iron spear inlaid in gold and hefting its bulk in both his hands he aimed at Vira·dhanvan's car and swung. Its deadly point transfixed the hero's heart and Bhárata he crashed from his chariot to the earth.

O majesty. The bold Tri·garta's fall presaged your army's wider collapse beneath the weight of the Pándava assault. For when the great Tri·garta hero fell your men began to give way. Scolding Saha·deva across the fray Dúrmukha
shot six arrows at Pandu's son. Madréya's blood was up and 107.20
brother to brother he struck Dúrmukha back hard with six sharp shafts as a grin spread across his face. Dúrmukha saw the fierce mood that was in him. O Bhárata Saha·deva took nine more of Dúrmukha's darts and then with great skill sent a barbed arrow right through his foe's standard and four honed arrows into his four steeds, then with another whittled from rosewood and hooked in the point he tore his horseman's head clean away, earrings flashing as it fell. With a single razorsharp shaft Saha·deva cut through the great bow that Káurava held before pummelling him with a
further five. O Bhárata Dúrmukha stumbled in a daze from 107.25
among his dead horses and clambered aboard Niramítra's car. But majesty rage was upon Saha·deva and he would

āruroha ratham rājan Niramitrasya Bhārata.
Sahadevas tataḥ kruddho Niramitraṃ mah"|āhave
jaghāna pṛtanā|madhye bhallena para|vīra|hā.
sa papāta rath'|ôpasthān Niramitro jan'|ēśvaraḥ
Trigarta|rājasya suto vyathayaṃs tava vāhinīm.
taṃ tu hatvā mahā|bāhuḥ Sahadevo vyarocata
yathā Dāśarathī Rāmaḥ Kharaṃ hatvā mahā|balam.
hāhākāro mahān āsīt Trigartānāṃ jan'|ēśvara
rāja|putraṃ hataṃ dṛṣṭvā Niramitraṃ mahā|ratham.
107.30 Nakulas te sutaṃ, rājan, Vikarṇaṃ pṛthu|locanam
muhūrtāj jitavān loke. tad adbhutam iv' âbhavat.
Sātyakiṃ Vyāghradattas tu śaraiḥ saṃnata|parvabhiḥ
cakre '|dṛśyaṃ s'|âśva|sūtaṃ sa|dhvajaṃ pṛtan"|ântare.
tān nivārya śarāñ śūraḥ Śaineyaḥ kṛta|hastavat
s'|âśva|sūta|dhvajaṃ bāṇair Vyāghradattam apātayat.
kumāre nihate tasmin Magadhasya sute prabho
Māgadhāḥ sarvato yattā Yuyudhānam upādravan.
visṛjantaḥ śarāṃś c' âiva tomarāṃś ca sahasraśaḥ
bhindipālāṃs tathā prāsān mudgarān musalān api
ayodhayan raṇe śūrāḥ Sātvataṃ yuddha|dur|madam.
107.35 tāṃs tu sarvān sa balavān Sātyaktir yuddha|dur|madaḥ
n' âtikṛcchrādd hasann eva vijigye puruṣa'|rṣabhaḥ.
Māgadhān dravato dṛṣṭvā hata|śeṣān samantataḥ
balaṃ te 'bhajyata, vibho, Yuyudhāna|śar'|ârditam.
nāśayitvā raṇe sainyaṃ tvadīyaṃ Mādhav'|ôttamaḥ
vidhunvāno dhanuḥ|śreṣṭhaṃ vyabhrājata mahā|yaśāḥ.
bhajyamānaṃ balaṃ rājan Sātvatena mah"|ātmanā
n' âbhyavartata yuddhāya trāsitaṃ dīrgha|bāhunā.

not let his enemies go. A single deadly shaft arced through the great arena and lodged fast in Niramítra and brought the lord of men and heir of Tri·garta down from the platform he rode in. We shuddered to see it. As when Rama son of Dasha·ratha had slain the bold demon Khara, Saha·deva raised his mighty arms and shone in his kill while o lord of men a ululation rose from the Tri·gartas to see their scion Niramítra cut down.

O king. Your child Vikárna stood gaping at the sight 107.30
and truth be told it took just a moment for Nákula to cast
him down. Deeper in the host Sátyaki's car disappeared
horses driver totem and all as Vyaghra·datta hid them beneath his knotless darts. Shini's powerful grandson had a
nimble hand and he pushed back Vyaghra·datta's volley and
upturned his car, driver, steed and pole with arrows of his
own. Highness when their young prince had been brought
down the Mágadhas rode out as one for Yuyudhána and
casting before them a thousand arrows and javelins and
bolts, darts and hammers and clubs they crashed against the
Sátvata. But his mead was war and drunk now he smiled 107.35
and without a struggle Sátyaki bull in the herd of men
crushed them all beneath his might. O lord. The few Mágadhas that still breathed fled for their lives as more arrows
from Yuyudhána's hand went carving through their ranks.
His fine bow quivered and glories burst around him as the
Mádhava champion shattered his way through the host. O
majesty the army did not stand to face the Sátvata's might
but fell away in fear beneath the blows of his arching fists.

tato Droṇo bhṛśaṃ kruddhaḥ sahas" ôdvṛtya cakṣuṣī
Sātyakiṃ satya|karmāṇaṃ svayam ev' âbhidudruve.

SAMJAYA uvāca:

108.1 DRAUPADEYĀN mah"|ēṣv|āsān Saumadattir mahā|yaśāḥ
ek'|âikaṃ pañcabhir viddhvā punar vivyādha saptabhiḥ.
te pīḍitā bhṛśaṃ tena raudreṇa sahasā vibho,
pramūḍhā n' âiva vividur mṛdhe kṛtyaṃ sma kiṃ cana.
Nākuliś ca Śatānīkaḥ
Saumadattiṃ nara'|rṣabham
dvābhyāṃ viddhv" ânadadd hṛṣṭaḥ
śarābhyāṃ śatru|karśaṇaḥ.
tath" êtare raṇe yattās tribhis tribhir a|jihma|gaiḥ
vivyadhuḥ samare tūrṇaṃ Saumadattim a|marṣaṇam.
108.5 sa tān prati mahā|rāja cikṣepa pañca sāyakān
ek' âikaṃ hṛdi c' âjaghne ek' âikena mahā|yaśāḥ.
tatas te bhrātaraḥ pañca śarair viddhā mah"|ātmanā
parivārya raṇe vīraṃ vivyadhuḥ sāyakair bhṛśam.
Ārjunis tu hayāṃs tasya caturbhir niśitaiḥ śaraiḥ
preṣayām āsa saṃkruddho Yamasya sadanaṃ prati.
Bhaimasenir dhanuś chittvā Saumadatter mah"|ātmanaḥ
nanāda balavan nādaṃ vivyādha ca śitaiḥ śaraiḥ.
Yaudhiṣṭhirir dhvajaṃ tasya cchittvā bhūmāv apātayat
Nākuliś c' âtha yantāraṃ ratha|nīḍād apāharat.
108.10 Sāhadevis tu taṃ jñātvā bhrātṛbhir vi|mukhī|kṛtam
kṣurapreṇa śiro rājan nicakarta mahā|manāḥ.
tac chiro nyapatad bhūmau tapanīya|vibhūṣitam
bhrājayantaṃ raṇ'|ôddeśaṃ bāla|sūrya|sama|prabham.
Saumadatteḥ śiro dṛṣṭvā nihataṃ tan mah"|ātmanaḥ
vitrastās tāvakā rājan pradudruvur an|ekadhā.
Alambuṣas tu samare Bhīmasenaṃ mahā|balam

It fell to Drona. He raised his eyes and they flashed in anger and he rode out to stay Sátyaki's violent passage himself.

SÁNJAYA spoke:

WITH FIVE arrows each Saumadátti the glorious struck 108.1
the great bowmen born to Dráupadi then struck them all again with flights of seven apiece, and o majesty the sheer force of his sudden attack left his enemies reeling and insensate. Then the son of Nákula Shataníka summoned his strength and struck back twice at Soma·datta's taurine heir and he let out a cry as he harrowed his foe. Saumadátti stood firm in the fray as his enemies rose to his challenge and sent at him their trueflying arrows in pulses of three.
His glory was great and o king he let fly five arrows more 108.5
and each of the Draupadéyas took one in the chest. Wearing his shafts the five brothers drew in around the bold fighter and loosed another flight of reeds. With four sharp darts Árjuni drove Saumadátti's horses down to Death's abode and breaking his bow Bhaimaséni hollered and harrowed the hero with whetted darts. When Yudhi·shthira's boy had cut his flags to the earth and Nákuli knocked his driver from
the car, Saha·deva's haughty son saw how he struggled and 108.10
o king with a single razorlike shaft he sheared the warrior's head clean away. All decorated in heated gold it fell to earth and lit up the battlefield like a newly risen sun. O king the severed head of Soma·datta's son landed among your men and the sight of it pitched them into terrified dismay.

Across the fighting Alámbusha found Bhima·sena as Rávana's child had once found Lákshmana, and demon met

yodhayām āsa saṃkruddho Lakṣmaṇaṃ Rāvaṇir yathā.
samprayuddhau raṇe dṛṣṭvā tāv ubhau nara|rākṣasau
vismayaḥ sarva|bhūtānāṃ praharṣaṃ samajāyata.
108.15 Ārṣyaśṛṅgiṃ tato Bhīmo navabhir niśitaiḥ śaraiḥ
vivyādha prahasan, rājan, rākṣas'|êndram a|marṣaṇam.
tad rakṣaḥ samare viddhaṃ kṛtvā nādaṃ bhay'|âvaham
abhyadravat tato Bhīmaṃ ye ca tasya pad'|ânugāḥ.
sa Bhīmaṃ pañcabhir viddhvā śaraiḥ saṃnata|parvabhiḥ
bhaumān parijaghān' āśu rathāṃs tri|śatam āhave.
punaś catuḥ|śatān hatvā Bhīmaṃ vivyādha patriṇā.
so 'tividdhas tathā Bhīmo rākṣasena mahā|balaḥ
niṣasāda rath'|ôpasthe mūrchay" âbhipariplutaḥ.
108.20 pratilabhya tataḥ saṃjñāṃ Mārutiḥ krodha|mūrchitaḥ
vikṛṣya kārmukaṃ ghoraṃ bhāra|sādhanam uttamam
Alambuṣaṃ śarais tīkṣṇair ardayām āsa sarvataḥ.
sa viddho bahubhir bāṇair nīl'|âñjana|cay'|ôpamaḥ
śuśubhe sarvato rājan praphulla iva kiṃśukaḥ.
sa vadhyamānaḥ samare Bhīma|cāpa|cyutaiḥ śaraiḥ
smaran bhrātṛ|vadhaṃ c' âiva Pāṇḍavena mah"|ātmanā
ghoraṃ rūpam atho kṛtvā Bhīmasenam abhāṣata.
«tiṣṭh' êdānīṃ raṇe Pārtha paśya me 'dya parākramam.
Bako nāma su|durbuddhe rākṣasa|pravaro balī
parokṣaṃ mama tad vṛttaṃ yad bhrātā me hatas tvayā.»
108.25 evam uktvā tato Bhīmam antar|dhāna|gatas tadā
mahatā śara|varṣeṇa bhṛśaṃ taṃ samavākirat.
Bhīmas tu samare rājann a|dṛśye rākṣase tadā
ākāśaṃ pūrayām āsa śaraiḥ saṃnata|parvabhiḥ.
sa vadhyamāno Bhīmena nimeṣād ratham āsthitaḥ

man in a battle to shock and to thrill any who had eyes for
it. With a mocking laugh Bhima pierced the wrathful de- 108.15
mon king with nine of his whetted shafts. Rishya·shringa's
child bellowed terribly at the blow and he fell upon Bhima
and the men at his side. Five knotless shafts found Bhima
as the demon smashed three hundred of his cars into the
dust. He tore through four hundred more and turned back
to Bhima and let fly another feathered dart. Mighty Bhima
swayed and swooned beneath the demon's attack and sunk
into the floor of his car. Then his head swam with anger 108.20
and gathering his wits the Storm God's son got back on his
feet and drew back his fine fearful and unfailing bow and
harrowed Alámbusha hard with biting darts. The demon
was black as antimony and o king as arrows pierced his skin
he flowered with wounds like a flame of the forest in bloom.

The arrows whistled from Bhima·sena's bow and found their mark and with them the image of his brother's death at the Pándava's hand came back to Alámbusha, and flaring up into a fearsome shape he called across at his adversary.

"O Partha stay your hand and look upon me. You may somewhere in your ravaged mind recall a great king of night's denizenry who now is fallen. His name was Baka, and he was my brother. I will reward you now for his murder."*

So he spoke to Bhima and then he burst forth with a 108.25
massive pulse of arrows and disappeared. Even as the demon vanished Bhima filled the air o king with wellwhittled
shafts. Caught in Bhima's volley Alámbusha appeared again
for a moment in his chariot and then down on the ground
and then like a bee darted up into the sky. He began to shift

jagāma dharaṇīṃ c' êva kṣudraḥ khaṃ sahas" âgamat.
ucc'|âvacāni rūpāṇi cakāra su|bahūni ca
aṇur bṛhat punaḥ sthūlo nādān muñcann iv' âmbu|daḥ.
ucc'|âvacās tathā vāco vyājahāra samantataḥ
nipetur gaganāc c' âiva śara|dhārāḥ sahasraśaḥ,
108.30 śaktayaḥ kaṇapāḥ prāsāḥ śūla|paṭṭiśa|tomarāḥ
śataghnyaḥ parighāś c' âiva bhindipālāḥ paraśvadhāḥ
śilāḥ khaḍgā guḍāś c' âiva ṛṣṭīr vajrāṇi c' âiva ha,
sā rākṣasa|visṛṣṭā tu śastra|vṛṣṭiḥ su|dāruṇā
jaghāna Pāṇḍu|putrasya sainikān raṇa|mūrdhani.
tena Pāṇḍava|sainyānāṃ mṛditā yudhi vāraṇāḥ
hayāś ca bahavo, rājan, pattayaś ca tathā punaḥ.
rathebhyo rathinaḥ petus tasya nunnāḥ sma sāyakaiḥ.
śoṇit'|ôdāṃ rath'|āvartāṃ hasti|grāha|samākulām
chatra|haṃsāṃ kardaminīṃ bāhu|pannaga|saṃkulām,
108.35 nadīṃ prāvartayām āsa rakṣo|gaṇa|samākulām
vahantīṃ bahudhā rājaṃś Cedi|Pāñcāla|Sṛñjayān.
taṃ tathā samare rājan vicarantam a|bhītavat
Pāṇḍavā bhṛśa|saṃvignāḥ prāpaśyaṃs tasya vikramam.
tāvakānāṃ tu sainyānāṃ praharṣaḥ samajāyata
vāditra|ninadaś c' ôgraḥ su|mahāṃl roma|harṣaṇaḥ.
taṃ śrutvā ninadaṃ ghoraṃ tava sainyasya Pāṇḍavaḥ
n' âmṛṣyata yathā nāgas tala|śabdaṃ samīritam.
tataḥ krodh'|âbhitāmr'|âkṣo nirdahann iva pāvakaḥ
saṃdadhe Tvāṣṭram astraṃ sa svayaṃ Tvaṣṭ" êva Mārutiḥ.
108.40 tataḥ śara|sahasrāṇi prādur āsan samantataḥ.
taiḥ śarais tava sainyasya vidravaḥ su|mahān abhūt.
tad astraṃ preritaṃ tena Bhīmasenena saṃyuge
rākṣasasya mahā|māyāṃ hatvā rākṣasam ārdayat.

his shape. He shrank then stretched and expanded and we
heard his roars like thunder in the air. His cries echoed high
and low and all around and arrows came gushing from the
heavens. Then came spears and halberds and pikes, mallets, 108.30
lances, stakes and spikes, maces, slingshots and axes, stones,
swords, clubs and knives and bolts. The demon's bladed
rain fell into the very heart of the melée and crashed upon
the heads of Bhima·sena's men. All around him the Pándava's elephants and horses and soldiers were pummelled to
the ground and warriors were cast down from their cars as
the deluge formed a bloodred river upon the marshy plain
where chariots bobbed and parasols nested like geese and
elephants swam like sharks. A tangle of severed arms were
its watersnakes and its banks were host to packs of vam- 108.35
pires. The bodies of Chedis, Panchálas and Srínjayas rolled
down along its course.

O majesty. Bhima·sena's brothers watched the demon's bold and ranging attack unfold across the plain and they felt sick at heart. But as the excitement spread through our host and the musicians struck up their songs, the dread and spinetingling chorus reached the ears of the Pándava and as a snake breaks its stillness at the sound of a clap his eyes flushed crimson and all aflame the Storm God's son drew forth the Craftsman's Arrow as if he were the very deity who had fashioned it.

Arrows massed in their thousands overhead and men ran 108.40
for cover on the ground below. Bhima·sena's counterattack
had dispelled the demon's sorcery and now he turned his
aim on the creature that had wrought it. As Bhima·sena's

sa vadhyamāno bahudhā Bhīmasenena rākṣasaḥ
saṃtyajya samare Bhīmaṃ Droṇ'|ânīkam upādravat.
tasmiṃs tu nirjite, rājan, rākṣas'|êndre mah"|ātmanā
anādayan siṃha|nādaiḥ Pāṇḍavāḥ sarvato|diśam.
apūjayan Mārutiṃ ca saṃhṛṣṭās te mahā|balam
Prahrādaṃ samare jitvā yathā Śakraṃ Marud|gaṇāḥ.

SAṂJAYA uvāca:

109.1 ALAMBUṢAṂ TATHĀ yuddhe vicarantam a|bhītavat
Haiḍimbiḥ prayayau tūrṇaṃ, vivyādha niśitaiḥ śaraiḥ.
tayoḥ pratibhayaṃ yuddham āsīd rākṣasa|siṃhayoḥ
kurvator vividhā māyāḥ Śakra|Śambarayor iva.
Alambuṣo bhṛśaṃ kruddho Ghaṭotkacam atāḍayat.
tayor yuddhaṃ samabhavad rakṣo|grāmaṇi|mukhyayoḥ
yādṛg eva purā vṛttaṃ Rāma|Rāvaṇayoḥ prabho.
109.5 Ghaṭotkacas tu viṃśatyā nārācānāṃ stan'|ântare
Alambuṣam atho viddhvā siṃhavad vyanadan muhuḥ.
tath" âiv' Âlambuṣo rājan
Haiḍimbiṃ yuddha|dur|madam
viddhvā viddhv" ânadadd hṛṣṭaḥ
pūrayan khaṃ samantataḥ.
tathā tau bhṛśa|saṃkruddhau rākṣas'|êndrau mahā|balau
nir|viśeṣam ayudhyetāṃ māyābhir itar'|êtaram.
māyā|śata|sṛjau nityaṃ mohayantau paras|param
māyā|yuddheṣu kuśalau māyā|yuddham ayudhyatām.
yāṃ yāṃ Ghaṭotkaco yuddhe māyāṃ darśayate nṛ|pa
tāṃ tām Alambuṣo, rājan, māyay" âiva nijaghnivān.

onslaught fell upon him Alámbusha abandoned the fight and ran back for Drona's line. The other Pándavas watched as the demon king fled and majesty they filled the air with their cheers and sang their great brother's praises. Victory was his, as it had been Shakra's when he had gathered the storm gods and blasted Prahráda back from the battlefield.

SÁNJAYA spoke:

BUT IT WAS NOT long before Alámbusha was back in the 109.1
fray. This time Haidímbi went to cross his fearless course and pierced him with whetted shafts. Alámbusha hit back hard and fast against Ghatótkacha, and like Shakra and Shámbara the bold demons began a battle full of magic dark and strange. O highness they were lords of the night kingdom and they fought as Rama and Rávana had fought of old.

Roaring like a lion Ghatótkacha sent twenty iron darts 109.5
thudding into Alámbusha's chest. Back came Alámbusha's bolts again and again, and majesty his bellows filled the sky as he pierced his wardrunk foe. The two demon kings were a match in wrath and main and their magic blended as they dizzied each other with a thousand enchantments. They were masters of the black arts and their battle was woven from these secrets. Ghatótkacha would conjure something and strike and Alámbusha would overwhelm him o majesty with a trick of his own.

109.10 tam tathā yudhyamānaṃ tu māyā|yuddha|viśāradam
Alambuṣaṃ rākṣas'|êndraṃ dṛṣṭv" âkrudhyanta Pāṇḍavāḥ.
ta enaṃ bhṛśa|saṃvignāḥ sarvataḥ pravarā rathaiḥ
abhyadravanta saṃkruddhā Bhīmasen'|ādayo nṛ|pa.
ta enaṃ koṣṭhakī|kṛtya ratha|vaṃśena māriṣa
sarvato vyakiran bāṇair ulkābhir iva kuñjaram.
sa teṣām astra|vegaṃ taṃ pratihaty' âstra|māyayā
tasmād ratha|vrajān mukto vana|dāhād iva dvipaḥ.
sa visphārya dhanur ghoram Indr'|âśani|sama|svanam
Mārutiṃ pañcaviṃśatyā Bhaimaseniṃ ca pañcabhiḥ,
Yudhiṣṭhiraṃ tribhir viddhvā Sahadevaṃ ca saptabhiḥ,
109.15 Nakulaṃ ca tri|saptatyā, Draupadeyāṃś ca māriṣa
pañcabhiḥ pañcabhir viddhvā ghoraṃ nādaṃ nanāda ha.
taṃ Bhīmaseno navabhiḥ Sahadevas tu pañcabhiḥ
Yudhiṣṭhiraḥ śaten' âiva rākṣasaṃ pratyavidhyata,
Nakulas tu catuḥ|ṣaṣṭyā Draupadeyās tribhis tribhiḥ.
Haiḍimbo rākṣasaṃ viddhvā yuddhe pañcāśatā śaraiḥ
punar vivyādha saptatyā nanāda ca mahā|balaḥ.
tasya nādena mahatā kampit" êyaṃ vasuṃ|dharā
sa|parvata|vanā rājan sa|pādapa|jal'|âśayā.
so 'tividdho mah"|ēṣv|āsaiḥ sarvatas tair mahā|rathaiḥ
prativivyādha tān sarvān pañcabhiḥ pañcabhiḥ śaraiḥ.
109.20 taṃ kruddhaṃ rākṣasaṃ yuddhe pratikruddhas tu rākṣasaḥ
Haiḍimbo Bharata|śreṣṭha śarair vivyādha saptabhiḥ.
so 'tividdho balavatā rākṣas'|êndro mahā|balaḥ
vyasṛjat sāyakāṃs tūrṇaṃ rukma|puṅkhāñ śilā|śitān.
te śarā nata|parvāṇo viviśū rākṣasaṃ tadā

Such was Alámbusha's sorcery that the Pándavas would 109.10
not let pass the demon king's tricks and Bhima·sena and his
brothers drove their royal cars forth o highness to join the
fight. They blocked the demon in with their cars and rained
arrows down upon him like men corralling an elephant
with firebrands. Alámbusha breached their attack with his
sorcery and shot from among them as if from a burning
wood, and snapping his bowstring loud and formidable
as Indra's thunderclap he first found Máruti with five and
twenty shafts and then his son with five. He roared and
pierced Yudhi·shthira with three of his darts and Saha·deva
with seven, Nákula with a full seventythree and the Drau- 109.15
padéyas with five and five again. Back at the demon came
nine from Bhima·sena's hand, five from Saha·deva and a
hundred from Yudhi·shthira's bow. Nákula found the king
with sixtyfour before the Draupadéyas pierced him with
three and three again, and Haidímbi first sent a volley fifty
strong arcing through the fray and then struck him with
seven more. Hidímbi yelled as he did so with a sound o king
to the shake the flowery earth and the trees and hills and all
the creatures that walk on its surface or swim in its seas.

Though Alámbusha was now suffering badly he sent at
each one of his foes five arrows then five again. Seven arrows 109.20
flew back from Haidímbi's bow and o best of the Bharatas
those arrows bit cruelly into the nightwalker king as the battle gained pace. Alámbusha notched darts fletched in feathers flecked gold and honed to a hiss and sent them sliding
into his adversary like snakes between stones. O king. The
Pándavas were desperate now. They and Ghatótkacha sent
their keen shafts up to fill the sky. Alámbusha felt the full

ruṣitāḥ pannagā yadvad giri|śṛṅgaṃ mahā|balāḥ.
tatas te Pāṇḍavā, rājan, samantān niśitāñ śarān
preṣayām āsur udvignā Haiḍimbaś ca Ghaṭotkacaḥ.
sa vadhyamānaḥ samare Pāṇḍavair jita|kāśibhiḥ
martya|dharmam anuprāptaḥ kartavyaṃ n' ânvapadyate.
109.25 tataḥ samara|śauṇḍo vai Bhaimasenir mahā|balaḥ
samīkṣya tad|avasthaṃ taṃ vadhāy' âsya mano dadhe.
vegaṃ cakre mahāntaṃ ca rākṣas'|êṇdra|rathaṃ prati
dagdh'|âdri|kūṭa|śṛṅg'|ābhaṃ bhinn'|âñjana|cay'|ôpamam.
rathād ratham abhidrutya kruddho Haiḍimbir ākṣipat
udvavarha rathāc c' âpi pannagaṃ garuḍo yathā.
samutkṣipya ca bāhubhyām āvidhya ca punaḥ punaḥ
niṣpipeṣa kṣitau kṣipraṃ pūrṇa|kumbham iv' âśmani.
bala|lāghava|sampannaḥ sampanno vikrameṇa ca
Bhaimasenī raṇe kruddhaḥ sarva|sainyāny abhīṣayat.
109.30 sa visphārita|sarv'|âṅgaś cūrṇit'|âsthir vibhīṣaṇaḥ
Ghaṭotkacena vīreṇa hataḥ Śālakaṭaṅkaṭaḥ.

tataḥ su|manasaḥ Pārthā hate tasmin niśā|care
cukruśuḥ siṃha|nādāṃś ca vāsāṃsy ādudhuvuś ca ha.
tāvakāś ca hataṃ dṛṣṭvā rākṣas'|êndraṃ mahā|balam
Alambuṣaṃ tathā śūrā viśīrṇam iva parvatam
hāhā|kāram akārṣuś ca sainyāni Bharata'|rṣabha.
janāś ca tad dadṛśire rakṣaḥ kautūhal'|ânvitāḥ
yadṛcchayā nipatitaṃ bhūmāv aṅgārakaṃ yathā.

Ghaṭotkacas tu tadd hatvā rakṣo balavatāṃ varam
mumoca balavan nādaṃ Balaṃ hatv" êva Vāsavaḥ.

force of the Pándavas' bunched fists and death opened its door to him and he no longer knew what to do. Bhima· 109.25
sena's mighty son saw through a blood mist how Alámbusha suffered and decided then that he would be the one to finish him off. On rolled the demon king's car tall as a mountain tipped in ash or black crystal and with a sudden burst of speed Ghatótkacha tore towards it. He knocked against it with his own and then with fury in his eyes hauled its passenger out like Gáruda snatching a worm from the earth. Grappling with Alámbusha he pummelled him over and over with his fists then lifted him up and smashed him viciously against the ground. Alámbusha broke like a clay pot against a rock. The force and speed of Bhaimaséni's attack and its sheer ferocity and rage chilled us all to the bone. Ghatótkacha stepped back. Shalakatánkata's horrible 109.30
corpse lay in pieces, with its limbs all twisted and its bones snapped apart.

The nightwalker was dead. The Parthas were overjoyed and they pulled off their breastplates and whooped. Once a great king of demonkind Alámbusha was now just a heap of broken stone and o bull of the Bharatas your men looked down upon him and howled in despair. He could barely be recognised. He looked like a pile of charcoal lying there on the earth.

Few could have matched the demon's main and Ghatótkacha cried out exultant as Indra to have slain him.

109.35 sa pūjyamānaḥ pitṛbhiḥ sa|bāndhavair
Ghaṭotkacaḥ karmaṇi duṣ|kare kṛte
ripuṃ nihaty' âbhinananda vai tadā hy
alambuṣaṃ pakvam Alambuṣaṃ yathā.

tato ninādaḥ su|mahān samutthitaḥ
sa|śaṅkha|nānā|vidha|bāṇa|ghoṣavān:
niśamya taṃ pratyanadaṃs tu Kauravās
tato dhvanir bhuvanam ath' âspṛśad bhṛśam.

Honour upon him from friend and father: 109.35
The deadly deed done Ghatótkacha
Basked in it, his foe's life plucked
Like fruit from a fruittree's branch.*

Uproar from the crowd,
Horns and a thousand trumpets and drums:
The Káuravas drowned them with moans
That rippled out across the land.

NOTES

Bold *references are to the English text;* ***bold italic*** *references are to the Sanskrit text. An asterisk (*) in the body of the text marks the word or passage being annotated.*

55.38 **To the mighty seer**: Vyasa now recounts the histories of a series of mythic kings whom he depicts as exemplars of their kind. He describes in great detail their wildly extravagant sacrifices. These ornate exhibitions of wealth in the name of religious observance are known as *Śrauta* ceremonies, and their elucidation and exegesis form the main substance of Vedic literature. Although differing greatly in scale, complexity and intent, the general methods by which these ceremonies were conducted were quite consistent. The organiser of the sacrifice, called the *yajamāna*, was never the officiant: he would hire the priests to perform the ritual on his behalf. No ritual would ever be performed purely for its social or public benefit, and its effects were thought to return exclusively to the *yajamāna* himself. However, the priests would receive a *dakṣiṇā*, a payment for their services, and we can see in Vyasa's description how the grandeur of a king's offerings to the gods would shade into the largesse he displayed to his priests, since prestige would attach to the scale of both. For more on these rites, see the Introduction, pp. xv–xx.

55.39 **Thronged his halls**: a crucial stage in a *Śrauta* ritual involved extending an invitation to the gods. If circumstances were propitious, the deities would come to the event in person, gathering at a plot on the shriven ground especially reserved for their attendance. There they would be entertained by praise and song, and offered food directly in the form of oblations. See JAMISON (1991: 18–19).

60.6 **She became a kind of son**: the Sanskrit here is extremely obscure and can be read in different ways with mostly bizarre results. What seems to be the idea is that the huge crowd of people and animals that the king is giving the priests as payment for officiating at his rite descend to the bank of the Ganges for their ritual ablutions, and that the river is forced under the pressure into a new course. The epithet *urvaśī* I thus take in its primordial sense as **uru-aś* "widely extending:" it is more conventionally used as a name for the dawn.

60.12 **To abide with him**: the meaning in this verse is quite opaque. I take it as an analogy between the plant kingdom and the kingdom of heaven, both of whose inhabitants seek to abide where they "take root."

61.3 **Its golden ring and clasp**: the *yūpa*, or "wooden stake," was the great central symbol of solemn ritual. The sacrificial animal would be tied to the *caṣāla*, the wooden ring attached to the top of the pole, before immolation.

61.3 The **ápsarases** are comparable to the nymphs of ancient Greece, supernatural denizens of the sky and consorts of the *gandharva*s.

62.6 **The gods decided to call the boy Mandhátri**: a pun that becomes obscured in translation. When the gods find the baby Indra says *māṃ dhāsyati*, literally "he will suckle me." In Sanskrit *māndhātṛ* sounds roughly like "Me-drinker."

62.15 **Gandhárvas**: a group of supernatural beings who dwell in the heavens. Originally associated with Soma and the moon, they are the heavenly musicians and singers who perform at the feasts of the gods.

67.4 **Animals stepped up to the blade**: there were various approaches developed in Vedic ritual which were intended to subdue the inherent violence of sacrifice by eliciting the consent of a sacrificial victim. The constant reference to the necessity of securing an animal's permission to immolate it, necessarily unobtainable in practice, is testament to how profound this anxiety was.

67.5 **The Charmánvati got its name**: the river's name in Sanskrit does seem literally to translate as "bearer of animal hides."

72.20 ***arbhakam***: Árjuna's choice of the rare diminutive *arbhaka* to describe his son is a poignant one, presaging his growing awareness of the truth of what has happened in his absence.

72.46 **Had been sucked into the sea**: Árjuna is said to cry out *bhinna/ poto vaṇig yathā*, literally "like a merchant with a broken boat." Though in English it may seem odd to compare a semidivine warrior to a figure as modest and unassuming as a merchant, the analogy is indeed just as awkward in Sanskrit. Its peculiarity has a dissonance that renders Árjuna's emotion suddenly very human and "unheroic."

72.70 **The dance of war**: Among the many words for "war" that Krishna uses in this passage, one in particular contains in its etymology a fascinating double meaning that epitomises many of the epic's curious ambiguities: *raṇaḥ* translates as both "war" and "joy." Perhaps this double meaning results from an etymological fusion between the three verbs √*raṇ*, "to enjoy," √*raṇ* "to move about" and √*raṇ* "to clatter" or "ring."

75.27 **Splinter and lotus**: Krishna here referes to the arum array as made up of two parts. See the description of Drona's formation at note to 87.22.

76.8 **The dice in this contest**: the term *dyūtam* is a polyvalent term that contains within it several of many contradictions of the "Maha·bhárata": it translates as "game" or "gambling" but also "battle" and "spoils" or "prize." To have the *dyūtam baddham* would be to have the game "wrapped up," or even to load the dice. See the Introduction, pp. xx–xxi.

77.12 **O daughter of the rams**: Krishna and his sister and the rest of their tribe are known as the Vrishnis, after their patriarch, the youngest of the four sons of Bhima Sátvata, a ruler of the Yádava kingdom in northwest India. Vrishni literally translates as "Ram."

79.4 **Nightpiece**: Árjuna and Krishna have just performed a nocturnal rite together. A *naiśaṃ* means a "night-thing:" I take it to refer to some remnant of the ritual become a kind of charm that Árjuna passes at the rite's conclusion to his "priest," in place of a *dakṣiṇā*. See note to 55.38.

80.63 **O great one**: Árjuna pays homage to Rudra by reciting his names in a hieratic register. This sounds very much like a ritual formula, and as these names rarely occur elsewhere they are not included in the glossary at the end of the volume. Using the correct formulae to address a god was important, especially in an exchange of this kind. We can understand this interlude with reference to a Vedic model of ritual action. See the Introduction, pp. xv–xx.

84.21 **Set out to hunt him down**: Brihas·pati is the chief priest or *purohita* of the gods. His wife is called Tara or Táraka, "Star." The reference here is to an episode in the mythic system that first comes down to us in its entirety in the "Vishnu Purána." When Soma's conquests and glory drive him to abduct Táraka in arrogance, the gods declare war on him to steal her back. The Daityas and Dánavas join forces with Soma, and a fierce battle begins. Only when Brahma intervenes do the combatants lay down their arms. It is interesting that this episode is mentioned here in particular, as earlier in the epic Jayad·ratha has tried to abscond with Dráupadi. See Introduction, n. 9.

85.26 **Dice game to go ahead**: Dhrita·rashtra refers here to the gambling match to which Duryódhana challenges Yudhi·shthira, and during which the Pándava forfeits all that he has.

85.31 **Half of this seabounded land**: it is interesting to note that in KINJAWADEKAR's text Dhrita·rashtra refers to the whole of the earth, rather than just a part of it. I prefer the note of equivocation present in the Calcutta reading, although the variant does itself show how contested these nuances were by the epic's different compilers. It is as if Dhrita·rashtra is still hesitating to concede that his dynasty has no claim at all on the kingdom.

87.22 **An arum lily**: an arum is a genus of plant belonging to the *Araceae* family of aroids: it is characterised fittingly enough by sagittate or hastate leaves and a tubular, conelike flower called a spathe that enfolds a central spadix. The spadix is formed from an upper stipe and a lower section hidden in the spathe tube made up of the staminodes and pistillodes. To understand the description that follows, we must imagine the flower collapsed into two dimensions as an army is spread across a plain. The men in Drona's array can thus be pictured in two formations, the broader droplike perimeter of the spathe coming to a point with the army's commander at its tip, and a narrower, needlelike formation of the spadix contained within that, densely folded at its base and at the rear of the army, where we can imagine Jayad·ratha is stationed to ensure a maximal distance from the enemy frontline.

88.26 **A gruesome hoot from the monkey's muzzle**: this is a rather unusual reference to one of the deities that inhabit the battle standards of the warriors. These effigies and ensigns were not simply there to scare off the opposition: they were invested with totemic spirits who rode with the fighters, and now we actually hear the living sounds from one of them. For more on this see 'Drona,' volume I, note to 23.48.

93.61 **Shrutáyus of Ambáshtha**: the text presents us with a puzzle at this point. Either there has been some sort of corruption of an event that has spawned a doppelgänger of the Shrutáyus who fell at 93.24, or we can simply assume that it was a more common name than might be expected. Duryódhana's words at 94.30 seem to support the latter conclusion.

94.14 **Thorns in the jar**: this is Duryódhana's repeated refrain to Drona: that he is partial to the Pándavas, and secretly plots their victory. See 'Drona,' volume I, canto 33.

96.13 **Rained down upon him**: a rather eccentric metaphor to say the least. Bahlíka is compared to the *ātman*, the organising principle of the human soul, and the Draupadéyas to the five sense organs that it normally is thought to control.

98.9 **He has left his grimoires at home**: Literally "he has defaulted on his own duties:" Yuyudhána mocks Drona's warrior credentials, giving voice to the widespread grievance that *kṣatriya* characters often bear towards their brahmin peers. The caste divisions in the time of the epic were, however, far from clear-cut. See 'Drona,' volume 1, note to 7.1.

101.19 **The curving desert**: though *maru/dhanvan* translates simply as "desert," as a compound it rather perfectly expresses the wilderness of bows through which Árjuna and Krishna have passed.

102.11 **Though you did him no wrong**: Krishna addresses Árjuna with the epithet *an/agha*, an honorific literally meaning "sinless one." It is often thought that the position of such words and their choice is purely metrical. But this is simplistic. Krishna chooses the term quite carefully here and twists it to his rhetorical advantage. For another example see 72.47, where Árjuna's use of the word *Kuru/nandana* takes on a savage irony.

102.13 **That have corrupted his noble blood**: Krishna calls Duryódhana *an/āryaṃ*, literally a "non-Aryan," stripping him of his genealogy and placing him among the aboriginals outside the hallowed ground of the Vedic society.

108.24 **For his murder**: Alámbusha is the brother of a marauding demon slain by Bhima for his crimes against the brahmins in the first book of the epic.

109.35 **Like fruit from a fruittree's branch**: an *alambuṣa* is a kind of fruitbearing plant whose true identity is now lost to us. It is this meaning on which the text of the demon's epitaph plays.

GLOSSARY OF COMMON NAMES AND EPITHETS

Ábhibhu Ruler of Kashi.

Abhimányu Son of Árjuna and Subhádra. Also known as Árjuni, Saubhádra.

Abhisháha A people allied to the Káuravas.

Achárya The Teacher: a name for Drona.

Áchyuta Krishna.

Achyutáyus A warrior allied to the Káuravas.

Áditi One of the daughters of Daksha and the mother of the Adítyas.

Adítya Matronymic for a son of Áditi.

Agni God of fire.

Agni·veshya A seer and teacher known to Drona.

Ajagava Name of Prithu's bow.

Ajáta·shatru Yudhi·shthira.

Alámbusha A demon allied to the Kurus.

Aláyudha A demon fighting for the Káuravas.

Ámara·raja Indra.

Amarávati The House of the Gods.

Ambáshtha A people and their king (also called Shrutáyus), allied to the Káuravas.

Amúrta·rayas Father of Gaya.

Ándhaka A demon killed by Rudra. Also an ancestor of Krishna in the lineage of Yadu and the people descended from him.

Anga A people and their king, allied to the Káuravas.

Ángiras Born from Brahma's mouth, a divine seer named as the composer of hymns, laws and a treatise on astronomy.

Anuvínda A prince of Avánti, allied to the Káuravas. Brother of Vinda.

Árjuna Third of the five Pándava brothers, son of Pandu and Kunti. Also known as Bibhátsu, Dhanan·jaya, Guda·kesha, Jishnu, Kauntéya, Kirítin, Paka·shásani, Pándava, Partha, Phálguna, Savya·sachin.

Árjuni Patronymic of Árjuna's sons Abhimányu and Shruta·kirti.

Arúndhati Wife of Vasíshtha.

Áshmaka Name of people, some of whom follow Duryódhana, some Yudhi·shthira.

Ashvatthámen Son of Drona and Kripi.

Ashvins Twin gods, healers of the devas. Fathers of Saha·deva and Nákula by Madri.

Ásita An ancient king, defeated by Mandhátri.

Ásita Dévala The Black Priest, a mysterious figure descended from the Vedic seer Káshyapa.

Atisára The "muck men," allied to the Káuravas.

Avánti A people and a place.

Avántya People or king of Avánti.

Avíkshita An ancestral king.

Bahlíka King of Bahli (modern-day Balkh) and halfbrother of Shántanu, thus great uncle to Dhrita·rashtra and Pandu. He and his people fight with the Káuravas.

Baka Brother of Alámbusha.

Baláhaka One of Krishna's horses.

Bali A demon, son of Viróchana and father of Bana.

Bhaga An Adítya who was blinded by Rudra.

Bhagi·ratha An ancestral king, father of the Ganges.

Bhaimaséni Patronymic for Bhima·sena's sons Suta·soma and Ghatótkacha.

BHARAD·VAJA An ancient seer, father of Drona and grandfather of Ashvattháman.

BHARADVÁJA Patronymic for Drona.

BHÁRATA Descendant of Bharata.

BHARATA Primordial ruler of North India and ancestor of most of the characters in the "Maha·bhárata." Any of his descendents, and thus most of the characters of the epic, can be called a Bharata or Bhárata.

BHÁRGAVA Párashu·rama.

BHAVA Rudra.

BHIMA Bhima·sena.

BHIMA·SENA Second of the five Pándava brothers, son of Pandu and Kunti. Also known as Bhima, Kauntéya, Pándava, Partha, Vrikódara.

BHISHMA Son of Shántanu and Ganga, leader of the Káurava forces until his demise at the end of the book preceding 'Drona.'

BHOJA Name of a people and their king (also called Krita·varman), allied to the Káuravas.

BHRIGU A seer who was the ancestor of one of the chief brahmin families.

BHURI·SHRAVAS A son of Soma·datta, allied to the Káuravas.

BIBHÁTSU Árjuna.

BRAHMA Creator and supreme deity.

BRIHAD·BALA King of Kósala, allied to the Káuravas.

BRIHAD·RATHA An ancient king defeated by Mandhátri.

BRIHÁNTA A Kuru warrior, brother of Kshema·dhurti.

BRIHAS·PATI Deity of prayer and devotion, and priest to the gods.

BRIHAT·KSHATRA A Kékaya king allied to the Pándavas.

BUDHA Ancient seer descended from Soma and identified with the planet Mercury.

CHARMÁNVATI A river. In modern times called the Chambal.

CHEDI A people.

CHEKITÁNA A Vrishni warrior allied to the Pándavas.

CHITRA·RATHA King of the gandharvas.

CHITRA·SENA A son of Dhrita·rashtra.

DAITYA Demonic offspring of Diti.

DAKSHA An Adítya who performed the archetypal sacrifice, to which he failed to invite Rudra and thus incurred the god's wrath.

DÁNAVA Demonic offspring of Danu.

DANTA·KRURA A king killed by Párashu·rama.

DANU Daughter of Káshyapa and progenitrix of the Dánavas.

DÁRADA A people allied to the Káuravas.

DÁRUKA Krishna's charioteer.

DARVA The "wood people," allied to the Káuravas.

DASHA·RATHA Rama's father.

DASHÁRHA A people. Used as a name for Krishna, a chief of the Dashárhas.

DAUHSHÁSANI Patronymic for Duhshásana's son, killer of Abhimányu.

DEVA·DATTA Árjuna's conch.

DEVA·YANI One of Yayáti's wives: daughter of Úshanas.

DÉVAKI Daughter of Dévaka, wife of Vasu·deva and mother of Krishna.

DHANAN·JAYA Árjuna.

DHARMA A god, and Yudhi·shthira's father.

DHARMA·RAJA Yudhi·shthira.

DHARTARÁSHTRA Patronymic for the sons of Dhrita·rashtra.

DHATRI A deity related to Brahma and commonly identified as one of the twelve Adítyas.

DHRISHTA·DYUMNA Son of the Panchála king Drúpada, born from a sacrificial fire. Brother of Dráupadi and general of the Pándava army.

DHRISHTA·KETU A Chedi prince allied to the Pándavas.

DHRITA·RASHTRA Blind king of the Kurus. Son of Krishna Dvaipáyana and Ámbika. Father of Duryódhana and a hundred other children.

DHUNDHU·MARA The "slayer of Dhundhu." An ancestral monarch.

DILÍPA An ancestral king, son of Ílavila.

DIRGHÁYUS Son of Achyutáyus.

DITI Progenitrix of the Daityas.

DRAUNI Patronymic for Ashvattháman.

DRAUPADÉYA Metronymic for the sons of Dráupadi.

DRÁUPADI Daughter of Drúpada and wife of the five Pándava brothers.

DRÁVIHAS A barbarian people allied to the Káuravas.

DRONA Son of Bharad·vaja, husband of Kripi and father of Ashvattháman. Drona is the Achárya, the teacher of the sons of Pandu and Dhrita·rashtra, and he is general of the Káurava forces during the course of 'Drona.'

DRÚPADA King of the Panchálas and father of Dhrishta·dyumna. Sworn enemy of Drona.

DUHSHÁSANA A son of Dhrita·rashtra.

DÚRJAYA A son of Dhrita·rashtra.

DURMÁRSHANA A son of Dhrita·rashtra.

DÚRMUKHA A son of Dhrita·rashtra.

DURYÓDHANA Eldest son of Dhrita·rashtra and Gandhári. Also known as Suyódhana and Dhartaráshtra.

DUSHYÁNTA Father of Bharata.

DVI·MURDHAN A demon.

GANDHÁRA A people and country of great antiquity, ruled in the epic's time by Shákuni.

GANDÍVA Árjuna's bow.

GANÉSHA God of wisdom, and of the placing and removing of obstacles.

GANGA The Ganges river, goddess and mother of Bhishma.

GÁRUDA Bird god.

GÁUTAMA Kripa.

GAYA An ancestral king.

GHATÓTKACHA Semidemonic son of Bhima and Hidímba. Also called Haidímbi and Bhaimaséni.

GO·PALA A people allied to the Káuravas.

GO·VÁSANA A Shibi king.

GO·VINDA Krishna.

GÓTAMA Father of Kripa.

GUDA·KESHA Árjuna.

HIDÍMBA Demonic mother of Ghatótkacha.

HAIDÍMBI Metronymic of Ghatótkacha.

HÁIHAYA A people wiped out by Párashu·rama.

HARA Rudra or Vishnu.

HARDÍKYA Patronymic for Krita·varman.

HRÍDIKA Father of Krita·varman.

HRISHI·KESHA Krishna.

IKSHVÁKU An ancestral king and son of Manu.

ÍLAVILA Father of Dilípa.

INDRA King of the gods. Also known as Ámara·raja, Mághavat, Shakra, Vásava, Shata·kratu.

JALA·SANDHA A son of Dhrita·rashtra.

JAMAD·AGNI A seer, father of Párashu·rama.

JAMBHA A demon, sometimes said to have led the demons in the war against the gods.

JAMBU The name of a river.

JANAM·ÉJAYA Son of Paríkshit. At his sacrifice Vaishampáyana recites the "Maha·bhárata" for the first time. Also the name of an ancestral king.

JANÁRDANA Krishna.

JAYA A son of Dhrita·rashtra.

JAYAD·RATHA King of the Sindhus, allied to the Káuravas.

JISHNU Árjuna.

KAIKÉYA One of the five chieftains of the Kékaya people allied to the Pándavas. Also Vinda and Anuvínda, Kékaya kings of Avánti allied to the Káuravas.

KALA Name of a mountain mentioned in the Rig Veda.

KALÍNGA A people and their king.

KAMBÓJA A people and their king, allied to the Káuravas.

KANVA A mythical seer and priest.

KARNA Son of Surya (the sun) and Kunti. Adopted by the charioteer Ádhiratha and his wife Radha. Also called Vaikártana.

KARTA·VIRYA A king killed by Párashu·rama.

KARTTIKÉYA Skanda.

KASHI A people, a place and its king.

KASHMÍRA A people, obviously connected to present Kashmir.

KÁSHYAPA An ancient seer who performed rites for Párashu·rama.

KAUMÓDAKI The name of Krishna's mace.

KAUNTÉYA Metronymic for Yudhi·shthira, Bhima or Árjuna.

KÁURAVA Descendant of Kuru. Often refers to Dhrita·rashtra's sons and their followers, although the Pándavas are also sometimes called Káuravas.

KAUSÁLYA Brihad·bala, king of Kósala.

KÉKAYA A people and their princes, some allied to Yudhi·shthira, others to Duryódhana.

KÉSHAVA Krishna.

KHARA Demon killed by Rama.

KHATVÁNGA Rudra.

KIRÍTIN Árjuna.

KÓSALA A people.

KRIPA Son of Sharádvat and grandson of Gótama. Allied to the Káuravas.

KRISHNA Son of Vasu·deva and Dévaki, identified with Vishnu/Naráyana. Also known as Áchyuta, Go·vinda, Hrishi·kesha, Janárdana, Késhava, Madhu·súdana, Pundaríkáksha, Shauri, Vasudéva, Varshnéya.

KRITA·VARMAN A Vrishni prince and son of Hrídika, allied to the Káuravas.

KSHATRA·DHARMAN Son of Dhrishta·dyumna.

KSHEMA·DHURTI Brother of Brihánta, allied to the Káuravas.

KSHÚDRAKA A people.

KUBÉRA Originally the chief of the spirits of darkness, and in later theology the god of riches.

KUNTI A people, but more also and more importantly the wife of Pandu. Mother of the three of the Pándavas and Karna. Also known as Pritha.

KUNTI·BHOJA Adoptive father of Kunti, allied to the Pándavas. Also called Púrujit.

KURU Ancestor of the Bháratas. The Kurus are the descendants of Kuru and include both the Káuravas and the Pándavas, although the name largely refers to Dhrita·rashtra's sons and their followers.

KURU·JÁNGALA Name of a country.

KURU·KSHETRA The plain upon which the battle between the Pándavas and Káuravas is taking place.

LÁKSHMANA Rama's brother.

LAKSHMI Goddess of fortune and beauty.

LALÍTTHA A people linked to the Tri·gartas.

LOKÉSHA "Lord of the World:" a deity often equated with Brahma.

MÁDHAVA A people, and used to refer variously to Krishna, Sátyaki and Krita·varman.

MADHU The Sanskrit for "honey," and the name of a demon killed by Krishna.

MADHU·SÚDANA Slayer of Madhu. Another name for Krishna.

MADRA/MÁDRAKA A people.

MADRÉYA Metronymic for Saha·deva or Nákula.

MADRI Second wife of Pandu. Princess of the Madras, sister of Shalya and mother of the twins Nákula and Saha·deva by the two Ashvin gods.

MÁGADHA A people.

MAHÉNDRA Indra. Also the name of a mountain peak in northern India.

MAHÉSHVARA Rudra.

MAINÁKA Name of a mountain.

MÁLAVA A people and its king.

MÁNDARA A mountain used as a staff by the gods to churn the ocean. The dwelling place of Rudra.

MANDHÁTRI An ancestral king, son of Yuvanáshva.

MANU The primordial human, grandfather of the human race.

MARÍCHA Father of Káshyapa.

MARTTIKÁVATAKA A people and a country.

MÁRUTA Vayu.

MARUT Storm god, follower of Indra.

MARÚTTA An ancestral king.

MÁTALI Indra's charioteer.

MATSYA A people.

MAVÉLLAKA A people linked to the Tri·gartas.

MEGHA·PUSHPA One of Krishna's horses.

MERU Mountain at the center of the cosmos.

MITRA A Vedic god often invoked with Váruna.

NÁHUSHA Father of Yayáti.

NÁKULA One of the Pándava brothers (twin of Saha·deva).

NÁKULI Patronymic for Shataníka, Nákula's son.

NÁRADA A divine seer considered an intermediary between gods and men.

NARÁYANA The god Vishnu, often linked with Nara. Identified with Krishna. At the same time the name of a people.

NIRAMÍTRA A king allied to the Káuravas.

NIVÁTA·KÁVACHAS A tribe of demons destroyed by Árjuna.

NIYUTÁYUS Son of Shrutáyus.

NRIGA An ancient king, defeated by Mandhátri.

PANCHA·JANA Demon slain by Krishna.

PANCHA·JANYA Conch carried by Krishna, obtained from the demon Pancha·jana.

PANCHÁLA A people allied to the Pándavas and sworn enemies of Drona.

PANCHÁLI Dráupadi.

PÁNDAVA A son of Pandu, so Yudhi·shthira, Bhima, Árjuna, Nákula or Saha·deva. The "Pándavas" as a whole are the sons of Pandu, their relatives and their followers.

PANDU Son of Krishna Dvaipáyana, half brother of Dhrita·rashtra and Vídura and "father" of the Pándavas. In the plural it refers to the Pándava army as a whole.

PAKA·SHÁSANI Tamer of the Fire, a name for Árjuna.

PÁRADA Name of a barbarian people allied to the Káuravas.

PÁRASHU·RAMA Son of Jamad·agni and Rénuka, and a hero of legend who once wiped out the warrior caste. Also called Rama, Bhárgava.

PARNÁSHA Name of a river, mother of Shrutáyudha

PÁRSHATA Patronymic for Dhrishta·dyumna and Drúpada.

PARTHA Son of Pritha, so Yudhi·shthira, Bhima·sena or Árjuna. Also refers to the followers of the sons of Pritha.

PÁRVATA A divine seer.

PASHU·PATA Name of a magic weapon obtained by Árjuna from Rudra.

PAULÁSTYA Rávana.

PÁURAVA Descendant of Puru. Name of a people and king, and their ancestral monarch: associated with the Angas.

PHÁLGUNA Árjuna.

PRADYÚMNA God of love.

PRAHRÁDA A demon king, father of Viróchana.

PRAJA·PATI God of creation.

PRÍSHATA Father of Drúpada, grandfather of Dhrishta·dyumna.

PRITHA Kunti.

PRITHU An ancestral king.

PULÁSTYA Father of Rávana.

PUNDARÍKÁKSHA Lotuseye, ie Krishna.

PUNDRA A barbarian people allied to the Káuravas.

PURAN·DARA Indra.

PURU An ancient king.

PURU·MITRA A warrior allied to the Káuravas.

PÚRUJIT A Kunti chieftain.

PUSHAN A Vedic deity, associated with Soma and the sun.

RAHU A demon thought to swallow the sun and moon and so cause eclipses.

RAKSHO·VAHA A people wiped out by Párashu·rama.

RAMA Hero of the epic the Ramáyana. Also an abbreviation for Párashu·rama.

RANTI·DEVA An ancestral king.

RÁVANA A king of the demons.

RISHYA·SHRINGA Father of Alámbusha.

RUDRA The fierce deity later known as Shiva. Also called Sharva, Shánkara, Bhava, Try·ámbaka, and a huge number of other names besides: see the eightieth canto for a selection of them.

SAHA·DEVA One of the Pándava brothers, twin brother of Nákula.

SÁINDHAVA Principally Jayad·ratha, King of the Sindhus, but also his father Vriddha·kshatra.

SAMÁNTA·PÁNCHAKA The place where Párashu·rama was said to have killed all the warrior caste.

SÁNJAYA Son of Gaválgana and charioteer of Dhrita·rashtra, to whom he narrates the events of the great battle.

SÁNKRITI Father of Ranti·deva.

SAMVÁRTA Marútta.

SARÁSVATI A river goddess, deity of wisdom.

SÁTVATA A people from the south of India connected to the Shinis, Vrishnis and Yádavas. Used in the singular for one of their kings, and for Krita·varman, Sátyaki and Krishna.

SATYA·VRATA One of the Tri·garta princes.

SÁTYAKA Father of Yuyudhána.

SÁTYAKI Patronymic for Yuyudhána, a Vrishni king allied to the Pándavas.

SÁUBALA Patronymic for Shákuni.

SAUBHÁDRA Metronymic for Abhimányu.

SAUMADÁTTI Patronymic for a son of Soma·datta.

SAUVÍRA A people associated with the Sindhus.

SAVYA·SACHIN Árjuna.

SHACHI Indra's wife.

SHAINÉYA Patronymic for Sátyaki, grandson of Shini.

SHAIVYA One of Krishna's horses.

SHAKA Name of a barbarian people allied to the Káuravas.

SHAKRA Indra.

SHÁKUNI Son of the Gandhára king Súbala and father of Ulúka.

SHAKÚNTALA Mother of Bharata.

SHALA Son of Soma·datta, and brother of Bhuri and Bhuri·shravas. Allied to the Káuravas.

SHALAKATÁNKATA Alámbusha.

SHALVA A people allied to the Pándavas.

SHALYA King of the Madras, brother of Madri. Also known as Artáyani.

SHÁMBARA A demon slain by Indra.

SHÁNKARA Rudra.

SHARMÍSHTHA One of Yayáti's wives.

SHARVA Rudra.

SHASHA·BINDU An ancestral king.

SHATA·KRATU Indra.

SHATANÍKA Son of Nákula and Dráupadi.

SHAURI Patronymic for Krishna.

SHIBI A people and their ancestral king: the Shibis were all but wiped out by Párashu·rama. Their descendents fight for the Káuravas.

SHIKHÁNDIN Son (originally daughter) of Drúpada. Allied to the Pándavas and pivotal in Árjuna's victory over Bhishma.

SHINI Father of Sátyaka and grandfather of Sátyaki, and the name of his race.

SHONÁSHVA Warrior of the red horses, namely Drona.

SHRUTA·KIRTI Son of Árjuna and Dráupadi.

SHRUTÁYUS There are at least two men by this name who are allied to the Káuravas: one is king of the Ambáshthas, and the other is Achyutáyus's brother. Both are killed in this volume by Árjuna. See note to 93.61.

SHRUTÁYUDHA A king born to Váruna and allied to the Káuravas.

SHUKRA Bhrigu's son and teacher of the Daityas. Identified with the planet Venus.

SHURA·SENA A people allied to the Káuravas.

SHVETÁSHVA Warrior of the white horses, namely Árjuna.

SHVAITYA Son of Srínjaya.

SINDHU A people, allied to the Káuravas. Their king is Jayad·ratha.

SKANDA A protean deity, son of Shiva or Agni in the Veda and god of war.

SOMA A plant used as an intoxicant in Vedic religious practice, and venerated as a deity associated with the moon.

SOMA·DATTA Father of Bhuri·shravas, allied to the Káuravas.

SÓMAKA A people allied to the Pándavas, linked to the Panchálas. Their patriarch Sómaka was an ancestor of Drúpada.

SRÍNJAYA A people often grouped with the Panchálas. Also their ancestral king.

SUBÁHU One of Dhrita·rashtra's sons, and also a Tri·garta warrior.

SUBHÁDRA Mother of Abhimányu.

SUDÁKSHINA Prince of Kambója.

SUDHÁNVAN A Panchála king. Also an ancient monarch defeated by Mandhátri.

SUGRÍVA One of Krishna's horses.

SUHÓTRA Ancestral king of Kuru·jángala.

SUTA·SOMA Son of Bhima and Dráupadi.

SUYÓDHANA Duryódhana.

SVADHA The libation offered to departed ancestors, personified as a daughter of Daksha.

SVAHA The burnt offering of Vedic sacrifice, personified as a daughter of Daksha.

TÁKSHAKA A shadowy figure, perhaps identified with Vishva·karman, the gods' blacksmith.

TAMRA·LÍPTAKA "The Ones Covered in Darkness." The name of a people slain by Párashu·rama.

TÁRAKA Brihas·pati's wife, for whom the gods went to war against the demons.

TRI·GARTA A people and the five brothers who are their chieftains.

TRY·ÁMBAKA The Three Eyed God, namely Rudra.

TVASHTRI The great craftsman deity, blacksmith and armourer to the gods. Also a magical attack named after him.

ÚSHANAS An ancient seer.

USHI·NARA An ancient people from central India.

UTTAMÁUJAS A Panchála warrior allied to the Pándavas. Brother of Yudha·manyu.

ÚTTARA Vairáti.

VAIDÉHI A name of Sita, Rama's wife.

VAIKÁRTANA Patronymic for Karna, son of the sun.

VAIKÚNTHA Vishnu.

VAINATÉYA Gáruda.

VAIRÁTI Daughter of Viráta, wife of Abhimányu.

VAIRÓCHANI Bali.

VAIVÁSVATA Yama.

VANGA A people.

VÁRADA The Giver. Sometimes used as a name for Rudra.

VARSHNÉYA Krishna.

VARSHNÉYI Subhádra.

VÁRUNA One of the greatest of the Vedic gods.

VASÁTIS A people allied to the Káuravas.

VÁSAVA Indra.

VASÍSHTHA A divine seer, son of the god Váruna.

VASU·DEVA Father of Krishna.

VASUDÉVA Patronymic for Krishna.

VASV·OKASÁRA The name of Kubéra's palace.

VAYU God of the wind.

VENA Father of Prithu.

VIDÉHA A people.

VIDHÁTRI Brother of Dhatri.

VÍDURA Half brother of Dhrita·rashtra and Pandu.

VIKÁRNA A son of Dhrita·rashtra.

VINDA Brother of Anuvínda and prince of Avánti, allied to the Káuravas.

VINDHYA A mountain god.

VIRA·DHANVAN A king allied to the Káuravas.

VIRÁTA The king of the Matsyas.

VIRÓCHANA A demon.

VISHNU One of the major gods in the Hindu pantheon, incarnated in Krishna.

VISHVAK·SENA Krishna.

VISHVA·RUCHI Name of a divine being, probably a gandharva.

VISHVA·VASU One of the gandharvas.

VITI·HOTRA A people wiped out by Párashu·rama.

VIVÁSVAT The Brilliant One: the sun.

VIVÍNSHATI A son of Dhrita·rashtra.

VRIKÓDARA Bhima.

VRISHA·DHVAJA Ganésha or Rudra, depending upon whether the "mark" is a rat or bull.

VRISHA·SENA A son of Karna.

VRISHÁNKA Rudra.

VRISHNI A Yádava people connected with the Ándhakas and the Bhojas and descended from a patriarch who bore their name. Krishna, Sátyaki and Krita·varman are all Vrishnis.

VRITRA A demon slain by Indra.

VYAGHRA·DATTA A warrior allied to the Pándavas.

VYASA A seer, supposed to have compiled the "Maha·bhárata."

YÁDAVA A people descended from Yadu and linked with the Vrishnis.

YADU Ancestor of Krishna and patriarch of the Yádavas.

YAJNYA·SENA Drúpada.

YAJNA·SENI Patronymic for Shikhándin and Dhrishta·dyumna.

YAMA God of the dead, son of Vivásvat.

YÁMUNA A river, the present Jamna.

YÁVANA A people whom scholars have connected with the ancient Greeks.

YAYÁTI An ancestral king.

YUDHA·MANYU A Panchála warrior allied to the Pándavas. Brother of Uttamáujas.

YUDHI·SHTHIRA Eldest of the Pándava brothers. Also known as Ajáta·shatru, Dharma·raja, Partha, Pándava, Kauntéya.

YUVANÁSHVA Father of Mandhátri.

YUYUDHÁNA Pándava warrior also known as Sátyaki.

YUYÚTSU Son of Dhrita·rashtra and a woman of the merchant caste. Allied to the Pándavas.

THE CLAY SANSKRIT LIBRARY

The volumes in the series are listed here in order of publication.
Titles marked with an asterisk* are also available in the Digital Clay Sanskrit Library (eCSL).
For further information visit www.claysanskritlibrary.org

1. The Emperor of the Sorcerers (*Bṛhatkathāślokasaṃgraha*) (vol. 1 of 2) by *Budhasvāmin*. Sir James Mallinson
2. Heavenly Exploits (*Divyāvadāna*). Joel Tatelman
3. Maha·bhárata III: The Forest (*Vanaparvan*) (vol. 4 of 4)* William J. Johnson
4. Much Ado about Religion (*Āgamaḍambara*) by *Bhaṭṭa Jayanta*. Csaba Dezső
5. The Birth of Kumára (*Kumārasaṃbhava*) by *Kālidāsa*. David Smith
6. Ramáyana I: Boyhood (*Bālakāṇḍa*) by *Vālmīki*. Robert P. Goldman
7. The Epitome of Queen Lilávati (*Līlāvatīsāra*) (vol. 1 of 2) by *Jinaratna*. R.C.C. Fynes
8. Ramáyana II: Ayódhya (*Ayodhyākāṇḍa*) by *Vālmīki*. Sheldon I. Pollock
9. Love Lyrics (*Amaruśataka, Śatakatraya & Caurapañcāśikā*) by *Amaru, Bhartṛhari & Bilhaṇa*. Greg Bailey & Richard Gombrich
10. What Ten Young Men Did (*Daśakumāracarita*) by *Daṇḍin*. Isabelle Onians
11. Three Satires (*Kaliviḍambana, Kalāvilāsa & Bhallaṭaśataka*) by *Nīlakaṇṭha, Kṣemendra & Bhallaṭa*. Somadeva Vasudeva
12. Ramáyana IV: Kishkíndha (*Kiṣkindhākāṇḍa*) by *Vālmīki*. Rosalind Lefeber
13. The Emperor of the Sorcerers (*Bṛhatkathāślokasaṃgraha*) (vol. 2 of 2) by *Budhasvāmin*. Sir James Mallinson
14. Maha·bhárata IX: Shalya (*Śalyaparvan*) (vol. 1 of 2)* Justin Meiland

15. Rákshasa's Ring (*Mudrārākṣasa*)*
by *Viśākhadatta*. Michael Coulson
16. Messenger Poems (*Meghadūta, Pavanadūta & Haṃsadūta*)
by *Kālidāsa, Dhoyī & Rūpa Gosvāmin*. Sir James Mallinson
17. Ramáyana III: The Forest (*Araṇyakāṇḍa*)
by *Vālmīki*. Sheldon I. Pollock
18. The Epitome of Queen Lilávati (*Līlāvatīsāra*) (vol. 2 of 2)
by *Jinaratna*. R.C.C. Fynes
19. Five Discourses on Worldly Wisdom (*Pañcatantra*)*
by *Viṣṇuśarman*. Patrick Olivelle
20. Ramáyana V: Súndara (*Sundarakāṇḍa*) by *Vālmīki*.
Robert P. Goldman & Sally J. Sutherland Goldman
21. Maha·bhárata II: The Great Hall (*Sabhāparvan*)
Paul Wilmot
22. The Recognition of Shakúntala (*Abhijñānaśākuntala*) (Kashmir Recension) by *Kālidāsa*. Somadeva Vasudeva
23. Maha·bhárata VII: Drona (*Droṇaparvan*) (vol. 1 of 4)*
Vaughan Pilikian
24. Rama Beyond Price (*Anargharāghava*)
by *Murāri*. Judit Törzsök
25. Maha·bhárata IV: Viráta (*Virāṭaparvan*)
Kathleen Garbutt
26. Maha·bhárata VIII: Karna (*Karṇaparvan*) (vol. 1 of 2)
Adam Bowles
27. "The Lady of the Jewel Necklace" & "The Lady who Shows her Love" (*Ratnāvalī & Priyadarśikā*) by *Harṣa*.*
Wendy Doniger
28. The Ocean of the Rivers of Story (*Kathāsaritsāgara*) (vol. 1 of 7)
by *Somadeva*. Sir James Mallinson
29. Handsome Nanda (*Saundarananda*)*
by *Aśvaghoṣa*. Linda Covill
30. Maha·bhárata IX: Shalya (*Śalyaparvan*) (vol. 2 of 2)*
Justin Meiland
31. Rama's Last Act (*Uttararāmacarita*) by *Bhavabhūti*.
Sheldon Pollock. Foreword by Girish Karnad

32. "Friendly Advice" (*Hitopadeśa*) by *Nārāyaṇa* &
"King Víkrama's Adventures" (*Vikramacarita*). JUDIT TÖRZSÖK
33. Life of the Buddha (*Buddhacarita*)
by *Aśvaghoṣa*. PATRICK OLIVELLE
34. Maha·bhárata V: Preparations for War (*Udyogaparvan*) (vol. 1 of 2)
KATHLEEN GARBUTT. Foreword by GURCHARAN DAS
35. Maha·bhárata VIII: Karna (*Karṇaparvan*) (vol. 2 of 2)
ADAM BOWLES
36. Maha·bhárata V: Preparations for War (*Udyogaparvan*) (vol. 2 of 2)
KATHLEEN GARBUTT
37. Maha·bhárata VI: Bhishma (*Bhīṣmaparvan*) (vol. 1 of 2)*
Including the "Bhagavad Gita" in Context
ALEX CHERNIAK. Foreword by RANAJIT GUHA
38. The Ocean of the Rivers of Story (*Kathāsaritsāgara*) (vol. 2 of 7)
by *Somadeva*. SIR JAMES MALLINSON
39. "How the Nagas were Pleased" (*Nāgānanda*) by *Harṣa* &
"The Shattered Thighs" (*Ūrubhaṅga*) by *Bhāsa*.*
ANDREW SKILTON
40. Gita·govínda: Love Songs of Radha and Krishna (*Gītagovinda*)*
by *Jayadeva*. LEE SIEGEL. Foreword by SUDIPTA KAVIRAJ
41. "Bouquet of Rasa" & "River of Rasa" (*Rasamañjarī & Rasataraṅgiṇī*) by *Bhānudatta*. SHELDON POLLOCK
42. Garland of the Buddha's Past Lives (*Jātakamālā*) (vol. 1 of 2)*
by *Āryaśūra*. JUSTIN MEILAND
43. Maha·bhárata XII: Peace (*Śāntiparvan*) (vol. 3 of 5)*
"The Book of Liberation" (*Mokṣadharma*). ALEXANDER WYNNE
44. The Little Clay Cart (*Mṛcchakaṭikā*) by *Śūdraka*.
DIWAKAR ACHARYA. Foreword by PARTHA CHATTERJEE
45. Bhatti's Poem: The Death of Rávana (*Bhaṭṭikāvya*)*
by *Bhaṭṭi*. OLIVER FALLON

46. "Self-Surrender," "Peace," "Compassion," and "The Mission of the Goose": Poems and Prayers from South India (*Ātmārpaṇastuti, Śāntivilāsa, Dayāśataka & Haṃsasaṃdeśa*) by *Appayya Dīkṣita, Nīlakaṇṭha Dīkṣita & Vedānta Deśika.* YIGAL BRONNER & DAVID SHULMAN
Foreword by GIEVE PATEL
47. Maha·bhárata VI: Bhishma (*Bhīṣmaparvan*) (vol. 2 of 2)* ALEX CHERNIAK
48. How Úrvashi Was Won (*Vikramorvaśīya*) by *Kālidāsa* VELCHERU NARAYANA RAO & DAVID SHULMAN
49. The Quartet of Causeries (*Caturbhāṇī*) by *Śūdraka, Śyāmilaka, Vararuci & Īśvaradatta.* CSABA DEZSŐ & SOMADEVA VASUDEVA
50. Garland of the Buddha's Past Lives (*Jātakamālā*) (vol. 2 of 2)* by *Āryaśūra.* JUSTIN MEILAND
51. Princess Kadámbari (*Kādambarī*) (vol. 1 of 3) by *Bāṇa.* DAVID SMITH
52. The Rise of Wisdom Moon (*Prabodhacandrodaya*)* by *Kṛṣṇamiśra.* MATTHEW T. KAPSTEIN
Foreword by J.N. MOHANTY
53. Maha·bhárata VII: Drona (*Droṇaparvan*) (vol. 2 of 4)* VAUGHAN PILIKIAN
54. Maha·bhárata X & XI: Dead of Night & The Women (*Sauptikaparvan & Strīparvan*).* KATE CROSBY
55. Seven Hundred Elegant Verses (*Āryāsaptaśatī*)* by *Govardhana.* FRIEDHELM HARDY
56. Málavika and Agni·mitra (*Mālavikāgnimitram*) by *Kālidāsa.* DÁNIEL BALOGH & ESZTER SOMOGYI